Massenerschießungen.
Der Holocaust zwischen
Ostsee und Schwarzem Meer 1941 – 1944

Mass Shootings.
The Holocaust from
the Baltic to the Black Sea 1941 – 1944

Stiftung Denkmal für die ermordeten Juden Europas
Stiftung Topographie des Terrors

Massenerschießungen.
Der Holocaust zwischen Ostsee und Schwarzem Meer 1941 – 1944

Mass Shootings.
The Holocaust from the Baltic to the Black Sea 1941 – 1944

Inhalt

Content

- 6 — Grußwort / Message
- 8 — Vorwort / Preface

Ausstellung / Exhibition

- 11 — Historische Einführung / Historical introduction
- 32 — Karte / Map
- 35 — Die Zerstörung einer Gemeinde – Mizocz in Wolhynien 1941 bis 1944 / Eradication of a community – Mizocz in Volhynia 1941 – 1944
- 53 — Die Deutsche Besatzung in Mizocz – Befehlswege und Täterschaft / The German occupation of Mizocz – perpetrators and chains of command
- 69 — Die Verbrechen in Mizocz und die Erinnerung an den Holocaust / The crimes in Mizocz and remembrance of the Holocaust
- 79 — Täter und Massenmord / Perpetrators and mass murder
- 89 — Juristische Aufarbeitung / Judicial investigation
- 111 — Zwischen Widerstand und Ohnmacht / Between resistance and paralysis
- 123 — Schicksale / Biographies
- 181 — Ständige Erschießungsorte / Permanent killing sites

Essays / Essays

- 272 — Martin Cüppers. Die Erschießungen in der Sowietunion 1941 – 1944 / Shootings in the Soviet Union, 1941 – 1944
- 288 — Andrej Angrick. Die Aktion 1005 oder Vom Verschwinden der Massengräber / Operation 1005: On the disappearance of mass graves
- 302 — Michaela Christ. Gewaltbilder. Über das Zeigen und Betrachten von Fotografien der Extreme / Photographs of violence. Exhibiting and viewing images of brutality and suffering

Grußwort

Frank-Walter Steinmeier, Bundesminister des Auswärtigen

Vor 75 Jahren griff Nazideutschland die Sowjetunion an – und begann damit einen rassistisch, antislawisch und antisemitisch motivierten Vernichtungs- und Eroberungskrieg. Das Ausmaß der Wunden dieses Krieges, der mit bis dahin ungekannter Brutalität und Grausamkeit geführt wurde, lässt immer wieder erschaudern: 25 Millionen Menschen in der Sowjetunion – Weißrussen, Ukrainer, Russen und andere, verloren ihr Leben. Soldaten, Kriegsgefangene, aber größtenteils Zivilisten, darunter allein zwei Millionen Juden. Schon in den ersten Tagen nach dem Angriff gingen vereinzelte Massaker in eine systematische Judenvernichtung über, zumeist durch Massenerschießungen seitens des SS- und Polizeiapparats. Nicht nur die Juden, die auf dem Gebiet der ehemaligen Sowjetunion lebten, sondern auch deutsche, tschechische und österreichische Juden, die aus dem Deutschen Reich nach Osten verschleppt wurden, wurden getötet.

Die Ausstellung »Massenerschießungen. Der Holocaust zwischen Ostsee und Schwarzem Meer 1941–1944« widmet sich diesem schrecklichen Kapitel deutscher Geschichte. Dass zwei Millionen Juden durch Massenerschießungen getötet wurden, ist auch 71 Jahre nach Kriegsende noch nicht allgemein bekannt. Vielmehr werden mit dem Begriff Holocaust primär Auschwitz und andere Vernichtungslager verbunden. Hier leistet die Ausstellung Aufklärungsarbeit.

Die historischen Fotografien, die in der Ausstellung gezeigt werden, wurden von Tätern oder Zuschauern aufgenommen. Diese Bilder ermöglichen heute, dass wir uns ein Bild vom Grauen machen können, das vor 75 Jahren begann. Sie zeigen die Opfer, wie sie zusammengetrieben dastehen, nur wenige Stunden vor ihrer Erschießung – und danach. Es sind Bilder, deren Anblick man fast nicht erträgt. Und wir wissen, dass diese Bilder bereits damals weitergereicht wurden und damit Zeugnis ablegten von den begangenen Verbrechen.

Es hat lange gedauert, bis Deutschland die Dimension dieses Vernichtungskriegs und seine Verantwortung dafür anerkannt hat. Dies verdanken wir unermüdlichen Wissenschaftlern, die auch Jahrzehnte nach Kriegsende noch Zeitzeugen und Überlebende befragen, um so Gegenstände und Erzählungen einzuordnen, Archive auswerten und die deutsche Geschichte aufarbeiten. Die Ausstellung trägt damit nicht nur zu notwendiger Aufklärung bei, sondern auch dazu, dass sich die betroffenen Menschen und Staaten einander nähern.

Ich danke den Ausstellungsmachern, den Stiftungen Denkmal für die ermordeten Juden Europas und Topographie des Terrors, sehr herzlich für ihre wichtige Arbeit und wünsche der Ausstellung sowohl in Berlin als auch in den weiteren Städten, in denen sie gezeigt wird, zahlreiche Besucher.

Message

Frank-Walter Steinmeier, Federal Minister for Foreign Affairs

Seventy five years ago, Nazi Germany attacked the Soviet Union – and began a racially motivated anti Slavic and antisemitic war of extermination and conquest. The extent of the wounds left by this war, unprecedented in its cruelty and brutality, still has the power to horrify: over 25 million people in the Soviet Union – Belarusians, Ukrainians, Russians and others – lost their lives. Soldiers, prisoners of war, but for the most part civilians, including two million Jews. It was not long, in the first few days after the invasion, until isolated massacres turned into the systematic extermination of Jews, usually in the form of mass shootings by German SS and police units. Not only the Jews living in the territory of the then Soviet Union were killed, but also German, Czech and Austrian Jews who had been transported from the German Reich to the east.

The exhibition »Mass Shootings. The Holocaust from the Baltic to the Black Sea 1941 – 1944« looks at this dreadful chapter of German history. Even now, 71 years after the end of the War, the fact that two million Jews were killed in mass shootings is not yet universally known. The term Holocaust is, rather, associated primarily with Auschwitz and other extermination camps. The exhibition provides much needed information.

The historic photographs displayed in the exhibition were taken either by perpetrators or onlookers. Today these pictures enable us to get an idea of the terror that began 75 years ago. They show the victims, herded together, just a few hours before being shot – and afterwards. Looking at these pictures is almost unbearable. And we know that these images were passed on at the time, as evidence of the crimes committed.

It took a long time for Germany to recognise the dimensions of this war of extermination and to acknowledge its responsibility. That it did so is thanks to the untiring scholars who, decades after the end of the War, are still interviewing contemporary witnesses and survivors in order to classify objects and stories, who are evaluating archives and making a reckoning with Germany's history. This exhibition will help not only to provide very necessary education and information, but also to bring the people and countries affected closer together.

I would like to thank the designers of the exhibition, the Foundation Memorial to the Murdered Jews of Europe and the Topography of Terror Foundation, very much indeed for their important work. I hope the exhibition will have many visitors, both in Berlin and in the other cities where it will be on display.

Vorwort

Uwe Neumärker, Stiftung Denkmal für die ermordeten Juden Europas
Andreas Nachama, Stiftung Topographie des Terrors

Lange Zeit war der Angriff auf die Sowjetunion in Deutschland kein Gegenstand einer kritischen historischen Auseinandersetzung. In Westdeutschland wurde er schlicht beschwiegen und verdrängt, in der DDR einem ritualisierten Gedenken unterworfen. Im Jahr 1991 präsentierte die Stiftung Topographie des Terrors erstmals ihre Ausstellung »Der Krieg gegen die Sowjetunion 1941 – 1945«. Sie zeichnete ein neues Bild dieses auf Vernichtung und Versklavung ausgerichteten Weltanschauungskriegs – lange bevor die Ausstellung »Verbrechen der Wehrmacht. Dimensionen des Vernichtungskrieges 1941 – 1944« das Bild einer »sauberen« Wehrmacht in der deutschen Öffentlichkeit nachhaltig veränderte. Inzwischen wird das Thema auch in den Dauerausstellungen der Stiftungen Denkmal für die ermordeten Juden Europas und Topographie des Terrors dokumentiert. Der Ort der Information unter dem Holocaustdenkmal stellt die Thematik vor allem anhand einzelner Familienschicksale dar. Die Dauerausstellung »Topographie des Terrors. Gestapo, SS und Reichssicherheitshauptamt in der Wilhelm- und Prinz-Albrecht-Straße« schildert den Krieg in Polen und auf den Gebieten der Sowjetunion mit zahlreichen Text- und Bilddokumenten.

Mit der Ausstellung »Massenerschießungen. Der Holocaust zwischen Ostsee und Schwarzem Meer 1941 – 1944« unternehmen beide Häuser einen weiteren Schritt, um die Verbrechen deutscher Einheiten und ihrer einheimischen Hilfswilligen einer breiten Öffentlichkeit bekannt zu machen und würdevoll an die Opfer zu erinnern. Hierzu sollen Biografien den Besuchern auch die persönliche Dimension der Mordpolitik nahebringen. So wird in der Ausstellung an Judyta Wyszniacka erinnert, ein Mädchen aus dem ostpolnischen (heute weißrussischen) Ort Byten. Am 31. Juli 1942 schrieb sie an ihren in den USA lebenden Vater: »Wir möchten so gerne leben, doch man lässt uns nicht, wir werden umkommen«. Wenige Tage zuvor hatten die deutschen Besatzer in Byten innerhalb von drei Stunden über 800 Menschen erschossen. Judytas Mutter Złata war es gelungen, mit ihren beiden Kindern in die Wälder zu flüchten. Doch auch hier waren die drei nicht sicher; die Deutschen und einheimische Hilfspolizisten machten Jagd auf Überlebende der Erschießungen. Judyta, ihre Mutter und ihr Bruder kamen am 20. Januar 1943 auf unbekannte Weise ums Leben.

Anders als in Deutschland (und Österreich) spielten die Massenerschießungen in der Erinnerungskultur der Sowjetunion schon früh eine große Rolle. An hunderten Orten entstanden Denkmäler. Künstler wie Dmitri Schostakowitsch (1906 – 1975) mit seiner Symphonie Nr. 13 b-Moll op. 113 »Babij Jar«, auf Grundlage des gleichnamigen Gedichts von Jewgenij Jewtuschenko (*1932), beschäftigten sich mit der Dimension der Verbrechen. Allerdings verschwieg die offizielle sowjetische Geschichtsschreibung, dass es sich bei den Opfern der Massenerschießungen vorwiegend um Juden gehandelt hatte. In den Nachfolgestaaten der Sowjetunion und in Polen wird mittlerweile auch der jüdischen Ermordeten gedacht; die Erinnerung an die Erschießungen hat weiterhin große Bedeutung. Die nun erstellte Ausstellung will geschichtspolitische Brücken schlagen. Wir hoffen, dass die Ausstellung nach ihrer Präsentation in Berlin an vielen weiteren Orten zu sehen sein wird.

An dieser Stelle sei den Kuratoren der Ausstellung – Dr. Ulrich Baumann, Paula Oppermann und Christian Schmittwilken – ebenso gedankt wie der Gestalterin Ursula Wilms, sowie allen, die zum Gelingen der Ausstellung beigetragen haben. Ein besonderer Dank gilt dem Auswärtigen Amt, das durch seine großzügige finanzielle Unterstützung die Ausstellung erst möglich gemacht hat.

Preface

Uwe Neumärker, Foundation Memorial to the Murdered Jews of Europe
Andreas Nachama, Topography of Terror Foundation

For many years after the war, German historical discourse failed to address the invasion of the Soviet Union. In West Germany, this aspect of the Second World War was mostly ignored or repressed and in East Germany it was subsumed into ritualised commemoration. The first presentation on the invasion produced by the Topography of Terror Foundation was the exhibition »The War against the Soviet Union 1941 – 1945« opened in 1991. It shed new light on the ideological war that had sought to annihilate or enslave its victims, several years before the exhibition »War of Annihilation. Crimes of the Wehrmacht 1941 to 1944« transformed the prevailing view that the Wehrmacht had had »no blood on its hands«. The invasion of the Soviet Union now also features in the permanent exhibitions at the Memorial to the Murdered Jews of Europe and the Topography of Terror Documentation Center. The subterranean Information Centre at the Memorial to the Murdered Jews of Europe mainly approaches the theme through the biographies of individual families. The permanent exhibition »Topography of Terror: Gestapo, SS and Reich Security Main Office on Wilhelm- and Prinz-Albrecht-Straße« presents a wealth of texts and photographs to document the war in Poland and on Soviet territory.

The Topography of Terror Foundation and the Foundation of Memorial to the Murdered Jews of Europe have designed the exhibition »Mass Shootings. The Holocaust from the Baltic to the Black Sea 1941 – 1944« to heighten public awareness of the crimes committed by German units and local collaborators and to pay a dignified tribute to the victims. It includes a number of biographies to demonstrate how the policy of murder affected individuals. One such individual was Judyta Wyszniacka, a young girl from the village of Byten in eastern Poland (now Belarus). In a letter dated 31 July 1942 she wrote the following to her father, who was living in the US: »We so much want to live, but they won't let us. We are going to die«. A few days before, German occupiers in Byten had shot over 800 people in the space of three hours. Judyta's mother Złata had managed to escape into the woods with her two children. However they were not safe here either as the Germans and local auxiliary police continued to hunt down any survivors of the shootings. Judyta, her mother, and her brother all died on 20 January 1943 in unexplained circumstances.

In contrast to Germany (and Austria), the mass shootings became an integral feature of Soviet commemorative culture soon after the war. Memorials were constructed in many places. Artists also confronted the mass atrocities through their work, one example being Symphony No. 13 in b flat minor op. 113 »Babi Yar« by Dmitri Shostakovich (1906 – 1975), which was inspired by the eponymous poem by Yevgeny Yevtushenko (*1932). However, the official Soviet version of events did not acknowledge that most of the victims of the mass shootings had been Jews. Poland and the successor states of the Soviet Union do now commemorate the Jewish victims and remembrance of the mass shootings remains significant in these countries. This exhibition aims to foster historical and political understanding. We hope that it will be shown in many other places after Berlin.

We would like to extend our sincere thanks to the curators of the exhibition – Dr Ulrich Baumann, Paula Oppermann and Christian Schmittwilken – as well as to Ursula Wilms, who designed it. Our thanks also go to everyone else who has contributed to the exhibition. We are particularly grateful to the German Foreign Office for its generous financial assistance, without which the exhibition would not have been possible.

Historische Einführung
Historical introduction

Historische Einführung

Von der Machtübernahme der Nationalsozialisten bis zum Beginn des Zweiten Weltkriegs

Am 30. Januar 1933 wird Adolf Hitler, der »Führer« der NSDAP, Reichskanzler. Die Nationalsozialisten verhaften, foltern und ermorden politische Gegner oder zwingen sie ins Exil. Im »Antibolschewismus« des Regimes verbinden sich extremer Antikommunismus und Judenhass. Antisemitismus wird erstmals Bestandteil des Regierungsprogramms eines modernen Staats. Zugleich betreiben die Machthaber eine aggressive Außenpolitik: Im März 1938 marschiert die Wehrmacht in Österreich ein. Bald darauf zerschlägt das »Dritte Reich« die Tschechoslowakei. Im August 1939 schließen die deutsche und die sowjetische Führung eine Vereinbarung, einander nicht anzugreifen – den »Hitler-Stalin-Pakt«. In einem geheimen Zusatzprotokoll halten sie die Aufteilung Ostmitteleuropas fest. Eine Woche später greift die Wehrmacht Polen an. Damit beginnt der Zweite Weltkrieg. Nach der Niederlage der polnischen Armee fällt der Westen an das Deutsche Reich, in den Osten rückt die Rote Armee ein. Bis 1940 werden zudem Litauen, Lettland, Estland und Teile Rumäniens sowjetisch.

From the National Socialists' seizure of power up to the start of the Second World War

On 30 January 1933, Adolf Hitler, »Führer« of the National Socialist German Workers' Party (NSDAP), took office as Chancellor of the Reich. The Nazis arrested, tortured, and killed political opponents or forced them into exile. The regime's »anti-Bolshevik« sentiment combined extreme anti-Communism and hatred of Jews. For the first time, a modern state adopted antisemitism as part of its government programme. Simultaneously, the National Socialists pursued a very aggressive foreign policy: In March 1938, the Wehrmacht marched into Austria. Soon after, the »Third Reich« destroyed Czechoslovakia. In August 1939, German and Soviet leaders signed a non-aggression treaty – the »Molotov-Ribbentrop Pact«. In a secret protocol, they agreed on a partition of East Central Europe. A week later, the Wehrmacht invaded Poland, marking the start of the Second World War. After the Polish Army's defeat, western Poland remained occupied by Germany and the Red Army moved into the country's eastern provinces. In addition, Lithuania, Latvia, Estonia and parts of Romania became part of the Soviet Union until summer 1940.

Instytut Pamięci Narodowej, Warschau

Tucheler Heide (Bory Tucholskie) bei Danzig (Gdańsk), 27. Oktober 1939: Erschießung des 40-jährigen katholischen Pfarrers Piotr Sosnowski und anderer durch den »Volksdeutschen Selbstschutz«, der aus Angehörigen der deutschen Minderheit besteht. Besatzer und Volksdeutsche ermorden große Teile der polnischen Oberschicht. Auch tausende Patienten psychiatrischer Anstalten fallen systematischen Erschießungen zum Opfer.

Bory Tucholskie near Gdańsk, 27 October 1939: The shooting of 40-year-old Catholic priest Piotr Sosnowski and others by a »German self-protection force«, made up of members of the German ethnic minority. Together with the German occupiers, they murdered large parts of the Polish elites. Thousands of patients in psychiatric clinics also fell victim to systematic shootings.

Historical introduction

Państwowe Muzeum Auschwitz-Birkenau

Ostrów Mazowiecka (Polen), 11. November 1939: Über 360 Juden der Kleinstadt werden von Angehörigen des 4. Polizeibataillons als ›Vergeltung‹ für eine Brandstiftung erschossen. Es ist die erste ›Totalliquidierung‹ einer jüdischen Gemeinde während des Holocaust.
Die Mehrheit der polnischen Juden wird nicht erschossen, sondern mit Giftgas ermordet.

Ostrów Mazowiecka (Poland), 11 November 1939: More than 360 Jews from this small town were murdered by members of the 4th Police Battalion in ›reprisal‹ for a case of arson. This was the first ›total liquidation‹ of a Jewish community during the Holocaust.
Most Polish Jews were murdered with poison gas, not shot.

Historische Einführung

Vorbereitung des Vernichtungskriegs gegen die Sowjetunion

Im Juli 1940 teilt Hitler der Wehrmacht seinen Entschluss mit, »Rußland zu erledigen«. Die Nationalsozialisten beabsichtigen, den angeblichen Hort des »jüdischen Bolschewismus« zu vernichten und dort ein deutsches Kolonialreich zu errichten. Um dieses Ziel schnell zu erreichen, ist die Beseitigung der kommunistischen Funktionärsschicht geplant, unter der die Nationalsozialisten einen hohen Anteil Juden erwarten. Wehrmacht, SS- und Polizeiapparat verständigen sich über ihre Zuständigkeiten bei der Besatzungspolitik: So soll die Wehrmacht gefangen genommene politische Offiziere der Roten Armee erschießen. Eigens aufgestellte »Einsatzgruppen« haben in Zusammenarbeit mit anderen SS- und Polizeiverbänden den Auftrag, vor allem zivile kommunistische Funktionäre ins Visier zu nehmen.

Preparations for the war of annihilation against the Soviet Union

In July 1940, Hitler informed the Wehrmacht of his decision to »finish off Russia«. The National Socialists intended to destroy the alleged stronghold of »Jewish Bolshevism« and set up a German colonial empire. In order to achieve this aim swiftly, they planned to eliminate the communist functionaries, most of whom they assumed to be Jews. The Wehrmacht and the leadership of SS and police agreed on jurisdictions within occupation policy: Accordingly the Wehrmacht was to shoot Red Army political officers who had been taken prisoner. Specially-created mobile killing squads (Einsatzgruppen), along with other SS and police units, had the task of targeting above all civilian communist functionaries.

Transkription (Auszug) des Schreibens des Chefs der Sicherheitspolizei und des SD, Reinhard Heydrich (1904 – 1942), an die Höheren SS- und Polizeiführer (HSSPF) für die Sowjetunion, 2. Juli 1941: Heydrich informiert die HSSPF über die zuvor an die Einsatzgruppen ausgegebenen Weisungen unter anderem zur Ermordung aller »Juden in Partei- und Staatsstellungen«.

2 July 1941, transcript (excerpt) of a letter by the Chief of the Security Police and the SD, Reinhard Heydrich (1904 – 1942), to the Higher SS and Police Leaders (HSSPF) for the Soviet Union: Heydrich was informing the HSSPF about the directions issued to the Einsatzgruppen, including the execution of all »Jews in Party or State positions«.

```
4.) Exekutionen:

Zu exekutieren sind alle

Funktionäre der Komintern (wie
überhaupt die kommunistischen
Berufspolitiker schlechthin)

die höheren, mittleren und radikalen
unteren Funktionäre der Partei, der
Zentralkomitees, der Gau- und
Gebietskomitees

Volkskommissare

Juden in Partei- und Staatsstellungen

sonstigen radikalen Elemente
(Saboteure, Propandeure,
Heckenschützen, Attentäter, Hetzer usw.)
```

```
4.) Executions:

All the following are to be executed:

Comintern officials (together with
professional Communist politicians
in general)

Top and medium-level officials and radical
lower-level officials of the Party, of the
Central Committee and of the district and
sub-district committees

People's Commissars

Jews in Party or State positions

Other radical elements
(saboteurs, propagandists,
snipers, assassins, inciters, etc.)
```

BArch R 58/241 fol. 315 – 316

Historical introduction

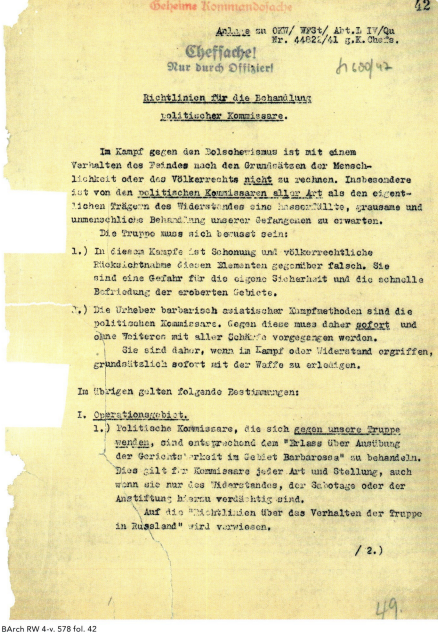

BArch RW 4-v. 578 fol. 42

Erste Seite des sogenannten Kommissarbefehls, 6. Juni 1941. Er schafft die Grundlage für die Ermordung politischer Kommissare der Roten Armee. Der zuvor verordnete, sogenannte Kriegsgerichtsbarkeitserlass hebt die Ahndung von Kriegsverbrechen von Wehrmachtsangehörigen auf und überlässt die Strafverfolgung sowjetischer Zivilisten der Willkür deutscher Offiziere.

First page of the so-called Commissar Order, 6 June 1941. This provided the basis for the liquidation of Red Army political commissars. The so called Jurisdiction Decree introduced beforehand suspended punishment of German soldiers for war crimes and left the legal prosecution of Soviet civilians up to the arbitrary decisions of German officers.

Historische Einführung

Der Überfall auf die Sowjetunion

Am 22. Juni 1941 greift das Deutsche Reich gemeinsam mit seinen Verbündeten die Sowjetunion an. In kurzer Zeit erobern sie weite Gebiete Osteuropas. Zahlreiche Einheimische begrüßen die Wehrmacht begeistert, denn die sowjetische Besatzung seit 1939/40 hatte für Hunderttausende Enteignung und Deportation bedeutet. Viele nichtjüdische Polen, Ukrainer, Litauer oder Letten geben Juden eine Mitschuld an der Unterdrückung durch die Sowjetunion; das Feindbild des »jüdischen Bolschewismus« verbindet sich mit bestehenden antisemitischen Vorurteilen. Unmittelbar nach dem Abzug der Roten Armee greifen vor allem Nationalisten ihre jüdischen Nachbarn an. Angehörige der Wehrmacht und des SS- und Polizeiapparats schüren die Pogrome. Zugleich erschießen sie systematisch jüdische Männer und Nichtjuden, die sie für Kommunisten halten.

Invasion of the Soviet Union

On 22 June 1941, Germany and its allies invaded the Soviet Union. Within a short time, they had conquered large parts of Eastern Europe. A considerable proportion of the local population greeted the Wehrmacht enthusiastically, since hundreds of thousands of people had been expropriated and deported under Soviet occupation since 1939/40. Many non-Jewish Poles, Ukrainians, Lithuanians, and Latvians blamed the Jews for the Soviet oppression; the concept of »Jewish Bolshevism« as an enemy merged with existing antisemitic prejudices. Immediately after the Red Army's withdrawal, local non-Jews, in particular nationalists, attacked their Jewish neighbours. Members of the Wehrmacht, the SS, and the police fueled the pogroms. At the same time, they systematically shot Jewish men and non-Jews they considered to be communists.

Libau (Liepāja, Lettland, ab 1940 sowjetisch besetzt), Juli 1941: Standbilder eines Films einer Erschießung jüdischer Männer. Der Marineangehörige Reinhard Wiener filmt, wie die Männer von einem LKW absteigen und in eine Grube laufen müssen. Dort werden sie von Angehörigen der Einsatzgruppe A erschossen.

Liepāja (Libau, Latvia, occupied by the Soviet Union in 1940), July 1941: Stills from a film showing the shooting of Jewish men. Reinhard Wiener, member of German Navy, filmed the men being forced to climb down from a truck and descend into a pit, where they were shot by members of Einsatzgruppe A.

BArch 162 Bild-04997　　BArch B 162 Bild-05001　　BArch B 162 Bild-05005

Historical introduction

Lemberg (Lwów/Lwiw, Polen, ab 1939 sowjetisch besetzt), Leon-Sapieha-Straße, Anfang Juli 1941: Angriff auf einen jüdischen Mann, ein deutscher Ordnungspolizist sieht zu. Die Deutschen beschuldigten die Juden, Morde begangen zu haben, die tatsächlich aber der sowjetische Geheimdienst zu verantworten hatte.

Lviv (Lemberg/Lwów, Poland, occupied by the Soviet Union in 1939), Leon-Sapieha-Street, early July 1941: Attack on a Jewish man, a German policeman looks on. The Germans had accused the Jews of murders that in fact had been committed by the Soviet Secret Service.

Zydowski Instytut Historyczny im. Emanuela Ringelbluma, Warschau

Kaunas (Litauen, ab 1940 sowjetisch besetzt), Lietukis-Garage, zwischen 25. und 27. Juni 1941: Ein Litauer erschlägt Juden im Beisein deutscher Soldaten und Einheimischer.

Kaunas (Lithuania, occupied by the Soviet Union in 1940), Lietukis garage, between 25 and 27 June 1941: A Lithuanian kills Jews in the presence of German soldiers and local inhabitants.

BArch B 162 Bild-04128

Kaunas, VII. Fort, Ende Juni/Anfang Juli 1941: Jüdische Männer vor ihrer Erschießung durch litauische Nationalisten und deutsche Polizei.

Kaunas, VII Fort, late June/early July 1941: Jewish men before being shot by Lithuanian nationalists and German police.

BArch B 162 Bild-04135

Historische Einführung

Übergang zum Völkermord

Ohne zentralen schriftlichen Befehl der NS-Führung erschießen einzelne SS- und Polizeieinheiten ab Ende Juli 1941 erstmals unterschiedslos jüdische Männer, Frauen und Kinder. Ganze jüdische Gemeinden werden in der Folgezeit ermordet. Die Verbrechen markieren den Übergang zum Völkermord. Ab Herbst 1941 setzen die Einsatzgruppen auch eigens gebaute Gaswagen ein, in denen sie ihre Opfer mit Abgasen ersticken.
Trotz gelegentlicher Konflikte arbeiten Wehrmacht, SS und Polizei bei der Planung und Durchführung der Erschießungen eng zusammen. Dabei geht die Wehrmacht immer wieder über die mit SS und Polizei getroffenen Vereinbarungen hinweg und erschießt eigenständig Zivilisten. Nicht selten eignen sich die Täter im Umfeld der Erschießungen Wertsachen an, erzwingen sexuelle Handlungen oder schlagen ihre Opfer. An den Mordstätten entwickelt sich ein regelrechter Erschießungstourismus: Zehntausende nicht direkt beteiligte Besatzer und Einheimische werden zu Zuschauern der Vernichtung.

Transition to genocide

Starting in late July 1941, individual SS and police units shot Jewish men, women, and children indiscriminately without any central written order from the Nazi leadership. In the following months, entire Jewish communities were murdered. These crimes mark the transition to genocide. Starting in autumn 1941, the Einsatzgruppen deployed specially-built gas vans to suffocate their victims with exhaust fumes.
Despite occasional disagreements, the Wehrmacht, the SS, and the police cooperated closely in planning and carrying out shootings. At the same time, the Wehrmacht repeatedly infringed agreements with the SS and the police and shot civilians of its own accord. It was not uncommon for the perpetrators to pocket valuables from the victims, or to sexually abuse or beat them up first. At the killing sites, a kind of ›shooting tourism‹ set in: thousands of members of the occupying forces and locals who were not directly involved came to watch the mass murder.

Historical introduction

Privatbesitz Mirek

Bei Pinsk (Pińsk, Polen, ab 1939 sowjetisch besetzt), Anfang August 1941: durch das 2. SS-Kavallerieregiment ermordete Juden. Am Morgen des 6. August werden etwa 8.000 Juden von SS-Reitern vor die Stadt getrieben. Die SS beginnt, sie mit Genickschüssen zu töten. Als sich die Dämmerung abzeichnet, befürchtet Hauptsturmführer Stefan Charwat (1908 – 1942), das Verbrechen nicht am selben Tag abschließen zu können. Die SS-Männer schießen daraufhin mit Maschinengewehren in die Menge der noch Lebenden.
Das Regiment und andere Mordverbände stehen in engem Kontakt mit dem Reichsführer-SS, Heinrich Himmler (1900 – 1945), der mit immer neuen Befehlen die Bereitschaft seiner Einheiten zum Massenmord erprobt. Der vollzogene Massenmord bestätigt ihm, dass sich die Vernichtung auf diese Weise umsetzen lässt.
Der Fotograf der Aufnahme ist der kommunistisch gesinnte Wehrmachtssoldat Erich Mirek (1912 – 2004).

Near Pińsk (Poland, occupied by the Soviet Union in 1939), early August 1941: Jews murdered by the 2nd SS Cavalry Regiment. On the morning of 6 August, around 8,000 Jews were driven out of town by SS horsemen. The SS began by shooting the Jews individually at the base of the skull. As dusk set in, SS captain Stefan Charwat (1908 – 1942) feared that they would not complete the crime that day, so the SS men fired into the crowd of those who were still alive using machine guns.
The regiment and other killing units were in close contact with the leader of the SS, Heinrich Himmler (1900 – 1945), who continually issued new orders to test the willingness of his units to commit mass murder. He was eventually convinced that extermination plans could be carried out in this way.
The photograph was taken by German soldier, Erich Mirek (1912 – 2004), who was a communist sympathiser.

Historische Einführung

United States Holocaust Memorial Museum, Washington, D.C.

Kamenez-Podolsk (Kamjanez-Podilskyj, Ukraine), 27./28. August 1941: Menschenkolonnen, die vor die Stadt getrieben werden. In Kamenez halten sich mehrere tausend Juden auf, die zuvor von Ungarn – einem Bündnispartner der Deutschen – abgeschoben worden waren. Die Wehrmacht drängt zunächst auf ihre »Rücknahme«. Der Höhere SS- und Polizeiführer Friedrich Jeckeln entwickelt in dieser Lage eine Politik des Massenmords. Gegenüber der Wehrmacht äußert er, er hoffe »die Liquidation dieser Juden bis zum 1.9.1941 durchgeführt zu haben«. Zwei Tage später meldet er die Erschießung von 23.600 Juden nach Berlin. Zu den Opfern zählen neben den Abgeschobenen auch ortsansässige Juden.

Kamianets-Podilsky, Ukraine, 27/28 August 1941: columns of people are marched out of the city. At the time, several thousand Jews who had been deported by Hungary, one of Germany's allies, were staying in Kamianets. Initially the Wehrmacht insisted on their »return«. In view of the situation, Higher SS and Police Leader Friedrich Jeckeln developed a policy of mass murder. He explained to the Wehrmacht that he hoped to have »completed liquidation of these Jews by 1.9.1941«. Two days later, he reported the shooting of 23,600 Jews to Berlin. The victims included not only the deported Jews from Hungary but also local Jews.

Die Aufnahmen stammen von dem Budapester Juden Gyula Spitz (1902 – 1945), der als Fahrer in der ungarischen Armee dient. Er fotografiert heimlich aus seinem Fahrzeug. Zwischen 1940 und 1942 transportiert er im Auftrag ungarischer Offiziere Güter, die diese in der besetzten Sowjetunion geplündert hatten. Nach der Besetzung Ungarns durch die Deutschen wird Spitz deportiert. Er stirbt im Konzentrationslager Mauthausen an Typhus.

These photographs were taken by Gyula Spitz (1902 – 1945), a Jew from Budapest who served in the Hungarian army as a driver. He took the photographs secretly from his vehicle. Between 1940 and 1942, he transported goods that Hungarian officers had looted in the occupied Soviet Union. After Germany occupied Hungary, Spitz was deported. He died of typhoid fever at concentration camp Mauthausen.

Historical introduction

Kiew (Kyjiw), Schlucht von Babij Jar, Oktober 1941:
Am 29. und 30. September 1941 ermorden Angehörige des Sonderkommandos 4a und des Gruppenstabs der Einsatzgruppe C sowie des Polizeiregiments Rußland-Süd nach Angaben einer »Ereignismeldung« 33.771 Menschen. Eine wesentliche Verantwortung für den Mord trägt auch hier Friedrich Jeckeln.

Die Fotos gehören zu einer Reihe von 29 Farb-Diapositiven von Johannes Hähle (1906 – 1944), Fotograf einer Propagandakompanie der Wehrmacht. Er übergibt sie nicht seiner Dienststelle. Sie enthält Nahaufnahmen des Besitzes der Erschossenen und Aufnahmen, die offenbar die Planierung des Massengrabes durch Kriegsgefangene zeigen.

Kiev, Babi Yar ravine, October 1941: On 29 and 30 September 1941, members of Sonderkommando 4a and the Group Command Staff of Einsatzgruppe C, along with the Police Regiment Russia South murdered 33,771 people, according to an »events report«. Higher SS and Police Leader Friedrich Jeckeln bore considerable responsibility for the murders.

The photos are part of a series of 29 colour slides taken by Johannes Hähle (1906 – 1944), photographer of a Wehrmacht propaganda unit. He did not hand them over to his superiors. The pictures show close-ups of the victims' possessions, as well as prisoners-of-war filling in the mass grave and apparently levelling the ground.

Archiv des Hamburger Instituts für Sozialforschung / Fotograf: Johannes Hähle

Historische Einführung

Verhalten der einheimischen nichtjüdischen Bevölkerung

Die Deutschen gliedern in weiten Gebieten, so im Baltikum und in der Ukraine, lokale Nationalisten in ihren Besatzungsapparat ein. Viele beteiligen sich als Schützen freiwillig an den Verbrechen. Einheimische unterstützen die Besatzer auch bei der Suche nach Juden, die den fortgesetzten Erschießungen durch Flucht, beispielsweise in umliegende Wälder, zu entkommen suchen. Dabei spielt nicht nur Judenhass eine Rolle. Viele Nichtjuden folgen aus Furcht den Regeln und Erwartungen der Besatzer. Nur wenige gewähren den Verfolgten Hilfe, verstecken und versorgen sie. Die Mehrheit der nichtjüdischen Bevölkerung verhält sich passiv zum Schicksal ihrer Nachbarn, manche bereichern sich an deren Eigentum.

Attitude of the local, non-Jewish population

The Germans incorporated local nationalists into their occupation apparatus in large parts of the occupied territories, such as the Baltic States and Ukraine. Many took part voluntarily in the killing as shooters. Locals also helped the occupiers to hunt down Jews who had fled into the woods to escape the shootings. Not all of them did this out of hatred for Jews. Many non-Jews were following regulations and trying to anticipate the occupiers' expectations out of fear. Very few of them offered to help the persecuted Jews by hiding them or providing them with food. The majority of the non-Jewish population remained passive in view of their neighbours' fate. Some enriched themselves by appropriating the possessions of the Jews.

Smolensk (Russland), undatiert: Laut einer Zeugenaussage führt dieser litauische Schutzmann jüdische Frauen zur Erschießung. Die Schutzmannschaften aus Einwohnern der besetzten Länder stehen unter deutscher Führung.

Smolensk (Russia), no date: According to an eye-witness, this Lithuanian auxiliary policeman is leading Jewish women to the killing squad. The auxiliary police, consisting of residents of the occupied countries, were under German command.

BArch B 162/4352 fol. 70

Historical introduction

Latvijas Okupācijas Muzejs, Riga / Fotograf: Georg Josef Gundlach

Durben (Durbe) bei Libau (Lettland), Ende Juni 1941: Eine lettische Frau begrüßt deutsche Soldaten. Viele Einheimische erhoffen sich die Wiedererlangung der Eigenstaatlichkeit mit Hilfe der Deutschen.

Durbe near Liēpaja (Latvia), end of June 1941: A Latvian woman greets German soldiers. Many locals hoped to regain national sovereignty with the help of the Germans.

Historische Einführung

Ausweitung der Massenmorde

Im Dezember 1941 beginnen die deutschen Besatzer in Polen mit der systematischen Ermordung von Juden durch Giftgas. Die deutsche Führung entwickelt ihre Pläne zur Ermordung aller europäischen Juden weiter. Bis zum Frühjahr 1942 lässt sie in Polen fünf Vernichtungsstätten errichten. Im Sommer 1942 wird vor allem Auschwitz zum Ziel von Deportationen aus mittel- und westeuropäischen Staaten, die unter deutscher Herrschaft stehen. Zugleich weiten die Deutschen ihre Mordpolitik in der besetzten Sowjetunion noch einmal aus. Bestehende Ghettos werden geräumt, ihre Insassen oft vor Ort erschossen. Abseits der Front führen diese Verbrechen vor allem Angehörige der neu geschaffenen stationären SS- und Polizeidienststellen aus. In Frontnähe erschießen die mobilen Einheiten von SS und Polizei sowie die Wehrmacht weiterhin jüdische und nichtjüdische Zivilisten.

Escalation of mass murder

In December 1941, the German occupation authorities in Poland commenced the systematic murder of Jews using poison gas. The German leadership continued to develop plans to murder all European Jews. By early 1942, the Germans had created five extermination sites in Poland. In the summer of 1942, Auschwitz became the main destination for deportations from those central and western European countries ruled by Germany. At the same time, the Germans escalated their policy of murder in the occupied Soviet Union further. Existing ghettos were ›liquidated‹ and the inmates were often shot on site. Away from the front, these killings were carried out mainly by members of the recently created stationary SS and police offices. Near the front, the mobile SS and police units as well as the Wehrmacht continued shooting Jewish and non-Jewish civilians.

Stadtarchiv Bielefeld

Bielefeld, 13. Dezember 1941: Bilder aus der Kriegschronik der Stadt Bielefeld von der Deportation von Juden aus Ostwestfalen-Lippe sowie aus den Regierungsbezirken Osnabrück und Münster nach Riga. Auch aus anderen Städten des Deutschen Reichs verschleppt das Reichssicherheitshauptamt Juden in die lettische Hauptstadt. Um Platz im Rigaer Ghetto zu schaffen, lässt der Höhere SS- und Polizeiführer Friedrich Jeckeln etwa 27.000 lettische Juden erschießen. Auch die Mehrheit der angekommenen mitteleuropäischen Juden wird in den folgenden Monaten ermordet.

Bielefeld, 13 December 1941: Photographs from the war chronicle of the town of Bielefeld showing the deportation of Jews from Ostwestfalen-Lippe and the administrative regions of Osnabrück and Münster to Riga. The Reich Security Main Office deported Jews from other cities in the Reich to the Latvian capital as well. To create space in Riga Ghetto, Higher SS and Police Leader Friedrich Jeckeln had approximately 27.000 Latvian Jews shot. The majority of the central European Jews who arrived in Riga was killed in the following months.

Historical introduction

Magyar Nemzeti Múzeum, Budapest

Tschernigow (Tschernihiw, Ukraine), 18. Februar 1942:
Aufnahmen eines ungarischen Soldaten von den Vorbereitungen
einer Erschießung. Deutsche Ordnungspolizei und Hilfspolizisten
bringen Juden an einen Waldrand in der Nähe der Stadt. Sie
zwingen sie dazu, sich zu entkleiden. Anschließend werden sie
erschossen und in einer Grube verscharrt.

Chernihiv (Ukraine), 18 February 1942: Photos by a Hungarian
soldier showing preparations for a shooting. German Order
Police and auxiliary police bring Jews to the edge of the woods
outside the town. They force them to undress before killing them
and burying them in a pit.

Yad Vashem, Jerusalem

Sowjetunion, unbekannter Ort, Beschriftung der Bildrückseite:
»Zigeuner vor der Erschießung. Herbst 1942«. Das Foto stammt
aus Beständen der sowjetischen »Außerordentlichen Staatlichen
Kommission« zur Untersuchung der nationalsozialistischen
Verbrechen.

Soviet Union, place unknown, writing on the back of this photo:
»Gypsies before shooting. Autumn 1942«. The photo was found
in the holdings of the Soviet »Extraordinary State Commission«
formed to investigate National Socialist crimes.

Historische Einführung

Kenntnis von den Verbrechen

Durch Zeugenberichte und Geheimdienstinformationen besitzen die Alliierten schon im Sommer 1941 Kenntnis der deutschen Verbrechen. Die im Krieg gegen Deutschland verbündeten Regierungen verurteilen die Massenmorde allerdings erst am 18. Dezember 1942 in einer gemeinsamen Erklärung. Im Deutschen Reich stehen die Verbrechen »im Osten« offiziell unter strenger Geheimhaltung. Dennoch tragen viele Tatbeteiligte ihr Wissen über die Erschießungen in die Heimat. Bald machen Gerüchte über die Ermordung der Juden die Runde. Die Bevölkerung bewegt sich zwischen Wissen, Halbwissen und mangelnder Vorstellungskraft. Wer offizielle Verlautbarungen, private Schilderungen von Soldaten und Meldungen verbotener ausländischer Radiosender in Beziehung setzt, kann sich ein einigermaßen genaues Bild machen. Solche Anstrengungen unternehmen aber die wenigsten Deutschen.

Awareness of the crimes

Thanks to eyewitness accounts and information from their secret services, the Allies were aware of the German crimes in summer 1941 already. Despite this, the governments that had joined forces in the war against Germany did not condemn the mass killings until 18 December 1942, when they issued a joint statement to this effect. Within the German Reich, the crimes committed »in the east« were officially kept secret. Nonetheless, many of the individuals involved in the crimes shared their knowledge of the shootings with friends and relatives at home. Soon rumours began to spread about the murder of Jews. The population was caught between certain knowledge, half-truths, and the inability to even imagine that such deeds were possible. Anyone correlating official statements, the private accounts of soldiers, and reports by prohibited foreign radio broadcasts could gain a fairly detailed idea of what was happening. But only a few Germans took the trouble to do so.

The New York Times vom 26. Oktober 1941

The New York Times, 26. Oktober 1941:
Artikel über die Massenerschießung in Kamenez-Podolsk. Berichte über Massenmorde an Juden sind in der US-Presse zu dieser Zeit noch selten.
Der Artikel befindet sich auf Seite 6 der Zeitung, eingerahmt von Anzeigen, darunter eine für das bekannte Pelz- und Modegeschäft *Russeks*. Den Inserenten, der jüdischen Familie Nemerow-Russek, war die Platzierung der Anzeige vermutlich nicht mitgeteilt worden.

The New York Times, 26 October 1941:
Article on the massacre of Kamianets-Podilsky. At this time, reports on the mass murder of Jews were not very common in US newspapers.
The article was published on page 6 of the newspaper, among various advertisements, including one for the well-known fur and fashion shop, *Russeks*. Presumably, the newspaper did not inform the Jewish family Nemerow-Russek where their advertisement was going to be placed.

Historical introduction

Das Reich vom 16. November 1941

Das Reich, 16. November 1941:
Kommentar des Reichspropagandaministers Joseph Goebbels (1897 – 1945); darin spricht er von einem »allmählichen Vernichtungsprozess«, den das »Weltjudentum« erleide. Als die Alliierten die Verbrechen Ende 1942 offen anprangern, werden diese von der deutschen Propaganda nicht geleugnet. Damit verfolgt das Regime offenkundig das Kalkül, die Deutschen insgesamt zu Komplizen zu machen.

Das Reich, 16 November 1941:
Commentary by Reich propaganda minister Joseph Goebbels (1897 – 1945); here he speaks of a »gradual process of annihilation«, affecting »world Jewry«. When the Allies openly condemned the crimes at the end of 1942, German propaganda did not deny them. The regime's obvious intention was to turn all Germans into accomplices.

Historische Einführung

Partisanenkrieg

Die vorhandenen Verbände reichen den deutschen Besatzern nicht aus, um ihre Herrschaft in der Sowjetunion durchzusetzen und Widerstand zu unterdrücken. Zur Abschreckung setzen sie daher von Beginn an auf gezielten Terror gegen die Zivilbevölkerung. Der Kampf gegen Partisanen dient als Vorwand, den rassistischen Vernichtungskrieg weiter auszudehnen.
Wehrmacht, SS und Polizei führen gemeinsam mit einheimischen Verbänden »Aktionen« gegen Partisanen durch. Diese verfehlen meistens ihr Ziel, da die Partisanen rechtzeitig fliehen können. Hingegen sterben unbeteiligte Zivilisten: Unzählige Dörfer werden verwüstet, die Bewohner getötet oder als Zwangsarbeiter verschleppt. Im Rahmen des Partisanenkriegs treiben die Deutschen auch den systematischen Völkermord an den Juden weiter voran: Sie erschießen die Mitglieder noch bestehender jüdischer Gemeinden und Ghettoinsassen.

Partisan war

The forces available to the German occupation authorities were insufficient to maintain control of the Soviet Union and to suppress resistance. From the start, they relied on targeted terror against the civilian population as a deterrent. The struggle against partisans was used as a pretext to further expand the racist war of annihilation.
The Wehrmacht, the SS, and police assisted by local forces, carried out »operations« against partisan fighters. These mostly failed to achieve their goal, since the partisans were able to flee in time. Uninvolved civilians died instead: countless villages were devastated and their inhabitants killed or deported as forced labourers. In the course of the partisan war, the Germans continued to push ahead with their systematic genocide on the Jews: They shot members of any Jewish communities that still existed and ghetto inmates.

Auszug aus der Propaganda-Zeitschrift *Die deutsche Polizei*, Ausgabe Ordnungspolizei vom 1. Oktober 1943.

Excerpt from the propaganda magazine *Die deutsche Polizei*, Ausgabe Ordnungspolizei, 1 October 1943, reporting »A bandits' camp is destroyed!«

Ein Banditenlager wird vernichtet, in: *Die deutsche Polizei* 11 (1943), H. 19, S. 391.

Historical introduction

Württembergische Landesbibliothek / Bibliothek für Zeitgeschichte, Stuttgart

Weißrussland, unbekannter Ort, 5./6. Juni 1942: Dia aus der Sammlung *Kampf im Osten* eines Majors der Wehrmacht. Das Bild zeigt Wehrmachtssoldaten im Rahmen des »Antipartisanenunternehmens Frühlingsfeier«. Die Deutschen brennen ganze Dörfer mit dem Ziel nieder, den Rückhalt der Partisanen zu schwächen.

Belarus, place unknown, 5/6 June 1942: Slide from the collection of a Wehrmacht major. The photo shows Wehrmacht soldiers taking part in the »anti-partisan operation Spring Festival«. The Germans burnt down entire villages with the aim of undermining support for the partisans.

Weißrussland, 1942: Angehörige der 13. Kompanie des Sumyer Partisanenverbands nach dem Überfall auf eine Gruppe von Wehrmachtssoldaten. Die Partisanen entkleiden die Toten, um sich deren Uniformen anzueignen. Der immer stärkeren Partisanenbewegung gelingt es, schrittweise die Hoheit über einen Teil der besetzten Gebiete zu erlangen.

Belarus, 1942: Members of the 13th company of the Sumy partisan formation after ambushing a group of German soldiers. The partisans took off the dead soldiers' uniforms for their own use. The increasingly strong partisan movement succeeded in gradually gaining supremacy over part of the occupied territory.

Rossijskij Gosudarstwennyj Archiv Kinofotodokumentow, Krasnogorsk

Historische Einführung

Rückzugsverbrechen und Kriegsende

Ab Anfang 1943 zwingt die Rote Armee die Wehrmacht endgültig zum Rückzug. Die Deutschen hinterlassen dabei »verbrannte Erde«: Sie begehen weitere Massenmorde, vor allem an nichtjüdischen Zivilisten, und zerstören die Infrastruktur. Jüdische Zwangsarbeiter des »Sonderkommandos 1005« müssen in der besetzten Sowjetunion Massengräber öffnen und die Leichen verbrennen, um so Spuren zu beseitigen. Danach werden sie ermordet.
Während die Rote Armee weiter vorrückt, treiben die deutschen Besatzer einen großen Teil der Häftlinge aus den Lagern im Osten in Richtung der Konzentrationslager im Reichsinneren. Noch nach der Kapitulation der Wehrmacht am 8. Mai 1945 sterben viele ehemalige Häftlinge an den Folgen der Lagerhaft. In der Sowjetunion fallen der deutschen Besatzungspolitik 14 Millionen Zivilisten zum Opfer. Unter ihnen sind mindestens 17.000 Patienten psychiatrischer Anstalten, bis zu 30.000 Roma und etwa zwei Millionen Juden, fast ein Drittel aller unter deutscher Herrschaft ermordeten europäischen Juden.

Crimes committed during the retreat and at the end of the war

In early 1943, the Red Army forced the Wehrmacht into final retreat. The Germans employed »scorched earth« tactics. They committed yet more mass murders, killing above all non-Jewish civilians, and destroying the infrastructure. In the occupied Soviet Union, Jewish forced labourers in »Special Commando 1005« had to open mass graves and burn the corpses in order to destroy all traces of German crimes. Then they were murdered.
While the Red Army advanced, the German occupiers drove large numbers of prisoners from the camps in the east towards concentration camps located in the centre of the Reich. Even after the Wehrmacht capitulated on 8 May 1945, many former prisoners perished as a result of conditions in the camps. In the Soviet Union, 14 million civilians fell victim to the German occupation policy. Among them were at least 17,000 patients from psychiatric institutions, up to 30,000 Romani, and around two million Jews, almost a third of all European Jews murdered under German rule.

Memorial Schertwam Faschistskogo Konzlagerja w Osaritschach, Osaritschi / Fotograf: E. Podschiwalow

Historical introduction

Derschawnij Archiv Odeskoj Oblasti, Odessa

Bogdanowka (Bohdanivka, Ukraine), 1944: Angehörige einer sowjetischen Untersuchungskommission öffnen ein Massengrab. Das Gebiet, in dem Bogdanowka liegt, steht ab Sommer 1941 unter Hoheit des deutschen Bündnispartners Rumänien. Die Besatzer pferchen hier über 54.000 Juden in Schweineställe. Viele verhungern, nahezu alle Überlebenden werden Ende Dezember 1941 erschossen oder lebendig verbrannt. Insgesamt sterben unter rumänischer Hoheit bis zu 300.000 Juden und etwa 12.500 Roma.

Bohdanivka (Ukraine), 1944: Soviet investigators open up a mass grave. The area around Bohdanivka had been under the jurisdiction of Germany's ally Romania since summer 1941. Here, the occupiers crammed more than 54,000 Jews into pigsties. Many of them starved. Nearly all the survivors were either shot or burned alive at the end of December 1941. In all, as many as 300,000 Jews and around 12,500 Romani died under Romanian rule.

Latvijas Valsts vēstures arhīvs, Riga

Rumbula (Lettland), Herbst 1944: Massengrab im Wald von Rumbula bei Riga, fotografiert vor den Grabungen der sowjetischen Untersuchungskommission. Hier waren am 30. November und 8. Dezember 1941 bis zu 27.000 Juden erschossen worden. Nach 1945 gerät Rumbula nahezu in Vergessenheit. Ein offizielles Gedenken an die Opfer der deutschen Massenerschießungen in der Sowjetunion beginnt erst Jahrzehnte nach Kriegsende.

Rumbula (Latvia), autumn 1944: Mass grave in the woods of Rumbula, close to Riga, picture taken before excavation by the Soviet investigators. On 30 November and 8 December 1941, as many as 27,000 Jews were shot here. After 1945, Rumbula was almost forgotten. The first official commemoration of the victims of German massacres in the Soviet Union did not take place until decades after the war.

Bei Osaritschi (Weißrussland), 18./19. März 1944: Aufnahme eines sowjetischen Militärberichterstatters vom Sterbelager Osaritschi. Vor ihrem Rückzug sperren Wehrmacht und Angehörige der Einsatzgruppe B hier über 40.000 kranke und schwache Zivilisten in drei eingezäunte Waldgebiete und verminen die Umgebung. In den drei Wochen bis zur Befreiung sterben dort über 9.000 Menschen an Hunger, durch Kälte oder bei Fluchtversuchen.

Near Ozarichi (Belarus), 18/19 March 1944: Photo of the Ozarichi camp, taken by a Soviet military reporter. Prior to retreat, the Wehrmacht and members of Einsatzgruppe B confined more than 40,000 sick and weak civilians to three fenced-off areas of a forest and mined the surroundings. In the three weeks before the camp was liberated by the Red Army, more than 9,000 inmates died of hunger, exposure, or the mines.

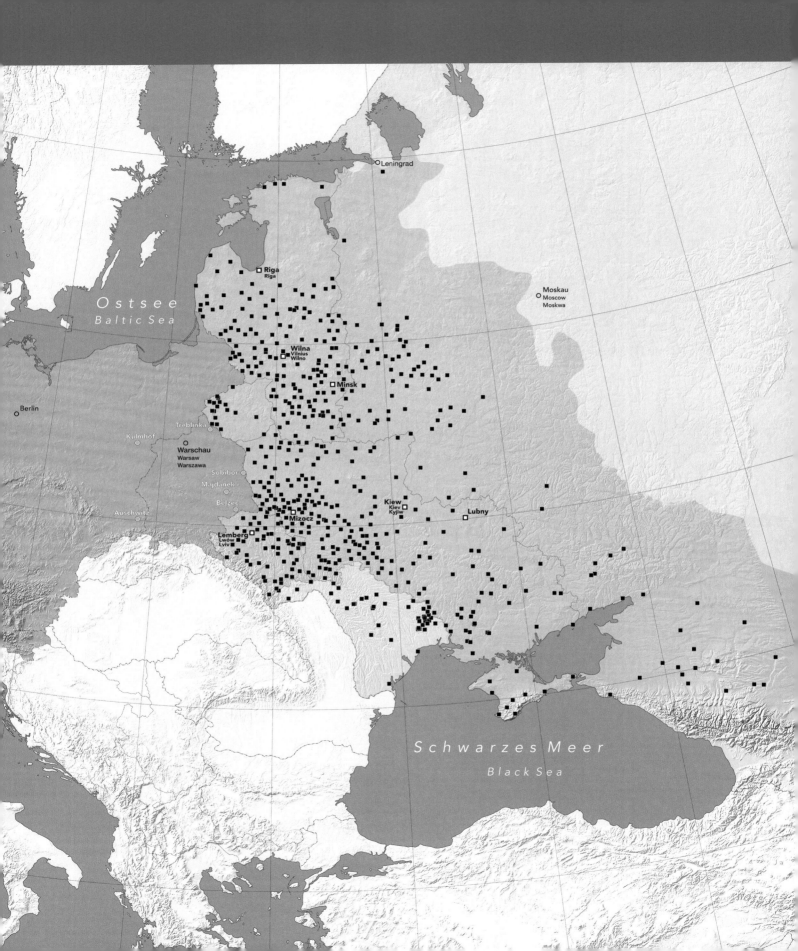

Massenerschießungen in der besetzten Sowjetunion
Mass shootings in the occupied Soviet Union

Deutsches Reich in den Grenzen von Juni 1941
German Reich within the borders of June 1941

Deutsche Besatzungsgebiete in der Sowjetunion
in ihrer größten Ausdehnung
German occupation on Soviet territories
at its greatest extent

Städte und Dörfer, in denen die Deutschen und lokale Helfer
zwischen 1941 und 1944 jeweils 500 oder mehr jüdische Kinder,
Frauen und Männer erschossen. An vielen Tatorten wurden
darüber hinaus auch Nichtjuden ermordet – kommunistische
Funktionäre, Roma oder Patienten psychiatrischer Anstalten.
Verzeichnet sind 573 Orte mit etwa 1,52 Millionen Opfern.

Häufig erschossen die Täter auch kleinere Gruppen oder einzelne
Personen. Aufgrund der großen Zahl dieser Verbrechen und ihrer
bis heute unzureichenden Erforschung sind sie auf der Karte nicht
kenntlich gemacht

Towns and villages where Germans and local collaborators shot
dead 500 or more Jewish men, women and children between
1941 and 1944. Many non-Jews were also killed, including
Communist functionaries, Roma or psychiatric patients. The map
shows 573 locations and a total of around 1.52 million victims.

In addition, the perpetrators frequently shot small groups or
individuals. These murders are not shown on the map as they
were so vast in number and have not yet been adequately
researched.

Deutsche Vernichtungslager im besetzen Polen
German extermination camps in occupied Poland

Mizocz, 14. Oktober 1942:
Vor der Erschießung jüdischer Kinder, Frauen und Männer.

Mizocz, 14 October 1942:
Before the shooting of Jewish children, women, and men.

Národní archiv, Prag, ČVKSNVZ, Az. 338/75 / Fotograf: Gustav Hille

Die Zerstörung einer Gemeinde – Mizocz in Wolhynien 1941 bis 1944
Eradication of a community – Mizocz in Volhynia 1941 – 1944

Über 1.000 jüdische Gemeinden fallen der nationalsozialistischen Vernichtungspolitik in der besetzten Sowjetunion zum Opfer. Zu ihnen zählt auch jene in der Kleinstadt Mizocz (Misotsch) in Wolhynien. Im 18. Jahrhundert, zur Zeit der polnisch-litauischen Adelsrepublik, hatten sich hier die ersten jüdischen Familien angesiedelt. In den 1920er Jahren machten sie rund die Hälfte der Ortsbevölkerung aus. Als Folge des »Hitler-Stalin-Pakts« fällt das Schtetl 1939 unter sowjetische Besatzung, im Juni 1941 marschiert die Wehrmacht ein. Unmittelbar danach beginnt die Verfolgung der jüdischen Einwohner. Im Oktober 1942 erschießt ein Kommando der Sicherheitspolizei und des Sicherheitsdienstes der SS innerhalb von zwei Tagen bis zu 1.500 Juden in Mizocz. Das Schicksal dieser jüdischen Kinder, Frauen und Männer steht hier stellvertretend für die Ermordung von etwa zwei Millionen Juden in der besetzten Sowjetunion.

More than 1,000 Jewish communities were destroyed during Nazi Germany's occupation of the Soviet Union. One of them was that of the small town of Mizocz (Mizoch) in Volhynia. The first Jewish families settled here during the 18th century, at the time of the Polish-Lithuanian Commonwealth (Kingdom of Poland and Grand Duchy of Lithuania). By the 1920s, around half of the town's population was Jewish. As a result of the »Molotov-Ribbentrop Pact«, the shtetl was occupied by Soviet forces in 1939. In June 1941, the Wehrmacht invaded the region. Persecution of Jewish inhabitants began immediately. In October 1942, a detachment of the Security Police and the Security Service of the SS (SD) shot as many as 1,500 Jews in Mizocz within two days. The murder of these Jewish men, women and children, is described here as an example of the fate of around two million Jews in the occupied Soviet Union.

Die Zerstörung einer Gemeinde – Mizocz in Wolhynien 1941 bis 1944

Eradication of a community – Mizocz in Volhynia 1941 – 1944

Jüdische Bevölkerungsanteile in der westlichen Sowjetunion bis Mitte 1941
Jewish share of the population in the western Soviet Union as of mid-1941

Jüdische Bevölkerungsanteile in der westlichen Sowjetunion in den Grenzen von Juni 1941, hervorgehoben sind einzelne Orte. Die Darstellung fußt auf den Volkszählungen in Rumänien (1930), Estland (1934), Lettland (1935) und in der Sowjetunion (1939). Die Zahlen zu Litauen entstammen einer sowjetischen Schätzung zum 1. Januar 1941. Die Darstellung zu Ostpolen bezieht sich auf die polnische Volkszählung von 1931 und auf Schätzungen der Historiker Andrej Umansky und Alexander Kruglow für das Jahr 1941.

Jewish share of the population in the western Soviet Union within the borders of June 1941, with individual localities highlighted. The presentation is based on census data from Romania (1930), Estonia (1934), Latvia (1935), and the Soviet Union (1939). The figures for Lithuania come from a Soviet estimate as of 1 January 1941. The presentation regarding eastern Poland reflects the Polish census of 1931 and estimates by historians Andrej Umansky and Alexander Kruglov for 1941.

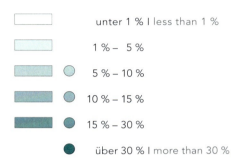

unter 1 % I less than 1 %
1 % – 5 %
5 % – 10 %
10 % – 15 %
15 % – 30 %
über 30 % I more than 30 %

Massenerschießungen in der besetzten Sowjetunion
Mass shootings in the occupied Soviet Union

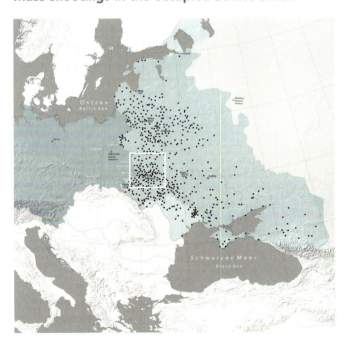

Wolhynien
Volhynia

Erklärungen siehe Karte Seite 32 I Explanations see map page 32

Die Zerstörung einer Gemeinde – Mizocz in Wolhynien 1941 bis 1944

Misozka Miska Biblioteka, Mizocz

Privatbesitz Boren

Das jüdische Ehepaar Joseph und Anne Langer (rechts). Anne und ihre Tochter Chaja zählen zu den wenigen Überlebenden.
The Jewish couple, Joseph and Anne Langer (right). Anne and her daughter Chaja were two of the few survivors.

Mizocz, Hauptplatz, vor 1939: In der Stadt wohnen Juden, Polen, Ukrainer und Tschechen. Die jüdische Gemeinde lebt unter anderem vom überregionalen Obsthandel und gilt als wohlhabend. Unter den sowjetischen Besatzern müssen private Betriebe schließen. Zahlreiche Juden aus dem deutsch besetzten West- und Zentralpolen treffen in der Stadt ein; viele Flüchtlinge werden von den sowjetischen Behörden nach Sibirien deportiert.

Mizocz, main square, before 1939: the town's population consisted of Jews, Poles, Ukrainians, and Czechs. The Jewish community lived largely from the fruit trade and was regarded as wealthy. Under Soviet occupation, private businesses had to close down. Numerous Jews from those parts of west and central Poland occupied by the Germans arrived in the town. The Soviet authorities deported many refugees to Siberia.

Privatbesitz Michaltschuk

Graf Józef Dunin-Karwicki (1870 – 1940, hinten, 3.v.r.). Der polnische Adlige wird von sowjetischen Behörden verschleppt.
Count Józef Dunin-Karwicki (1870 – 1940, back, 3rd from right). The Polish aristocrat was deported by the Soviet authorities.

Eradication of a community – Mizocz in Volhynia 1941 – 1944

Mizocz; sefer zikaron. Tel Aviv 1961.

Die chassidische Familie Kotel. Ihre Mitglieder werden von den Deutschen ermordet. Abbildung aus dem Erinnerungsbuch zur jüdischen Gemeinde (*Mizocz: Sefer zikaron*).
The Hasidic Kotel family. The entire family was murdered by the Germans. Photograph from the memorial book of the Jewish community (*Mizocz: Sefer zikaron*).

Mizocz; sefer zikaron

Marsch des zionistischen Jugendverbands Beitar auf dem Hauptplatz.
March of the Beitar zionist youth movement on the main square.

Mizocz; sefer zikaron

Angehörige der sozialistisch-zionistischen Jugendbewegung Gordonia. Auf dem Schild steht »Arbeitergruppe«.
Members of the socialist-youth zionist movement Gordonia. The sign says »workers group«.

Misozka Miska Biblioteka, Mizocz

Kindergarten mit katholischen Schwestern, 1933.
Kindergarten with Catholic nuns, 1933.

Misozka Miska Biblioteka, Mizocz

Kleinstadtspaziergang, 1939.
A walk in the town, 1939.

Privatbesitz Michaltschuk

Schloss der Dunin-Karwickis, nach dem deutschen Einmarsch Wehrmachtlazarett. Juden müssen hier Zwangsarbeit leisten.
Dunin-Karwicki Palace – used as a hospital for the Wehrmacht after the German invasion. Jews were subjected to forced labour here.

Privatbesitz Michaltschuk

Orangerie der gräflichen Schlossanlage.
Orangery of the count's palace.

Privatbesitz Michaltschuk

Zuckerfabrik. In ihrer Nähe finden im Oktober 1942 die Massenerschießungen statt.
Sugar factory. The mass shootings of October 1942 were carried out not far from here.

Die Zerstörung einer Gemeinde – Mizocz in Wolhynien 1941 bis 1944

1941

Chronik der Ereignisse
Chronicle of events

27. Juni

Wehrmachtverbände erreichen Mizocz; etwa 300 Juden können die Stadt zuvor noch verlassen.

Bei einer jüdischen Beerdigung bewerfen Ukrainer die Trauernden mit Steinen.

Wehrmacht troops reach Mizocz; around 300 Jews are able to flee from the town before the troops arrive.

At a Jewish funeral, Ukrainians throw stones at the mourners.

Das Verhältnis zwischen Polen und Ukrainern, das unter der sowjetischen Besatzung trotz anti-polnischer Propaganda nicht gelitten hatte, verschlechtert sich. Viele Ukrainer erhoffen sich die Eigenstaatlichkeit mit Hilfe der Deutschen.

The relationship between Poles and Ukrainians, which had not suffered from the Soviet occupation despite anti-Polish propaganda, deteriorates. Many Ukrainians hope that the Germans will help them gain sovereignty.

27 June

BArch B 162 Bild 04233 / Fotograf: Hanns Pilz

Eradication of a community – Mizocz in Volhynia 1941 – 1944

29. Juni

Pogrom von Ukrainern gegen Juden, mehrere Juden werden ermordet. Die Deutschen unterbinden weitere Ausschreitungen. Zugleich zwingen sie die Juden zum Tragen von Kennzeichen an der Kleidung. Ein Judenrat muss seine Arbeit aufnehmen.

Pogrom by Ukrainians against Jews, several Jews are murdered. The Germans stop the excesses. Jews are forced to wear special markings on their clothes and are required to form a Jewish council.

4. August

In Ostróg (Ostroh) erschießen Einheiten der 1. SS-Infanteriebrigade mindestens 2.000 jüdische Männer, Frauen und Kinder.
Am 1. September 1941 werden nochmals etwa 2.100 jüdische Männer aus Ostróg ermordet.

In Ostróg (Ostroh), units of the 1st SS Infantry Brigade shoot at least 2,000 Jewish men, women and children.
On 1 September 1941, another 2,100 Jewish men from Ostróg are murdered.

7. August

In Zdołbunów (Sdolbuniw) erschießt ein Kommando der Einsatzgruppe C mehrere hundert jüdische Männer.

In Zdołbunów (Zdolbuniv), a commando from Einsatzgruppe C kills several hundred Jewish men.

September / Oktober

Die Firma *Josef Jung* setzt zahlreiche jüdische Zwangsarbeiter aus Mizocz ein. Der leitende Ingenieur Hermann Friedrich Gräbe (1900 – 1986) versucht unter großem persönlichem und finanziellem Einsatz, Juden zu retten.

The *Josef Jung* company makes use of numerous Jewish forced labourers. With great personal commitment and at great expense, chief engineer Hermann Friedrich Gräbe (1900 – 1986) tries to rescue some of them.

29 June   **4 August**   **7 August**   **September / October**

BArch B 162 Bild 04235 / Fotograf: Hanns Pilz

BArch B 162 Bild 04237 / Fotograf: Hanns Pilz

Die Zerstörung einer Gemeinde – Mizocz in Wolhynien 1941 bis 1944

1941

7. November **1941 / 1942**

Über 20.000 Rownoer Juden werden in einen Kiefernwald getrieben und dort von Angehörigen der Einsatzgruppe C und Einheiten der Ordnungspolizei erschossen.

More than 20.000 Jews from Równe (Rivne) are driven into the surrounding woods and are shot there by members of Einsatzgruppe C and battalions of the Order Police.

Nichtjuden meiden die jüdischen Nachbarn. Die von den Deutschen aufgestellte ukrainische Schutzmannschaft bedrängt und beraubt Juden. Zwei Angestellte der Firma *Josef Jung* prügeln Zeugen zufolge Zwangsarbeiter zu Tode.

Non-Jews shun their Jewish neighbours. The Ukrainian auxiliary police set up by the Germans harasses and robs Jews. According to witness accounts, two *Josef Jung* employees beat forced labourers to death.

7 November **1941 / 1942**

Vorige Seite:
Bei Rowno (Równe/Riwne, Polen, ab 1939 sowjetisch besetzt), 16. November 1941: Fotos des Wehrmachtsangehörigen Hanns (Johann) Pilz (1898 – 1964). 1959 sagt er aus: »Nach den Erschiessungen bin ich mit meinem Freund Strauss bei der Hinrichtungsstätte gewesen und habe noch bei herrlichem Sonnenschein die Ukrainer fotographiert, wie sie den Boden nach Wertstücken absuchten. Viele waren entsetzt, es gab aber auch eine ganze Reihe von gleichgültigen.«

Previous page:
Near Równe (Rivne, Poland, occupied by the Soviet Union in 1939), 16 November 1941: Photos taken by Wehrmacht soldier Hanns (Johann) Pilz (1898 – 1964). In 1959, he testified: »After the shootings I went to the execution site with my friend Strauss. The sun was shining, and I took photos of the Ukrainians as they searched the ground for valuables. Many were horrified, but there were quite a few who were indifferent.«

Eradication of a community – Mizocz in Volhynia 1941 – 1944

1942 >

Frühjahr

Auf Veranlassung des deutschen Gebietskommissariats müssen die Juden in Mizocz, Zdołbunów und Ostróg in Ghettos umziehen.

By order of the German District Commissar's office, Jews living in Mizocz, Zdołbunów and Ostróg are forced to move into ghettos.

13. Juli

Hermann Friedrich Gräbe erfährt von der bevorstehenden Ermordung der Ghettobewohner in Rowno. Er kann 74 seiner Arbeiter und deren Frauen von dort abziehen, darunter 60 Mizoczer.

Hermann Friedrich Gräbe learns about the imminent killing of the inhabitants of the Równe ghetto and succeeds in removing 74 of his workers and their wives from there, including 60 inhabitants of Mizocz.

14. Juli

5.000 Rownoer Juden werden erschossen.

5,000 Jews from Równe are shot.

August

Auf Befehl des Gebietskommissariats Sdolbunow wird der jüdische Metzger Sejde Gelman auf dem Marktplatz von Mizocz gehängt.

By order of the District Commissar's office for Zdołbunów, Jewish butcher Sejde Gelman, is hanged in the market square of Mizocz.

Spring   13 July   14 July   August

Yad Vashem, Jerusalem

Zdołbunów, Juni 1942: Einige Wochen vor der Erhängung von Sejde Gelman lässt Gebietskommissar Georg Marschall den jüdischen Tischler Josef (Jakob) Diener hinrichten. Diener trägt dabei ein Schild mit der Aufschrift: »Ich habe einen Befehl des Gebietskommissars nicht befolgt.« Der Fotograf ist unbekannt; 1947 übergibt der Überlebende Jakob Segal die Aufnahme an die Historische Kommission im Displaced Persons-Lager in Landsberg am Lech.

Zdołbunów, June 1942: A few weeks before Sejde Gelman was executed, District Commissar Georg Marschall had Jewish carpenter Josef (Jakob) Diener hanged. Diener was forced to wear a sign saying: »I did not follow the District Commissar's orders.« The photographer is not known; in 1947, survivor Jakob Segal handed the photograph over to the Historic Commission in the Displaced Persons camp in Landsberg am Lech.

Die Zerstörung einer Gemeinde – Mizocz in Wolhynien 1941 bis 1944

1942

16. August

Die deutsche Führung verschärft ihre Ausplünderungspolitik. Zukünftig soll die gesamte Wehrmacht ihren Lebensmittelbedarf aus der besetzten Sowjetunion decken. Der Reichskommissar der Ukraine, Erich Koch, dringt auf die baldige Ermordung aller noch lebenden Juden, um die Zahl der Nahrungsmittelverbraucher drastisch zu senken.

The German leadership intensifies its policy of exploitation. The entire Wehrmacht is now to cover its food supplies from the Soviet Union. Reich Commissar Ukraine, Erich Koch, urges to kill the remaining Jews in order to radically lower the number of food consumers.

16 August

28. bis 31. August

Tagung der Gebietskommissare. Die Zivilverwaltung vereinbart mit dem Kommandeur der Sicherheitspolizei und des SD (KdS) Rowno, Dr. Karl Pütz, innerhalb von fünf Wochen alle Juden in Wolhynien mit Ausnahme von 500 Fachkräften umzubringen.

Meeting of the District Commissars. The civil administration agrees with the Commanding Officer of the Security Police and the SD (KdS) Rowno, Dr. Karl Pütz, to eliminate all the Jews in Volhynia within five weeks, with the exception of 500 skilled workers.

From 28 till 31 August

21. September

Die Mizoczer Juden begehen den Feiertag Jom-Kippur. Mit Beteiligung des Judenrats unter Abe Stievel bildet sich eine Widerstandsgruppe: Jugendliche bewaffnen sich mit Äxten, Messern und Eisenstangen.

The Jews of Mizocz observe the Jewish holiday of Yom-Kippur. A resistance group is formed with the participation of the Jewish Council led by Abe Stievel: Youths arm themselves with axes, knives, and iron bars.

21 September

Anfang Oktober

Der KdS Rowno kündigt dem Gebietskommissariat die Ermordung der Juden von Zdołbunów, Mizocz und Ostróg an. Der Leiter des deutschen Arbeitsamts in Zdołbunów, Hans Raabe (1904 – 1974), wird informiert, »um hinsichtlich des weiteren Arbeitseinsatzes disponieren zu können«.

KdS Rowno announces the plan to murder the Jews of Zdołbunów, Mizocz, and Ostróg to the District Commissariat. The head of the German labour office in Zdołbunów, Hans Raabe (1904 – 1974), is informed of this »in order to plan future work assignments accordingly«.

Early October

Eradication of a community – Mizocz in Volhynia 1941 – 1944

	Um den 11. Oktober	**12. Oktober**	**13. Oktober**
Der polnische Inhaber der Mizoczer Zuckerfabrik beobachtet einen Gendarmen, der sich nach Gruben umsieht. Er warnt seinen jüdischen Arbeiter Idel Bronstein; dieser benachrichtigt den Judenrat. Auf Nachfrage wiegeln deutsche Stellen ab.	Der Bezirksleutnant der Gendarmerie, Joseph Paur, erhält vom KdS Rowno den Befehl, die drei Ghettos durch Gendarmerie und ukrainische Schutzmannschaften umstellen zu lassen.	Hermann Friedrich Gräbe sucht Gebietskommissar Georg Marschall auf, nachdem er gerüchteweise von der Aushebung von Gruben bei Zdołbunów erfahren hat. Marschall verweist auf seinen Stellvertreter Otto Köller (1908 – 1965). Dieser gibt keine Auskunft.	Nach einer späteren Zeugenaussage von Ernestine Schmitt, Küchenleiterin bei der Firma *Josef Jung*, werden Leuchtraketen über dem Ghetto in Zdołbunów abgeschossen. Im Verlauf des Tages erschießt ein Kommando der Sicherheitspolizei und des SD außerhalb der Stadt über 1.500 Juden.
The Polish owner of the Mizocz sugar factory observes a gendarme looking for pits. He warns his Jewish worker, Idel Bronstein, who in turn informs the Jewish Council. Asked about this, German authorities play down the issue.	District-gendarmerie lieutenant, Joseph Paur, receives an order from KdS Rowno to have the three ghettos surrounded by the gendarmerie and the Ukrainian auxiliary police.	Hermann Friedrich Gräbe visits the District Commissar, Georg Marschall, after hearing rumours about pits being dug near Zdołbunów. Marschall refers him to his deputy, Otto Köller (1908 – 1965), who refuses to provide any information.	According to a later testimony by Ernestine Schmitt, head of the canteen at the *Josef Jung* company, rocket flares are shot into the air over the Zdołbunów ghetto. In the course of the day, a commando of the Security Police and the SD shoot more than 1,500 Jews outside the town.
	Around 11 October	**12 October**	**13 October**

Die Zerstörung einer Gemeinde – Mizocz in Wolhynien 1941 bis 1944

1942

13. Oktober, 3.30 Uhr

Abriegelung des Mizoczer Ghettos. Ukrainische und deutsche Polizisten suchen nach Versteckten. Auf Fliehende wird geschossen. Jüdische Bewohner legen Feuer; sie hoffen, in dessen Schutz zu entkommen und wollen verhindern, dass ihr Besitz an die Verfolger fällt.

The Mizocz ghetto is cordoned off. Ukrainian and German police start looking for people in hiding. Anyone seen fleeing is shot. Jewish inhabitants lay fires in the hope that this will assist their escape, and also to prevent their possessions falling to their persecutors.

13 October 3.30 a.m.

Auf Anordnung der Deutschen müssen sich die Ghettoinsassen mit Proviant für drei Tage auf dem Marktplatz sammeln.

The Germans force the ghetto inmates to assemble in the market square and to bring food for three days.

13. Oktober, 9.00 Uhr

Die Feuerwehr wird nach Mizocz gerufen, um die Brände zu löschen.

The fire brigade is called to Mizocz to put out the fires.

13 October 9.00 a.m.

13. Oktober, tagsüber

Schaulustige strömen nach Mizocz. Hunderte ermordete Juden liegen am Straßenrand und am Fluss Stubła.

Onlookers flock to Mizocz. Hundreds of murdered Jews line the streets and the banks of the River Stubła.

**13 October
In the course of the day**

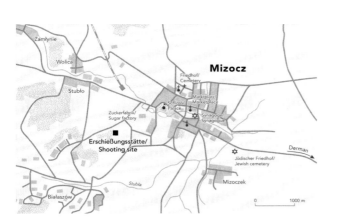

46

Eradication of a community – Mizocz in Volhynia 1941 – 1944

14. Oktober, morgens

Die auf dem Marktplatz Versammelten werden zum Fußballplatz getrieben. Nach abweichenden Erinnerungen werden sie bereits an den Erschießungsort geführt; den Zug führt ein deutscher Gendarm mit Motorrad und Maschinengewehr an.

Those assembled in the market square are forced to walk to the football field. Other witnesses claim that they were taken to the killing site immediately, led by a German policeman on a motorcycle and carrying a machine gun.

Die Ukrainer feiern das Schutzfest der Jungfrau Maria. Viele Menschen gehen in die Kirche.

Ukrainians observe the Feast of the Mother of God. Many people go to church.

14. Oktober tagsüber

Das Tötungskommando der Sicherheitspolizei und des SD trifft ein. Die festgehaltenen Juden werden gruppenweise in eine Geländesenke getrieben und gezwungen, ihre Kleider abzulegen.

The killing squad of the Security Police and the SD arrives. The detained Jews are herded into a hollow in groups and are forced to undress.

Die Schützen töten Kinder, Frauen und Männer durch Genickschüsse. Manche Opfer müssen offenbar zuvor über ein Brett gehen und fallen dann getroffen in vorbereitete Gruben. Andere werden gezwungen, sich auf die Toten oder Verletzten zu legen, bevor das Mordkommando auch sie erschießt.

The killing squad shoots men, women and children, one by one, in the base of the skull. Apparently, some of the victims first have to walk across a board so that they drop into the prepared pits as they are hit. Others are forced to lie down on top of the dead or injured victims before being shot as well.

14 October Morning

**14 October
In the course of the day**

Die Zerstörung einer Gemeinde – Mizocz in Wolhynien 1941 bis 1944

1942

15. Oktober

Deutsche und Ukrainer machen Jagd auf Juden. Die Aufgefundenen werden bei den Gruben erschossen. Die nichtjüdische Bevölkerung sammelt die Kleidungsstücke der Toten ein. Das ehemalige Ghetto wird geplündert.

Germans and Ukrainians hunt down Jews. Those who are found are shot next to the pits. The non-Jewish population collects the clothes of the corpses. The former ghetto is looted.

Die Auslöschung der jüdischen Gemeinde von Ostróg beginnt. Dort werden allein am 15. Oktober 1942 etwa 2.000 Menschen erschossen.

Extermination of the Jewish community of Ostróg begins. On 15 October 1942 alone, around 2,000 people are shot there.

Herbst 1942

Mizoczer Juden, teilweise ganze Familien, suchen Zuflucht in der Umgebung. Einzelne Ukrainer, Polen und Tschechen verstecken sie. Zeitweise bieten auch selbstgegrabene Unterstände in den Wäldern Schutz.

Jews from Mizocz, sometimes entire families, try to hide in the surrounding areas. In isolated cases, Ukrainians, Poles, and Czechs hide them. Some Jews find refuge in dugouts in the forests.

Ende 1942

Die Ukrainische Aufständische Armee (UPA) gewinnt an Zulauf. Sie bekämpft die Deutschen, aber auch polnische und sowjetische Partisanen. Viele UPA-Angehörige sind vom Feindbild des »jüdischen Bolschewismus« durchdrungen und ermorden versteckte jüdische Kinder, Frauen und Männer.

The Ukrainian Insurgent Army (UPA) is gaining supporters. It fights the Germans, but also Polish and Soviet partisans. Many UPA members are imbued with the enemy image of »Jewish Bolshevism«. They murder Jewish men, women and children in hiding.

15 October **Autumn 1942** **End of 1942**

Eradication of a community – Mizocz in Volhynia 1941 – 1944

1943 >

31. Dezember

Das Generalkommissariat Wolhynien-Podolien meldet: »Judentum. Die Bereinigung des Gebietes steht vor dem Abschluß.« Zwischen Mai und Dezember 1942 werden allein in Wolhynien etwa 160.000 Juden ermordet.

The General Commissariat of Volhynia and Podolia reports: »Jewry. Clearance of the area almost completed.« Between May and December 1942, some 160,000 Jews are killed in Volhynia alone.

2. April

Einige Mizoczer Juden feiern Pessach im Wald. Mit der Handmühle eines Bauern mahlen sie Mehl für ungesäuerte Brote. »Angesichts der Erinnerung an bessere Zeiten wurden wir sehr traurig«, erinnert sich der Überlebende Nachum Kopyt (1907 – 1992).

Some of the Jews from Mizocz celebrate Passover in the woods. Using a hand-mill given to them by a farmer, they grind flour for unleavened bread. »Recalling better times, everyone became very sad«, survivor Nachum Kopyt (1907 – 1992) remembers.

31 December

2 April

Národní archiv, Prag, ČVKSNVZ, Az. 338/75 / Fotograf: Gustav Hille

Mizocz, 14. Oktober 1942: Erschießung jüdischer Kinder, Frauen und Männer. Fotograf der Aufnahmen ist der aus dem Sudetenland stammende Gustav Hille (1899 – 1956), der von Herbst 1941 bis Mitte 1943 beim Gendarmerieposten Mizocz stationiert ist.

Mizocz, 14 October 1942: Shooting of Jewish children, women, and men. The photographer is Gustav Hille (1899 – 1956) from the Sudetenland, who was stationed at the Mizocz gendarmerie post from autumn 1941 to mid-1943.

Die Zerstörung einer Gemeinde – Mizocz in Wolhynien 1941 bis 1944

1943

Frühjahr

Viele Polen fliehen aus Angst vor der UPA aus der Umgebung nach Mizocz; sie ziehen in leerstehende Häuser der Mizoczer Juden.

Out of fear of the UPA, many Poles flee the surrounding area and head for Mizocz; they move into houses vacated by the Jews.

Spring

3. August

Die Deutschen exhumieren im Rahmen der »Aktion 1005« vielerorts die Leichen ermordeter Juden und verbrennen sie, um Spuren zu beseitigen. Die Dienststelle des KdS Rowno versendet ein Rundschreiben an örtliche Polizeiposten. Darin bittet sie, alle Massengräber anzugeben. 200 solcher Stellen werden gemeldet.

As part of »Aktion 1005«, the Germans exhume the corpses of murdered Jews in many areas and burn them in order to destroy evidence. The office of KdS Rowno sends out a circular asking police offices on site to inform it of the locations of all mass graves. 200 such graves are reported.

3 August

Ende August

Die UPA greift Mizocz an. Ihre Kämpfer ermorden über 100 Polen. Große Teile der Stadt brennen ab. Die überlebenden Polen werden mit der Eisenbahn nach Zdołbunów evakuiert. Der Vertreibungs- und Mordpolitik von Ukrainern fallen in Wolhynien zwischen 1942 und 1945 40.000 bis 60.000 Polen zum Opfer.

The UPA attacks Mizocz. Its combatants murder more than 100 Poles. Large sections of the town burn down. The surviving Poles are evacuated to Zdołbunów by train. Between 1942 and 1945, 40,000 – 60,000 Poles in Volhynia fall victim to displacement and murder by Ukrainians.

End of August

Eradication of a community – Mizocz in Volhynia 1941 – 1944

1944

Februar

Die Rote Armee erreicht die Gegend um Mizocz. Die wenigen überlebenden Mizoczer Juden verlassen ihre Verstecke, unter ihnen 13 Personen, die sich zuletzt in dem von Tschechen bewohnten Dorf Borszczówka aufgehalten haben. Etwa 100 jüdische Überlebende sammeln sich in Zdołbunów.

The Red Army reaches the Mizocz area. The few surviving Jews from Mizocz come out of hiding, including 13 people last seen in the village Borszczówka, inhabited by Czechs. Around 100 Jewish survivors gather in Zdołbunów.

February

Mizocz; sefer zikaron

Mizocz, undatiert: der Ort der Massenerschießung. Abbildung aus dem 1961 erschienenen Erinnerungsbuch der ehemaligen jüdischen Einwohner von Mizocz.

Mizocz, no date: the killing site. Photo from the memorial book of the former Jewish inhabitants of Mizocz, which was published in 1961.

Die Deutsche Besatzung in Mizocz – Befehlswege und Täterschaft
The German occupation of Mizocz – perpetrators and chains of command

Wie an vielen anderen Orten beruht das Verbrechen in Mizocz vor allem auf der Zusammenarbeit zwischen dem SS- und Polizeiapparat und der deutschen Zivilverwaltung. Zwischen den Führern der Besatzungsorgane treten zwar immer wieder Spannungen auf, weil ihre Zuständigkeiten bewusst ungenau abgegrenzt sind, die Zusammenarbeit auf den unteren Ebenen läuft jedoch ohne größere Konflikte.

Die Grundlage für die Verfolgungs- und Mordpolitik legt die Wehrmacht, die Ende Juni 1941 in das Städtchen einrückt. Bei der Ermordung der Juden spielt sie im Gegensatz zu anderen Orten keine direkte Rolle – zum 1. September 1941 gibt das Militär seine Zuständigkeit an die deutsche Zivilverwaltung ab. Mizocz ist fortan Teil des Gebietskommissariats Sdolbunow im Reichskommissariat Ukraine. Deutsche Gendarmen patrouillieren nun in den Straßen, bald unterstützt von einer ukrainischen Schutzmannschaft. Diese Polizeikräfte treiben am 13. Oktober 1942 die Mizoczer Juden aus dem Ghetto. Die Massenerschießungen in den folgenden Tagen werden von einem angereisten Kommando der Sicherheitspolizei und des SD verübt.

As in many other places, the crimes committed in Mizocz can be largely attributed to cooperation between the SS and police forces and the German civil administration. Although tensions frequently arose between the leaders of the occupation authorities because their responsibilities were intentionally vaguely defined, there were no major conflicts in cooperation at lower levels.

The basis for this policy of persecution and murder was laid by the Wehrmacht, which entered the small town at the end of June 1941. As opposed to other places, however, the Wehrmacht did not play a direct role in the murder of the Jewish population – on 1 September 1941, the military handed over responsibility to the German civil administration. Mizocz was from now on part of the District Commissariat Sdolbunow in the Reich Commissariat Ukraine. German gendarmes patrolled the streets, soon supported by a unit of the Ukrainian auxiliary police. These police forces drove Jews out of the Mizocz ghetto on 13 October 1942. The mass shootings that took place in the following days were carried out by a commando of the Security Police and the Security Service, which had come to Mizocz specifically for this purpose.

Die Deutsche Besatzung in Mizocz – Befehlswege und Täterschaft

Zivilverwaltung in der Ukraine

Die Zivilverwaltung unter Reichskommissar Erich Koch soll vor allem die Grundlage zur systematischen Ausbeutung der Ukraine schaffen. Die Politik vor Ort betreiben Gebiets- und Stadtkommissare, die Koch unterstellt und zum Teil von ihm persönlich ausgesucht sind. Sie erfassen die jüdische Bevölkerung zur Zwangsarbeit, richten Ghettos ein und sind häufig an der Planung der Massenmorde beteiligt. Leiter des Gebietskommissariats Sdolbunow, zu dem auch Mizocz gehört, wird im Oktober 1941 Georg Marschall.

Civilian administration in Ukraine

The main task of the civil administration under the leadership of Reich Commissar Erich Koch was to lay the groundwork for systematic exploitation of Ukraine. Local politics were the responsibility of District Commissars and Town Commissars, who reported to Koch and were partly hand-picked by him. They registered the Jewish population for forced labour, set up the ghettos, and they were often involved in planning mass shootings. Georg Marschall was appointed head of the District Commissariat Sdolbunow, to which Mizocz belonged, in October 1941.

BArch Bild 146-1994-006-30A

BArch B 162 Bild 04245 und 04246

Kiew, Höhlenkloster, ohne Datum: Der Reichsminister für die besetzten Ostgebiete Alfred Rosenberg (1893 – 1946, Mitte) mit dem ihm unterstellten Erich Koch (1896 – 1986, rechts). Koch wird von Hitler gegen Rosenbergs Willen eingesetzt. Mehrfach umgeht er die Anweisungen seines Vorgesetzten und versucht, sich aus dessen Unterstellung zu lösen.

Kiev, Monastery of the Caves, no date: Reichsminister for the Occupied Eastern Territories, Alfred Rosenberg (1893 – 1946, centre), with his subordinate, Erich Koch (1896 – 1986, right). Hitler appointed Koch against Rosenberg's will. Koch bypassed the orders of his superior several times and tried to free himself of the status of a subordinate.

Rowno, 20. April 1942: Erich Koch bei einer Parade am Geburtstag Adolf Hitlers. Koch ist seit 1928 Gauleiter von Ostpreußen und hält sich nur selten an seinem zweiten Dienstsitz in der Ukraine auf. Bei seinen Besuchen lebt er wie ein König, hält sich eigens einen Fischreferenten und lässt ganze Dörfer zwangsumsiedeln, um sich ein Jagdrevier einzurichten.

Równe, 20 April 1942: Erich Koch at a parade on Adolf Hitler's birthday. Koch had been Gauleiter (regional Nazi party leader) in East Prussia since 1928 and was seldom present at his second office in Ukraine. When he did visit Ukraine, he lived like a lord, had his own fish officer and had entire villages relocated in order to create hunting grounds for his own use.

The German occupation of Mizocz – perpetrators and chains of command

Deutsche Dienststelle (WASt) Berlin

Staatsarchiv Nürnberg 2004-01-Nr. 199 /
Fotograf: Bruno Jebramek (1912 - 1989)

Georg Marschall (1903 – 1985), 1938: Der Handelslehrer tritt 1930 in die NSDAP und die SA ein. Spätestens ab 1937 unterrichtet er auf der Ordensburg Vogelsang (Eifel) den Führungsnachwuchs der Partei. Bei Kriegsbeginn meldet er sich freiwillig zur Wehrmacht. 1941 wird er für die Tätigkeit in der Zivilverwaltung zurückgestellt; er übernimmt das Amt des Gebietskommissars in Zdołbunów.

Georg Marschall (1903 – 1985), 1938: The business teacher joined the NSDAP and the SA in 1930. From 1937 on, at the latest, he instructed the party's future leaders at the Castle of the Order Vogelsang. When war began, he volunteered for the Wehrmacht. In 1941, he was released from duty for a job in the civil administration; he was appointed District Commissar for Zdołbunów.

Stade, Februar 1960, Zeitungsfoto: Das Landgericht Stade verurteilt Marschall wegen der Erhängung von Josef (Jakob) Diener zu lebenslanger Haft. Das Strafmaß wird 1967 in einem neuen Verfahren auf fünf Jahre herabgesetzt, da Marschall das Gericht überzeugt, auf Befehl gehandelt zu haben.

Stade, February 1960, Newspaper photograph: The State Court of Stade sentenced Marschall to lifelong imprisonment for the hanging of Josef (Jakob) Diener. In 1967, the sentence was reduced to five years in a second trial after Marschall convinced the court that he was only acting on orders.

Zdołbunów, Januar 1942: Hermann Friedrich Gräbe (links) mit dem stellvertretenden Gebietskommissar Erich Habenicht während eines Besuchs von dessen Ehefrau. Bei seinen Rettungsbemühungen für Juden nutzt Gräbe seine Stellung als Vertreter seiner Baufirma, die für die Wehrmacht arbeitet. Es gelingt ihm, Einfluss auf die Zivilverwaltung zu gewinnen.

Zdołbunów, January 1942: Hermann Friedrich Gräbe (left) with Deputy District Commissiar, Erich Habenicht, during a visit by the latter's wife. Gräbe used his position as representative of his construction company, which worked for the Wehrmacht, to help Jews. He managed to gain influence over the civil administration.

Staatsarchiv Nürnberg 2004-01-Nr. 176

Die Deutsche Besatzung in Mizocz – Befehlswege und Täterschaft

Der Reichsführer-SS und Chef der Deutschen Polizei

Seit 1936 unterstehen Heinrich Himmler sämtliche deutsche Polizei- und SS-Verbände. Nach dem Überfall auf die Sowjetunion beansprucht er die zentrale Leitung des Völkermords. Er vergewissert sich dabei immer wieder Hitlers Zustimmung. Seine Befehle geben meist nur einen Rahmen vor. Auch der Entschluss zur Erschießung der Mizoczer Juden geht maßgeblich auf die Initiative der Täter vor Ort zurück.

Reich SS Leader and Chief of the German Police

Since 1936, Heinrich Himmler had been chief of all German police and SS forces. After Germany invaded the Soviet Union, he laid claim to central management of the genocide. He always made sure that he had Hitler's approval. The orders given to his local representatives were usually left vague and provided merely a framework for action. The decision to murder the Jews of Mizocz was also taken mainly at the initiative of perpetrators on site.

BArch Bild 101III-Bueschel-010-06A / Fotograf: Büschel

Bei Lyck (Ostpreußen, heute Ełk), 5. Juli 1941: Propagandaaufnahme eines Besuchs Himmlers beim 1. SS-Kavallerieregiment. Himmler ist fast durchgehend auf Reisen und trifft Entscheidungen bevorzugt vor Ort.

Near Lyck (today Ełk), 5 July 1941: Propaganda photo of a visit by Himmler to the 1st SS Cavalry Regiment. Himmler was almost permanently underway and preferred to make decisions on site.

Höhere SS- und Polizeiführer

Den Höheren SS- und Polizeiführern (HSSPF) unterstehen alle SS- und Polizeieinheiten ihres Bereichs. Als Himmlers regionale Stellvertreter lenken sie die Terrorpolitik gegen die Zivilbevölkerung und den Massenmord an den Juden. Dem HSSPF Ukraine und Rußland-Süd Hans-Adolf Prützmann wird die Zuständigkeit in »Judenfragen« offiziell durch Reichskommissar Koch übertragen, der damit gegen den Willen seines Vorgesetzten Alfred Rosenberg handelt. Koch unterstützt Prützmann bei der Planung der Erschießungen und regt diese immer wieder auch selbst an.

Higher SS and Police Leaders

All SS and police units in a region reported to a Higher SS and Police Leader (HSSPF). As Himmler's representatives, these leaders steered the spread of terror against the civilian population and the mass murder of Jews. Reich Commissar Koch delegated responsibility for »Jewish questions« to Hans-Adolf Prützmann, HSSPF for Ukraine and Russia South, and in doing so acted against the will of his superior, Alfred Rosenberg. Koch supported Prützmann in planning the shootings and personally encouraged such actions repeatedly.

BArch Bild 101III-Alber-083-03A / Fotograf: Kurt Alber

Heinrich Himmler (2.v.r.) mit Hans-Adolf Prützmann (2.v.l., 1901 – 1945). Wie alle HSSPF wird Prützmann von Himmler persönlich ausgewählt. Dabei zählen weniger Ausbildung und Erfahrung als ›Treue und Gehorsam‹. Der studierte Landwirt Prützmann war 1930 der SS beigetreten. Kurz nach Kriegsende nimmt er sich in britischer Haft das Leben.

Heinrich Himmler (2nd from r.) with Hans-Adolf Prützmann (2nd from l., 1901 – 1945). Like all other HSSPF, Prützmann was hand-picked by Himmler. Training and experience were not as important as ›loyalty and obedience‹. Prützmann, who had studied agriculture, joined the SS in 1930. He committed suicide in British custody shortly after the war.

Die Deutsche Besatzung in Mizocz – Befehlswege und Täterschaft

Kommandeur der Sicherheitspolizei und des SD

Mit Einrichtung der Zivilverwaltung werden aus den mobilen Einsatzgruppen stationäre Dienststellen der Kommandeure der Sicherheitspolizei und des SD (KdS) gebildet. HSSPF Prützmann überträgt ihnen die Ermordung eines großen Teils der jüdischen Bevölkerung. Als KdS Wolhynien-Podolien mit Sitz in Rowno wird der Jurist Dr. Karl Pütz eingesetzt. Angehörige seiner Dienststelle erschießen im Oktober 1942 nahezu alle Mizoczer Juden.

Commanding Officer of the Security Police and the Security Service (SD)

Once a civil administration had been set up, stationary offices reporting to the Commanding Officer of the Security Police and the Security Service (KdS) were formed from the ranks of the mobile killing squads. HSSPF Prützmann assigned them the task of murdering a large part of the Jewish population. Karl Pütz, who held a PhD in law, was appointed KdS Volhynia-Podolia with headquarters in Równe. Men from his department shot almost all the Jews in Mizocz in October 1942.

BArch R_9361_III_156264

Aufnahme von Dr. Karl Pütz (1911 – 1945) aus den Unterlagen des Rasse- und Siedlungshauptamts. Pütz tritt 1933 der SA und der NSDAP bei und schlägt nach Abschluss seiner Ausbildung eine Laufbahn bei der Geheimen Staatspolizei ein. In der Sowjetunion und in Polen ist Pütz für die Ermordung hunderttausender Juden verantwortlich. Zwei Tage vor Kriegsende erschießt er sich in St. Märgen im Schwarzwald.

Photograph of Dr. Karl Pütz (1911 – 1945) taken from the files of the SS Race and Settlement Main Office. Pütz joined the SA and the NSDAP in 1933, and after completing his training, began a career with the Secret State Police (Gestapo). Pütz was responsible for the murder of hundreds of thousands of Jews in the Soviet Union and Poland. Two days before the end of the war, he shot himself in Sankt Märgen in the Black Forest.

Národní archiv, Prag, ČVKSNVZ, Az. 338/75 / Fotograf: Gustav Hille

Mizocz, 14. Oktober 1942: Der Bildausschnitt zeigt Angehörige der Dienststelle des KdS Rowno vor der Erschießung der jüdischen Gemeinde. Ihre Identität konnte im Rahmen bundesdeutscher Ermittlungsverfahren nicht festgestellt werden.

Mizocz, 14 October 1942: This image detail shows members of the KdS Rowno office shortly before shooting the Jewish community. Investigations in West Germany failed to identify them.

Gendarmerie

In kleineren Orten unter Zivilverwaltung werden deutsche Gendarmerieposten eingerichtet. Die dort stationierten Polizisten setzen die Besatzungsordnung durch und überwachen die jüdische Bevölkerung. Bei den Massenerschießungen sperren sie meist die Ghettos und Erschießungsstätten ab. Einige beteiligen sich freiwillig als Schützen an den Verbrechen. Bei einer Einwohnerzahl von etwa 5.000 Menschen (1941) sind in Mizocz der Postenführer Oskar Drews (1899 – 1960) und zwei deutsche Reservepolizisten tätig.

Gendarmerie

In smaller towns and villages under civil administration, local German gendarmerie posts were set up. The police stationed there were responsible for ensuring that the occupation regulations were adhered to and for keeping the Jewish population under surveillance. Before mass shootings, they usually sealed off the ghettos and the killing sites. Some participated voluntarily as shooters. The head of the gendarmerie post, Oskar Drews (1899 – 1960), and two German reserve police constables were stationed in Mizocz, which had a population of around 5,000 (1941).

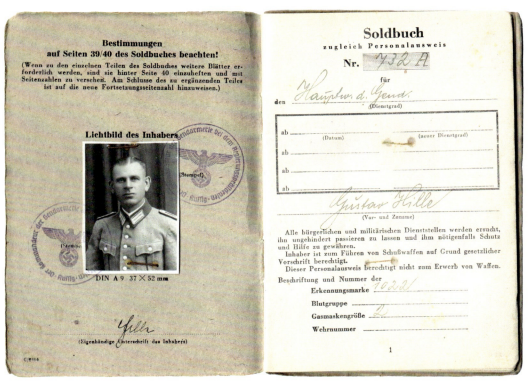

Privatbesitz Hille

Soldbuch von Gustav Hille (1899 – 1956): Er wird nach Beginn des Zweiten Weltkriegs zur Reservepolizei einberufen und wahrscheinlich im Herbst 1941 zum Gendarmerieposten Mizocz versetzt. Dort fotografiert er die Massenerschießungen.

Pay book of Gustav Hille (1899 – 1956): After the start of the Second World War, he was conscripted to the reserve police force and was sent to the gendarmerie in Mizocz, probably in autumn 1941, where he photographed the mass shootings.

Die Deutsche Besatzung in Mizocz – Befehlswege und Täterschaft

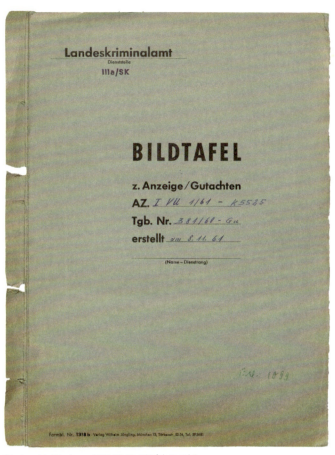

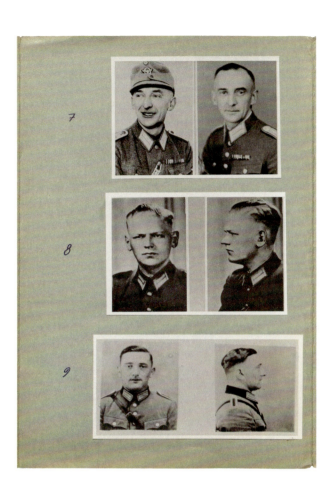

Staatsarchiv Nürnberg, 2004-01-Nr. 188 fol. 1 und 4

Teil einer Bildtafel des Bayerischen Landeskriminalamts; Zeugen erkennen unter Nr. 7 Joseph Paur (1899 – 1975): Paur wird als Soldat im Ersten Weltkrieg verwundet. Er schlägt eine Polizeilaufbahn ein und leitet verschiedene Gendarmerieposten im Reichsgebiet, bevor er 1942 den Befehl über die Polizei in Zdołbunów, Ostróg und Mizocz übernimmt. Das Landgericht Nürnberg-Fürth verurteilt ihn 1963 unter anderem wegen der Ermordung der Mizoczer Juden zu sieben Jahren Haft.

Part of a photo panel of the Bavarian office of criminal investigation; witnesses recognised number 7 as being Joseph Paur (1899 – 1975): Paur was wounded as a soldier in the First World War. He joined the police and was head of several local gendarmerie posts on Reich territory before taking command of the police in Zdołbunów, Ostróg and Mizocz in 1942. The State Court of Nürnberg-Fürth sentenced him to seven years imprisonment in 1963 for various crimes, including the murder of Jews in Mizocz.

Ukrainische Schutzmannschaft

Die Deutschen binden Hilfspolizisten aus den besetzten Gebieten in ihren Besatzungsapparat ein. In Mizocz sind bis zu 30 Ukrainer in einer Schutzmannschaft zusammengefasst. Sie unterstehen dem örtlichen Gendarmerieposten und sind auch an der Räumung des Ghettos und der Absperrung der Erschießungsstätte beteiligt. Im Sommer 1943 werden die Ukrainer durch Polen ersetzt, da sie den Deutschen aufgrund der stärker werdenden ukrainischen Nationalbewegung nicht mehr zuverlässig scheinen.

Ukrainian auxiliary police

The Germans incorporated auxiliary police from the occupied territories into their local structures. In Mizocz, as many as 30 Ukrainians were organised in the auxiliary police force. They reported to the local gendarmerie and participated in driving the inmates out of the ghetto and cordoning off the killing site. In summer 1943, they were replaced by Poles, since the Germans feared that Ukrainians were no longer reliable due to the increasing strength of the Ukrainian national movement.

Národní archiv, Prag, ČVKSNVZ, Az. 338/75 / Fotograf: Gustav Hille

Mizocz, 14. Oktober 1942: Unbekannte Angehörige der Mizoczer Schutzmannschaft. Sie tragen zur Erkennung weiße Armbinden und sind mit eingesammelten langen Mänteln und sowjetischen Beutewaffen ausgestattet. Vermutlich muss sich nach Kriegsende kaum einer der hier beteiligten Schutzmänner gerichtlich verantworten.

Mizocz, 14 October 1942: Unknown members of the Mizocz auxiliary police. They are wearing white armbands as identification, and are dressed in long coats and carrying weapons captured from Soviet troops. It is presumed that hardly any of the auxiliary police involved in this crime faced trial after the end of the war.

Die Deutsche Besatzung in Mizocz – Befehlswege und Täterschaft

Unterstellungsverhältnisse und Ämterbesetzungen

Schematische Übersicht der Unterstellungsverhältnisse und Ämterbesetzungen (Reichsführung bis zur lokalen Ebene in Mizocz) zum Zeitpunkt der Erschießung im Oktober 1942. Die hier wiedergegebenen, offiziellen Befehlswege wurden in der Praxis immer wieder umgangen und Absprachen auf persönlicher Ebene beispielsweise beim gemeinsamen Mittagessen getroffen.

Chains of command and officeholders

Outline of the chains of command and officeholders (from Reich leadership to the local level in Mizocz) at the time of the shootings in October 1942. In practice, official chains of command, shown here, were repeatedly by-passed, and agreements were reached at a personal level, for example, during lunch meetings.

Grundsätzliche Unterstellung
Official hierarchy

Zur polizeilichen Sicherung der besetzten Ostgebiete: Befehle an den Reichskommissar über den Reichsminister für die besetzten Ostgebiete, bei Gefahr direkt an den Reichskommissar
To ensure police control over the occupied Eastern territories, orders were sent to the Reich Commissioner via the Reich Minister for the Occupied Eastern Territories. In urgent cases, the Reich Commissioner received orders directly.

In allgemeinpolitischer und verwaltungstechnischer Hinsicht
General political and administrative hierarchy

In sicherheitsrelevanten Fragen
Responsibility for security affairs

Dienstaufsichtlich und ausbildungsmäßig
Responsibility for supervision and training

Einsatzmäßig
Responsibility for the deployment of troops

The German occupation of Mizocz – perpetrators and chains of command

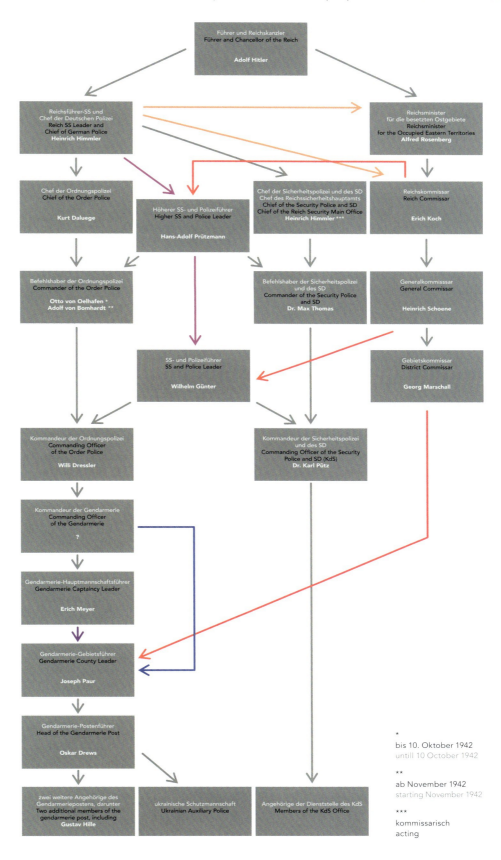

Die Deutsche Besatzung in Mizocz – Befehlswege und Täterschaft

Nachbarn

Die deutschen Besatzer verstärken überall in Osteuropa bestehende antijüdische Strömungen. In Mizocz ist das Verhältnis zwischen Juden, Polen und Ukrainern bis zum Beginn des Zweiten Weltkriegs offenbar friedlich. Mit dem deutschen Einmarsch im Sommer 1941 gerät es aus dem Gleichgewicht; Ukrainer äußern sich polenfeindlich und greifen Juden an. Die Deutschen stärken die ukrainische Bevölkerungsgruppe, indem sie aus deren Reihen eine Schutzmannschaft aufbauen. Die Hoffnung ukrainischer Nationalisten auf staatliche Unabhängigkeit zerschlägt sich jedoch. Die Besatzungsbehörden plündern erbarmungslos und verschleppen Hunderttausende zur Zwangsarbeit. Vor diesem Hintergrund und angesichts drohender Strafen erhalten die verfolgten jüdischen Nachbarn kaum Hilfe. Die Mehrheit der Nichtjuden verhält sich nach den Regeln der Besatzer. Darunter fällt auch, Versteckte zu verraten.
Helfern droht nicht nur von deutscher Seite Gefahr. Ab Oktober 1942 machen ukrainische Milizen Jagd auf Juden und ihre Unterstützer. Über das Verhalten der polnischen Bevölkerung, die 1943 aus Mizocz vertrieben wird, gegenüber den Juden, ist kaum etwas bekannt.

Neighbours

The German occupiers intensified already existing anti-Jewish sentiment everywhere in Eastern Europe. In Mizocz, Jews, Poles, and Ukrainians apparently got along with each other peacefully up until the Second World War. The situation destabilised by the German invasion in summer 1941; Ukrainians started to make hostile remarks about Poles and attacked Jews. The Germans strengthened the Ukrainian side by recruiting them into the auxiliary police. The Ukrainian nationalists' hopes for independence were dashed, however. The occupation authorities ruthlessly plundered the country and deported hundreds of thousands of civilians as forced labourers. In view of all this, and the threat of punishment, the persecuted Jews received little assistance from their neighbours. The majority of non-Jews followed the occupiers' rules and regulations. These included the order to report anyone they found hiding.
Not only the Germans presented a danger to anyone who dared to help Jews. From October 1942 onwards, Ukrainian paramilitary forces hunted down Jews and their supporters. Little is known about how the Polish population, which was driven out of Mizocz in 1943, behaved towards the Jews.

Portraitaufnahmen von Angehörigen der Familie Slobodjuk. Hunderte Mizoczer Juden fliehen aus dem brennenden Ghetto. Einigen wenigen gelingt es, mit Hilfe von Nichtjuden zu überleben. Unter den Geretteten ist Sofia Gorstein. Sidor (unten links) und Justina Slobodjuk (oben, rechts im Bild) und ihre Tochter Maria (unten rechts) verstecken Sofia zwischen Oktober 1942 und Juli 1943. Auch nachdem Sofia bei anderen Helfern unterkommt, hält Sidor Slobodjuk Kontakt zu ihr. Ukrainische Nationalisten ermorden ihn deswegen. Sofia überlebt und erreicht später die Ehrung der Slobodjuks als »Gerechte unter den Völkern«.

Portraits of members of the Slobodiuk family. Hundreds of Jews from Mizocz fled the burning ghetto. A few of them managed to survive with the help of non-Jews. One of those who were saved was Sofia Gorstein. Sidor (bottom, left) and Yustyna Slobodiuk (top, right in the photo) and their daughter Maria (bottom, right) hid Sofia between October 1942 and July 1943. Sidor Slobodiuk tried to keep up contact with Sofia after she moved to another hiding place. Ukrainian nationalists murdered him as a result. Sofia survived and later succeeded in getting the Slobodiuks honoured as »Righteous among the Nations«.

The German occupation of Mizocz – perpetrators and chains of command

Yad Vashem, Jerusalem

Yad Vashem, Jerusalem

Yad Vashem, Jerusalem

Die Deutsche Besatzung in Mizocz – Befehlswege und Täterschaft

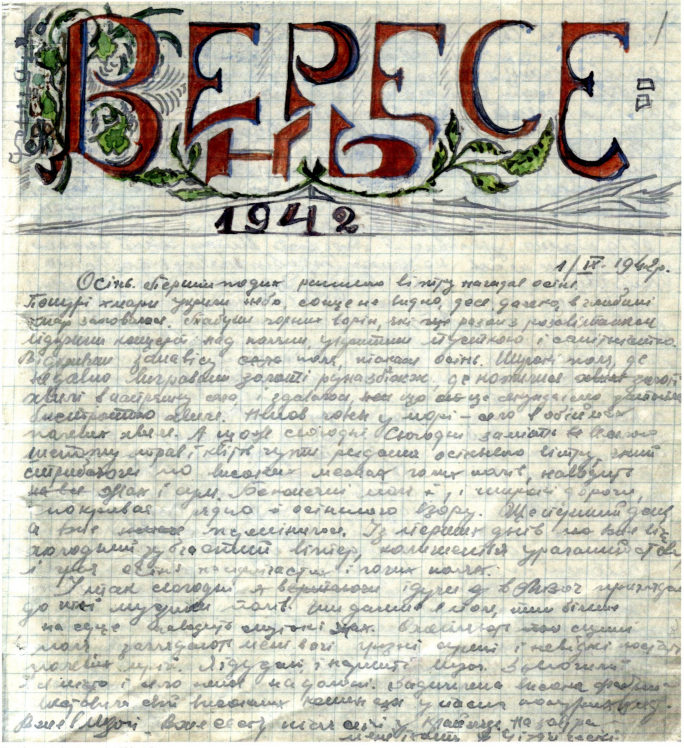

Derschawnij Archiv Riwnenskoj Oblasti, Rowno

Ausschnitt aus dem Tagebuch eines 20-jährigen Mitglieds der ukrainischen Unabhängigkeitsbewegung OUN. Die Abbildung zeigt das Blatt des ersten Eintrags vom 1. September 1942. Nur sein Vorname, Semen, ist bekannt; er wohnt im benachbarten Dorf Derman. Unter dem 13. Oktober schreibt er über die Räumung des Mizoczer Ghettos und dessen Brand. Er fährt an diesem Tag mit dem Fahrrad nach Mizocz, um das um sich greifende Feuer zu beobachten. Dort wird er selbst zum Täter, als er eine flüchtende Jüdin und ihr Kind an einen ukrainischen Hilfspolizisten verrät. Die Frau wird vor seinen Augen erschossen, über das Schicksal des Kindes schreibt er nichts. Am Nachmittag kehrt er nach Mizocz zurück. Erneut besucht der Autor Mizocz am 14. Oktober.

Excerpt from the diary of a 20-year-old member of the Ukrainian independence movement, OUN. The image shows the first entry of 1 September 1942. Only the first name of the author, Semen, is known; he lived in the neighbouring village of Derman. On 13 October he wrote about how the Mizocz ghetto was set on fire. On this day, he rode his bike to Mizocz to watch the fires. There, he became a perpetrator himself by betraying a fleeing Jewish woman and her child to the Ukrainian auxiliary police. The woman was shot before his very eyes. He did not mention what happened to the child. In the afternoon he returned to Mizocz. The author visited Mizocz again on 14 October.

13. Oktober 1942
»Die Leute sagen, auf dem Marktplatz sitzen die bereits Zusammengetriebenen und warten auf ihren sicheren Tod. Gegen Abend werden sie zur Hinrichtung an eine vorbereitete Stelle im Kiefernwald hinter der Fabrik gebracht. (…) Die Leute beginnen, die noch nicht abgebrannten Häuser leerzuräumen. Weiber schleppen schweißüberströmt ganze Fuhren alter jüdischer Klamotten weg. Genau. In der Hölle, in der die Juden umkommen, erblicken die Christen das Paradies. Da zappelt einer noch mit den Gliedern, und schon zieht ihm ein Bauer die Lumpen aus und lässt ihn nackt liegen. (…) Und die Ukrainer sehnen sich seit Jahren danach, ihrem Hass auf die jüdischen Feinde freien Lauf zu lassen. Die Zeit der Abrechnung ist gekommen, die Ukrainer offenbaren ihren Eifer an den Juden. (…) Für alles, alles ist das Ende gekommen. Die Strafe ist gekommen für Europas Feind (…).«

14. Oktober 1942
»Wir kommen an die Brücke, an den Stadtrand. Am Fluss liegt eine fürchterliche, mit Blut befleckte Leiche einer Jüdin. Sie ist barfuß, die Kleidung ganz im Blut. Die Arme zu beiden Seiten ausgestreckt, liegt sie mit dem Gesicht zum Boden. Ein schreckliches Bild, dieses getrocknete Blut löst Schauder aus. Aber Du überwindest Dich und schaust mit Verachtung hinunter, wie auf einen Besiegten.«

13 October 1942
»They're saying that those already rounded up are sitting in the market square, awaiting certain death. Towards evening, all of them are led to their execution at a prepared place in the pine woods behind the factory. (…) They're starting to clean out the houses that have not burned down. Dripping with sweat, women are carrying cartloads of various Jewish rags on their backs. Yes. The Christians see paradise in the hell where the Jews are dying. One of them is still twitching, but in no time a peasant has stripped him of his rags and left him lying there naked. (…) The Ukrainian has longed to vent his fervour on the Jewish enemies for many years. Now that hour has come, the fire of reckoning ignited, the Ukrainians are showing the Jews their indignation. (…) An end has come to everything, the end has come. Europe's enemy has been punished (…).«

14 October 1942
»We arrive at the little bridge, at the edge of town. The horrible corpse of a Jewish woman, covered in blood, is lying by the river. Barefoot, her clothing soaked in blood. She fell face first, arms stretched out to the side. A gruesome sight meets the eye – all this bubbled blood makes you shiver. But you overcome your hesitation and look again with contempt, as if on the vanquished.«

Die Verbrechen in Mizocz und die Erinnerung an den Holocaust
The crimes in Mizocz and remembrance of the Holocaust

Im Februar 1944 beendet die Rote Armee die deutsche Besatzung in Mizocz. Die Stadt verbleibt bei der Sowjetunion und wird nicht wieder polnisch. Wie überall im Land ermittelt eine Untersuchungskommission zu den Verbrechen der deutschen Besatzer. Die Erschießungen im Raum Zdołbunów finden im Nürnberger Hauptkriegsverbrecherprozess durch eine Aussage Hermann Friedrich Gräbes Erwähnung. In der Bundesrepublik beginnt die juristische Aufarbeitung erst Ende der 1950er Jahre. Ein Prozess gegen Angehörige des KdS Rowno, die die Massenerschießung verübten, kommt nicht zustande.

Die während des Verbrechens aufgenommenen Fotos befinden sich seit 1946 im Besitz tschechoslowakischer Behörden. Der bundesdeutschen Justiz liegt zunächst nur eines der Lichtbilder vor, allerdings ohne Ortsangabe. 1970 erhält sie aus Prag die gesamte Serie und kann den Fotografen sowie den Ort ermitteln. Die Fotos sind heute in Museen zum Holocaust zu sehen und zu einer ›Ikone‹ der Erinnerung geworden.

In February 1944, the Red Army ended the German occupation of Mizocz. The town remained part of the Soviet Union and was not returned to Poland. As everywhere else in the country, a commission of enquiry investigated the crimes of the German occupiers. The mass shootings in and around Zdołbunów were mentioned in the testimony of Hermann Friedrich Gräbe during the Nuremberg Trial of the Major War Criminals. Legal proceedings against the perpetrators were not initiated in West Germany until the late 1950s. Efforts to put members of KdS Rowno, who carried out the mass shootings, on trial were unsuccessful.

Photographs taken of this crime had been in the possession of the Czechoslovakian authorities since 1946. At first, the West German judiciary had only one of the photos, but lacked the name of the location. In 1970, the entire series was sent from Prague, and it was possible to identify both the photographer and the location. The photos can now be seen in Holocaust museums and have become one of the ›icons‹ of remembrance.

Die Verbrechen in Mizocz und die Erinnerung an den Holocaust

> **Der Landrat**
>
> Tagebuch Nr. Ref. I
>
> Bei Antwortschreiben angeben.
>
> Hof (Saale), den 5. Febr. 1946
> Theresienstraße 29
> Fernruf 2746
> J/R.
>
> Bescheinigung.
>
> Herr Gustav H i l l e , geb. 16.2.1899 in Schönborn Krs. Warnsdorf/Sudeten, hat am 8. September 1945 beim Landrat in Hof vorgesprochen und ihm folgendes eröffnet:
>
> Als Polizeibeamter im Osteinsatz hatte er Gelegenheit, fotografische Aufnahmen über die Juden-Massaker in der Ukraine zu machen. Er verfolgte dabei die Absicht, diese grauenhaften Vorkommnisse als Dokumente aufzubewahren und gegebenenfalls davon Gebrauch zu machen, obwohl ein solches Vorgehen unter dem Hitlerregime mit den schwersten Strafen bedroht war. Herr Hille erklärt sich bereit, diese fotographischen Dokumente, die er an seinem Wohnsitz Jablonetz No. 5 in einem eisernen Kasten aufbewahrt hat, zur gerichtlichen Untersuchung gegen die Kriegsverbrecher zur Verfügung zu stellen.
>
> Im Interesse der weiteren Verfolgung dieser Angelegenheit, die gegenwärtig auch im Nürnberger Prozess eine große Rolle spielt, wird gebeten, Herrn Gustav Hille Gelegenheit zu geben, diese fotographischen Dokumente beim Landratsamt Hof abzugeben, damit sie dem Gerichtshof der Vereinten Nationen zur Verfügung gestellt werden können.
>
> Der Landrat
> Joël

Privatbesitz Hille

Bescheinigung des bayerischen Landratsamts Hof (Saale) vom 5. Februar 1946: Es ist nicht sicher, ob die hier wiedergegebene Aussage Hilles über seine Beweggründe, »Aufnahmen über die Judenmassaker in der Ukraine« zu machen, zutrifft.

Attestation by the Bavarian District Office in Hof (Saale) dated 5 February 1946. Hille said that he had taken the photos with the intention of »preserving documentary evidence of these horrific events« and using them as a proof if necessary. It is not clear whether this statement is true.

Der Fotograf

Fünf Fotografien der Massenerschießung in Mizocz sind erhalten. Nach Ermittlungen der bundesdeutschen Justiz kann als bewiesen angesehen werden, dass der deutsche Gendarm Gustav Hille sie aufnahm. Der gelernte Maurer ist als Portier in der Strumpffabrik *J. Kunert & Söhne* in Warnsdorf (Sudetenland) tätig, bis er 1940 zur Polizei eingezogen und vermutlich im Herbst 1941 nach Mizocz abgeordnet wird. Drei Zeitzeugen erwähnen ihn namentlich im Zusammenhang mit der Ghettoräumung 1942. In dem 1963 laufenden Prozess gegen deutsche Polizisten und Angehörige der Zivilverwaltung im Raum Zdołbunów wird sein Verhalten nicht näher untersucht, da er bereits verstorben ist.

The photographer

Five photographs of the mass shooting in Mizocz have been preserved. According to investigations by the West German legal authorities, it is more or less certain that the German gendarme Gustav Hille took them. Hille, a mason, was employed as a doorman at the *J. Kunert & Söhne* hosiery factory in Varnsdorf in Sudetenland, when he was conscripted to the police force in 1940 and sent to Mizocz, presumably in autumn 1941. Three separate witnesses mentioned him in connection with the clearing of the ghetto in 1942. In the 1963 trial against German policemen and members of the civil administration in the area around Zdołbunów, his role in the crimes was not investigated any further because he had already died.

Privatbesitz Hille

Gustav Hille, um 1944.

Gustav Hille, around 1944.

Die Verbrechen in Mizocz und die Erinnerung an den Holocaust

Privatbesitz Kunert

Fabrikationsstätten der Firma *J. Kunert & Söhne GmbH* in Warnsdorf (Varnsdorf, Tschechoslowakei, 1938 – 1945 Deutsches Reich), undatiert: Die Firma ist vor dem Zweiten Weltkrieg der größte Strumpfhersteller Europas. Hier arbeitet Gustav Hille als Portier.

Production sites of *J. Kunert & Söhne GmbH* in Varnsdorf, Czechoslovakia (Warnsdorf, German Reich 1938 – 1945), no date: Before the Second World War, the company was the largest hosiery manufacturer in Europe. Gustav Hille worked here as a doorman.

Der Verbleib der Bilder

1944 oder Anfang 1945 zeigt Gustav Hille die Bilder seinem ehemaligen Arbeitgeber, dem Fabrikbesitzer Heinrich Kunert. Der Industrielle bittet ihn, die Bilder behalten zu dürfen, die abgebildeten Verbrechen empören ihn und er will sie einer kirchlichen Organisation übergeben. Kunert händigt die Fotos seinem Firmenanwalt Dr. Alois Knötig aus, der sie nach eigener Aussage über einen Mittelsmann an das Päpstliche Sekretariat nach Rom sendet. Ein zweiter Verbindungsmann bringt nach Knötigs späterer Aussage »die Lichtbilder mit der Bemerkung zurück, daß in Rom Vorfälle dieser Art bereits bekannt seien«. Knötig bewahrt die Bilder bei sich zu Hause auf. Nach Kriegsende – Warnsdorf gehört zur wiedererstandenen Tschechoslowakei – werden sie bei einer Hausdurchsuchung beschlagnahmt. Ob Hille weitere Abzüge bei sich behalten hatte, ist unklar.

History of the photos

In 1944 or at the beginning of 1945, Gustav Hille showed the photos to his former employer, factory owner Heinrich Kunert, who asked Hille if he would allow him to keep the photos. Kunert was revolted by the crimes they depicted and intended to hand them over to a church organisation. He gave the photos to the company lawyer, Dr. Alois Knötig, who, according to his own information, sent them to the Pontifical Secretariat in Rome via an intermediary. According to a later statement by Knötig, a second intermediary »brought the photographs back with the remark that Rome was already aware of events of this kind«. Knötig kept the photos at his home. After the end of the war – Varnsdorf was now part of the restored state of Czechoslovakia – they were confiscated during a search of his house. It is not known whether Hille kept further copies.

Heinrich Kunert (1899 – 1982), Aufnahme aus den 1960er Jahren. Kunert ist Mitinhaber des Unternehmens mit bis zu 7.000 Beschäftigten; ihm zeigt Hille die Bilder.

Heinrich Kunert (1899 – 1982), photograph taken in the 1960s. Kunert was co-owner of the company, which had as many as 7,000 employees; Hille showed him the photographs.

Dr. Alois Knötig (1895 – 1972), Aufnahme aus der Nachkriegszeit. Knötig ist von 1934 bis 1938 Bürgermeister von Warnsdorf. Anschließend arbeitet er als Rechtsanwalt (Syndikus) der Firma *Kunert*.

Dr. Alois Knötig (1895 – 1972), post-war photograph. Knötig was mayor of Varnsdorf from 1934 to 1938. After this, he worked as company lawyer for *Kunert*.

Privatbesitz Kunert

Privatbesitz Kunert

Mappe des tschechoslowakischen Innenministeriums mit den Bildern von Gustav Hille; Beschriftung des Aktendeckels »Dokumentation zu Massentötungen«. Erst die Ermittlungen der bundesdeutschen Justiz ergeben, dass es sich um das Verbrechen in Mizocz handelt.

Dossier of the Czechoslovakian Ministry of the Interior containing the photographs by Gustav Hille; writing on the cover »Documentation of mass killings«. It was not until the West German legal authorities started investigations that Mizocz was identified as the site of these crimes.

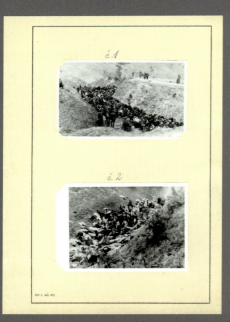
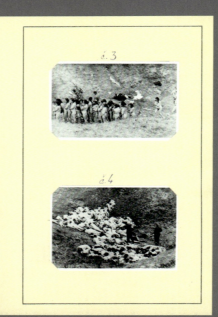
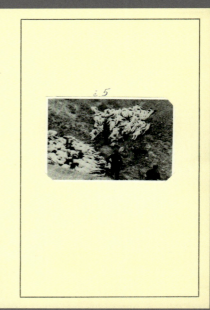

Národní archiv, Prag, ČVKSNVZ, Az. 338/75 / Fotograf: Gustav Hille

The crimes in Mizocz and remembrance of the Holocaust

Erinnerung und Aufklärung vor Ort

In den 1980er Jahren wird in Mizocz ein Denkmal errichtet, ein Zeitungsartikel beschreibt die Verbrechen. Umfassend dokumentiert werden sie in ukrainischer Sprache durch den lokalen Historiker Roman Michaltschuk, der seine Ergebnisse 2010 in einem Buch veröffentlicht. Forschungen gehen 2007/08 auch von *Yahad – In Unum* (hebräisch und lateinisch »gemeinsam«) aus. Diese in Paris ansässige, internationale Vereinigung sucht Orte von Massenerschießungen in der ehemaligen besetzten Sowjetunion, in Polen und in Rumänien. Anders als die sowjetische Außerordentliche Staatliche Kommission beachtet *Yahad* die Vorschrift der jüdischen Religion, nach der die sterblichen Überreste von Menschen unversehrt bleiben müssen. Folglich nimmt die Organisation keine Grabungen vor, sondern gewinnt Erkenntnisse durch Zeitzeugenbefragungen und Archivrecherchen.

Remembrance and on-site investigations

In the 1980s, a memorial stone was erected in Mizocz and a newspaper article reported on the atrocities that happened there. These were documented in detail in Ukrainian by local historian, Roman Mikhalchuk, who published his findings in a book in 2010. *Yahad – In Unum* (meaning »together« in both Hebrew and Latin) also carried out research into the crime in 2007/08. This international association with headquarters in Paris visits the sites of mass shootings in those parts of the former Soviet Union that were occupied by Germany, in Poland and in Romania. As opposed to the Soviet Extraordinary State Commission, *Yahad* observes the rule of the Jewish religion, namely that the mortal remains of humans must remain intact. For this reason, the organisation does not carry out excavations, but gathers information on crimes in interviews with eyewitnesses and by researching in historical archives.

Gosudarstwennyj Archiv Rossiskoj Federatsii, Moskau

Mizocz, 20. bis 27. November 1944: Aufnahme der sowjetischen Untersuchungskommission. Beschriftung auf der Bildrückseite: »Anblick der Grube, in der 3.500 jüdische Menschen vergraben wurden.« Eine Woche lang ermittelt die Kommission in Mizocz. Sie befragt Zeugen und exhumiert Leichen. Die angegebene Opferzahl ist vermutlich zu hoch angesetzt.

Mizocz, 20 to 27 November 1944: Photograph taken by Soviet investigators. Writing on the back of the photo: »View of the pit where 3,500 Jews were buried«. The commission spent a week investigating crimes in Mizocz. It interviewed eyewitnesses and exhumed corpses. The stated number of victims is probably too high.

Die Verbrechen in Mizocz und die Erinnerung an den Holocaust

Yahad – In Unum, Paris France

Mizocz, Sommer 2007: Erstmals besucht die Vereinigung *Yahad – In Unum* unter Leitung ihres Gründers, des katholischen Priesters Patrick Desbois, im Juli und August 2007 die Region Rowno, zu der auch Mizocz gehört. Die Aufnahme zeigt die Mulde, in der mindestens eines der Bilder von Gustav Hille entstanden ist.

Mizocz, summer 2007: In July and August 2007, the association *Yahad – In Unum*, led by its founder Patrick Desbois, a Catholic priest, visited the region of Rivne, to which Mizocz belongs, for the first time. The photograph shows the hollow where at least one of Gustav Hille's photos was taken.

Mizozc, Januar 2008: Ein ukrainischer Augenzeuge mit Mitarbeitern von *Yahad – In Unum* in der Mulde. Im Hintergrund werden Videoaufnahmen erstellt. Bild rechts: Ein von *Yahad – In Unum* interviewter Zeitzeuge mit Kopien der Fotos von Gustav Hille.

Mizozc, January 2008: A Ukrainian eyewitness with members of *Yahad – In Unum* in the hollow. There are people taking videos in the background. Right: An eyewitness interviewed by *Yahad – In Unum*, being shown copies of Gustav Hille's photographs.

Yahad – In Unum, Paris France

The crimes in Mizocz and remembrance of the Holocaust

Privatbesitz

Malerei von Alexej Slobodjuk nach den Erinnerungen seiner Tante Maria, 1992/93: Das Bild zeigt die Ermordung der Mizoczer Juden. Maria versteckt mit ihren Eltern zwischen Oktober 1942 und Juli 1943 die Jüdin Sofia Gorstein.

Painting by Alexej Slobodiuk based on the memories of his aunt Maria, 1992/93: The picture depicts the murder of the Mizocz Jews. Together with her parents, Maria hid the Jewish girl Sofia Gorstein from October 1942 to July 1943.

Fotograf: Christian Schmittwilken

Mizocz. Gedenktafel für die Opfer der Massenerschießung von Mizocz. Ende der 1980er Jahre wird nahe der Erschießungsstätte ein Denkmal errichtet. Die Inschrift lautet: »In Erinnerung an die Opfer des Holocaust des Jahres 1942«.

Mizocz. Plaque commemorating the victims of the Mizocz mass shooting. In the late 1980s, a memorial was erected near to the site of the shooting. The wording on the plaque says: »In memory of the victims of the Holocaust in 1942«.

Täter und Massenmord
Perpetrators and mass murder

Nach dem Zweiten Weltkrieg behaupteten viele deutsche Täter, sie hätten sich an den Erschießungen in der besetzten Sowjetunion beteiligt, weil sie den Befehlen ihrer Vorgesetzten hätten folgen müssen. Jedoch ist kein Fall bekannt, bei dem eine Verweigerung des Befehls eine erhebliche Strafe zur Folge gehabt hätte. Warum wurden tausende Deutsche zu Massenmördern? Nur wenige dieser Männer waren vor ihrem Einsatz begeisterte Nationalsozialisten oder durch besondere Gewalttätigkeit aufgefallen. Erkenntnisse darüber, was sie dazu brachte, sich in den Prozess des massenhaften Tötens einzugliedern, haben Historiker, Soziologen und Psychologen in den vergangenen Jahren gewonnen.

After the end of the Second World War, many German perpetrators claimed they had only taken part in the shootings in the occupied Soviet Union because they had to follow the orders of their superiors. However, not one single case is known in which the refusal to follow orders would have led to severe punishment. Why did thousands of Germans become mass murderers? Only a few of these men were ardent National Socialists or were known for violent behaviour before deployment. Over the years, historians, sociologists, and psychologists have gained insight into why the perpetrators cooperated in carrying out mass murder.

Das Denken

Antisemitismus

Judenfeindliche Hetze hatte das Zusammenleben von Juden und Nichtjuden in Deutschland lange vor 1933 überschattet. Unter den Nationalsozialisten wurde Hasspropaganda allgegenwärtig. Die Mehrheit der Deutschen grenzte die jüdischen Nachbarn zunehmend aus. Straßengewalt, Gesetze und endgültig der reichsweite Terror im November 1938 zerstörten deren Teilhabe am gesellschaftlichen Leben. Das jahrelang propagierte Bild von Juden als »Volksfeinden« beeinflusste auch die Täter an den Erschießungsstätten. Wer nicht aus persönlichem Judenhass mordete, erkannte die »Entfernung der Juden« als scheinbare Notwendigkeit an.

Antisemitism

The coexistence of Jews and non-Jews in Germany had been overshadowed by anti-Jewish sentiment long before 1933. Under the National Socialist regime, hate propaganda was omnipresent. The majority of Germans increasingly marginalised their Jewish neighbours. Street violence, anti-Jewish legislation, and finally the nationwide terror in November 1938, prevented them from taking part in social life. The image of Jews as »enemies of the people«, as propagated for many years, also influenced the perpetrators at the shooting sites. Those who did not murder Jews out of personal hatred regarded the »removal of all Jews« as seemingly necessary.

Deutsches Historisches Museum, Berlin / Fotograf: Joseph Schorer

Hamburg, 1. April 1933: SA-Männer und Sympathisanten blockieren die Tür zum Laden eines jüdischen Kaufmanns in der Grindelallee 79. Für diesen Tag rufen die Nationalsozialisten zu einem reichsweiten Boykott gegen jüdische Kaufleute, Ärzte und Rechtsanwälte auf.

Hamburg, 1 April 1933: SA storm troopers and sympathisers block the door of a Jewish shop at Grindelallee 79. The Nazis had called for a nationwide boycott of all Jewish merchants, doctors, and lawyers on this day.

Instytut Pamięci Narodowej, Warschau

Warta (Polen), vermutlich 1939: Die Gendarmen Lasch (links) und Dreger schneiden Hersz Laskowski die Schläfenlocken ab. Er muss sich dabei mit geöffneter Hose fotografieren lassen. Im April 1942 wird er mit seinem Vater, dem Rabbiner Eliasz Laskowski, und acht weiteren Juden erhängt. Die antisemitische Gewalt der Nationalsozialisten, die während der Übergriffe im November 1938 reichsweit etwa 100 Todesopfer zur Folge hatte, radikalisiert sich nach dem Überfall auf Polen weiter.

Warta (Poland), probably 1939: The Gendarmerie members Lasch (left) and Dreger cutting off Hersz Laskowski's sidelocks. He was forced into being photographed with his trousers open. In April 1942, he was hanged together with his father, Rabbi Eliasz Laskowski, and eight other Jews. The antisemitic violence, which in November 1938 led to abut 100 deaths across Germany, grew increasingly radical stage after the invasion of Poland.

The mentality

Rassistischer Herrschaftsanspruch

Bereits mit dem Einmarsch in Polen im September 1939 offenbarten die Besatzer nicht nur ihren Antisemitismus, sondern auch ihre tief sitzende Slawenfeindlichkeit. Das deutsche »Herrenmenschen«-Bewusstsein verband sich in der Sowjetunion mit dem Hass auf den kommunistischen Gegner. Die lokale Bevölkerung und die Kriegsgefangenen waren dem Allmachtgefühl und der Willkür der deutschen Besatzer schutzlos ausgeliefert.

Claim to racial supremacy

With the invasion of Poland in September 1939, the occupiers manifested not only their antisemitic but also their deeply-rooted anti-Slavic sentiment. In the Soviet Union, the Germans' conviction that they were a »master race« merged with their hatred of the communist enemy. The local population and prisoners of war were entirely at the mercy of the German occupiers' feeling of omnipotence and arbitrary exercise of authority.

ullstein bild / Fotograf: Walter Frentz

Weißrussland, Juli 1941: Karl Brandt (1904 – 1948), Begleitarzt Hitlers und einer der Hauptverantwortlichen für die Ermordung kranker und behinderter Menschen (»Euthanasie«), untersucht das Gebiss eines internierten Soldaten der Roten Armee. Allein bis Ende 1941 lässt die Wehrmacht etwa zwei Millionen sowjetische Kriegsgefangene verhungern. Aufnahme von Walter Frentz (1907 – 2004), der als Fotograf und Kameramann zum engen Umkreis Hitlers gehört.

Belarus, July 1941: Karl Brandt (1904 – 1948), Hitler's personal physician was one of the responsible for murdering ill and disabled persons (»euthanasia«). He is looking at the teeth of an interned Red Army soldier. Up to the end of 1941 alone, the Wehrmacht let two million prisoners of war starve to death. Picture by Walter Frentz (1907 – 2004), a photographer and cameraman who belonged to Hitler's circle of close.

Beit Lohamei Haghetaot, Kibbuz der Ghettokämpfer

Unbekannter Ort, 13. Juli 1941: Bildbeschriftung »Langst mit einer Zigeunerin«. Nähere Angaben zu den Abgebildeten liegen nicht vor. Mit ihrer Aufstellung und Mimik demonstrieren die Wehrmachtssoldaten ihr Überlegenheitsgefühl gegenüber der Romnia.

Place unknown, 13 July 1941: inscription »Langst with a gypsy«. No further details of the people on the picture are known. The German soldiers show by their pose and the looks on their faces that they consider themselves to be superior to the Roma woman.

Das Umfeld

Krieg

Die Männer der Erschießungskommandos nahmen sich als Teil der kämpfenden Truppe wahr, obwohl sie nicht gegen feindliche Soldaten kämpften, sondern Zivilisten ermordeten. Sie betrachteten deren Tötung als militärische Handlung und rechtfertigten ihre Verbrechen als Beitrag zum Kriegsgeschehen, bei dem von ihnen verlangt werde, Gegner zu töten.

War

Shooting commando members considered themselves a part of the combat troops, even though they were not fighting enemy soldiers, but were murdering civilians. They considered the killing a military act and justified their crimes a contribution to the war effort, which in their opinion called for them to kill enemies.

Białowieża-Wald (Polen), 11. Juli 1941: Ordensverleihung durch Generalleutnant Johann Pflugbeil (1882 – 1951) an einen Angehörigen des Polizeibataillons 309. Die Einheit unterstand der Wehrmacht. Sie hatte zuvor in der Stadt Białystok hunderte Juden in einer Synagoge verbrannt und weitere erschossen.

Białowieża forest (Poland), 11 July 1941: Lieutenant General Johann Pflugbeil (1882 – 1951) awards medals to members of Police Battalion 309. The unit was subordinate to the Wehrmacht and had previously burned hundreds of Jews alive in a synagogue in Białystok and shot many more.

Landesarchiv NRW – Abteilung Rheinland – RWB 18258/3

Kameradschaft

Die Erschießungen fanden fernab der Heimat der deutschen Schützen statt. In der Fremde wurde die eigene Einheit zum wichtigsten Bezugspunkt. Wer sich den Erschießungen entzog, konnte das Gefühl haben, den ihm zugedachten Anteil am Verbrechen seinen Kameraden aufzubürden, diese zu verärgern und deshalb ausgegrenzt zu werden. Das gemeinsame Töten war somit Ausdruck des Zusammenhalts und stiftete zugleich ein Gemeinschaftsgefühl.

Comradeship

The shootings took place far away from the hometowns of the German shooters. In the field, the unit became the most important point of reference. Anyone refusing to participate in the shootings could feel that he was imposing that part of the crime intended for him onto his comrades and in doing so antagonise them and bring about his ostracism. Killing collectively was therefore an expression of cohesion and promoted a sense of community.

Region Lublin (Polen), um 1942: Angehörige des in Hamburg aufgestellten Polizei-Reservebataillons 101 bei einem Kameradschaftsabend. Das Schild »Jetzt geht's los im ›Trapp‹ Und alles fühlt sich ›Wohlauf‹« spielt auf die Vorgesetzten Wilhelm Trapp (1889 – 1948) und Julius Wohlauf (1913 – 2002) an. Die etwa 500 Männer des Bataillons ermorden zwischen 1942 und 1943 mindestens 38.000 Juden.

Lublin region (Poland), around 1942: Members of Reserve Police Battalion 101 from Hamburg at a camaraderie evening. The sign is a play on words referring to commanding officers Wilhelm Trapp (1889 – 1948) and Julius Wohlauf (1913 – 2002). The men of this battalion, roughly 500, murdered at least 38,000 Jews between 1942 and 1943.

Staatsarchiv Hamburg, Best. 213-12 Staatsanwaltschaft Landgericht – Nationalsozialistische Gewaltverbrechen Nr. 0021 Band 45

The setting

Zuschauer

Die meisten Erschießungen fanden am helllichten Tag und häufig in Seh- und Hörweite umliegender Ortschaften statt. Offiziell sollten die Opfer unter Ausschluss der Öffentlichkeit erschossen werden. Zuschauer wurden jedoch nur selten ferngehalten. Unter ihnen waren Soldaten, deutsche Zivilisten und Einheimische. Ihre Anwesenheit zeigte den Schützen ihre Zustimmung. Die Täter konnten sich dadurch in ihrem Handeln bestätigt sehen und es erschien ihnen rechtmäßig.

Spectators

Most of the killings were carried out in broad daylight and frequently within sight and hearing distance of surrounding towns and villages. Orders stipulated that the victims were to be shot out of public view, but spectators were rarely kept away. These included Wehrmacht soldiers and German civilians as well as locals. The shooters interpreted the presence of spectators as a sign of approval. The perpetrators could see themselves confirmed in their actions and the killing seemed lawful to them.

Alkohol

Teilweise wurde vor und während der Erschießungen Schnaps ausgeschenkt, um den Schützen Hemmungen zu nehmen. Der gemeinsame Alkoholkonsum diente auch dazu, nach den Erschießungen Ablenkung zu finden.

Alcohol

The men were sometimes given hard liquor to drink before and during the shootings in order to reduce their inhibitions. The collective consumption of alcohol also served as a distraction after the shootings.

Vermutlich bei Schaulen (Šiauliai, Litauen), undatiert: Aushebung einer Grube und Erschießung. Im Hintergrund: Deutsche in Uniform und sitzende Zivilisten. Das Verbrechen wird von einem weiteren Fotografen festgehalten.

Probably near Šiauliai (Lithuania), no date: Digging of a pit before a shooting, Germans in uniform and seated civilians in the background. The crime was also documented by a second photographer.

Rossijskij Gosudarstwennyj Archiv Kinofotodokumentow, Krasnogorsk

Das Töten

Einbindung

Die Erschießungen wurden teilweise zunächst nach dem Schema militärischer Hinrichtungen durchgeführt. Dabei schossen mehrere Schützen auf ein Opfer. Dies konnte dem Einzelnen das Gefühl der persönlichen Verantwortung für den Mord nehmen. Zugleich entsprach diese Methode in den Augen der Täter dem Bild der Vernichtung von »Volksfeinden«, die ihnen notwendig und gerechtfertigt erschien.

Involvement

At first, some of the shootings were carried out like military executions. Several marksmen fired at one victim. This gave each shooter the feeling that he was not solely responsible for the murder. At the same time, in the eyes of the perpetrators this method corresponded with the concept of destroying »enemies of the people«, something that seemed to them necessary and justified.

Arbeit und Arbeitsteilung

An den Erschießungsstätten herrschte eine klare Aufgabenteilung: Eine Gruppe der Täter zwang die Opfer sich zu entkleiden, die nächsten trieben sie zur Grube, andere erschossen sie. Die Täter fassten ihr Morden als Arbeit auf, die erledigt werden musste, machten gemeinsam Pausen und begingen den Feierabend. Dies gab den Erschießungen einen offiziellen Charakter und verdrängte, dass es sich um ein Verbrechen handelte.

Work and division of labour

At the killing sites, the tasks were clearly divided: one group forced the victims to take off their clothes, another group herded them towards the pit, and others shot them. The perpetrators saw the murder as work that had to be done, they took breaks, and called it a day at the end of working hours. This made the shootings seem like an official activity and helped repress the fact that it was a crime.

Imperial War Museum, London

Dubossary (Dubăsari, Moldauische SSR), 14. September 1941: Ein Teilkommando der Einsatzgruppe D bei einer Massenerschießung. Jeweils zwei Schützen schießen auf ein Opfer. Der Führer des Kommandos, Max Drexel (1914 – ?), an der Stirnseite der Schützenreihe, gibt den Schießbefehl.

Dubăsari (Moldavian SSR), 14 September 1941: A squad from Einsatzgruppe D killing at a mass shooting. Two shooters fire at each victim. The squad leader, Max Drexel (1914 – ?), at the head of the killing squad, gives the order to fire.

The act of killing

Schweizerisches Bundesarchiv, Bern E27#1000/721#9928-3*#1

Schweizerisches Bundesarchiv, Bern E27#1000/721#9928-3*#2

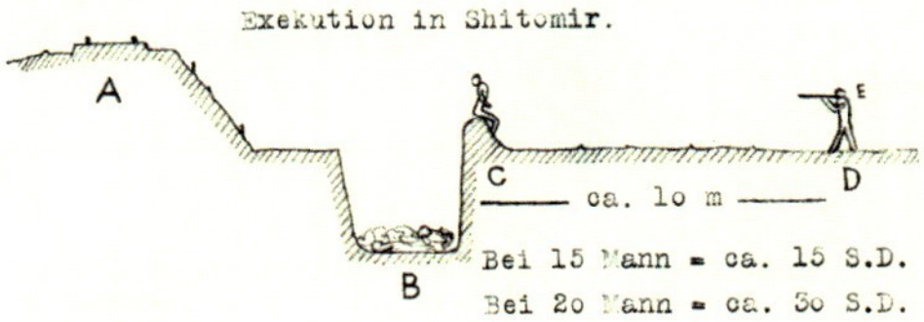

Skizze und Beschreibung einer Erschießung in Shitomir (Ukraine), 1941, angefertigt vom Schweizer Nachrichtendienst bei der Vernehmung des desertierten Wehrmachtssoldaten Wilhelm Josef Stättner (1916 – 1967), 28. Februar 1942.

Sketch and description of a mass shooting in Zhytomyr (Ukraine), 1941, prepared by the Swiss intelligence service during the interrogation of a deserted Wehrmacht soldier, Wilhelm Josef Stättner (1916 – 1967) on 28 February 1942.

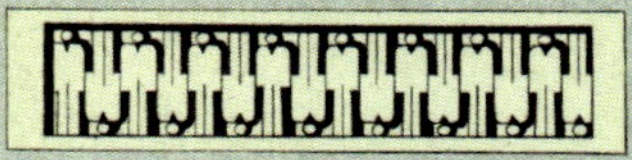

Skizze und Beschreibung der Erschießung von Juden in Orel (Russland) aus dem Vernehmungsprotokoll des in die Schweiz desertierten Obergefreiten Anton Brandhuber (1914 – 2008), 27. April 1942. Die Skizze stellt dar, in welcher Position die Opfer »mit Gewalt in die Gräben gelegt bezw. geworfen« wurden, »und zwar so, dass sie zu liegen kamen, wie Sardinen in der Büchse«.

Sketch and description of the shooting of Jews in Orel (Russia) from the interrogation, on 27 April 1942, of Lance Corporal Anton Brandhuber (1914 – 2008), who deserted to Switzerland. The sketch shows the position in which the victims were »forcibly placed or thrown into the pits«, namely, »so that they ended up lying like sardines in a tin«.

Der Einzelne

Frauen

Frauen gehörten nicht den Erschießungskommandos an, waren jedoch als Sekretärinnen an den Morden beteiligt oder sortierten die Wertsachen der Getöteten. Indem sie den Tätern Kaffee und Kuchen servierten oder sie zu Erschießungen begleiteten, vermittelten sie den Männern das Gefühl, der Mord sei etwas Alltägliches und werde von der eigenen Gesellschaft unterstützt.

Women

Women did not belong to the shooting commandos, but they were complicit in the murder through their work as secretaries, or they sorted through the belongings of those who were killed. By serving coffee and cake to the perpetrators or accompanying them to the shootings, they gave the impression that the killing was something routine and supported by society.

Männlichkeit

Manche Täter hatten anfänglich Hemmungen, die Verbrechen zu begehen. Sie empfanden das Töten als unangenehm, stellten den Massenmord als solchen aber nicht in Frage. Sich dazu zu überwinden, hilflose Menschen zu erschießen, wurde mit persönlicher Härte und Willensstärke gleichgesetzt. Wer nicht mitschoss, galt als unmännlich und schwach.

Masculinity

Some of the perpetrators initially had scruples about committing these crimes. They found the act of killing unpleasant, but they did not question the mass murder as such. Overcoming one's inhibitions about shooting helpless people was seen as a sign of toughness and strong willpower. Anyone who refused to participate was considered to be unmanly and weak.

Staatsarchiv Hamburg, Best. 213-12 Staatsanwaltschaft Landgericht – Nationalsozialistische Gewaltverbrechen Nr. 0021 Band 45

Region Lublin (Polen), Sommer 1942: Angehörige des Polizei-Reservebataillons 101 und Wera Wohlauf (1912 – 2003, Bildmitte), die Gattin des Bataillonskommandeurs Julius Wohlauf (1913 – 2002). Ehefrauen von Offizieren dürfen in die besetzten Ostgebiete reisen. Einige werden Zeuginnen der Massenmorde. Die dem Bild beigefügten Nummern stammen aus einem Strafverfahren gegen Julius Wohlauf und andere.

Lublin region (Poland), summer 1942: members of Reserve Police Battalion 101 with Wera Wohlauf (1912 – 2003, centre), the wife of battalion commander Julius Wohlauf (1913 – 2002). Officers' wives were allowed to travel to the occupied Eastern territories. Some of them witnessed the mass murders. The numbers on the picture were entered in the course of a trial against Julius Wohlauf and others.

The individual

Grausamkeit

Nicht alle Täter kostete es Überwindung, Gewalt anzuwenden und zu morden. Aus eigenem Antrieb demütigten, vergewaltigten und misshandelten sie Männer, Frauen und Kinder im Umfeld der Erschießungen.

Cruelty

Not all perpetrators had scruples about using violence and murdering people. Some of them humiliated, raped, and mistreated men, women, and children of their own accord in connection with the shootings.

Kein Zurück?

Je häufiger die Männer mordeten, desto schwieriger wurde es für sie, die Teilnahme an Erschießungen zu verweigern. Sie hätten sich selbst eingestehen müssen, ein Verbrechen begangen zu haben. Stattdessen töteten sie weiter.

No turning back?

The more the men committed murder, the more difficult it became for them to refuse further participation in the shootings. They would have had to admit to themselves that they had committed a crime. Instead, they kept on killing.

Vermutlich Winniza (Ukraine), Datum unbekannt: Erschießung durch Männer einer Einsatzgruppe. Im Hintergrund sind Wehrmachtssoldaten und Angehörige des Reichsarbeitsdienstes zu sehen.

Probably Vinnytsia (Winniza, Ukraine), no date: Shooting by the members of an Einsatzgruppe. Soldiers from the Wehrmacht and members of the Reich Labour Service can be seen in the background.

Iwangorod (Ukraine, Ortsname existiert mehrfach), 1942: Ein deutscher Ordnungspolizist zielt auf seine Opfer. Das Foto wird von einem deutschen Soldaten mit der Bildunterschrift »Ukraine 1942, Judenaktion, Ivangorod« nach Hause geschickt und in einem Warschauer Postamt von Mitgliedern des polnischen Widerstands abgefangen.

Ivanhorod (Ukraine, several places with the same name), 1942: A member of the German Order Police aims at his victims. The photo with the caption »Ukraine 1942, action against Jews, Ivangorod« was sent home by a German soldier and was intercepted at a Warsaw post office by members of the Polish resistance.

Instytut Pamięci Narodowej, Warschau

United States Holocaust Memorial Museum, Washington, D.C.

Juristische Aufarbeitung
Judicial investigation

Juristische Aufarbeitung

Juristische Aufarbeitung in der Sowjetunion

Schon während des Kriegs führt der sowjetische Staat Prozesse gegen einheimische Kollaborateure und einige wenige deutsche Täter. Erste öffentliche Verfahren im Jahr 1943 stoßen international auf großes Interesse. Nach Kriegsende müssen sich weitere Deutsche vor sowjetischen Gerichten verantworten. Die Massenerschießungen von Juden werden in den Verhandlungen immer wieder erwähnt, jedoch als Teil der deutschen Vernichtungspolitik gegen die sowjetische Bevölkerung dargestellt. Eine öffentliche Auseinandersetzung mit dem antisemitischen Charakter der Verbrechen findet nicht statt. Die Prozessführung genügt häufig nicht rechtsstaatlichen Ansprüchen. Zudem werden ganze Bevölkerungsgruppen wie Krimtataren oder Tschetschenen unter dem Vorwurf der Kollaboration nach Osten verschleppt. Bis zum Ende der Sowjetunion verurteilen die Gerichte tatsächliche und vermeintliche Täter zu langer Lagerhaft oder zum Tode.

Judicial investigation in the Soviet Union

The Soviet state held trials of local collaborators and a few German perpetrators during wartime already. The first public trials in 1943 generated considerable international interest. After the war, more Germans had to answer to Soviet courts for their actions. The mass shootings of Jews were repeatedly mentioned in court proceedings, but were described as part of Germany's policy of annihilation directed against the Soviet population. There was no public discussion about the antisemitic nature of the crimes. Proceedings often did not meet the norms of a fair trial. In addition, entire ethnic groups such as Crimean Tatars or Chechens were deported to the Soviet interior as alleged collaborators. Right up to the end of the Soviet Union, the courts were still sentencing either actual or supposed perpetrators to long terms in prison camps or to death.

Charkow (Charkiw, Ukraine), Dezember 1943: Erster öffentlicher sowjetischer Prozess gegen drei deutsche und einen russischen Täter wegen ihrer Beteiligung an Massenerschießungen und Morden mit Gaswagen. Alle vier Angeklagten werden zum Tode verurteilt und vor zehntausenden Zuschauern gehängt.

Kharkiv (Ukraine), December 1943: First public Soviet trial of three Germans and a Russian for participation in mass shootings and murders using gas vans. All of the accused men were sentenced to death and hanged before tens of thousands of spectators.

Yad Vashem, Jerusalem

Juristische Aufarbeitung in Polen

Mit dem Vorrücken der Roten Armee endet im Frühjahr 1945 die deutsche Besatzung in Polen; bereits 1944 war der polnische Staat als Volksrepublik unter kommunistischer Führung wiedererstanden. Noch vor Kriegsende wird im März 1945 die »Hauptkommission zur Untersuchung der deutschen Verbrechen in Polen« gegründet. Sie befragt Zeugen und sammelt Beweise. Kurz darauf beginnt die »Polnische Militärmission zur Untersuchung der deutschen Kriegsverbrechen« im besetzten Deutschland nach Verantwortlichen zu fahnden. Die meisten Prozesse gegen Deutsche und einheimische Täter finden bis 1947 statt. Die Mehrzahl der Verurteilten wird nach 1956 amnestiert. Trotzdem werden bis in die 1980er Jahre immer wieder Verfahren eingeleitet. In der Regel beruhen die Urteile auf einem persönlichen Tatnachweis und befolgen so rechtsstaatliche Prinzipien. Zugleich befinden sich jedoch Zehntausende, darunter viele »Volksdeutsche«, ohne Verurteilung in Lagerhaft. Ihnen können meist keine Verbrechen nachgewiesen werden – viele sind unschuldig. Nach dem Ende der Volksrepublik 1989 werden erneut einzelne Verfahren geführt.

Judicial investigation in Poland

With the advance of the Red Army, the German occupation of Poland came to an end in early 1945. The Polish state had already been re-established in 1944 as a People's Republic under communist leadership. In March 1945, before the end of the war, the »Main Commission for the Investigation of German Crimes in Poland« was founded. It interviewed witnesses and collected evidence. Shortly thereafter, the »Polish Military Mission for the Investigation of German War Crimes« started searching in occupied Germany to find those responsible. Most of the trials of Germans and local perpetrators took place before 1947. The majority of those convicted were granted amnesty after 1956. Nevertheless, criminal proceedings continued to be launched well into the 1980s. Generally, the convictions based on provided evidence of personal involvement in a crime, and this followed standards of a fair trial. At the same time, tens of thousands, including many ethnic Germans, were interned in prison camps, without ever having been tried or sentenced. In most cases, it could not be proven that they had committed a crime. Many were innocent. A few individual trials were still held after the end of the People's Republic in 1989.

Beit Lohamei Haghetaot, Kibbuz der Ghettokämpfer

Warschau, Oktober 1958 bis März 1959: Prozess gegen Erich Koch. Er wird 1950 aus der Bundesrepublik nach Polen ausgeliefert und für seine als Gauleiter von Ostpreußen in Polen begangenen Verbrechen zum Tode verurteilt. Seine mörderische Tätigkeit als Reichskommissar Ukraine wird nicht geahndet. Koch ist bemüht, vor Gericht ein mitleiderregendes Bild abzugeben. So weigert er sich, für den Prozess Hemd und Anzug zu wechseln. Das Urteil wird später in lebenslange Haft umgewandelt, in der Koch 1986 stirbt.

Warsaw, October 1958 to March 1959: Trial of Erich Koch. He was extradited to Poland from the Federal Republic of Germany in 1950 and sentenced to death for crimes committed in Poland as Gauleiter in East Prussia. He was not punished for his murderous activities as Reich Commissar in Ukraine. Koch tried to make a pitiful impression, for example, by refusing to change his shirt and suit for the trial. The sentence was later commuted to life imprisonment. Koch died in jail in 1986.

Juristische Aufarbeitung

Der Nürnberger Hauptkriegsverbrecherprozess

Im Herbst 1945 eröffnet der Internationale Militärgerichtshof ein Strafverfahren gegen 24 führende Vertreter des Deutschen Reichs. Zwar erwähnt die Anklageschrift das Ziel der Nationalsozialisten, »nationale, rassische oder religiöse Gruppen, insbesondere Juden, Polen, Zigeuner usw. zu vernichten«. Der Völkermord wird jedoch als allgemeines Kriegsverbrechen verstanden und steht nicht im Mittelpunkt der Verhandlungen. In diesem Rahmen tragen die amerikanischen Anklagevertreter den größten Anteil zur Aufklärung des Massenmords bei. Großbritannien scheut, den Punkt aufzugreifen, vor allem weil es fürchtet, dass Juden daraufhin vermehrt Anspruch auf Einreise nach Palästina erheben könnten. Auch Frankreich schreckt davor zurück, das Verbrechen zu verhandeln, da viele Franzosen an Deportationen beteiligt gewesen waren. Die sowjetischen Anklagevertreter erbringen eine Reihe von Beweisen für die deutschen Verbrechen, benennen Juden aber nicht als eigene Opfergruppe.

Nuremberg Trial of the Major War Criminals

In autumn 1945, the International Military Tribunal opened criminal proceedings against 24 leading representatives of the German Reich. The indictment did mention the goal of the National Socialists, destroying »national, racial, or religious groups, particularly Jews, Poles, Gypsies and others«. But genocide was considered to be a general war crime and was not at the focus of the proceedings. In this context, American prosecutors made the greatest contribution to investigating of the mass murders. Great Britain hesitated to raise the issue, in particular because it feared Jews would increasingly claim the right to enter Palestine. France, too, backed away from dealing with the atrocities, because many Frenchmen had participated in deportations. Soviet prosecutors provided a good deal evidence for the German crimes, but did not name Jews as a distinct group of victims.

Vordere Reihe von links | Front row, from l. to r.:
Hermann Göring (1893 – 1946), Rudolf Heß (1894 – 1987), Joachim von Ribbentrop (1893 – 1946), Wilhelm Keitel (1882 – 1946), Ernst Kaltenbrunner (1903 – 1946), Alfred Rosenberg (1893 – 1946), Hans Frank (1900 – 1946).
Hintere Reihe von links | Back row, from l. to r.:
Karl Dönitz (1891 – 1980, halb verdeckt | partly hidden), Hjalmar Schacht (1877 – 1970), Baldur von Schirach (1907 – 1974), Fritz Sauckel (1894 – 1946), Alfred Jodl (1890 – 1946), Franz von Papen (1879 – 1969), Arthur Seyß-Inquart (1892 – 1946), Albert Speer (1905 – 1981).

Stadtarchiv Nürnberg A 65 Nr. III-RA-262-D

Nürnberg, 20. November 1945 bis 1. Oktober 1946: Angeklagte im Prozess gegen die Hauptkriegsverbrecher. Es ergehen zwölf Todesurteile, sieben Haftstrafen und drei Freisprüche. Erstmals wird nicht nur gegen Einzelpersonen verhandelt: Das Gericht erklärt die SS mit dem SD, die Gestapo und das Führerkorps der NSDAP zu »verbrecherischen Organisationen«.

Nuremberg, 20 November 1945 – 1 October 1946: The accused in the Trial of Major War Criminals. Twelve of the accused were sentenced to death, seven were given prison sentences, and three were acquitted. For the first time ever, not only individual persons were indicted: The courts considered the SS, together with the SD, the Gestapo, and the leadership of the NSDAP to be »criminal organisations«.

Der Nürnberger Einsatzgruppenprozess

Nach der Verurteilung der Hauptkriegsverbrecher kommen keine weiteren gemeinsamen Prozesse der Alliierten zustande. Die vier Besatzungsmächte beginnen jedoch in ihren jeweiligen Zonen eigenständige Verfahren, auch gegen Verantwortliche aus Wehrmacht, Polizei und SS. Der in der amerikanischen Besatzungszone geführte Nürnberger Einsatzgruppenprozess macht als einziger die Massenerschießungen zum Hauptanklagepunkt. Verhandelt wird allerdings nur gegen 24 führende Angehörige der Einsatzgruppen der Sicherheitspolizei und des SD. Im April 1948 fällt das Gericht 14 Todesurteile und verhängt acht Haftstrafen. Nur vier Angeklagte werden tatsächlich hingerichtet, die letzten Verurteilten 1958 vorzeitig entlassen.

Nuremberg Einsatzgruppen trial

After the major war criminals had been sentenced, no more joint trials involving all the Allies were held. The four occupying powers held trials in their respective zones, including trials against members of the Wehrmacht, the police and the SS. The Nuremberg Einsatzgruppen trial held in the US zone of occupation was the only trial to make mass shootings the main charge of indictment. However, the case involved only 24 leading members of the Einsatzgruppen. In April 1948, the court passed 14 death sentences and eight prison sentences. Only four of the accused were actually executed. The last prisoners were released in 1958, after serving only part of their sentence.

United States Holocaust Memorial Museum, Washington, D.C.

Nürnberg, 1947/48: Chefankläger Benjamin Ferencz (*1920) beim Einsatzgruppenprozess, links neben ihm Dr. Friedrich Bergold (1899 – 1983), Anwalt von Ernst Biberstein, rechts Dr. Rudolf Aschenauer (1913 – 1983), Anwalt von Otto Ohlendorf. Aschenauer, der mit rechtsradikalen Kreisen verbunden ist, wird in den folgenden Jahren zu einer Schlüsselfigur bei der Kampagne für die Begnadigung der Verurteilten alliierter Gerichte.

Nuremberg, 1947/48: Chief prosecutor Benjamin Ferencz (*1920) at the Einsatzgruppen trial, to the left of him Dr. Friedrich Bergold (1899 – 1983), lawyer for Ernst Biberstein, to the right Dr. Rudolf Aschenauer (1913 – 1983), lawyer for Otto Ohlendorf. Aschenauer, who was associated with radical right-wing circles, became a key figure in the next few years in the campaign for the pardoning of those sentenced by Allied courts.

Juristische Aufarbeitung

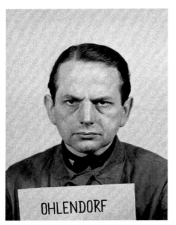

Otto Ohlendorf
(1907 – 1951)

Führer Einsatzgruppe D,
Todesstrafe, vollstreckt.

Commanding Officer of
Einsatzgruppe D,
death sentence, executed.

Heinz Jost
(1904 – 1964)

Führer Einsatzgruppe A,
lebenslänglich, entlassen 1952.

Commanding Officer of
Einsatzgruppe A,
life imprisonment,
released in 1952.

Erwin Schulz
(1900 – 1981)

Führer Einsatzkommando 5
Einsatzgruppe C,
20 Jahre, entlassen 1954.

Commanding Officer of
Einsatzkommando 5 of
Einsatzgruppe C,
20 years imprisonment,
released in 1954.

Prof. Dr. Franz Alfred Six
(1909 – 1975)

Führer Vorkommando Moskau
Einsatzgruppe B,
20 Jahre, entlassen 1952.

Commanding Officer of
Vorkommando Moscow of
Einsatzgruppe B,
20 years imprisonment,
released in 1952.

Dr. Martin Sandberger
(1911 – 2010)

Führer Einsatzkommando 1a
Einsatzgruppe A,
Todesstrafe, entlassen 1958.

Commanding Officer of
Einsatzkommando 1a of
Einsatzgruppe A,
death sentence,
released in 1958.

Willi Seibert
(1908 – 1976)

Stellvertretender Führer
Einsatzgruppe D,
Todesstrafe, entlassen 1954.

Deputy commanding Officer of
Einsatzgruppe D,
death sentence,
released in 1954.

United States Holocaust Memorial Museum, Washington, D.C.

Judicial investigation

Erich Naumann
(1905 – 1951)

Führer Einsatzgruppe B,
Todesstrafe, vollstreckt.

Commanding Officer of
Einsatzgruppe B,
death sentence, executed.

Dr. Dr. Otto Rasch
(1891 – 1948)

Führer Einsatzgruppe C,
verhandlungsunfähig.

Commanding Officer of
Einsatzgruppe C,
unfit to stand trial.

Paul Blobel
(1894 – 1951)

Führer Sonderkommando 4a
Einsatzgruppe C,
Todesstrafe, vollstreckt.

Commanding Officer of
Sonderkommando 4a of
Einsatzgruppe C,
death sentence, executed.

Dr. Walter Blume
(1906 – 1974)

Führer Sonderkommando 7a
Einsatzgruppe B,
Todesstrafe, entlassen 1955.

Commanding Officer of
Sonderkommando 7a of
Einsatzgruppe B,
death sentence,
released in 1955.

Eugen Steimle
(1909 – 1987)

Führer Sonderkommando 7a
Einsatzgruppe B,
Führer Sonderkommando 4a
Einsatzgruppe C,
Todesstrafe, entlassen 1954.

Commanding Officer of
Sonderkommando 7a of
Einsatzgruppe B,
Commanding Officer of
Sonderkommando 4a of
Einsatzgruppe C,
death sentence,
released in 1954.

Ernst Biberstein
geb. I née Szymanowski
(1899 – 1986)

Führer Einsatzkommando 6
Einsatzgruppe C,
Todesstrafe, entlassen 1958.

Commanding Officer of
Einsatzkommando 6 of
Einsatzgruppe C,
death sentence,
released in 1958.

Juristische Aufarbeitung

Dr. Werner Braune
(1909 – 1951)

Führer Sonderkommando 11b
Einsatzgruppe D,
Todesstrafe, vollstreckt.

Commanding Officer of
Sonderkommando 11b of
Einsatzgruppe D,
death sentence, executed.

Dr. Walter Haensch
(1904 – ?)

Führer Sonderkommando 4b
Einsatzgruppe C,
Todesstrafe, entlassen 1955.

Commanding Officer of
Sonderkommando 4b of
Einsatzgruppe C,
death sentence,
released in 1955.

Eduard Strauch
(1906 – 1955)

Führer Einsatzkommando 2
Einsatzgruppe A,
Todesstrafe, anschließend nach
Belgien ausgeliefert und erneut
zum Tode verurteilt. Verstirbt in
Haft.

Commanding Officer of
Einsatzkommando 2 of
Einsatzgruppe A,
death sentence, then extradited
to Belgium and again sentenced
to death. Died in prison.

Emil Haussmann
(1910 – 1947)

Offizier im Einsatzkommando 12
Einsatzgruppe D,
Suizid.

Officer in Einsatzkommando 12
of Einsatzgruppe D,
committed suicide.

Waldemar von Radetzky
(1910 – 1990)

Stellvertretender Führer
Sonderkommando 4a
Einsatzgruppe C,
20 Jahre, entlassen 1951.

Deputy commanding Officer of
Sonderkommando 4a of
Einsatzgruppe C,
20 years imprisonment,
released in 1951.

Felix Rühl
(1910 – ?)

Offizier im Sonderkommando 10b
Einsatzgruppe D,
10 Jahre, entlassen 1951.

Officer of Sonderkommando 10b
of Einsatzgruppe D,
10 years imprisonment,
released in 1951.

United States Holocaust Memorial Museum, Washington, D.C.

Judicial investigation

Gustav Nosske
(1902 – 1990?)

Führer Einsatzkommando 12
Einsatzgruppe D,
lebenslänglich, entlassen 1951.

Commanding Officer of
Einsatzkommando 12 of
Einsatzgruppe D,
life imprisonment,
released in 1951.

Adolf Ott
(1904 – ?)

Führer Sonderkommando 7b
Einsatzgruppe B,
Todesstrafe, entlassen 1958.

Commanding Officer of
Sonderkommando 7b of
Einsatzgruppe B,
death sentence,
released in 1958.

Waldemar (Woldemar) Klingelhöfer
(1900 – ?)

Angehöriger Sonderkommando 7b
Einsatzgruppe B,
Führer Vorkommando Moskau
Einsatzgruppe B,
Todesstrafe, entlassen 1956.

Member of Sonderkommando 7b
of Einsatzgruppe B,
Commanding Officer of
Vorkommando Moscow of
Einsatzgruppe B,
death sentence,
released in 1956.

Lothar Fendler
(1913 – 1983)

Stellvertretender Führer
Sonderkommando 4b
Einsatzgruppe C,
10 Jahre, entlassen 1951.

Deputy commanding Officer of
Sonderkommando 4b of
Einsatzgruppe C,
10 years imprisonment,
released in 1951.

Heinz Schubert
(1914 – 1987)

Offizier Einsatzgruppe D,
Todesstrafe,
entlassen 1951.

Officer of Einsatzgruppe D,
death sentence,
released in 1951.

Matthias Graf
(1903 – ?)

Offizier Einsatzkommando 6
Einsatzgruppe C,
3 Jahre, gilt bei
Urteilsverkündung als verbüßt.

Officer of Einsatzkommando 6 of
Einsatzgruppe C,
3 years imprisonment, already
served by the time judgment
was passed.

Juristische Aufarbeitung

Unterstützung für die Verurteilten

Die westalliierten Verfahren, die auf den Nürnberger Hauptkriegsverbrecherprozess folgen, stoßen in Westdeutschland zunehmend auf Ablehnung; sie werden als »Siegerjustiz« wahrgenommen. Kritik am Vorgehen der Alliierten äußern zunächst vor allem Vertreter der Kirchen. Sie machen sich zudem für großzügige Haftentlassungen und die Aussetzung von Todesurteilen stark. Die kirchliche Fürsprache erstreckt sich auch auf einzelne Angeklagte des Einsatzgruppenprozesses. Politischen Einfluss gewinnt ein Juristenkreis, der sich um ehemalige Verteidiger der Nürnberger Prozesse bildet. Nach der Gründung der Bundesrepublik 1949 gewinnt die Frage nach dem Umgang mit den Verurteilten an politischer Bedeutung. Die Bundesregierung nutzt ihre Rolle als Partner der Westmächte im Kalten Krieg, um auf die Freilassung der Häftlinge zu drängen. 1953 nehmen gemeinsame Kommissionen aus Vertretern der Bundesrepublik und der Westalliierten ihre Arbeit auf. Sie bearbeiten zahlreiche Gnadengesuche und erwirken bis 1958 die Entlassung aller verbliebenen Häftlinge.

Support for those who were sentenced

Trials held by the Western Allies in the wake of the Nuremberg Trial of the Major War Criminals met with growing disapproval in West Germany; they were seen as »victor's justice«. Initially, it was above all, church representatives who criticised the Allies' course of action. Churches also campaigned for early prison releases and for the suspension of death sentences. The support of the churches also extended to some of the accused in the Einsatzgruppen trial. A group of attorneys around the criminal defence lawyers from the Nuremberg trials gained political influence. After the founding of the Federal Republic of Germany in 1949, the question of how to deal with those sentenced gained political significance. The West German government used its role as a partner of the Western powers during the Cold War to press for the release of the prisoners. In 1953, joint commissions made up of representatives of the Federal Republic and the Western Allies were set up. These processed the numerous petitions for pardons and obtained the release of all remaining prisoners by 1958.

Vorherige Seiten:
Justizfotos der Verurteilten des Einsatzgruppenprozesses. Die Männer werden vor allem als Befehlshaber ihrer Einheiten angeklagt. Für das Strafmaß ist ausschlaggebend, ob ihnen das Gericht eine aktive Rolle beim Massenmord nachweisen kann. Todesstrafen werden nur verhängt, wenn der Angeklagte seine Verantwortung gesteht und nicht vorgibt, keine andere Wahl gehabt zu haben. 1951 wandeln die US-Amerikaner die meisten Todesstrafen in Haftstrafen um. Bis 1958 werden alle noch in Haft befindlichen Verurteilten begnadigt oder auf Bewährung entlassen.

Previous pages:
Official court photos of the men sentenced in the Einsatzgruppen trial. The men were accused, above all, of acts committed in their function as commanders of their units. The severity of the sentence depended on whether the court was able to prove that they played an active role in the mass murders. The death penalty was only passed if the accused admitted to his responsibility and did not claim that he had no other choice. In 1951, the Americans converted most of the death sentences into prison sentences. By 1958, all those who had been sentenced and were still in prison were pardoned or released on parole.

Judicial investigation

Stadtarchiv Landsberg am Lech Bild A 2687

Landsberg (Bayern): In der Stadt befindet sich ein US-amerikanisches Militärgefängnis, in dem zahlreiche verurteilte Nationalsozialisten einsitzen. Etwa 4.000 Menschen versammeln sich am 7. Januar 1951 auf dem Hauptplatz, um gegen die Hinrichtung Ohlendorfs und anderer zu protestieren. 300 Holocaustüberlebende sind zu einer Gegendemonstration gekommen. Als sie versuchen, durch Zwischenrufe zu stören, schlägt ihnen »Juden raus!« entgegen; einige jüdische Gegendemonstranten werden verhaftet.

Landsberg (Bavaria): The town housed a US military prison where many Nazis served their sentences. A crowd of about 4,000 gathered in the main square on 7 January 1951 to protest the execution of Ohlendorf and other prisoners. 300 Holocaust survivors arrived for a counterdemonstration. When they tried to disrupt the main demonstration by heckling, some in the crowd shouted »Jews out!«; several of the Jewish counterdemonstrators were arrested.

Juristische Aufarbeitung

München, 15. Januar 1951: Helene Elisabeth Prinzessin von Isenburg (1900 – 1974) und Weihbischof Johannes Neuhäusler (1888 – 1973) bei einer Pressekonferenz. Isenburg, die »Mutter der Landsberger« genannt wird, und Neuhäusler, ehemaliger Häftling im Konzentrationslager Dachau, gehören im gleichen Jahr zu den Mitbegründern der »Stillen Hilfe für Kriegsgefangene und Internierte«. Diese unterstützt inhaftierte Kriegsverbrecher.

Munich, 15 January 1951: Helene Elisabeth Princess of Isenburg (1900 – 1974) and Auxiliary Bishop Johannes Neuhäusler (1888 – 1973) at a press conference. Isenburg, who was called the »Mother of the Landsbergers«, and Neuhäusler, a former prisoner of Dachau concentration camp, were among the founders of the organisation »Silent Aid for Prisoners of War and Interned Persons«, which was established in the same year. The organisation provided support to imprisoned war criminals.

Treysa (Hessen), 31. August 1945: Der erste Ratsvorsitzende der Evangelischen Kirche in Deutschland, Theophil Wurm (1868 – 1953, links), und sein Stellvertreter Martin Niemöller (1892 – 1984). Beide waren mit den Nationalsozialisten in Konflikt geraten, Niemöller hatte mehrere Jahre in Konzentrationslagerhaft verbracht. Nach dem Krieg kritisieren sie die Prozesse der Alliierten. So behauptet Wurm, die Angeklagten im Nürnberger Einsatzgruppenprozess seien durch Folter zu Aussagen gezwungen worden. Er ist Mitbegründer der »Stillen Hilfe«. Diese erhält über Pastor Friedrich von Bodelschwingh (1902 – 1977) Kleider und Lebensmittel aus Bethel, der Bielefelder Anstalt für Kranke und behinderte Menschen.

Treysa (Hessia), 31 August 1945: The first chairman of the Council of the Protestant Church in Germany, Theophil Wurm (1868 – 1953, to the left), and his deputy, Martin Niemöller (1892 – 1984). Both had come into conflict with the Nazis. Niemöller had spent several years in concentration camps. After the war, the two men criticised the trials held by the Allies. Wurm, for example, claimed that statements had been obtained from the accused in the Nuremberg Einsatzgruppen trial under torture. He was also a founding member of »Silent Aid«. Through Pastor Friedrich von Bodelschwingh (1902 – 1977), this organisation obtained food and clothing from Bethel hospital for the ill and disabled people in Bielefeld.

dpa / Süddeutsche Zeitung Photo

epd-bild / Hephata-Archiv

Judicial investigation

Martin Sandberger (1911 – 2010) wird für die unter seiner Führung begangenen Verbrechen des Einsatzkommandos 1a zum Tode verurteilt. Die Beziehungen seiner Familie, seine kirchliche Bindung vor 1933 und sein Werdegang als Jurist verhelfen ihm zu prominenter Fürsprache, so durch Theophil Wurm. Sein Fall zeigt, wie stark sich Kirchen und Politik in Wetsdeutschland für Verurteilte alliierter Verfahren einsetzen.

Martin Sandberger (1911 – 2010) was sentenced to death for crimes committed by Einsatzkommando 1a under his command. His family's connections, his church involvement before 1933, and his career as a lawyer ensured him prominent support, for example, from Theophil Wurm. His case shows how vigorously the churches and political circles in Western Germany supported those who had been convicted in Allied proceedings.

United States Holocaust Memorial Museum, Washington, D.C.

Nürnberg 1948/49: Hellmut Becker (1913 – 1993). Auf Wunsch seines Freundes Carl-Friedrich von Weizsäcker (1912–2007), dessen Vater Ernst von Weizsäcker (1882 – 1951) er in Nürnberg verteidigt hatte, übernimmt der junge Anwalt Anfang der 1950er Jahre die Vertretung Sandbergers. Ab 1953 reicht Becker halbjährlich Gnadengesuche für ihn ein und verschafft sich Unterstützung durch Bonner Politiker. Becker prägt später wesentlich die Bildungsreformen der Bundesrepublik.

Nuremberg 1948/49: Hellmut Becker (1913 – 1993). At the request of his friend Carl-Friedrich von Weizsäcker (1912–2007), whose father Ernst von Weizsäcker (1882 – 1951) he had defended in Nuremberg, this young lawyer was appointed to represent Sandberger in the early 1950s. Starting in 1953, Becker submitted a petition for pardon every 6 months and won the support of politicians in Bonn. Later, Becker became one of the masterminds of educational reforms in West Germany.

Bonn, 1. Januar 1954: Bundespräsident Theodor Heuss (1884 – 1963, FDP, l.) mit Bundestagsvizepräsident Carlo Schmid (1896 – 1979, SPD). Beide setzen sich für Sandberger ein. Schmid, der ihn in den 1930er Jahren in der Referendarzeit betreut hatte, äußert, dass dieser »kein blindwütiger Fanatiker gewesen sein kann«. Sandberger kommt 1958 frei.

Bonn, 1 January 1954: German President Theodor Heuss (1884 – 1963, l.) with Vice-President of the German parliament Carlo Schmid (1896 – 1979). Both gave their support to Sandberger. Schmid, who had been Sandberger's supervisor during his legal clerkship in the 1930s, claimed that Sandberger »could not possibly have been a fanatic blind with rage«. Sandberger was released from prison in 1958.

Privatbesitz Becker

ullstein bild / Fotografin: Charlotte Willot

Juristische Aufarbeitung

Prozesse in der Bundesrepublik und der DDR

In beiden deutschen Staaten kommt die Strafverfolgung der Täter Anfang der 1950er Jahre weitgehend zum Erliegen. Die Bundesrepublik beginnt erst mit systematischen Ermittlungen, als die DDR die Wiedereingliederung ehemaliger Nationalsozialisten in die westdeutsche Gesellschaft anprangert und befreundete Staaten Druck ausüben. Gemessen am Umfang der Verbrechen werden in den folgenden Jahrzehnten jedoch nur wenige Prozesse geführt, die Urteile fallen meist milde aus. Die DDR klagt nur noch vereinzelt ausgesuchte Täter an. Die Verfahren dienen vor allem der Propaganda: Sie sollen vortäuschen, dass der Staat hart gegen ehemalige »Hitlerfaschisten« vorgeht. Im wiedervereinigten Deutschland wird bis heute gegen die Mörder ermittelt. Nur selten gelingt es, den Tätern ihre persönliche Beteiligung an den Verbrechen nachzuweisen. Es ist ein Wettlauf gegen die Zeit: Die meisten Zeugen und Täter sind inzwischen verstorben.

Trials in East and West Germany

In both German states, prosecution of the perpetrators more or less came to a halt in the early 1950s. West Germany did not start systematic investigations until the German Democratic Republic (GDR) began to criticise the rehabilitation of former Nazis in West German society and friendly countries exerted pressure. However, given the magnitude of the crimes committed, very few trials were held in the ensuing decades. Sentences tended to be mild. The East German state only indicated individual hand-picked perpetrators. Here, proceedings mainly served propaganda purposes: they were supposed to give the impression that the state was taking a hard line against former »Hitler fascists«. In reunited Germany, the murderers are still being investigated, but prosecutors rarely succeed in proving that the accused were personally involved in crimes. It is a race against time. Most witnesses and perpetrators have already passed away.

Harald von Koenigswald: *Im roten Schatten. Alltag in Mitteldeutschland*, 4. Auflage. München/Eßlingen 1964, S. 62.

Judicial investigation

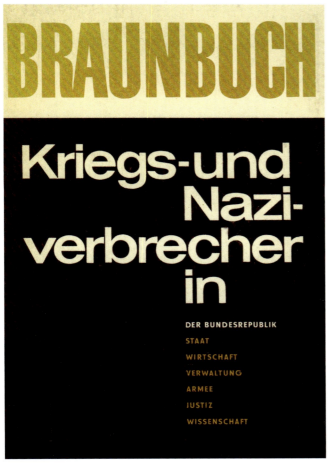

Braunbuch. Kriegs- und Naziverbrecher in der Bundesrepublik, 2. überarbeitete Auflage. Berlin 1965.

Titel des *Braunbuchs*: Mit verschiedenen Kampagnen macht die DDR auf ehemalige Nationalsozialisten in hohen Positionen in der Bundesrepublik aufmerksam. Abgesehen von einigen absichtlichen Falschmeldungen sind die Vorwürfe weitgehend berechtigt. Gleichzeitig deckt die DDR Belastete im eigenen Land.

Cover of the *Brown Book*: The GDR staged various campaigns drawing attention to former Nazis in high positions in West Germany. Apart from a few intentionally false reports, the accusations were justified. At the same time, the GDR was covering up the crimes of people living within its borders.

Waldheim, 1950: Häftlinge auf dem Hof der Strafvollzugsanstalt. Zwischen April und Juni verurteilt die DDR in der sächsischen Kleinstadt 3.324 Personen in Schnellverfahren und Schauprozessen zu meist langen Haftstrafen oder zum Tode. Ein persönlicher Tatnachweis wird nur selten erbracht. Die Verfahren sollen die Strafverfolgung in der DDR symbolisch abschließen. Die meisten Verurteilten werden noch in den 1950er Jahren amnestiert, mehrere hundert sterben in Haft.

Waldheim, 1950: Inmates in the prison courtyard. Between April and June, in this small Saxon town, East Germany sentenced 3,324 persons mostly to long imprisonment or death, either in summary proceedings or show trials. Proof of personal guilt was rarely presented. The trials were intended as a symbolic end to prosecution in the GDR. Most of those convicted were amnestied in the 1950s. Several hundred died in prison.

Juristische Aufarbeitung

Südwestpresse

Ulm, 1958: Angeklagte im sogenannten Ulmer Einsatzkommandoprozess. V.l.n.r.: Bernhard Fischer-Schweder, Pranas Lukys, Harm Willms Harms, Werner Hersmann.
Erstmals werden in der Bundesrepublik die Erschießungen von Juden im besetzten Osteuropa in einem öffentlichkeitswirksamen Verfahren geahndet. Die Angeklagten werden allerdings lediglich wegen »Beihilfe zum gemeinschaftlichen Mord« verurteilt, obwohl sie für die Ermordung von über 5.500 litauischen Juden verantwortlich sind.

Ulm, 1958: Accused in the so-called Ulm Einsatzkommando trial. From l. to r.: Bernhard Fischer-Schweder, Pranas Lukys, Harm Willms Harms, Werner Hersmann.
For the first time in West Germany, the shooting of Jews in occupied eastern Europe was the subject of a trial that raised great public interest. Nonetheless, the accused were only sentenced for »accessory to joint enterprise murder«, even though they were responsible for the murder of more than 5,500 Lithuanian Jews.

Judicial investigation

DER SPIEGEL 11/1965

Der Spiegel, 11/1965, 10. März 1965. Der Bundestag lehnt 1960 den Antrag ab, die geltenden Verjährungsfristen für Tötungsverbrechen aufzuheben. Vor 1945 begangener Totschlag kann damit nicht mehr geahndet werden. Da der Tatbestand des Mordes nach 20 Jahren verjährt, droht ab 1965 die Straffreiheit für Mörder des Holocaust. Nach heftigen Debatten wird die Verjährungsfrist für Mord mehrfach verlängert, 1979 ganz aufgehoben. Nur vor diesem Hintergrund kann bis heute gegen mutmaßliche Mörder ermittelt werden.

Der Spiegel, 11/1965, 10 March 1965: »Statute of Limitation?«. In 1960, the West German parliament rejected a motion to abolish existing statutes of limitations for homicide. This meant that manslaughter committed before 1945 could no longer be penalised. Since the statutory limitation period for murder was twenty years, there was a danger that the Holocaust murderers would go unpunished after 1965. Following heated discussions, the statute of limitations for murder was extended several times, and in 1979 was abolished altogether. As a result investigations against suspected murderers can still be carried out today.

Zentrale Stelle, Ludwigsburg

1958 wird die Zentrale Stelle der Landesjustizverwaltungen zur Aufklärung nationalsozialistischer Verbrechen ins Leben gerufen. Die Bundesrepublik reagiert damit zum einen auf eine Kampagne der DDR und den daraus entstehenden Druck aus dem In- und Ausland, zum anderen auf die Erfahrungen aus dem Ulmer Einsatzkommandoprozess. Dieser war nur durch einen Zufall zustande gekommen. Die Zentrale Stelle (Foto: Zentralkartei, 2015) besteht bis heute.

In 1958, the Central Office of the State Judicial Authorities for the Investigation of National Socialist Crimes was established. West Germany reacted to an East German campaign and to ensuing political pressure at home and abroad, as well as to the experience of the Ulm Einsatzkommando trial, which had come about more or less by chance. The Central Office (photo: central card catalogue, 2015) exists to this day.

Juristische Aufarbeitung

Für die juristische Ahndung ist es fast zu spät.
Es bleiben Erinnerung und Aufklärung.

Now it is almost too late for legal action.
What remains is to remember the victims and
inform future generations.

Stiftung Topographie des Terrors / Fotografin: Margret Nissen

Berlin, 1991: Ausstellung *Der Krieg gegen die Sowjetunion 1941 – 1945*. Sie zeigt den Krieg aus deutscher und sowjetischer Sicht und behandelt die deutschen Massenverbrechen. Von Juni bis Dezember 1991 ist sie auf dem Gelände der »Topographie des Terrors« zu sehen. Ab 1992 wandert sie durch die ehemalige Sowjetunion.

Berlin, 1991: Exhibition *The War against the Soviet Union 1941 – 1945*. This shows the war both from the German and from the Soviet perspective and addresses the mass crimes committed by Germans. It was on display at the »Topography of Terror« site from June to December 1991. Starting in 1992, it travelled through the former Soviet Union.

Süddeutsche Zeitung Photo / Fotograf: Karl-Heinz Egginger

Ausstellung *Vernichtungskrieg. Verbrechen der Wehrmacht 1941 bis 1944*. Zwischen 1995 und 1999 wird sie in 33 Städten gezeigt. Sie regt eine öffentliche Debatte über die Beteiligung der Wehrmacht an den Verbrechen an. Nach dem Vorwurf, einige Bilder seien falsch zugeordnet, wird die Ausstellung überarbeitet und von 2001 bis 2004 erneut gezeigt.

The Exhibition *War of Annihilation. Crimes of the Wehrmacht 1941 to 1944*. This exhibition was shown in 33 towns and cities between 1995 and 1999. It generated a public debate on the Wehrmacht's part in the crimes, including those committed in the Soviet Union. Following criticism that some photographs were wrongly attributed, the exhibition was revised and then shown again between 2001 and 2004.

Judicial investigation

Stiftung Denkmal für die ermordeten Juden Europas / Fotograf: Marko Priske

Berlin, Denkmal für die ermordeten Juden Europas. Das Denkmal geht auf eine bürgerschaftliche Initiative zurück; seine Verwirklichung erfolgt nach langjähriger öffentlicher Debatte und einem Beschluss des Deutschen Bundestags im Jahr 1999. Das Stelenfeld und der Ort der Information sind die zentrale deutsche Gedenkstätte zur Erinnerung an sechs Millionen ermordete Juden.

Berlin, Memorial to the Murdered Jews of Europe. The memorial was built at the initiative of a group of German citizens; the project was realised after many years of public debate and a decision by the German parliament in 1999. The field of stelae and the Information Centre make up Germany's main memorial site for remembering the six million murdered Jews.

Stiftung Topographie des Terrors / Fotograf: Stefan Müller

Berlin, Dokumentationszentrum Topographie des Terrors: Auf dem Gelände befanden sich vor 1945 das Geheime Staatspolizeiamt, die Reichsführung-SS, der Sicherheitsdienst (SD) der SS und ab 1939 das Reichssicherheitshauptamt. Seit 1987 informieren hier Ausstellungen über diese Zentralen des Terrors. Das Dokumentationszentrum wird 2010 eröffnet.

Berlin, Topography of Terror Documentation Centre: Before 1945, the Secret State Police Office, the Security Service (SD) of the SS, and, from 1939 onwards, the Reich Security Main Office were all located on this site. Ever since 1987, the site has been used for exhibitions informing visitors about these central institutions of terror. The Documentation Centre was opened in 2010.

Stiftung Denkmal für die ermordeten Juden Europas / Fotograf: Benno Auras

Stolpersteine für die Familie Bendix in der Lynarstaße 9, Berlin-Wilmersdorf, verlegt 2012: Elisabeth und Otto Bendix wurden am 30. November 1941 mit 1.051 anderen Berliner Juden in Riga erschossen. Ihr Sohn Peter war 1939 mit einem Kindertransport nach England gelangt. Die Messingsteine gedenken der Opfer der Nationalsozialisten an deren letzter Wohn- oder Wirkungsstätte. Seit 1995 sind europaweit über 50.000 Stolpersteine verlegt worden.

Stumbling stones for the Bendix family in Lynar Street 9, Berlin-Wilmersdorf, set in 2012: Elisabeth and Otto Bendix were shot in Riga on 30 November 1941 along with 1,051 other Berlin Jews. Their son Peter managed to reach England in a special children's transport in 1939. The brass bricks remind passers-by of the Nazis' victims and are set in the pavement outside the victim's last home or place of work. More than 50,000 of these stumbling stones have been placed throughout Europe since 1995.

Juristische Aufarbeitung

American Jewish Committee / Fotografin: Anna Voitenka

Judicial investigation

American Jewish Committee / Fotografin: Anna Voitenka

American Jewish Committee / Fotografin: Anna Voitenka

Eröffnung von Gedenkstätten an Orten von Massenerschießungen im besetzten Ostpolen (heute Ukraine), Sommer 2015. Links: Kisielin (Kysylyn), Mitte: Bachów (Bahiv), rechts: Ostrożec (Ostro). Die Gedenkorte, die im Rahmen von *Protecting Memory* entstehen, machen die Lage von Massengräbern sichtbar und informieren über die Geschichte der ausgelöschten jüdischen Gemeinden. Das Projekt beginnt 2010 auf Initiative des American Jewish Committee unter Beteiligung der Konferenz europäischer Rabbiner, des Ukrainischen Zentrums für Holocauststudien, des Ukrainischen Jüdischen Komitees und von *Yahad – In Unum*. Einen wesentlichen Anteil der Finanzierung übernimmt das deutsche Auswärtige Amt. Nach der Einweihung von fünf Gedenkorten sollen bis 2017 fünf weitere Massengräber, darunter eines ermordeter Roma, gesichert werden.

Opening of memorials at mass killing sites in occupied eastern Poland (now Ukraine), summer 2015. Left: Kysylyn, center: Bakhiv, right: Ostrozhets. The memorial sites, which were set up as part of the project *Protecting Memory*, show the locations of mass graves and inform visitors about the history of the Jewish communities that were destroyed. The project was started in 2010 at the initiative of the American Jewish Committee, supported by the Conference of European Rabbis, the Ukrainian Centre for Holocaust Studies, the Ukrainian Jewish Committee, and *Yahad – In Unum*. The German Foreign Ministry provided most of the funding. Five memorial sites have already been dedicated. Five more mass graves, including one of murdered Romani, are to be preserved by 2017.

Zwischen Widerstand und Ohnmacht
Between resistance and paralysis

Seit Jahrhunderten waren Juden in Osteuropa immer wieder Opfer lokaler antijüdischer Ausschreitungen geworden. Unter den deutschen Besatzern nahm die Gewalt andere Ausmaße an; sie planten einen systematischen Völkermord. Die jüdische Bevölkerung traf dies völlig unvorbereitet. Wohl niemand konnte sich vorstellen, dass das Ziel der Deutschen die Vernichtung aller Juden war. Unter den wenigen, denen die Flucht vor der herannahenden Wehrmacht gelang, waren vor allem junge Männer. Zurück blieben in der Mehrzahl Frauen, Kinder und Alte, auch in der Annahme, die Deutschen würden sie verschonen. Mit der Besetzung wurden Flucht und Widerstand beträchtlich erschwert, unmittelbar vor den Erschießungen nahezu unmöglich.

For centuries, the Jews of Eastern Europe repeatedly fell victim to local anti-Jewish excesses. Under the German occupation, the violence took on totally different dimensions. The Germans were planning systematic genocide. This caught the Jewish population entirely off-guard. Presumably no one could imagine that the Germans intended to annihilate all Jews. Those few who managed to escape the advancing Wehrmacht were above all young men. Most of those who stayed behind were women, children, and elderly people, often assuming the Germans would spare them. Once an area had been occupied, it became increasingly difficult to flee or to resist. Immediately before the shootings, it was practically impossible.

Zwischen Widerstand und Ohnmacht

Weg zur Erschießung
Before the shootings

Die jüdischen Gemeinden in Osteuropa waren zum Teil Monate vor ihrer Vernichtung unter unmenschlichen Bedingungen in Ghettos isoliert worden. Nur wenige Nichtjuden waren bereit, sich über die von den Deutschen erlassenen Verbote hinwegzusetzen und zu helfen. Vor den Erschießungen wurden die geschwächten Männer, Frauen und Kinder in großer Eile von Bewaffneten aus ihren Häusern getrieben. Häufig wussten sie nicht, was sie erwartete; sie waren orientierungs- und wehrlos. Einigen gelang es jedoch, Widerstand zu leisten. So wehrten sich Ghettoinsassen im litauischen Schagarren (Žagarė) im Oktober 1941 auf ein verabredetes Zeichen mit Waffengewalt gegen die Sammlung zur Erschießung. Sie wurden auf der Stelle ermordet.

Often months before they were eradicated, Jewish communities in Eastern Europe were isolated in ghettos under inhuman conditions. Very few non-Jews were willing to defy the bans imposed by the Germans and help their Jewish neighbours. Before the shootings, armed police hastily drove the weakened men, women, and children from their houses. Defenceless and disoriented they often did not know what awaited them. All the same, some managed to put up resistance. In October 1941, for example, inmates of the Žagarė ghetto in Lithuania refused to assemble, and upon an agreed signal resorted to force of arms. They were murdered on the spot.

Zwischen Widerstand und Ohnmacht

Kein Entkommen
No escape

Between resistance and paralysis

An der Erschießungsstätte mussten die Menschen häufig stundenlang verharren. Wer sich wehrte, lief Gefahr, vor den Augen seiner Angehörigen sofort getötet zu werden. Zuschauer verstärkten die von den Tätern ausgehende Todesdrohung: Ihre Anwesenheit verringerte die Möglichkeit zu fliehen. Die Umstehenden gaben den Zusammengetriebenen zu verstehen, dass sie nichts gegen die Erschießung einzuwenden hatten und von ihnen keinerlei Hilfe zu erwarten war.

People often had to endure hours of waiting at the killing site. Anyone who resisted risked being shot right in front of his or her family. Spectators increased the threat of death posed by the perpetrators: Their presence diminished the chance to escape. The bystanders made it clear to those who had been rounded up that they did not object the shooting, and no help could be expected from them.

Zwischen Widerstand und Ohnmacht

Im Angesicht des Todes
Looking death in the eye

Between resistance and paralysis

Der 13-jährige Kuki Kopelman überlebte im Oktober 1941 eine Massenerschießung von 9.200 Menschen nahe der litauischen Stadt Kaunas. Er floh zurück ins Ghetto zu seinem Freund Solly Ganor. Dieser gab nach dem Krieg wieder, was Kuki ihm erzählt hatte. Der Bericht beschreibt, was viele der Zusammengetriebenen gefühlt haben mögen: »Plötzlich zogen sich alle aus. Wenn du dem Tod so nah bist, ist jede Minute kostbar, als würde die nächste Sekunde die Begnadigung bringen. Schließlich standen wir alle nackt da und bedeckten unsere Scham mit den Händen und zitterten in der Kälte.« Viele fanden Trost im gemeinsamen Gebet und versuchten bis zuletzt, Kinder und schwächere Angehörige zu beschützen.

In October 1941, 13-year-old Kuki Kopelman survived the mass shooting of 9,200 people near the Lithuanian town of Kaunas. He fled back to the ghetto, to his friend Solly Ganor. After the war, the latter recalled what Kuki had told him. His report described what many of those who had been rounded up may have been thinking: »Suddenly, everyone was undressing. When you are so close to death, every minute is precious, as if the next second will bring reprieve. Finally, we were all standing there, naked, trying to cover private parts with our hands and shivering in the cold.« Many found comfort in joint prayer or tried to protect children and weaker family members right up to the end.

Zwischen Widerstand und Ohnmacht

Suche nach Auswegen
Trying to find a way out

Between resistance and paralysis

Alle Bilder: Archiv des Hamburger Instituts für Sozialforschung / Fotograf: Johannes Hähle

Angesichts der rassistischen Tötungsabsicht der Mordkommandos war es für die Zusammengetriebenen aussichtslos, ihre Unschuld zu beteuern oder auf Mitleid zu hoffen. Als Chance erschien einigen, der Denkweise der Mörder folgend zu erklären, nicht jüdisch zu sein. In Einzelfällen wurden sie herausgenommen und verhört, manche überlebten. Nur wenige konnten sich im letzten Moment verstecken, fliehen oder sich tot stellen und auf das Ende der Erschießung warten. In den darauffolgenden Monaten oder gar Jahren waren sie abhängig von nichtjüdischen Helfern. Viele zunächst Gerettete verloren durch Verrat ihr Leben.

In view of the murder squads' racist intend to kill it was pointless for those who had been rounded up to protest their innocence or hope for pity. Some saw their only chance in following the murderers' logic and declaring that they were not Jews. In some cases, they actually were taken out of the line and questioned, some survived. A few succeeded in hiding at the last moment, fleeing, or pretending to be dead until the shooting stopped. Those who did escape were dependent on non-Jewish helpers in the months or even years that followed. Many of those initially rescued were later betrayed and murdered after all.

Zwischen Widerstand und Ohnmacht

Die Ermordung der Juden von Lubny

Die gezeigten Bilder stammen aus dem ukrainischen Lubny. Am 13. September 1941 wird der 70 km östlich von Kiew gelegene Ort von deutschen Truppen besetzt. Hier ermorden am 16. Oktober 1941 Angehörige des Sonderkommandos 4a nach eigenen Angaben 1.865 Menschen. Die Aufnahmen stammen von dem Propagandafotografen Johannes Hähle (1906 – 1944). Sie zeigen, wie die Menschen aus der Stadt durch ein benachbartes Dorf zu einem Sammelplatz und dort vorbereiteten Gruben getrieben werden. Die physische Gewalt, die die Täter den Opfern vor der Ermordung zufügen, blenden die Bilder aus. Auch die Erschießungen hält Hähle nicht fest. Warum er in Lubny fotografiert, ist nicht bekannt.

The murder of the Jews of Lubny

The photos shown here were taken in the Ukrainian town of Lubny. On 13 September 1941, the town, located 70 km east of Kiev, was occupied by German troops. On 16 October 1941, members of Sonderkommando 4a by their own account killed 1,865 people. The photos were taken by propaganda photographer Johannes Hähle (1906 – 1944) and show how people were driven out of the town, through a neighbouring village, to a collection point where pits had been prepared. The photos do not show the brutality that the perpetrators inflicted on the victims before murdering them. Hähle did not photograph the actual shootings either. It is not known why he was taking pictures in Lubny.

Archiv des Hamburger Instituts für Sozialforschung

Johannes Hähle, vermutlich bei Charkow (Ukraine) 1941/42: Ab Sommer 1941 begleitet er als Fotograf der Propagandakompanie 637 eine Wehrmachtseinheit in die Ukraine. Anfang Oktober 1941 macht er Aufnahmen in Babij Jar, wo wenige Tage zuvor über 33.000 Kiewer Juden erschossen worden waren. Von Hähle stammen auch die Bilder aus Lubny vom 16. Oktober 1941. Anders als die offiziellen Propagandafotos des Kriegsgeschehens schickt er diese Bildserien nicht nach Berlin. Hähle kommt 1944 bei Kämpfen in Frankreich ums Leben. Erstmals werden seine Bilder 1995 einer breiten Öffentlichkeit durch die Ausstellung *Vernichtungskrieg. Verbrechen der Wehrmacht 1941 bis 1944* bekannt.

Johannes Hähle, probably near Kharkiv (Ukraine) 1941/42: From summer 1941 onwards, Hähle accompanied a Wehrmacht unit in Ukraine as photographer of the 637th Propaganda Company. At the beginning of October 1941, he took photos in Babi Yar, where more than 33,000 Jews from Kiev had been shot a few days earlier. The photos of Lubny taken on 16 October 1941 are also by Hähle. Unlike his official propaganda photos, he did not send these photos to Berlin. Hähle was killed in action in France in 1944. His photos became known to a wide public for the first time in 1995 as part of the exhibition *War of Annihilation. Crimes of the Wehrmacht 1941 to 1944*.

Between resistance and paralysis

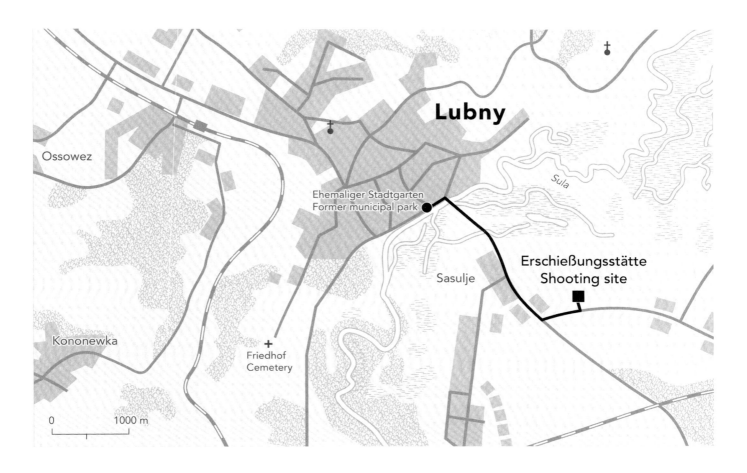

Die Wehrmachtsverwaltung fordert die Juden Lubnys und der Umgebung mit Plakaten auf, »sich Donnerstag den 16. Oktober 1941 bis 9 h früh zwecks Umsiedlung« mit Verpflegung und warmer Kleidung beim alten Stadtgarten einzufinden. Wer nicht erscheint, werde erschossen.

Die Deutschen und ukrainische Helfer treiben die Juden aus der Stadt. Einige Juden versuchen in den Fluss zu springen oder in den Wald zu fliehen. Nachbarn am Wegesrand, die jüdische Kinder retten wollen, werden von den Bewachern mit Schlägen daran gehindert.

Das Gelände hinter dem Fluss ist abgeriegelt. Die jüdischen Kinder, Frauen und Männer werden durch das Dorf Sasulje getrieben.

Unweit der Erschießungsstätte müssen die Juden Kleidung und Wertsachen ablegen. Danach ermorden Angehörige des Sonderkommandos 4a sie gruppenweise.

Heute erinnert vor Ort ein Denkmal an die Ermordeten.

On posters, the Wehrmacht administration calls on the Jews of Lubny and its surrounding area to gather at the former municipal park »on Thursday, 16 October 1941 until 9 a.m. for the purpose of resettlement«, equipped with food and warm clothing. Those who will not appear are threatened to be shot.

The Germans and Ukrainian helpers force the Jews out of the town. Some Jews try to jump into the river or to escape into the forest. The guards beat neighbours standing along the road who try to save Jewish children.

The area behind the river is cordoned off. The Jewish children, women and men are forced through the village Sasulye.

Near the killing site the Jews have to remove their clothes and valuables. Then, members of the Sonderkommando 4a kill them in groups.

Today, a memorial at the site commemorates the victims.

Schicksale
Biographies

14 Millionen Zivilisten wurden in der besetzten Sowjetunion von den Deutschen und ihren Helfern ermordet. Von der Mehrzahl der Kinder, Frauen und Männer sind nicht einmal die Namen bekannt. Ihre sterblichen Überreste fanden meist keine Begräbnisstätte, sie wurden verscharrt oder verbrannt. Die hier vorgestellten Biografien zeigen auf, wie sich der Vernichtungskrieg gegen Juden und Roma richtete, zugleich aber auch gegen sogenannte Asoziale, »Berufsverbrecher« sowie als Partisanen beschuldigte Zivilisten. Auch das Handeln der verantwortlichen Täter vor Ort wird dargestellt. Ein eigener Abschnitt ist den Bemühungen zur juristischen Aufarbeitung und der Erinnerung an die Verbrechen gewidmet.

14 million civilians were murdered in the occupied Soviet Union by Germans and local collaborators. We do not even know the names of most of the men, women and children who died. In most cases, their bodies were not transferred to proper burial sites but were instead cremated or left in shallow graves. The biographies presented here illustrate how the war of annihilation targeted Jews and Roma but also so-called asocials, »habitual criminals« and civilians accused of partisan activity. They also describe the actions of the perpetrators. A separate section deals with attempts to bring the crimes to justice and to preserve the memory of what happened.

Jekaterina **Danova Feldman**

»Ghetto im Schrank«

Jekaterina Feldman ist elf Jahre alt, als die Deutschen am 1. November 1941 die Stadt Simferopol auf der Halbinsel Krim einnehmen. Sie lebt nun in ständiger Angst. Anfang Dezember müssen sich alle Juden an einer Sammelstelle einfinden. Viele ahnen, dass sie getötet werden sollen. Jekaterinas Eltern werden ermordet, das Mädchen wird von einem russisch-armenischen Paar gerettet. Über zwei Jahre muss es sich tagsüber in einem Schrank verstecken. Im März 1944 fliehen sie gemeinsam zu den Partisanen, in deren Reihen sie die Rückeroberung Simferopols durch die Rote Armee erleben.

»A ghetto in a cupboard«

Yekaterina Feldman was eleven years old when the Germans took the Crimean city of Simferopol on 1 November 1941. From then on, she lived in permanent fear. In early December, all Jews were ordered to assemble at a given site. Many had a foreboding that they would be killed. Yekaterina' s parents were murdered, but the girl was saved by a Russian-Armenian couple. For more than two years, she had to hide in a cupboard during the daytime. In March 1944, she and her rescuers fled to the partisans. Serving in their ranks, they experienced the return of the Red Army to Simferopol.

Privatbesitz Danova Feldman

Vermutlich Simferopol (Russland), 1944: Jekaterina Feldman (*1930). Tagsüber muss sie sich in einem Schrank verstecken, da die Deutschen regelmäßig Wohnungen stürmen, um nach Juden zu suchen.

Probably Simferopol (Russia), 1944: Yekaterina Feldman (*1930). In the daytime she had to hide in a cupboard as the Germans regularly searched apartments looking for Jews.

Privatbesitz Danova Feldman

Jekaterina T. Kolesnikowa (1907 – 1993), undatiert: Gemeinsam mit ihrem Mann Sergej Danov versteckt die Mutter eines sechsjährigen Sohns Jekaterina Feldman ab Dezember 1941. Sie unterstützen die Untergrundbewegung in Simferopol. Als die Deutschen Anfang 1944 Razzien verstärken, flüchtet die Familie mit Jekaterina zu den Partisanen.

Yekaterina T. Kolesnikova (1907 – 1993), no date: Together with her husband, Sergei Danov, this mother of a six-year-old son, hid Yekaterina Feldman from December 1941 on. The couple supported the underground movement in Simferopol. When the Germans started intensifying raids at the beginning of 1944, the family fled to the partisans, taking Yekaterina Feldman with them.

Simferopol, 1941: Maria Feldman schreibt kurz vor ihrer Ermordung an ihre Tochter Jekaterina: »Glaube nicht an die Gerüchte, rege Dich nicht auf, wir arbeiten und kommen dann zurück. Bis dahin sei brav und gehorsam, pass auf Dich auf, gute Menschen retten Dich. Achte und liebe sie.« Erst nach dem Krieg gelangt der Brief über Umwege an Jekaterina Feldman.

Simferopol, 1941: Maria Feldman writes to her daughter Yekaterina shortly before she is murdered. »Don't believe the rumours, don't worry, we'll work and then come back. Until then, be a good girl and obedient. Take care of yourself. Good people are rescuing you. Love and respect them.« The letter reached Yekaterina Feldman only after the war by circuitous route.

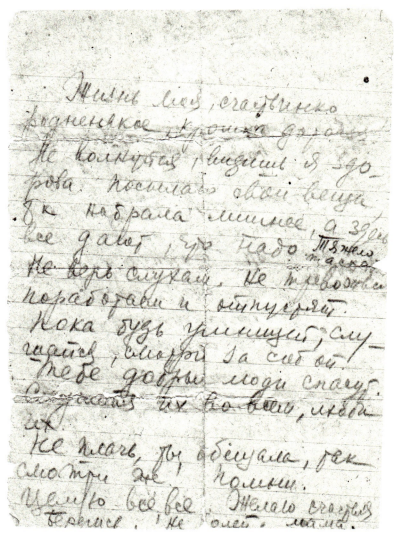

Privatbesitz Danova Feldman

Jekaterina **Danova Feldman**

Die Ermordung der Juden in Simferopol

Ab November 1941 befindet sich die Führung der Einsatzgruppe D in Simferopol. Sie verabredet mit der Ortsverwaltung der Wehrmacht, Juden als »unnütze Esser« zu ermorden. Am 9. Dezember erschießt das Sonderkommando 11b über 1.500 Angehörige der turksprachigen Gruppe der Krimtschaken, die als Juden angesehen werden. Vom 11. bis 13. Dezember töten Angehörige verschiedener Kommandos der Einsatzgruppe gemeinsam mit der Militärpolizei über 10.000 Juden. Es ist die umfangreichste Massenerschießung auf der Krim. Ab 1942 weiten die Tötungskommandos den Mord auf Roma, Patienten von Heil- und Pflegeanstalten, Partisanenverdächtige und weitere jüdische Gemeinden auf der gesamten Halbinsel aus.

Massacre of Jews in Simferopol

The leadership of Einsatzgruppe D was stationed in Simferopol from November 1941 onwards. It agreed with the local Wehrmacht administration that Jews were to be murdered as »extra mouths« to feed. On 9 December 1941, Sonderkommando 11b shot more than 1,500 members of the Turkic-speaking Krymchak minority, who were regarded as Jews. Between 11 and 13 December, members of various commandos of Einsatzgruppe D and the military police killed more than 10,000 Jews. It was the largest mass shooting on the Crimean peninsula. Starting in 1942, the killing squads expanded the killing to include Romani, patients of psychiatric hospitals, suspected partisans and additional Jewish communities on the entire peninsula.

BArch B 162 Bild-07620

Privatbesitz von Hentig

Privatbesitz von Hentig

Simferopol, Dezember 1941: Juden auf dem Weg zur »Sammelstelle« vor der Erschießung. Die Besatzer hatten in der Stadt verkünden lassen, dass Juden aufgrund der Versorgungslage »umgesiedelt« würden. Wer nicht erscheint, wird an den Folgetagen festgenommen und erhängt.

Simferopol, December 1941: Jews on the way to the »assembly point« before the shooting. The occupiers had announced that Jews would be »resettled« due to the supply situation. Those who did not report were apprehended and were hanged in the days that followed.

Werner Otto von Hentig (1886 – 1984, Gruppenbild, 3.v.l.). Er ist seit 1911 Diplomat und ab September 1941 Vertreter des Auswärtigen Amts auf der Krim. Hentig ist der einzige Gesandte im besetzten Osteuropa, der die Besatzungspolitik offen kritisiert. Die Massenerschießung in Simferopol bezeichnet er als »Schlächterei«. Seine Beschwerden bleiben folgenlos. Nach 1945 kann er sich – anders als viele Kollegen – nur schwer im diplomatischen Dienst der Bundesrepublik behaupten und wird auf unbeliebte Posten entsandt. Die Öffentlichkeit würdigt von Hentig bis heute als Kritiker der Nationalsozialisten, er selbst hatte in seinen Lebenserinnerungen vermieden, über die Massenerschießungen an Juden zu sprechen.

Werner Otto von Hentig (1886 – 1984, group photo, 3rd from left). A member of the diplomatic service since 1911 and Foreign Office representative in Crimea since September 1941, Hentig was the only Foreign Office envoy in occupied Eastern Europe to criticise the occupation policies openly. He described the Simferopol massacre as »slaughter«. His complaints had no effect. Unlike many of his colleagues, he had a hard time after 1945 holding his own in West Germany's diplomatic service and was given unpopular postings. Up to this day, Hentig is honoured by the general public for his criticism of the Nazis. In his memoires he avoided any mention of the mass shooting of Jews.

Jekaterina **Danova Feldman**

Aufarbeitung und Erinnerung

Im April 1944 erobert die Rote Armee Simferopol zurück. Sofort beschuldigt die sowjetische Regierung die nichtslawischen Minderheiten, mit den Deutschen zusammengearbeitet zu haben. Sie lässt über 200.000 Menschen in die östliche Sowjetunion deportieren. Unter ihnen ist Jekaterina Feldmans Retter, der Armenier Sergej Danov; sie sieht ihn nie wieder. Die sowjetische Führung diskriminiert auch Juden: Die Universität von Leningrad nimmt Jekaterina Feldman trotz guter Noten erst an, als sie ihre jüdische Herkunft verschweigt. Nach dem Zusammenbruch der Sowjetunion wandert sie nach Australien aus, wo sie sich bis heute für die Erinnerung an den Holocaust einsetzt. So beschreibt sie 2003 ihre Erlebnisse unter dem Titel »Ghetto im Schrank«. Sie trägt heute den Namen ihres Retters.

Judicial investigation and remembrance

In April 1944, the Red Army recaptured Simferopol. The Soviet government immediately accused the non-Slavic minorities of assisting the Germans. More than 200,000 alleged collaborators were deported to the eastern regions of the Soviet Union. Among them was Yekaterina Feldman's rescuer, the Armenian Sergei Danov; she never saw him again. The Soviet leadership also discriminated against Jews: despite her good marks, the University of Leningrad only accepted Yekaterina Feldman once she concealed her Jewish origins. After the collapse of the Soviet Union, she emigrated to Australia, where she to this day remains committed to remembering the Holocaust. In 2003, she described her experiences in an essay titled »A ghetto in a cupboard«. She added Danov's name to her own.

United States Holocaust Memorial Museum, Washington, D.C.

Nürnberg, 1947: Otto Ohlendorf (1907 – 1951, Mitte, stehend) beim Einsatzgruppenprozess. Als Leiter der Einsatzgruppe D ist der Jurist auch für den Mord an den Juden auf der Krim verantwortlich. Anfang der 1970er Jahre stehen weitere sieben Angehörige der Einsatzgruppe D für ihre Verbrechen in Simferopol in der Bundesrepublik und der DDR vor Gericht.

Nuremberg, 1947: Otto Ohlendorf (1907 – 1951, centre, standing up) at the Einsatzgruppen trial. As commander of Einsatzgruppe D, he was also responsible for the mass murder of Jews in Crimea. In the early 1970s, seven more members of Einsatzgruppe D were tried in both West and East Germany for their part in the crimes in Simferopol.

Simferopol **Simferopol**

Fotograf: Mikhail Tyaglyy

Simferopol, 2011: Das 1986 gebaute Denkmal für die ermordeten »sowjetischen Bürger«. Kurz nach Kriegsende legen Angehörige der Ermordeten einen Gedenkstein; 1964 errichten sie ein Denkmal. Im Laufe der Jahre fällt es der Witterung und der Zerstörung durch Grabräuber zum Opfer. 1986 muss die Regierung den Obelisken auf öffentlichen Druck erneuern. Erst ein 2002 von der jüdischen Gemeinde eingeweihtes Denkmal nennt die Identität der Opfer.

Simferopol, 2011: Memorial to the murdered »Soviet citizens«, erected in 1986. Shortly after the war, the families of those murdered laid a memorial stone, and in 1964, built a monument. Over the years, this was destroyed by the elements and grave robbers. In 1986, public pressure forced the government to rebuild the obelisk. The identity of the victims was not mentioned until the Jewish community dedicated another monument in 2002.

Privatbesitz Danova Feldman

Moskau (Moskwa, Russland), Israelische Botschaft, 1994: Jekaterina Danova Feldman nimmt die Urkunde und die Medaille entgegen, die Jekaterina T. Kolesnikowa als »Gerechte unter den Völkern« ehren. Die Retterin war kurz zuvor verstorben.

Moscow (Russia), Israeli Embassy, 1994: Yekaterina Danova Feldman accepts the certificate and medal honouring Yekaterina T. Kolesnikova as one of the »Righteous Among the Nations«. Ms Feldman's rescuer had passed away only a short time before.

Wanda **Jaskewitsch**

Opfer einer deutschen »Partisanenaktion«

Wanda Jaskewitsch lebt mit ihren Eltern und sechs Geschwistern in Chatyn, einem Dorf mit 26 Holzhäusern, etwa 60 Kilometer nördlich von Minsk. Am Vormittag des 22. März 1943 ereignet sich in der Nähe ein Gefecht zwischen Angehörigen des Schutzmannschaftsbataillons 118 und Partisanen, bei dem der Hauptmann der Schutzpolizei Hans Otto Woellke – 1936 Olympiasieger im Kugelstoßen –, ein weiterer Deutscher sowie drei ukrainische Schutzmänner sterben. Auf dem Rückmarsch erschießt das Bataillon etwa 25 Waldarbeiter, die angeblich den Partisanen geholfen hatten. Die 1. Kompanie fordert die SS-Sondereinheit Dirlewanger zur Verstärkung an. Gemeinsam riegeln sie am späten Nachmittag Chatyn ab.

Victim of a German »partisan operation«

Vanda Yaskevich lived with her parents and six brothers and sisters in Khatyn, a village with 26 wooden houses, approximately 60 kilometres north of Minsk. On the morning of 22 March 1943, a skirmish took place between members of Auxiliary Police Battalion 118 and partisans, during which police Captain Hans Otto Woellke – winner of the shot-put in the 1936 Olympics –, another German, and three Ukrainian auxiliary policemen were killed. On their way back, the battalion shot some 25 forest workers who allegedly helped the partisans. The 1st company requested reinforcement from the SS Special Battalion Dirlewanger. Together, they cordoned off Khatyn in the late afternoon.

Gosudarstwennyj Memorial'nyj Kompleks Chatyn

Das einzige erhaltene Foto der 20-jährigen Wanda Jaskewitsch (1923 – 1943).

The only remaining photograph of 20-year-old Vanda Yaskevich (1923 – 1943).

Vernichtung einer Dorfgemeinschaft

Nach der Abriegelung des Dorfes treiben Deutsche und Ukrainer etwa 149 Dorfbewohner – vom Säugling bis zum Greis – mit Gewehrkolbenschlägen in eine Scheune. Anschließend setzen die Deutschen die Scheune in Brand und schießen auf diejenige, die zu entkommen versuchen. Unter den Toten ist auch Wanda. Lediglich sechs Überlebende werden amtlich beurkundet, darunter Wandas Geschwister Wladimir (1930 – 2008) und Sofija (*1934), die sich verstecken konnten. Das Dorf wird geplündert und niedergebrannt. Chatyn ist einer von hunderten Orten in der Sowjetunion, die im Zuge von ›Vergeltungsaktionen‹ durch deutsche Einheiten und ihre Helfer ausgelöscht werden.

Annihilation of a village community

After cordoning off the village, Germans and Ukrainians used the butts of their rifles to drive an estimated 149 villagers – from infants to elderly persons – into a barn. The Germans then set the barn on fire and shot at anyone who tried to escape. One of the dead was Vanda. Only six survivors are recorded, including Vanda's brother Vladimir (1930 – 2008) and her sister Sofia (*1934), who had both managed to hide. The village was looted and burned to the ground. Khatyn is one of hundreds of towns and villages in the Soviet Union eradicated by German units and their auxiliaries as ›acts of reprisal‹.

BArch B 162 Bild-00218

Angehörige der SS-Sondereinheit Dirlewanger, undatiert: Die 1940 zusammengestellte Bewährungseinheit, benannt nach ihrem Kommandeur Oskar Dirlewanger (1895 – 1945), besteht aus Wilddieben, ehemaligen KZ-Häftlingen und Helfern aus den besetzten Gebieten. Sie wird im Januar 1942 nach Weißrussland versetzt und ermordet dort unter dem Vorwand der Partisanenbekämpfung unzählige Zivilisten.

Members of SS unit Dirlewanger, no date: This probation unit, named after its commander Oskar Dirlewanger (1895 – 1945), was formed in 1940 and made up mostly of convicted poachers, ex-concentration camp prisoners, and auxiliaries from the occupied territories. In January 1942, it was relocated to Belarus, where it murdered countless civilians under the pretext of fighting partisans.

Wanda **Jaskewitsch**

Erinnerung an die verbrannten Dörfer

In der Bundesrepublik erfolgt keine juristische Aufarbeitung des Verbrechens. 1975 stellt die Staatsanwaltschaft Itzehoe ein Ermittlungsverfahren gegen »Angehörige unbekannter deutscher Einheiten« ein. Die sowjetische Justiz verurteilt drei Täter wegen Kriegsverbrechen zum Tode, darunter den Ukrainer Grigorij Wasjura, der 1987 hingerichtet wird. Die Presse darf nicht berichten. In der sowjetischen Erinnerungskultur nimmt Chatyn allerdings einen zentralen Rang ein: Die 30 Hektar große, 1969 eingeweihte Gedenkstätte erinnert nicht nur an das Massaker am Ort, sondern auch an 433 weitere zerstörte Dörfer und an über 260 Vernichtungsstätten und Lager auf weißrussischem Boden.

Remembrance of the torched villages

The crime was never legally investigated in West Germany. In 1975, the Public Prosecutor of Itzehoe terminated investigations against »members of unknown German units«. The Soviet judiciary sentenced three perpetrators to death for war crimes, including the Ukrainian Grigory Vasiura, who was executed in 1987. The press was not allowed to report on the trial. Khatyn, however, played a central role in the Soviet culture of remembrance: The 30-hectare memorial site, dedicated in 1969, not only recalls the massacre that took place here, but also 433 other destroyed villages and more than 260 killing sites and prison camps on Belarusian soil.

Gosudarstwennyj Memorial'nyj Kompleks Chatyn

Gedenkstätte Chatyn (Weißrussland), 1985: Wandas Geschwister Wladimir (1930 – 2008, links) und Sofija Jaskewitsch (*1934, rechts) mit Wiktor Schelobkowitsch (*1934). Die drei Überlebenden stehen vor der symbolischen Nachbildung eines zerstörten Hauses in Chatyn.

Khatyn Memorial Site (Belarus), 1985: The survivors Vladimir (1930 – 2008, left) and Sofia Yaskevich (*1934, right), Vanda's siblings, with Viktor Zhelobkovich (*1934) in front of the symbolic reconstruction of a destroyed house in Khatyn.

Chatyn **Khatyn**

National Archives and Records Administration, College Park (MD)

Chatyn, 1. Juli 1974: Richard Nixon (1913 – 1994, Mitte), Präsident der USA, in der Gedenkstätte im Rahmen seines Staatsbesuchs in der Sowjetunion.

Khatyn, 1 July 1974: U.S.-President Richard Nixon (1913 – 1994, centre) visits the memorial site as part of his state visit to the Soviet Union.

Fotograf: Christian Dohnke

Chatyn, Staatliche Gedenkstätte, 2010: Die überlebensgroße Figur hat den Dorfschmied Josif Kaminskij zum Vorbild, der seinen sterbenden Sohn trägt. Im Hintergrund: »Friedhof der verbrannten Dörfer«.

Khatyn, National Memorial, 2010: The larger-than-life figure was modelled on village smith, Yozif Kaminsky, carrying his dying son. In the background: the »cemetery of torched villages«.

Familie **Krelitz**

Im Grenzort schutzlos ausgeliefert

Die jüdische Familie Krelitz lebt im litauischen Jurburg (Jurbarkas), nahe der Grenze zu Ostpreußen. Ende der 1930er Jahre treibt die Jurburger Juden die Angst vor einem Angriff Deutschlands um. Litauen wird 1940 von der Sowjetunion annektiert. Am 22. Juni 1941 rückt die Wehrmacht in Jurburg ein. Zwei Tage später ermächtigt der Führer der Einsatzgruppe A, Walter Stahlecker (1900 – 1942), die Staatspolizeistelle im ostpreußischen Tilsit (heute Sowetsk), Juden und Kommunisten im Grenzgebiet zum Deutschen Reich zu ermorden. Deutsche und litauische Polizei verhaften daraufhin Juden und kommunistische Funktionäre in Jurburg. Der SD-Abschnittsführer von Tilsit, Werner Hersmann (1904 – 1972), verabredet nach einem Besuch im Offizierskasino mit einem Angehörigen des dort stationierten deutschen Polizeibataillons, dass Angehörige dieser Einheit ein Erschießungskommando in Jurburg stellen.

Defenceless in a border town

The Krelitz family was a Jewish family living in the Lithuanian town of Jurbarkas near the border to East Prussia. At the end of the 1930s, fear of a German invasion spread among the Jews of Jurbarkas. In 1940, Lithuania was first annexed by the Soviet Union. The Wehrmacht marched into Jurbarkas on 22 June 1941. Two days later, the commanding officer of Einsatzgruppe A, Walter Stahlecker (1900 – 1942), authorised the State Police Office in the East-Prussian town of Tilsit (now Sovetsk) to murder Jews and communists along the border to the German Reich. Thereupon German and Lithuanian police detained Jews and communist functionaries in Jurbarkas. After a visit to the officers' canteen, the SD sector leader in Tilsit, Werner Hersmann (1904 – 1972), came to an arrangement with a member of the German police battalion stationed there that men from that unit should form a shooting squad in Jurbarkas.

Privatbesitz Sherman

Jurburg, um 1935: Die Geschwister Krelitz und unbekannte Personen am Seder (erster Abend des Pessachfestes). Vorn rechts Mosche Krelitz (um 1908 – ?), neben ihm seine Schwester Leah (1917 – 1983), ihm gegenüber sein Bruder Leib (um 1906 – ?).

Jurbarkas, around 1935: The Krelitz siblings and unidentified guests on Seder (the first night of Passover). Front right is Moshe Krelitz (around 1908 – ?), next to his sister Leah (1917 – 1983); his brother Leib (around 1906 – ?) is sitting at the other side of the table, facing him .

Memelufer, im Hintergrund Jurburg mit der Synagoge, am Fähranleger, v.r.n.l.: Mosche Krelitz, seine Schwester Leah und Freunde. Anfang 1939 schreibt Mosche seiner nach Mexiko ausgereisten Schwester angesichts der politischen Situation: »Und denk erst gar nicht über eine Rückkehr nach!«

Banks of the Neman river; standing on the ferry landing, from right to left: Moshe Krelitz, his sister Leah and friends of theirs. Jurbarkas with its synagogue can be seen in the background. In view of the political situation, Moshe wrote in 1939 to his sister who had left the country for Mexico: »…and don't even think of coming back!«

Dora Krelitz, Mosches Frau, mit der Tochter Esther (1938 – ?), um 1939.

Dora Krelitz, Moshe's wife, and their daughter Esther (1938 – ?), around 1939.

Privatbesitz Sherman

Jurburg, 1926: Holzsynagoge. Am 25. Juli 1941 zwingen die Deutschen die Juden, das Gebäude abzureißen, danach zu tanzen und zu singen. Dann wird ihnen befohlen, das rituelle Schlachthaus zu zerstören. Mit Geflügelblut und Federn bedeckt, werden sie zur Memel getrieben und müssen sich im Fluss waschen. Litauer misshandeln sie mit scharfen Metallharken.

Jurbarkas, 1926: The wooden synagogue. On 25 July 1941, the Germans forced the Jews to tear down the building, then dance and sing. After this, they were ordered to demolish the ritual slaughterhouse. They were smeared with the blood and feathers of fowl, then marched to the Neman, where they were forced to wash in the river. Lithuanians maltreated them with sharp rakes.

Familie **Krelitz**

Die Auslöschung der jüdischen Gemeinde Jurburg

Am 3. Juli 1941 treffen Gestapo- und SD-Angehörige im Ort ein. Sie lassen weitere Juden verhaften. Alle Festgenommenen werden zum jüdischen Friedhof getrieben. Der Kommandeur des von Hersmann vorgesehenen Polizeibataillons lehnt eine Beteiligung an der Erschießung ab. Gestapo- und SD-Männer holen daraufhin die Festgenommenen einzeln zu den ausgehobenen Gruben und erschießen sie eigenhändig. Zwei oder drei Gefangene, darunter ein mit dem deutschen Eisernen Kreuz ausgezeichneter Veteran des Ersten Weltkriegs, greifen die Täter an. Gestapo- und SD-Männer töten sie auf der Stelle. Über 300 Menschen sterben an diesem Tag auf dem Friedhof. Ende Juli und Anfang August finden weitere Erschießungen statt. Nach einer Zeugenaussage weist der deutsche Gebietskommissar Hans Gewecke (1906 – 1991) am 13. August 1941 die litauische Verwaltung an, »alle noch verbliebenen Juden« in seinem Einflussbereich mit Hilfe litauischer Schutzmänner töten zu lassen. Nahezu sämtliche Jurburger Juden kommen bis Mitte September 1941 um. Ein Überlebender berichtet, dass Frauen vor ihrer Erschießung gezwungen werden, sich gegenseitig zu treten, zu beißen und an den Haaren zu ziehen. Von Mosche, Dora und Esther Krelitz fehlt seit Sommer 1941 jede Spur.

Eradication of the Jewish community in Jurbarkas

Members of Gestapo and SD arrived in the town on 3 July 1941 and had more Jews imprisoned. All those detained were forcibly marched to the Jewish cemetery. The commander of the police battalion chosen by Hersmann to provide men for a killing squad refused to participate in the shootings. Members of the Gestapo and the SD thereupon took the detainees one by one to a pit dug in advance and shot them on their own. Two or three of the prisoners, one a veteran of the First World War who had been awarded the Iron Cross, attacked the perpetrators. They were killed on the spot by the SD and the Gestapo. On this day, more than 300 people perished in the cemetery. Further shootings took place at the end of July and the beginning of August. According to witness testimony, the German District Commissar Hans Gewecke (1906 – 1991) sent the Lithuanian administration an order on 13 August 1941 to kill »all remaining Jews« in his sphere of influence with the aid of the Lithuanian auxiliary police. By mid-September 1941, nearly all the Jews of Jurbarkas had perished. A survivor reported that women were forced to kick and bite one other and pull each others' hair before they were shot. There has been no trace of Moshe, Dora, and Esther Krelitz since summer 1941.

BArch VBS286_6400019172

Karl Jäger (1888 – 1959) überlebt den Krieg und arbeitet, ohne seinen Namen zu verschleiern, als Landarbeiter in der Region Heidelberg. Nach seiner Verhaftung erhängt er sich im Juni 1959.

Karl Jäger (1888 – 1959) survived the war and worked as an agricultural labourer in the vicinity of Heidelberg, without disguising his identity. He hanged himself in June 1959 after being arrested.

Rossijskij Gosudarstwennyj Woennyj Archiv, Moskau

Bericht von Karl Jäger vom 1. Dezember 1941 an seinen Vorgesetzten Walter Stahlecker, den Führer der Einsatzgruppe A. Jäger ist seit Juni 1941 Führer des Einsatzkommandos 3 und seit September 1941 Kommandeur der Sicherheitspolizei und des SD für das Generalkommissariat Litauen. Auf seinen Befehl werden zwischen Juli und Dezember 1941 etwa 137.000 Juden in Litauen ermordet.

Report sent by Karl Jäger on 1 December 1941 to his superior Walter Stahlecker, commanding officer of Einsatzgruppe A. Jäger had been head of Einsatzkommando 3 since June 1941 and Commanding Officer of the Security Police and SD in General Commissariat Lithuania since September 1941. Between July and December 1941, around 137,000 Jews were murdered in Lithuania on his orders.

Jurburg erscheint in Jägers Aufstellung vom 1. Dezember 1941 unter der Bezeichnung Georgenburg. Er vermerkt für den 6. September 1941 die »Exekution« »aller« jüdischen Frauen, Männer und Kinder. Eine Liste vom 12. September 1941 führt allerdings noch 272 Juden auf. Eine zwei Wochen später erstellte Übersicht enthält keine Namen jüdischer Einwohner mehr.

In Jäger's list of 1 December 1941, Jurbarkas was mentioned under the German name of Georgenburg. He notes the »execution« of »all« Jewish men, women, and children on 6 September 1941. However, a list dated 12 September 1941 names 272 Jews. Another list, compiled two weeks later, no longer contains the names of any Jewish inhabitants.

Aufarbeitung und Erinnerung

Die Erschießungen in Jurburg und in anderen Grenzorten werden 1958 in Ulm in einem Prozess gegen Angehörige des Tilsiter Einsatzkommandos untersucht. Es handelt sich um das erste öffentlichkeitswirksame Verfahren zu nationalsozialistischen Verbrechen, das in der Bundesrepublik geführt wird und ist eher einem Zufall geschuldet. In Litauen wird nach der Besetzung des Landes durch die Rote Arme und der erneuten Annexion schon in den 1940er Jahren gegen lokale Täter ermittelt. Eine historische Studie aus dem Jahr 1997 nennt 30 Litauer, die sich an Misshandlungen und Erschießungen Jurburger Juden beteiligt hatten, zehn von ihnen werden verurteilt.

Judicial investigation and remembrance

The mass shootings in Jurbarkas and other border settlements were investigated during the 1958 trial of members of the Tilsit Einsatzkommando. This was the first trial held in West Germany dealing with Nazi atrocities that generated public interest. It more or less came about by chance. After the occupation of Lithuania by the Red Army and re-annexation to the Soviet Union, the deeds of local perpetrators were investigated in the 1940s. A historical study from 1997 named 30 Lithuanians who participated in the maltreatment and shooting of Jewish inhabitants from Jurbarkas. Ten of the accused were convicted.

Südwestpresse

Ulm, 1958: Der Angeklagte Werner Hersmann (rechts) mit Anwalt Dr. Rudolf Aschenauer (1913 – 1983). Hersmann wird unter Einrechnung einer vorherigen Strafe zu 15 Jahren Zuchthaus verurteilt.

Ulm, 1958: The accused, Werner Hersmann (right) with his lawyer Dr. Rudolf Aschenauer (1913 – 1983). After taking into account a previous sentence, the court sentenced Hersmann to 15 years imprisonment.

Jurbakas **Jurburg**

Standbild aus einer Diskussion in einem litauischen Fernsehsender, 3. März 2012. Ein von der Stadtverwaltung in Auftrag gegebener Film über das jüdische Leben in Jurburg führt im Frühjahr 2012 zu lebhaften Diskussionen. Der Regisseur Saulius Berzhinis (links) nennt in der Dokumentation die Namen lokaler Täter, dies wird von der Auftraggeberin kritisiert. Es kommt zu einem öffentlichen Streit.

Excerpt from a discussion on a Lithuanian television channel on 3 March 2012. A film on Jewish life in Jurbarkas commissioned by the city administration provoked a lively debate in spring 2012. The director, Saulius Berzhinis (left), named local perpetrators in his documentary and was criticised by the city administration. A public argument was the result.

Jurburg, 2011: Das in den 1990er Jahren errichtete Denkmal für die im Holocaust ermordeten Juden auf dem jüdischen Friedhof, auf dessen Gelände 1941 eine Massenerschießung stattgefunden hatte. Es markiert die Konturen der Massengräber. Die Inschrift der Gedenktafeln ist in hebräischer und litauischer Sprache verfasst.

Jurbarkas, 2011: Memorial for the Jews murdered during the Holocaust on the Jewish Cemetery. Here, one mass shooting took place in 1941. The memorial, dedicated in the 1990s, marks the outlines of the mass graves. The plaque texts are written in Hebrew and Lithuanian.

Stiftung Denkmal für die ermordeten Juden Europas

Familie Krylow

Angriff auf eine »Zigeunerkolchose«

Marija Krylowa und ihre Schwester Lidija gehören zu den russischen Roma. Sie wachsen in der Umgebung von Smolensk auf. Während der Zarenzeit waren hier viele Angehörige der Minderheit sesshaft geworden. Marija lebt in Alexandrowka in der »Zigeunerkolchose *Stalinverfassung*«. Lidija arbeitet in Weißrussland. Als dort die Wehrmacht einmarschiert, kehrt sie nach Alexandrowka zurück. Auch die Kolchose fällt kurz darauf unter deutsche Besatzung. Am 24. April 1942 umstellen Angehörige des Trupp Smolensk – ein Kommando der Einsatzgruppe B – zusammen mit Smolensker Hilfspolizisten den Ort. Ihr Ziel ist die Ermordung der Roma.

Attack on a »gypsy kolkhoz«

Mariya Krylova and her sister Lidiya were Russian Romani and had grown up in the region around Smolensk. Many of this minority settled here during the tsarist era. Mariya lived in Alexandrovka on the »gypsy kolkhoz *Stalin Constitution*« and Lidiya worked in Belarus. When the Wehrmacht marched into Belarus, Lidiya returned to Alexandrovka, but soon thereafter, the kolkhoz was also occupied by the Germans. On 24 April 1942, members of Trupp Smolensk – a commando belonging to Einsatzgruppe B – and auxiliary police from Smolensk cordoned off the village. Their objective was to murder the Romani.

Privatbesitz Bessonow

Lidija Jegorowa, geborene Krylowa (1923 – 1998), Marijas Schwester, Jugendfoto.

Lidiya Yegorova, née Krylova (1923 – 1998), sister of Mariya, an early photo.

Privatbesitz Bessonow

Gruppenfoto von Roma aus Alexandrowka, Nachkriegszeit,
2. Reihe Mitte: Marija Schutschkow, geborene Krylowa (1916 – ?)
und ihr Mann Jakow Jegorowitsch Schutschkow (1910 – 1998).

Group photo of Romani from Alexandrovka, taken after the war,
2nd row, centre: Mariya Shuchkov, née Krylova (1916 – ?)
and her husband, Yakov Yegorovich Shuchkov (1910 – 1998).

Familie **Krylow**

Die Massenerschießung von Roma am 24. April 1942

Am Vorabend des Verbrechens verlangen deutsche Offiziere von der Kolchosbuchhalterin eine nach Familien und Nationalität sortierte Liste. Am folgenden Tag werden sämtliche Einwohner zusammengetrieben und in Roma und Russen getrennt, letztere kommen frei. Die Roma müssen zwei Gruben ausheben. Frauen, Kinder und schließlich auch die Männer durchleiden eine Art ›Begutachtung‹, bei der die Hautfarbe ausschlaggebend ist. 20 angeblich »slawisch« Aussehende kommen frei, darunter Marija mit ihrem Sohn. Lidija wird im letzten Moment offenbar durch einen Wehrmachtsoffizier gerettet. 176 Roma werden an diesem Tag in Alexandrowka erschossen.

Mass shooting of Romani on 24 April 1942

On the eve of this crime, German officers demanded the kolkhoz accountant to give them a list of all persons living there, sorted by family and nationality. The next day, all kolkhoz inhabitants were herded together and separated into two groups – Romani and Russians. The latter were released. The Romani were forced to dig two pits, after which the women, children, and finally the men were subjected to an ›inspection‹, in which skin colour was decisive. 20 people with a supposed »Slavic« appearance were released, among them Mariya and her son. Apparently, Lidiya was saved at the last moment by a Wehrmacht officer. 176 Romani were shot in Alexandrovka on this day.

Gosudarstwennyj Archiv Rossiskoj Federatsii, Moskau

Petition, 1943: Nach der Befreiung von Smolensk durch die Rote Armee fordern überlebende Romnia, unter ihnen Marija und Lidija Krylowa, eine Untersuchung des Verbrechens. Neun Frauen unterschreiben den Antrag namentlich. Der sowjetische Geheimdienst NKWD veranlasst daraufhin eine umfassende Untersuchung der Morde.

Petition, 1943: After the liberation of Smolensk by the Red Army, Romani survivors, among them Mariya and Lidiya Krylowa, demanded an investigation into the crime. Nine women signed the petition, giving their full names. In response, the Soviet secret service NKVD ordered a comprehensive investigation into the murders.

Nikolaj Federowitsch Alfjortschik, Registrierungsausweis, Innenseite, 1951. Neben den Angehörigen des Trupp Smolensk nehmen auch russische Hilfspolizisten an der Erschießung teil, darunter offenbar auch Alfjortschik (1917 – ?). Als Mitglied des antikommunistischen Bundes russischer Solidaristen gehört er zur Gruppe führender Unterstützer der Deutschen in Smolensk. Er soll eine zentrale Rolle bei der Folterung und der Ermordung von Juden, Roma und Partisanen gespielt haben.

Auf der Innenseite des Ausweises ist der Deckname Nikolaj Pavlov angegeben. Nach 1945 arbeitet Alfjortschik zunächst für den US-amerikanischen, dann für den australischen Geheimdienst. Dort ist man spätestens seit 1954 über seine Vergangenheit im Bilde. Ein von Alfjortschik in der Bundesrepublik geplantes Attentat auf den sowjetischen Staatschef Leonid Breschnew (1906 – 1982) wird vom Verfassungsschutz vereitelt.

Nikolai Federovich Alfiorchik, Certificate of Registration, inside pages, 1951. In addition to members of Trupp Smolensk, Russian auxiliary policemen also participated in the shooting. Alfiorchik (1917 – ?) was apparently among them. As a member of the anti-communist group Alliance of Russian Solidarists, he belonged to the Germans' key advocates in Smolensk. He reportedly played a central role in the torture and murder of Jews, Romani, and partisans.

The inside page of the ID card shows the alias Nikolai Pavlov. After 1945, Alfiorchik first worked for the US intelligence service, later for the Australian intelligence service. The latter had been aware of his past at the latest since 1954. An assassination attempt on Soviet leader Leonid Brezhnev (1906 – 1982) planned by Alfiorchik in West Germany was thwarted by West German domestic intelligence.

National Archives of Australia, Canberra, NAA: MT874/1, V1956/32393

Familie **Krylow**

Erinnerung an das Verbrechen

Marija und Lidija Krylowa bleiben nach Kriegsende im Dorf. Den Schwestern und anderen Roma aus dem Kreis Smolensk ist es ein Anliegen, über den Völkermord an ihrer Minderheit zu sprechen. Als 1982 ein Denkmal für die Ermordeten eingeweiht wird, begreifen sie dies als Anerkennung ihres Leids. Die Idee dazu entsteht bereits 1968. Die Initiatoren – Alexandrowker Roma – nehmen zunächst Kontakt mit dem Romatheater *Romen* in Moskau auf. Die Theaterleitung bittet das Exekutivkomitee des Smolensker Kreissowjets, ein offizielles Konto für den Bau des Denkmals einzurichten, und verspricht, selbst zur Finanzierung beizutragen. Auch die Roma in Alexandrowka spenden.

Remembrance of the atrocities

Mariya and Lidiya Krylova remained in the village after the end of the war. The two sisters and other Romani from the Smolensk region considered it important to talk about the genocide against their minority. In 1982, when a memorial for the victims was dedicated, they saw this as recognition of their suffering. The idea for this memorial emerged in 1968 already. The initiators, members of the Romani population of Alexandrovka, first contacted the Romani theatre *Romen* in Moscow. The theatre's management requested the executive committee of soviet the Smolensk region open an official bank account for the memorial's construction and promised to contribute to the project's funding. Romani from Alexandrovka donated money as well.

Fotograf: Nikolaj Bessonow

Alexandrowka, Denkmal, 2015: An den Massenmord an Roma erinnern in Europa jahrzehntelang keine eigenen Gedenkzeichen; in der Sowjetunion ist das Alexandrowker Denkmal aus dem Jahr 1982 vermutlich das erste. Die Inschrift lautet: »Hier sind 176 friedliche Einwohner des Dorfes Alexandrowka begraben, die am 24. April 1942 von den deutsch-faschistischen Eroberern erschossen wurden«.

Alexandrovka, memorial, 2015: For decades, there were no memorials anywhere in Europe to remember the mass murder of the Romani; this memorial, erected in 1982, was probably the first of its kind in the Soviet Union. The inscriptions reads: »Here lie 176 peaceful residents of the village of Alexandrovka who were shot by German-fascist invaders on 24 April 1942«.

Alexandrovka **Alexandrowka**

Privatbesitz Slitschenko

1985 führt *Romen* das Stück *Vögel brauchen den Himmel* auf, das die Geschichte der Roma von Alexandrowka behandelt.

In 1985, the *Romen* theatre staged a play called *Birds need the sky*, which tells the story of the Alexandrovka Romani.

Berlin, Denkmal für die im Nationalsozialismus ermordeten Sinti und Roma Europas. In der 2012 eröffneten Erinnerungsstätte erinnern beschriftete Bodenplatten an Orte, in denen Angehörige der Minderheit ermordet wurden, so auch an Alexandrowka.

Berlin, Memorial to the Sinti and Roma of Europe Murdered under the National Socialist Regime. At this memorial site, dedicated in 2012, engraved stone slabs recall places where members of this minority were murdered, among them Alexandrovka.

Stiftung Denkmal für die ermordeten Juden Europas / Fotograf: Marko Priske

Stiftung Denkmal für die ermordeten Juden Europas / Fotograf: Benno Auras

David **Zivcon**

Überleben im Versteck

Im ersten Jahr der Besatzung ermorden deutsche Einheiten und lettische Kollaborateure in der Hafenstadt Libau tausende Juden. Die wenigen Überlebenden zwingen sie im Juli 1942 in ein Ghetto. Einer von ihnen ist David Zivcon, der bei der Zwangsarbeit für die Außendienststelle der Sicherheitspolizei und des SD Fotos einer Massenerschießung findet. Es gelingt ihm, sie heimlich vervielfältigen zu lassen. Später fliehen Zivcon und seine Frau aus dem Ghetto und werden von einem lettischen Freund versteckt. Von etwa 5.700 Juden überleben nicht einmal 30 den Holocaust in Libau.

Survival in hiding

In the first year of the occupation, German units and Latvian collaborators murdered thousands of Jews in the port town of Liepāja. In July 1942, they forced the few survivors to move into a ghetto. Among these was David Zivcon, who discovered photos of a mass shooting while working as a forced labourer at the office of the Security Police and SD. He managed to have these copied secretly. Later, Zivcon and his wife escaped from the ghetto and were hidden by a Latvian friend. Of approximately 5,700 Jews from Liepāja, less than 30 survived the Holocaust there.

Privatbesitz Ivanova

David Zivcon (1914 – 1983), Januar 1940: Der Elektromechaniker spricht deutsch, jiddisch, lettisch und russisch. Nach der Flucht aus dem Ghetto versteckt er sich mit seiner Frau bei Robert Sedol.

David Zivcon (1914 – 1983), January 1940: David Zivcon, an electrician, spoke German, Yiddish, Latvian and Russian. After his escape from the ghetto, he and his wife hid at the home of Robert Sedol.

Libau (Lettland): David Zivcon im Kellerversteck bei den Sedols, 1945. Während des Kriegs repariert Zivcon hier Uhren und Radios; Sedol kann mit dem so verdienten Geld Nahrungsmittel beschaffen.

Liepāja (Latvia) 1945: David Zivcon in his cellar hideout at Sedol's home. During the war, Zivcon repaired watches and radios here. Sedol then bought food with the money earned.

Privatbesitz Zivcon Israeli

Henne Zivcon, geb. Friedländer (1921 – 2013), hinten links, mit ihrem Retter Robert Sedol (1906 – 1945).

Henne Zivcon, née Friedländer (1921 – 2013), back left, with rescuer Robert Sedol (1906 – 1945).

Privatbesitz Zivcon Israeli

Libau, vermutlich 1945, v.l.n.r.: Henne und David Zivcon, Johanna Sedol (1910 – 1987), Mischa Libauer, vorn Sedols Töchter Irida und Indra. Johanna Sedol übernimmt nach dem Tod ihres Mannes im März 1945 – Libau steht noch unter deutscher Besatzung – Schutz und Versorgung der versteckten Juden.

Liepāja, probably 1945, left to right: Henne and David Zivcon, Johanna Sedol (1910 – 1987), Misha Libauer. At the front are the Sedol daughters, Irida and Indra. After the death of her husband in March 1945, while Liepāja was still occupied by the Germans, Johanna Sedol took over protecting and providing for the hiding Jews.

Privatbesitz Ivanova

David **Zivcon**

Die Massenerschießung im Dezember 1941

Schon in den ersten Tagen der Besatzung Libaus begehen Angehörige der Einsatzgruppe A, der Kriegsmarine und des lettischen Selbstschutzes Morde. Im Juli 1941 wird in der Stadt eine Außenstelle des Kommandeurs der Sicherheitspolizei und des SD Lettland errichtet. Ihre deutschen und lettischen Angehörigen erschießen vom 15. bis 17. Dezember 1941 über 2.700 jüdische Kinder, Frauen und Männer am Strand von Schkeden außerhalb Libaus. Die Fotos, die David Zivcon findet, zeigen diese Erschießung. Er übergibt sie nach der Befreiung der Roten Armee.

The mass shootings of December 1941

Members of Einsatzgruppe A, the German Navy, and a local Latvian self-defence force started their murderous activities in the first days of the occupation of Liepāja. An outpost of the Commanding Officer of the Security Police and SD Latvia was established here in July 1941. The German and Latvian staff members shot more than 2,700 Jewish men, women, and children on the beach of Šķēde, just outside Liepāja, from 15 to 17 December 1941. The photos, later found by David Zivcon, show these shootings. He handed these photos over to the Red Army after liberation.

Kurzemes Vārds vom 12. Dezember 1941

Zeitung *Kurzemes Vārds*, 12. Dezember 1941: SS- und Polizei-Standortführer Fritz Dietrich (1898 – 1948) ordnet an, dass Juden ihre Häuser nicht verlassen dürfen. Damit trifft er Vorkehrungen für die der Massenerschießung vorausgehenden Verhaftungen. Die Zeitung druckt über seinem Erlass eine Regulierung der Preise für Weihnachtsbäume ab.

Clipping from the *Kurzemes Vārds* newspaper, 12 December 1941: SS and Police Base Leader Fritz Dietrich (1898 – 1948) instructed Jews to remain in their homes. This was in preparation for confining Jews in advance of the mass shooting. Printed above this decree is a regulation on the price of Christmas trees.

Schkeden (Šķēde) bei Libau, vermutlich 15. Dezember 1941.
Oben: Nach Aussage von Überlebenden sind auf dem Bild der 15-jährige Max Epstein, seine 18-jährige Schwester Mia und ihre Mutter Emma (v.l.n.r.) zu sehen.
Unten: Ganz links handelt es sich vermutlich um die zehnjährige Sorella Epstein. Sie versteckt ihr Gesicht. Die Frau neben ihr wurde als ihre Mutter Roza Epstein identifiziert.

Šķēde, near Liepāja, probably 15 December 1941.
Top: According survivors, the picture shows 15-year-old Max Epstein, his 18-year-old sister Mia, and their mother Emma (from left to right).
Lower picture: The child on the far left is probably ten-year-old Sorella Epstein. She is hiding her face. The woman next to her has been identified as Roza Epstein, her mother.

Alle Bilder: BStU, MfS, HA IX / 11, ZUV, Nr. 14,
Bd. 17,3, 17,4, 17,7, 17,10, 17,11

Schkeden, vermutlich 15. Dezember 1941:
Ein Abgleich mit Bildern von Mitgliedern der jüdischen Gemeinde lässt darauf schließen, dass es sich um Ruben-Aron Grinfeld (15 Jahre, dunkles Hemd), seine Mutter Ita-Beile (38 Jahre) und seine Schwestern Ester-Liebe (13 Jahre) und Cilla (9 Jahre, nur ihr Bein ist zu sehen) handelt. Sie befinden sich am Rand der Erschießungsgrube. Die weiteren Bilder zeigen ihre Ermordung.

Šķēde, probably 15 December 1941:
Comparison with other pictures of the Jewish community recalled that this photo shows Ruben-Aron Grinfeld (15 years old, dark shirt), his mother Ita-Beile (38 years old), and his sisters Ester-Liebe (13 years old) and Cilla (9 years old, only her leg is visible). They are at the edge of the pit. The other photos document their murder.

David **Zivcon**

Der Umgang mit der Vergangenheit

Bereits 1945 wird David Zivcon von sowjetischen Ermittlern als Zeuge der Verbrechen befragt. Seine Aussagen und die von ihm versteckten Bilder helfen Gerichten in der Bundesrepublik und der DDR Anfang der 1970er Jahre, Tatbeteiligte zu identifizieren. Zivcons Aussagen werden früh auch in sowjetischen Medien verbreitet, doch verschweigen diese meist, dass er als Jude verfolgt wurde.
Die Regierungen der Sowjetunion unterdrücken jüdisches kulturelles und religiöses Leben; erst nach dem Zusammenbruch der Sowjetunion und der Wiedererlangung der staatlichen Unabhängigkeit Lettlands 1991 kann eine neue jüdische Gemeinde in Libau gegründet werden.

Dealing with the past

David Zivcon was questioned by Soviet investigators as a witness already in 1945. His testimony and the pictures he managed to hide helped courts in West and East Germany to identify accomplices in the early 1970s. Zivcon's statements were also published in Soviet media at an early stage, but the reports usually concealed the fact that he was persecuted as a Jew. The Soviet regime suppressed Jewish cultural and religious life. It was not possible to found a new Jewish community in Liepāja until after the collapse of the Soviet Union and restoration of Latvian independence in 1991.

Stiftung Topographie des Terrors / Fotografin: Paula Oppermann

Denkmal in Schkeden, erbaut in den 1960er Jahren, 2015:
Mit »mehr als 19.000 sowjetischen Patrioten« nennt die Inschrift eine zu hohe Opferzahl und verschweigt, dass es sich um Juden handelt.

Memorial in Šķēde, set up in the 1960s, photo taken 2015:
By claiming the death of »more than 19,000 Soviet patriots«, the inscription exaggerates the number of victims and suppresses the information that these were Jews.

Liepāja **Libau**

Stiftung Topographie des Terrors / Fotografin: Paula Oppermann

Gedenkort für die Opfer der Massenerschießungen, Schkeden, 2015: Das Denkmal wird 2005 eingeweiht und seitdem schrittweise erweitert. Der Weg zur Gedenkanlage ist gesäumt von Stelen, die an die Retter von Libauer Juden erinnern. Daneben gedenkt eine Tafel der in Schkeden erschossenen Kriegsgefangenen und politischen Gegner der Nationalsozialisten.

Memorial site for victims of the mass shootings, Šķēde, 2015: This memorial was inaugurated in 2005 and has been gradually extended since then. The path to the memorial site is flanked by steles that recall those who rescued Jews from Liepāja. In addition, a plaque memorialises the prisoners of war and political opponents of National Socialism who were shot in Šķēde.

Fjodor Wasiljewitsch **Korso**

Psychiatriepatient unter deutscher Besatzung

Als Soldat erleidet der Arbeiter Fjodor Korso im sowjetisch-finnischen Winterkrieg 1939/40 eine schwere Kopfverletzung. In der Folge entwickelt er Beschwerden, die zu seiner Einweisung in die psychiatrische Klinik im weißrussischen Mogilew führen. Die Stadt wird im Juli 1941 von der Wehrmacht eingenommen, ihr folgen die Einsatzgruppe B und Polizeiverbände. Psychiatriepatienten gelten den Besatzern als »Erbkranke« und »unnütze Esser«, weil sie nicht als Arbeitskräfte ausgebeutet werden können. Die Militärverwaltung kürzt die Lebensmittelzuteilung und verlangt von der neuen Klinikleitung eine ›Selektion‹ der Insassen. Mitte September 1941 lässt der Leiter der Einsatzgruppe B, Arthur Nebe, eine Gaskammer auf dem Klinikgelände einrichten.

Psychiatric patient under German occupation

As a soldier during the Soviet-Finnish Winter War in 1939/1940, the labourer Fyodor Korso suffered a serious head injury. This led to disorders that resulted in his being commited to the psychiatric clinic in Mogilev, Belarus. In July 1941, the town was taken by the Wehrmacht, Einsatzgruppe B and police units followed. Psychiatric patients were deemed by the occupiers to be »hereditarily defective« and »extra mouths« to feed because they could not be exploited as labourers. The military administration shortened their food rations and demanded that the new hospital management should carry out a ›selection‹ of the patients. In mid-September 1941, Arthur Nebe, the commander of Einsatzgruppe B, had a gas-chamber installed on the hospital grounds.

Privatbesitz

Fjodor Wasiljewitsch Korso, Datum unbekannt: Sein Name befindet sich auf einer der Listen, die die Klinikleitung unter anderem nach dem Gesichtspunkt der Arbeitsfähigkeit für die Besatzer erstellen muss.

Fyodor Vasilevich Korso, date unknown: His name was on one of the lists that the hospital's management had to compile for the occupiers. One of the criteria for the lists was whether the patient was able to work.

BArch RH2/125 fol. 109

Kriegstagebuch von Generaloberst Franz Halder (1884 – 1972), Chef des Generalstabs des Heeres, 26. September 1941. »Nord« bedeutet Heeresgruppe Nord. Der Auszug fasst ein Gespräch Halders mit dem Generalquartiermeister des Heeres, Eduard Wagner (1894 – 1944), zusammen. 1953 behauptet Halder, der Eintrag habe lediglich die Äußerung eines SS-Manns wiedergegeben.

War diary of Colonel General Franz Halder (1884 – 1972), chief of General Staff of the Ground Forces, 26 September 1941. »North« refers to Army Group North. This excerpt sums up a discussion between Halder and Quartermaster-General of the Ground Forces Eduard Wagner (1894 – 1944). In 1953, Halder claimed that the entry simply repeated a statement made by an SS man.

h) Irrenanstalten bei <u>Nord.</u> Russen sehen Geistesschwache als heilig an. Trotzdem Toetung notwendig.

h) Mental asylums in <u>North.</u> Russians regard the feeble-minded as holy. Even so killing necessary.

Portrait Franz Halder, Aufnahme von Walter Frentz (1907 – 2004), der als Fotograf und Kameramann zum engen Umkreis Hitlers gehört.

Portrait of Franz Halder, picture by Walter Frentz (1907 – 2004). Photographer and cameraman Frentz belonged to Hitler's circle of close associates.

ullstein bild / Fotograf: Walter Frentz

Fjodor Wasiljewitsch **Korso**

Gasmord auf dem Krankenhausgelände

Mitte September 1941 lässt Arthur Nebe die ersten Mogilewer Patienten mit Autoabgasen, die in ein zugemauertes Zimmer geleitet werden, ersticken. Zwei bis drei Wochen später ermorden Angehörige des Einsatzkommandos 8 und ihre Helfer auf diese Weise die meisten Anstaltsbewohner. Im Januar 1942 werden die noch anwesenden, völlig ausgehungerten Patienten vor die Stadt gefahren und dort erschossen oder mit Handgranaten umgebracht. Die Angehörigen von Fjodor Korso versuchen, ihn zu retten, kommen aber zu spät. Wann er stirbt, ist unklar. Das leergemordete Krankenhaus wird der Wehrmacht zur Nutzung übergeben.

Murder by gas on the hospital grounds

In mid-September 1941, Arthur Nebe had the first patients in Mogilev killed by suffocating them with automobile exhaust fed into a bricked room. Two to three weeks later, members of Einsatzkommando 8 and accomplices murdered most of the hospital's patients in the same way. In January 1942, the remaining, completely starved patients were driven outside the city and shot or blown up by hand grenades. Fyodor Korso's relatives tried to save him, but it was too late. The time of his death is not known. The hospital, emptied by this act of murder, was handed over to the Wehrmacht for use.

Nowinki bei Minsk, 15. August 1941: Besuch Heinrich Himmlers (4.v.l.) in der psychiatrischen Klinik. Bei der Begehung soll er Arthur Nebe beauftragt haben, »die Kranken dort zu erlösen«. Mitte September 1941 lässt Nebe Minsker Psychiatriepatienten mit Sprengstoff töten. Die Mordmethode wird verworfen, weil sie zu unsicher erscheint und Leichenteile aufgesammelt werden müssen. Unmittelbar danach fährt Nebe mit seinen Mitarbeitern in die Anstalt in Mogilew (Mahiljou).

Novinki, near Minsk, 15 August 1941: Heinrich Himmler (4th from left) visits the psychiatric hospital. During inspection, Himmler reportedly instructed Arthur Nebe »to put the ill persons out of their misery«. In mid-September 1941, Nebe had psychiatric patients killed in Minsk using explosives as an experiment. This method of murder was rejected, because it was considered too unreliable, and because the parts of the corpses had to be collected. Nebe and his staff proceeded to the hospital in Mogilev immediately thereafter.

ullstein bild / Fotograf: Walter Frentz

Arthur Nebe (1894 – 1945), ab 1937 Leiter des Reichskriminalpolizeiamts. In dieser Funktion ist er am Patientenmord im Deutschen Reich beteiligt; 1941 wird er einige Monate Führer der Einsatzgruppe B. Nebe pflegt Kontakte zum Widerstand und taucht nach dem Umsturzversuch vom 20. Juli 1944 unter. Anfang 1945 wird er verhaftet und vom Volksgerichtshof zum Tode verurteilt.

Arthur Nebe (1894 – 1945), director of the Reich Office of Criminal Investigation from 1937 onwards. In this capacity he was involved in the murder of patients within the German Reich. In 1941, he held the post of commander of Einsatzgruppe B for several months. Nebe maintained contact to the German resistance and went into hiding after the assassination attempt on Hitler on 20 July 1944. He was arrested and sentenced to death by the People's Court in early 1945.

BArch Bild 101III-Alber-096-34 / Fotograf: Kurt Alber

Standfotos aus dem Film über die »Probevergasung« in Mogilew, September 1941: Sie zeigen die in die Mauer eingebrachten Rohre, die die Abgase ins Innere des zugemauerten Chirurgiezimmers leiten, sowie eines der verwendeten Fahrzeuge. Es handelt sich dabei möglicherweise um das Dienstfahrzeug von Arthur Nebes Mitarbeiter, dem Chemiker Albert Widmann (1912 – 1986). Auf hier nicht abgebildeten Teilen des Films sind völlig abgemagerte Patienten zu erkennen. Der Film wurde im Auftrag Nebes erstellt.

Stills from a film about »gassing experiments« in Mogilev, September 1941: They show the pipes leading through the wall, transporting the exhaust gases into the bricked-up operating room, as well as one of the vehicles used. This may be the staff vehicle of chemist Albert Widmann (1912 – 1986), one of Arthur Nebe's colleagues. Parts of the film, which are not displayed here, show completely emaciated patients. The film was commissioned by Arthur Nebe.

National Archives and Records Administration, College Park (MD)

Fjodor Wasiljewitsch **Korso**

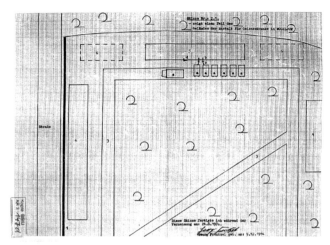

BStU, MfS, HA IX / 11, ZUV, Nr. 9, Bd. 13

Lageplan der zur Ermordung von Patienten genutzten Heilanstalt Mogilew: Die sechs Rechtecke stellen die Fahrzeuge dar, deren Auspuffgase in einen abgedichteten Raum der Klinik geleitet wurden. Zu erkennen sind die Rohre, die die Gaskammer mit den Fahrzeugen verbanden. Die Skizze fertigt der an den Gasmorden beteiligte Kraftfahrer und Angehörige des Einsatzkommandos 8 Georg Frentzel (1914 – 1979) während seiner Vernehmung durch die Staatssicherheit der DDR an. Frentzel verschweigt nach 1945 seine Zugehörigkeit zu den Einsatzgruppen. Als SED-Mitglied steigt er in verschiedenen DDR-Organisationen auf. 1968 wird er verhaftet und 1971 auch wegen der Morde in Mogilew zu lebenslanger Haft verurteilt.

Ground plan of the Mogilev clinic, which was used to murder patients: The six rectangles represent the vehicles from which exhaust fumes were pumped into a sealed room in the clinic. The sketch also shows the pipes connecting the vehicles to the gas chamber. It was drawn by Georg Frentzel (1914 – 1979) during his interrogation by the East German Secret Police. He had been complicit in the gassings as a driver and as a member of Einsatzkommando 8. After the war, Frentzel kept quiet about his role in the Einsatzgruppen. He joined the SED – the ruling party in the GDR – and rose through the ranks of various East German organisations. He was arrested in 1968 and sentenced to life in prison in 1971 after being found guilty of crimes including the murders in Mogilev.

Aufarbeitung und Erinnerung

1944 und 1948 finden in Weißrussland Prozesse gegen die Ärzte der Mogilewer Anstalt statt. Die juristische Aufarbeitung in Deutschland beginnt erst 1967 mit dem Verfahren des Landgerichts Stuttgart gegen den Chemiker Albert Widmann, der als Mitarbeiter Nebes den ersten Mord an Mogilewer Patienten geleitet hatte. 1969 führt das Bezirksgericht Karl-Marx-Stadt (heute wieder Chemnitz) ein Verfahren gegen einen ehemaligen Fahrer des Einsatzkommandos 8, Georg Frentzel. In Mogilew wird im Juli 2009 auf Initiative der Psychiatrischen Universitätsklinik Heidelberg und des Psychiatrischen Gebietskrankenhauses von Mogilew ein Mahnmal eingeweiht.

Judicial investigation and remembrance

Doctors from the Mogilev psychiatric hospital were put on trial in Belarus in 1944 and 1948. Judicial investigation in Germany did not get underway until 1967 with the trial of the chemist Albert Widmann at the State Court of Stuttgart. Widmann was a colleague of Nebe's staff and supervised the first murder of patients in Mogilev. In 1969, the District Court of Karl-Marx-Stadt (Chemnitz) tried Georg Frentzel, a former driver with Einsatzkommando 8. A memorial in Mogilev was dedicated in July 2009 at the initiative of Heidelberg University Hospital's Psychiatric Clinic and the Regional Psychiatric Hospital in Mogilev.

Mogilev **Mogilew**

Stuttgart, 1967: Albert Widmann (Mitte) bei dem gegen ihn geführten Prozess. Widmann kommt in Anrechnung bereits verbüßter Strafen und mit Zahlung von 4.000 Mark an eine Einrichtung für Menschen mit Behinderungen frei.

Stuttgart, 1967: Albert Widmann (centre) during his trial. After taking into consideration former convictions, Widmann was sentenced to pay 4,000 Marks to an institution for disabled persons.

ullstein bild – Heritage Images / Keystone Archives

Mogilew, Mahnmal für die ermordeten Psychiatriepatienten, 2009: Es ist das einzige Denkmal auf dem Gebiet der ehemaligen Sowjetunion, das an die Ermordung von Patienten psychiatrischer Kliniken während der deutschen Besatzung erinnert.

Mogilev, memorial for the murdered psychiatric patients, 2009: This is the only memorial in the entire former Soviet Union to remember psychiatric patients murdered during the German occupation.

Privatbesitz Hohendorf

Gert **Rosenthal**

Ein Berliner Waisenkind wird nach Riga deportiert

Gert Rosenthal wird 1932 in Berlin geboren. Nach dem frühen Tod der Eltern kommen Gert und sein älterer Bruder Hans im Januar 1942 in das Baruch Auerbach'sche Waisenhaus im Bezirk Prenzlauer Berg. Hier geht Gert zur Schule. Hans muss Zwangsarbeit in Brandenburg leisten, später gelingt es ihm, unterzutauchen. Bereits im Oktober 1941 hatte das Reichssicherheitshauptamt mit der systematischen Deportation deutscher Juden in den besetzten Osten begonnen. Nach Auflösung des jüdischen Waisenhauses wird auch Gert verhaftet und am 19. Oktober 1942 mit 958 anderen Berliner Juden im »21. Osttransport« nach Riga verschleppt.

A Berlin orphan is deported to Riga

Gert Rosenthal was born in Berlin in 1932. Following the early death of their parents, Gert and his elder brother, Hans, were taken to the Baruch Auerbach Orphanage in the Berlin borrow of Prenzlauer Berg in January 1942. Gert attended school there. Hans had to work in Brandenburg as a forced labourer. He later managed to go into hiding. In October 1941, the Reich Security Main Office had started the systematic deportation of German Jews to the occupied east. Gert was interned when the Jewish orphanage was closed down, and deported to Riga with the »21st transport to the east« on 19 October 1942, together with 958 other Jews from Berlin.

Stiftung Neue Synagoge Berlin – Centrum Judaicum

Gert und Hans Rosenthal, ca. 1940.

Gert and Hans Rosenthal, around 1940.

Jüdisches Museum Berlin, Schenkung von Leonie und Walter Frankenstein

Berlin, Baruch Auerbach'sches Waisenhaus, Ballspiel, nach 1936, Bildmitte (springend): Walter Frankenstein (*1924), der im Versteck überlebt.

Berlin, Baruch Auerbach Orphanage, children playing ball, after 1936, in the centre of the picture (jumping): Walter Frankenstein (*1924), who survived in hiding.

Güterbahnhof Moabit, am Berliner Nordring gelegen, um 1960: Von hier gehen 1942 auch die Deportationszüge nach Riga ab.

Moabit freight station on the northern side of Berlin's circle line, around 1960: This is where the deportation trains to Riga left from in 1942.

bpk

Gert **Rosenthal**

Tod sofort nach der Ankunft

Riga wird ab November 1941 zum Zielort von insgesamt 25 Deportationstransporten aus dem Deutschen Reich. Um Platz für die Verschleppten im Rigaer Ghetto zu schaffen, lässt der Höhere SS- und Polizeiführer Friedrich Jeckeln über 25.000 lettische Juden erschießen. Viele der aus dem Reich Deportierten überleben zunächst als Zwangsarbeiter. Gert Rosenthal und die meisten anderen Insassen des »21. Osttransports« kommen mit ihnen nicht in Kontakt: Sie werden unmittelbar nach ihrer Ankunft im Wald von Biķernieki erschossen. Nur etwa vier Prozent der nach Riga Verschleppten erleben das Kriegsende. Von den etwa 30.000 Rigaer Juden, die am Vorabend des deutschen Einmarsches in der Stadt verblieben waren, entkommen nur einige hundert den Morden.

Death upon arrival

From November 1941 onwards, Riga was the destination for a total of 25 deportation transports from the German Reich. In order to make room for the deportees in the Riga Ghetto, Higher SS and Police Leader Friedrich Jeckeln ordered the shooting of more than 25,000 Latvian Jews. Many of those deported from the Reich initially survived as forced labourers. Gert Rosenthal and most of the other deportees on the »21st transport« never got to meet them: They were shot in the Biķernieki Forest immediately upon arrival. Only about four percent of all Jews deported to Riga lived to war's end. Of some 30,000 Jews remaining in Riga on the eve of the German occupation of the city, only a few hundred escaped the mass murder.

BArch VBS286_6400019504

Friedrich Jeckeln (1895 – 1946): seit Ende Oktober 1941 Höherer SS- und Polizeiführer Rußland-Nord und Ostland mit Sitz in Riga, zuvor in gleicher Funktion in der Ukraine, wo er unter anderem für die Massaker in Kamenez-Podolsk und Babij Jar verantwortlich war. 1946 verurteilt ihn ein sowjetisches Gericht in Riga zum Tode.

Friedrich Jeckeln (1895 – 1946): Since late October 1941 Higher SS and Police Leader Russia North and Ostland, with headquarters in Riga, previously in the same post in Ukraine, where he was responsible for the massacres in Kamianets-Podilsky and at Babi Yar and other atrocities. He was sentenced to death by a Soviet court in Riga in 1946.

Riga (Lettland), ohne Datum: Hinrich Lohse (1896 – 1964), Reichskommissar Ostland (3.v.l.) und Friedrich Jeckeln (5.v.l.) sowie weitere Angehörige der Besatzungsmacht am Bahnhof.

Riga (Latvia), no date: Hinrich Lohse (1896 – 1964), Reich Commissar Ostland (3rd from left) and Friedrich Jeckeln (5th from left) at the railway station with other members of the occupation authority.

BArch Bild 146-1970-043-42

Transportliste

188

Lfd. Nr.	Name	Vorname	geb. am	Ort	Beruf	ledig	verh.	Alter	arbeits- fähig	Wohnung Ort / Straße	Kennkarten- Nr.	Kennzeichen- Nr.	Bemerkungen
241	Stroh	Ellen Sara	15.12.27	Heidelberg	ohne	ja		15	ja	N58, Schönh. Allee 162		19643	✓
242	Stein	Bertel Sara	13.2.28	Berlin	ohne	ja		14	ja	dto.		19644	✓
243	Stein	Ruth Sara	16.7.26	Berlin	ohne	ja		16	ja	dto.	Tr.P.II 3067/41	19645	✓
244	Strassner	Egon Jacob Israel	29.9.24	Berlin	ohne	ja		18	ja	dto.		19646	✓
245	Spiegel	Hans Israel	20.5.32	Friedrichsfelde	ohne	ja		10	n	dto.	A732979	19648	✓
246	Seelig	Arnold Israel	28.1.36	Berlin	ohne	ja		6	n	dto.	A043243	19649	✓
247	Salomon	Max Israel	8.10.33	Berlin	ohne	ja		9	n	dto.	A20803	19650a	✓
248	Sabor	Kurt Israel	30.3.30	Berlin	ohne	ja		12	n	dto.		19651	✓
249	Rowelski	Traute Sara	1.11.32	Königsberg	ohne	ja		10	n	dto.		19652	✓
250	Rothstein	Herbert Israel	4.9.28	Berlin	ohne	ja		14	n	dto.		19653	✓
251	Rosenthal	Gerd Israel	26.7.32	Berlin	ohne	ja		10	n	dto.	B198240	19654	✓
252	Rosenbaum	Rolf Israel	23.6.36	Berlin	ohne	ja		6	n	dto.	A485475	19655	✓
253	Reppen	Horst Israel	6.4.29	Berlin	ohne	ja		13	n	dto.	A732915	19656	✓
254	Rehfeld	Rut Sara	12.8.27	Berlin	ohne	ja		15	n	dto.	A022907	19657	✓
255	Reiss	Rudolf Alexander Israel	17.12.30	Berlin	ohne	ja		12	n	dto.	A201150	19658	✓
256	Pisetzki	Erwin Israel	25.2.27	Bonn	ohne	ja		15	ja	dto.		19659	✓
257	Neumann	Hans Joseph Isr.	8.3.33	Berlin	ohne	ja		9	n	dto.	A738817	19660	✓
258	Löbl	Grete Sara	26.7.32	Podersen	ohne	ja		10	n	dto.	A11986	19661	✓
259	Liniel	Fanni Sara	4.2.27	Dortmund	ohne	ja		15	ja	dto.		19662	✓
260	Lesser	Werner Israel	30.12.25	Berlin	ohne	ja		17	ja	dto.	A732861	19663	✓

Auszug Transportliste vom 19. Oktober 1942, Ordner 4, Seite 188 (Depot), ITS Bad Arolsen

Ausschnitt aus der Liste des »21. Osttransports« nach Riga. Unter den Verschleppten befindet sich eine große Zahl von Familien und 59 Kinder aus dem geschlossenen Baruch Auerbach'schen Waisenhaus.

Excerpt from the list of the »21st transport to the east« to Riga. The deportees included many families as well as 59 children from the Baruch Auerbach Orphanage, which had been closed down.

»Wo ich bin …« Erinnerung an Gert Rosenthal

Das Schicksal Gert Rosenthals wird einer breiteren Öffentlichkeit durch die Autobiografie seines Bruders Hans bekannt, der in der Bundesrepublik in den 1970er und 1980er Jahren zu den bekanntesten Fernsehshowmastern zählt. Hans Rosenthal hatte mit Hilfe von Nichtjuden in zwei verschiedenen Verstecken überlebt. An einer Mauer des ehemaligen Waisenhauses in Berlin wird seit 2014 namentlich Gert Rosenthals und der anderen Kinder gedacht. In Riga-Biķernieki besteht seit 2001 eine Gedenkanlage, die mit Mitteln der Bundesrepublik vom Volksbund Deutsche Kriegsgräberfürsorge errichtet wurde.

»Where I am …« In remembrance of Gert Rosenthal

The general public learned about Gert Rosenthal's fate due to the autobiography of his brother, Hans Rosenthal, one of West German television's most popular entertainers in the 1970s and 1980s. With the help of non-Jews, Hans Rosenthal survived the Nazi era in two different hiding places. Since 2014, the names of Gert Rosenthal and the other children stand engraved on a wall of the building of the former orphanage. At Riga-Biķernieki, a memorial site funded by the Federal Republic of Germany and built by the German War Graves Commission has been open to the public since 2001.

Stiftung Denkmal für die ermordeten Juden Europas / Fotograf: Ronnie Golz

Biķernieki, 2009: Mittelpunkt der Gedenkanlage. Zwischen 1941 und 1944 starben hier etwa 30.000 Menschen. Einer von ihnen war Gert Rosenthal.

Biķernieki, 2009: Centre of the memorial site. About 30,000 people died here between 1941 and 1944. Gert Rosenthal was one of them.

Berlin, Erinnerungsort Baruch Auerbach'sches Waisenhaus, 2014: Dort ist auch der Name Gert Rosenthals eingraviert.

Berlin, Memorial site Baruch Auerbach Orphanage, 2014: Gert Rosenthal's name and the names of the other children are engraved on the wall.

Stiftung Denkmal für die ermordeten Juden Europas

Riga **Riga**

Privatbesitz Rosenthal

Hans Rosenthal (1925 – 1987) und seine Assistentin Monika Sundermann (*1946) in der Sendung *Dalli Dalli*, Mitte der 1970er Jahre. In seinen Lebenserinnerungen schreibt er:

Hans Rosenthal (1925 – 1987) and his assistant Monika Sundermann (*1946) in the TV show *Dalli Dalli* in the mid-1970s. In his autobiography he writes:

»Als ich ein letztes Mal ins Waisenhaus ging, um Abschied zu nehmen, hatte Gert von seinen Ersparnissen fünfzig Postkarten gekauft. Er hielt sie stolz in der Hand und zeigte sie mir:
›Hansi‹, sagte er, ›auf diesen Postkarten steht schon deine Adresse. Ich habe sie alle vorbereitet. Alle zwei Tage werde ich dir schreiben, wo ich bin und wie es mir geht.‹
Ich habe nicht eine dieser Postkarten bekommen. Und ich habe Gert nie wiedergesehen.«

»When I went to the orphanage one last time to say goodbye, Gert had bought fifty postcards from his savings. He held them proudly in his hand and showed them to me:
›Hansi‹, he said, ›your address is already written on these postcards. I have prepared all of them. I will send you one every second day to tell you where I am and how I'm doing.‹
I never received any of these postcards. And I never saw Gert again.«

Aleksander Walt

Ermordung eines »Gewohnheitsverbrechers«

Aleksander Walt wird 1890 auf der estnischen Insel Ösel (Saaremaa) geboren und besucht dort die technische Oberschule. Über sein Leben geben heute einzig Polizeiakten Auskunft: Er wird ab 1923 wiederholt wegen Diebstahls und Einbrüchen verhaftet und verbringt mehr als zwölf Jahre im Gefängnis. Später arbeitet er als Elektromonteur in Reval (Tallinn), wo er im Oktober 1941 – nun unter deutscher Besatzung – wegen kleinerer Vergehen festgenommen wird. Die estnische Polizei betrachtet Walt als gefährlich und ersucht die deutsche Polizei um seine Einweisung in ein Konzentrationslager. Daraufhin ordnet diese an, den »Gewohnheitsverbrecher« Walt hinzurichten.

Murder of an »habitual criminal«

Aleksander Walt was born on the Estonian island of Saaremaa in 1890 and later attended the local technical high school. Today, police files are the only source of information about his life: From 1923 on, he was repeatedly arrested for theft and burglary and spent more than twelve years in jail. Later, he worked in Tallinn as an electrician and was arrested for minor offences in October 1941 – by this time Tallinn was under German occupation. The Estonian police considered Walt to be dangerous and requested the German police to send him to a concentration camp. Thereupon, the latter ordered the execution of Walt as a »habitual criminal«.

Rahvusarhiiv, Reval

Polizeiliches Erkennungsfoto von Aleksander Walt, Reval (Estland), Herbst 1941: Die Polizei beschuldigt ihn unter anderem, während der Kämpfe um Reval im August 1941 Werkzeug aus dem Hafen gestohlen zu haben. Er wird am 14. Januar 1942 hingerichtet.

Police photograph of Aleksander Walt, Tallinn (Estonia), autumn 1941: The police accused him, among other things, of stealing tools at the docks during the battle for Tallinn in August 1941. He was executed on 14 January 1942.

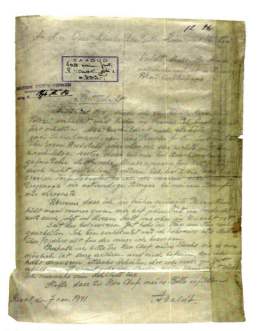

Rahvusarhiiv, Reval

Brief Aleksander Walts an die deutsche Sicherheitspolizei, November 1941: Walt streitet ab, Werkzeug gestohlen zu haben, und beklagt, dass er einzig aufgrund seiner Vorstrafen verdächtigt werde. Zudem müsse er für seine Frau und seine alte Mutter sorgen.

Letter by Aleksander Walt to the German Security Police, November 1941: Walt denied having stolen any tools and complained that he was only suspected on the basis of his previous convictions. He added that he had to care for his wife and elderly mother.

Rahvusarhiiv, Reval

Studentenausweis der Universität Dorpat (Tartu, Estland) von Enno Männik (1908 – 1981), 1937: Er ist unter sowjetischer und deutscher Besatzung als Polizist tätig. Basierend auf seinen Untersuchungen, gibt die estnische Polizei die Einschätzung ab, Walt sei gefährlich und ihn freizulassen »unerträglich«. Männik dient ab März 1943 in der Waffen-SS. Er erlebt das Kriegsende in Bayern und wandert später nach Australien aus.

Student ID card of Enno Männik (1908 – 1981) issued by the University of Tartu (Estonia), 1937: He worked as a policeman during the Soviet and German occupations. On the basis of his investigations, the Estonian police assessed Walt as dangerous and declared that releasing him was »intolerable«. Männik served in the Waffen SS from March 1943 on. He was in Bavaria at the end of the war and later emigrated to Australia.

BArch R_9361_III201302

Fritz Störtz (1912 – 1985). Der Stellvertreter des Kommandeurs der Sicherheitspolizei und des SD (KdS) Estland ist bereits vor 1933 Mitglied der SA und der NSDAP und tritt 1937 in die SS ein. Seine Anweisung zum Umgang mit Aleksander Walt lautet: »Er ist ein intelligenter, gefährlicher Einbrecher (…). Die deutsche Sicherheitspolizei verfügt daher die Exekution des Walt.«

Fritz Störtz (1912 – 1985). The Deputy Commanding Officer of the Security Police and SD (KdS) in Estonia was already a member of the SA and the NSDAP before 1933 and joined the SS in 1937. His instructions concerning Walt read as follows: »He is an intelligent, dangerous burglar (…). Therefore, the German Security Police orders Walt's execution.«

Aleksander Walt

Polizeiliche Zusammenarbeit bei der Verfolgung

Nach ihrem Einmarsch bauen die Deutschen gemeinsam mit estnischen Nationalisten eine Selbstverwaltung auf. Die Entscheidungshoheit bleibt jedoch bei den Besatzern. Dies gilt auch für die Kriminalpolizei. Meist ermitteln estnische Polizisten und sprechen Empfehlungen zum Umgang mit den Verhafteten aus. Auf dieser Grundlage entscheiden dann Deutsche über deren Schicksal. Estnische und deutsche Beamte teilen die Ansicht, dass Prostituierte, Alkoholkranke und Wiederholungstäter an einem erblichen Charakterdefekt leiden. Zahlreiche Menschen werden Opfer dieser Vorstellung.

Police cooperation in persecution

After their invasion, the Germans, in cooperation with Estonian nationalists, established the Estonian Self-Administration. The decision-making power remained in the hands of the occupiers. This also applied to the criminal investigation police. In most cases, Estonian policemen carried out the investigations and issued recommendations on how to deal with those arrested. Based on this, Germans then decided on the prisoners' fate. Estonian and German officials shared the view that prostitutes, alcoholics, and repeat offenders suffered from a genetic defect. Numerous people fell victim to this notion.

Dorpat (Estland), Rathausplatz, 11. Juli 1942: Feierlichkeiten zum Jahrestag der »Befreiung« durch deutsche Truppen, 2.v.l.: Martin Sandberger (1911 – 2010). Der in Tübingen promovierte Jurist ist ab Dezember 1941 Kommandeur der Sicherheitspolizei und des SD (KdS) Estland. Neben ihm der Bürgermeister von Dorpat, Karl Keerdoja (1896 – 1968), und Hjalmar Mäe (1901 – 1978), Direktor der estnischen Selbstverwaltung.

Tartu (Estonia), Town Hall Square, 11 July 1942: Celebrations to mark the anniversary of »liberation« by German troops, 2nd from left: Martin Sandberger (1911 – 2010). He earned a PhD in law at the University of Tübingen. In December 1941, he was appointed Commanding Officer of the Security Police and SD (KdS) in Estonia. Next to him, Tartu Mayor Karl Keerdoja (1896 – 1968) and Hjalmar Mäe (1901 – 1978), head of the Estonian Self-Administration.

Herder-Institut, Marburg. Bildarchiv. Inv.-Nr. 162237

Tallinn Reval

Vergessene Opfer

In den 1950er Jahren werden im sowjetisch besetzten Estland erste Denkmäler »für die Opfer des Faschismus« errichtet. Doch erst nach Wiedererlangen der Unabhängigkeit 1991 wird ausdrücklich erwähnt, dass es sich bei den Ermordeten vornehmlich um Juden handelte. Später wird auch der getöteten Roma gedacht. Im Jahr 2005 verurteilt die estnische Regierung die Beteiligung von Esten am Holocaust. Die Ermordung von Homosexuellen, »Asozialen« und »Gewohnheitsverbrechern« findet wie in vielen Ländern bis heute wenig Aufmerksamkeit.

Forgotten victims

The first memorials »to the victims of fascism« in Estonia were built in the 1950s. At the same time, the country was under Soviet occupation. The fact that the majority of those murdered were Jews was not expressly mentioned until Estonia regained independence in 1991. Later, the murdered Romani were memorialised. In 2005, the Estonian government condemned the involvement of Estonians in the Holocaust. However, as in many other countries, little attention has been given to the murder of homosexuals, »asocial persons«, and »habitual criminals«.

Reval, Wiru Straße 8, 2015: Dieses Haus war zum Zeitpunkt seiner Verhaftung als Aleksander Walts Adresse angegeben. Nichts erinnert an sein Schicksal.

Tallinn, Wiru Street 8, 2015: This was given as Aleksander Walt's address at the time of his arrest. Nothing here reminds the public of his fate.

Stiftung Topographie des Terrors / Fotografin: Paula Oppermann

Nikolaj **Walachanowitsch**

Weichenwärter im Widerstand

Nikolaj Walachanowitsch arbeitet als Weichenwärter am Bahnhof des weißrussischen Dorfes Negoreloe, 50 Kilometer südwestlich von Minsk. Ab April 1943 berichtet er über die verkehrenden Güter und den Bahnverkehr an Verbindungsleute der sowjetischen Aufklärung. Diese stellt Informationen für den Kampf gegen die deutschen Besatzer zusammen. Walachanowitsch wird am 20. Juni 1944 zusammen mit weiteren Dorfbewohnern unter dem Vorwurf der Partisanentätigkeit verhaftet. Am 29. Juni 1944 bringen die Besatzer ihn und viele andere in das nahegelegene Lager Malyj Trostenez. Zu diesem Zeitpunkt steht die Rote Armee bereits kurz vor Minsk.

A signalman in the resistance

Nikolai Valakhanovich worked as a signalman at the railway station of the Belarusian village of Negoreloe, 50 kilometres southwest of Minsk. In April 1943, he started reporting to liaisons from Soviet reconnaissance, providing them with information on transported freight and rail traffic. The Soviets collected this information for the struggle against the German occupiers. Valakhanovich was arrested on 20 June 1944, together with other villagers, on suspicion of partisan activity. On 29 June 1944, the occupiers transported him and many others to nearby Maly Trostenets camp. By this time, the Red Army had already reached the outskirts of Minsk.

Privatbesitz Walachanowitsch, in: Zeitzeugenarchiv der Geschichtswerkstatt Minsk

Nikolaj Walachanowitsch (1917 – 1989) mit seiner Frau Serafima (Mitte), der Schwester Tamara (links) und dem Bruder Alexander, etwa 1938.

Nikolai Valakhanovich (1917 – 1989) with his wife Serafima (centre), his sister Tamara (left), and his brother Alexander, around 1938.

Nikolaj **Walachanowitsch**

Massenmord in der Scheune

In der unmittelbaren Umgebung der ehemaligen Kolchose in Malyj Trostenez erschießen Angehörige der Sicherheitspolizei und des SD (KdS/BdS) zehntausende Menschen oder ersticken sie in Gaswagen – Kriegsgefangene, Juden aus Weißrussland und dem Deutschen Reich sowie Angehörige des Widerstands. Das Morden dauert bis in die letzten Tage der Besatzung an. Nikolaj Walachanowitsch wird nach seiner Ankunft in eine Scheune getrieben, in der bereits unzählige Leichen liegen. Er wird angeschossen und verliert ein Auge. Über einen Tag lang liegt er zwischen den Toten, dann kriecht er – die Erschießungen dauern noch an – ins Freie und versteckt sich. Kurze Zeit später wird die Scheune von den Wachmannschaften des Lagers in Brand gesetzt.

Mass murder in the barn

In the immediate vicinity of the former kolkhoz in Maly Trostenets, members of the Security Police and SD shot tens of thousands of people or suffocated them in mobile gas vans – prisoners of war, Jews from Belarus and the German Reich, as well as members of the resistance. The killing continued right up until the final days of German occupation. Upon arrival at Maly Trostenets, Nikolai Valakhanovich was herded into a barn, already full of corpses. He was wounded by a bullet and lost an eye. He lay among the dead for more than a day before crawling into the open and hiding. The shootings continued. Shortly after his escape, the barn was set on fire by the camp's guards.

Belorusskij Gosudarstwennyj Muzej istorii Welikoj Otetschestwennoj Woiny, Minsk

Malyj Trostenez, 1944: Warnschild am ehemaligen Lagerzaun und die abgebrannte Scheune mit Leichenresten. Beide Aufnahmen entstehen nach der Einnahme von Minsk durch die Rote Armee.

Maly Trostenets, 1944: Warning sign at the former fence of the camp and the burnt-down barn with remnants of corpses. Both pictures were taken after the capture of Minsk by the Red Army.

Stiftung Denkmal für die ermordeten Juden Europas

Georg Heuser (1913 – 1989) leitet die Abteilung IV (Gestapo) beim KdS in Minsk und ist ab Herbst 1943 mit der Überwachung der Partisanenaktivitäten betraut. Er bleibt bis kurz vor Eintreffen der Roten Armee in Minsk. Im August 1944 wird er zur Bekämpfung des Nationalaufstands in der Slowakei eingesetzt.

Georg Heuser (1913 – 1989) was head of Gestapo department within the KdS office in Minsk and was entrusted with monitoring partisan activities starting in autumn 1943. He stayed in Minsk until just before the Red Army's arrival. In August 1944, he was deployed to fight the Slovak national uprising.

Georg Heuser nach seiner Festnahme durch die Polizei am 23. Juli 1959.

Georg Heuser, after being arrested by the police on 23 July 1959.

Landeshauptarchiv Koblenz Best. 584,001 Nr. 8800 Bild Nr. 267

Nikolaj **Walachanowitsch**

Aufarbeitung und Erinnerung

In der Nachkriegszeit nimmt Nikolaj Walachanowitsch an Gedenkveranstaltungen in Malyj Trostenez teil und berichtet in Schulen von seinen Erlebnissen. Anfang der 1960er Jahre laden ihn die sowjetischen Behörden nach Moskau vor, um seine Zeugenaussage für einen Prozess gegen elf Angehörige des KdS Minsk in Koblenz aufzunehmen. Unter den Angeklagten befindet sich auch Georg Heuser, der zuletzt Leiter des rheinland-pfälzischen Landeskriminalamts gewesen ist. Das Verfahren erregt großes Aufsehen. Der Massenmord in der Scheune von Malyj Trostenez wird erwähnt, jedoch nicht weiter verhandelt. Das Gericht verurteilt Heuser 1963 wegen Beihilfe zum Mord in über zehntausend Fällen zu 15 Jahren Zuchthaus.

Judicial investigation and remembrance

In the post-war period, Nikolai Valakhanovich attended memorial services in Maly Trostenets and told school children his story. In the early 1960s, the Soviet authorities summoned him to appear in Moscow to provide his testimony for the trial of eleven former members of the KdS Minsk. One of the accused in the West German town of Koblenz was Georg Heuser, who most recently had been director of the Rhineland-Palatinate State Criminal Investigation Office. The proceedings generated a great deal of public interest. The mass murder at the barn of Maly Trostenets was mentioned, but was not part of the proceedings. In 1963, the court sentenced Heuser to 15 years in prison for accessory to more than ten thousand counts of murder.

Nikolaj Walachanowitsch, 1962.
Standbild aus dem sowjetischen Film
Die Opfer klagen an.

Nikolai Valakhanovich, 1962.
Still picture from the Soviet film
Victims are accusing.

Stiftung Denkmal für die ermordeten Juden Europas

Malyj Trostenez, 2014: Denkmal am Ort der niedergebrannten Scheune. Lange erinnert wenig an den Vernichtungsort. 1963 wird in einiger Entfernung vom eigentlichen Lagergelände ein Obelisk errichtet. In den 1980er Jahren entstehen Gedenksteine, auch für die Opfer des Mordes in der Scheune.

Maly Trostenets, 2014: Memorial at the site of the burnt-down barn. For a long time, there was little to remind people of this killing site. In 1963, an obelisk was erected some distance away from the actual site of the camp. Several memorial stones were erected in the 1980s, among them the memorial stone for those murder victims from the barn.

Malyj Trostenez **Maly Trostenets**

Privatbesitz Walachanowitsch, in: Zeitzeugenarchiv der Geschichtswerkstatt Minsk

Nikolaj Walachanowitsch (vorne mit Hut) gemeinsam mit seinem Sohn Leonid, 1962, auf dem Weg zur Kranzniederlegung in Bolschoj Trostenez anlässlich des Tages der Befreiung von Minsk.

Nikolai Valakhanovich (first row, the man with the hat) and his son, Leonid, 1962, on their way to a wreath-laying ceremony in Bolschoi Trostenets to mark the anniversary of the liberation of Minsk.

Internationale Bildungs- und Begegnungsstätte »Johannes Rau«, Minsk

Malyj Trostenez, 2015: Das ehemalige Lagergelände wird auf Initiative des weißrussischen Staates umgestaltet. Das zentrale Element der neuen Gedenkstätte bildet das »Tor der Erinnerung« – zwei etwa 15 Meter hohe Stelen, an denen Figuren hinter Stacheldraht zu erkennen sind.

Maly Trostenets, 2015: The former camp site is beeing turned into a memorial site at the initiative of the Belarusian government. The central element of the new memorial site is the »Gate of Remembrance« – two 15-metre-high steles showing figures behind barbed wire.

Judyta **Wyszniacka**

**»Wir möchten so gerne leben,
doch man lässt uns nicht«**

Judyta Wyszniacka ist noch ein Kind, als am 25. Juli 1942 fast alle Juden ihres Heimatorts Byten (Byteń) in Ostpolen von einem deutschen Mordkommando erschossen werden. Ihrer Mutter Złata gelingt es im letzten Augenblick, mit ihren zwei Kindern in die Wälder zu flüchten. Doch auch hier sind die drei nicht sicher; die Deutschen und einheimische Hilfspolizisten machen Jagd auf Überlebende der Erschießungen. Judyta, ihre Mutter und ihr Bruder kommen am 20. Januar 1943 auf unbekannte Weise ums Leben.

**»We so much want to live
but they won't let us«**

Judyta Wyszniacka was still a child when almost all the Jews from her home town of Byten (Byteń) in eastern Poland were shot by a German death squad on 25 July 1942. Her mother, Złata, managed to flee into the woods at the very last moment, together with her two children, but they were not safe there, either. The Germans and local auxiliary police hunted down those who survived the shootings. Judyta, her mother, and her brother died under unknown circumstances on 20 January 1943.

Pinkas Byten. Buenos Aires 1954.

Aufnahme von Judyta Wyszniacka aus dem Erinnerungsbuch *Pinkas Byten, der oyfkum un untergang fun a yidischer kehile (Das Buch von Byten, der Aufstieg und Untergang einer jüdischen Gemeinde).* Es wird 1954 von ausgewanderten Bytener Juden in Buenos Aires herausgegeben.

Photograph of Judyta Wyszniacka in the memorial book *The book of Byten (Pinkas Byten), the rise and fall of a Jewish community.* The book was published by Jewish emigres from Byten in Buenos Aires in 1954.

Pinkas Byten

Judytas Mutter Złata Wyszniacka und ihr Bruder Gordi, Fotos abgedruckt im Erinnerungsbuch *Pinkas Byten*.

Judyta's mother, Złata Wyszniacka, and her brother, Gordi, photographs published in the memorial book *Pinkas Byten*.

Einwohner von Byten in der Neuen Straße (jiddisch: naje gass), vermutlich 1930er Jahre, abgebildet im *Pinkas Byten*. In Byten herrscht vor dem Krieg ein reges jüdisches Leben mit eigenen Schulen und religiösen Einrichtungen. Viele Gemeindemitglieder unterstützen außerdem die Arbeiterbewegung.

Citizens of Byten at New Street, photo presumably taken in the 1930s, published in *Pinkas Byten*. Before the war, Byten had a vibrant Jewish community with its own schools and religious institutions. Many members of the community supported the workers' movement.

Pinkas Byten

Judyta **Wyszniacka**

Die Ermordung der Juden in Byten

Byten wird Ende Juni 1941 von der Wehrmacht besetzt und einige Wochen später Teil des Gebietskommissariats Slonim (Słonim), das von Gerhard Erren geleitet wird. Fast die Hälfte der 2.500 Einwohner sind Juden. Sie müssen einen Judenrat bilden, Zwangsarbeit verrichten und im Frühjahr 1942 in ein Ghetto ziehen. Als die Gemeinde von einer Massenerschießung im nahegelegenen Słonim erfährt, verstecken sich viele in selbstgebauten Bunkern. Doch deutsche Gendarmen finden sie mit Unterstützung litauischer und weißrussischer Hilfspolizisten. Am 25. Juli werden über 800 Menschen innerhalb von drei Stunden erschossen. Etwa 200 der 350 Überlebenden gelingt die Flucht in die Wälder zu den Partisanen. Die meisten von ihnen werden bis September 1942 von den Besatzern ermordet.

Murder of the Byten Jews

Byten was occupied by the Wehrmacht at the end of June 1941 and a few weeks later became part of the District Commissariat Slonim (Słonim), which was run by Gerhard Erren. Almost half of the 2,500 citizens were Jews. They had to establish a Jewish council, to work as forced labourers, and, in spring 1942, move into a ghetto. When the community heard of a mass shooting in the nearby town of Słonim, many of them hid in self-made bunkers. The German Gendarmerie still managed to find them with the help of Lithuanian and Belarusian auxiliary policemen. On July 25th, more than 800 people were shot in only three hours. About 200 of the 350 survivors managed to flee into the woods and join partisan groups. Most of them were killed by the occupiers before September 1942.

BArch VBS286_6400009396

Gerhard Erren (1901 – 1984), vom 1. September 1941 bis Juli 1944 Leiter des Gebietskommissariats Slonim, zu dem auch Byten gehört: Vom Gebietskommissariat geht wahrscheinlich der Befehl zur Erschießung der Bytener Juden im Juli 1942 aus. Erren schlägt und tötet immer wieder auch eigenhändig. Bei einer Dienstversammlung sagt er: »Wenn man es einmal gemacht hat, ist es so leicht, als würde man über einen Strohhalm springen.«

Gerhard Erren (1901 – 1984), head of the District Commissariat Slonim of which Byten was a part, from 1 September 1941 to July 1944: It was most probably the District Commissariat that ordered the shooting of the Byten Jews in July 1942. Erren repeatedly beat up and killed people himself. At an official meeting, he said: »After you have done it once, it's as easy as jumping over a straw.«

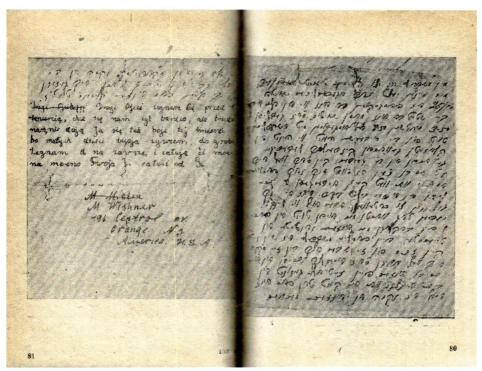

Merder fun felker

Abdruck eines Briefs von Złata und Judyta Wyszniacka. Mutter und Tochter schreiben am 31. Juli 1942 an den Vater in den USA. Złata Wyszniacka übergibt den Brief einem Nichtjuden mit der Bitte, ihn nach dem Krieg nach Amerika zu schicken. Er wird 1945 in Ilja Ehrenburgs (1891 – 1967) Sammlung *Merder fun felker* (Mörder der Völker) veröffentlicht. Diese enthält Dokumente über den Mord an den Juden in der Sowjetunion.

Unter die jiddischen Worte ihrer Mutter schreibt Judyta auf Polnisch:

»Lieber Vater!
Vor dem Tod nehme ich Abschied von Dir. Wir möchten so gerne leben, doch man lässt uns nicht, wir werden umkommen. Ich habe solche Angst vor diesem Tod, denn die kleinen Kinder werden lebend in die Grube geworfen.
Auf Wiedersehen für immer.
Ich küsse Dich inniglich.
Deine J.«

Copy of a letter by Złata and Judyta Wyszniacka. On 31 July 1942, mother and daughter wrote to Judyta's father who was living in the USA. Złata Wyszniacka gave this letter to a non-Jew and asked him to send it to America as soon after the war. The letter was published by Ilya Ehrenburg (1891 – 1967) in the collection *Merder fun felker* (murderers of peoples) in 1945. This book documents the murder of the Jews in the Soviet Union.

Beneath the Yiddish text written by her mother, Judyta writes in Polish:

»Dear Father!
Before I die I want say farewell to you. We so much want to live, but they won't let us. We are going to die. I'm so afraid of this kind of death, for the little children are thrown into the pit alive.
Farewell forever.
With kisses.
Your J.«

Judyta **Wyszniacka**

Versuche der Erinnerung und der Strafverfolgung

Nur 73 Bytener Juden erleben das Kriegsende. Fast alle wandern in die USA, nach Israel oder Argentinien aus. In Buenos Aires veröffentlichen Mitglieder der jüdischen Gemeinde 1954 ein Erinnerungsbuch über Byten. Darin wird der Brief von Złata und Judyta Wyszniacka abgedruckt, vermutlich als Faksimile einer früheren sowjetischen Veröffentlichung. In der Bundesrepublik vergehen weitere 20 Jahre, bis einer der Täter belangt wird: Das Landgericht Hamburg verurteilt den ehemaligen Gebietskommissar Gerhard Erren zu lebenslanger Haft wegen seiner Rolle bei der Ermordung von über 15.000 Juden in Słonim. Das Urteil wird wegen Verhandlungsfehlern aufgehoben. Es folgt keine neue Verfahrenseröffnung.

Efforts to remember and to prosecute

Only 73 Byten Jews survived the war. Most of them emigrated to the USA, Israel, or Argentina. In 1954, members of the Jewish community in Buenos Aires published a memorial book on Byten. The letter from Złata and Judyta Wyszniacka was also published here, presumably a facsimile of the previous Soviet publication. It took another 20 years before one of the perpetrators was brought to trial in West Germany: The State Court of Hamburg sentenced the former District Commissar, Gerhard Erren, to life in prison for his role in the killing of more than 15,000 Jews in Słonim. Later, the sentence was suspended due to procedural errors. No new trial was opened.

akg-images / Universal Images Group / Sovfoto

Moskau, 24. August 1941: Ilja Ehrenburg (vorne rechts) und andere jüdische Künstler verurteilen in einer Rundfunksprache die Verbrechen der Deutschen. Aus diesem Kreis geht später das Jüdische Antifaschistische Komitee (JAK) hervor. Nach einem Vorschlag Albert Einsteins (1879 – 1955) beginnt Ehrenburg 1942 gemeinsam mit Wassili Grossman (1905 – 1964) und anderen Mitgliedern des JAK, Dokumente für das *Schwarzbuch. Der Genozid an den sowjetischen Juden* zu sammeln. Teile dieses Materials veröffentlicht Ehrenburg 1944 unter dem Titel *Merder fun Felker*. Die sowjetische Führung verurteilt die Arbeit am *Schwarzbuch* als Ausdruck »nationalistischer Bestrebungen« und lässt Anfang der 1950er Jahre zahlreiche Mitglieder des JAK hinrichten.

Moscow, 24 August 1941: Ilya Ehrenburg (front right) and other Jewish artists condemn the crimes of the Germans in a radio address. Some artists from this group later formed the Jewish Anti-Fascist Committee (JAC). In 1942, at the suggestion of Albert Einstein (1879 – 1955), Ehrenburg together with Vassily Grossman (1905 – 1964) and other JAC members started collecting documents for the *Black Book. The ruthless murder of Jews by German-Fascist invaders*. Ehrenburg published parts of this material under the title *Merder fun Felker* in 1944. The Soviet leaders condemned work on the *Black Book* as an expression of »nationalist aspirations« and, in the early 1950s, ordered the execution of numerous JAC members.

Byten **Byten**

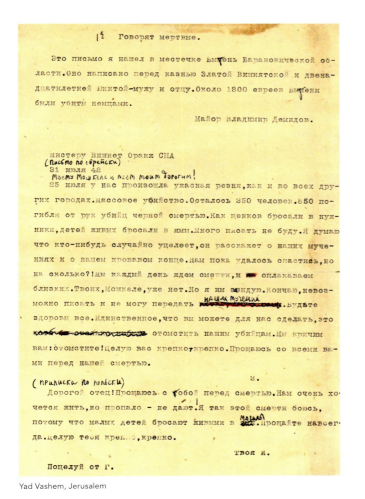

Yad Vashem, Jerusalem

Russische Übersetzung des Briefs von Złata und Judyta Wyszniacka für das *Schwarzbuch*. Der Text wird handschriftlich verändert: »Jama« (Grube) ist mit mit »Mogila« (Grab) überschrieben. Das Schwarzbuch soll über den Mord an den sowjetischen Juden aufklären. Die sowjetische Führung verbietet die Publikation 1947 unter anderem, weil das Buch nur das Leiden der Juden, nicht aber das anderer Opfer beschreibe. Das *Schwarzbuch* erscheint erstmals 1980 in Jerusalem.

Russian translation of the letter by Złata und Judyta Wyszniacka for the *Black Book*. The text is changed by hand: »yama« (pit) is replaced by »mogila« (grave). The *Black Book* provides information about the murder of the Soviet Jews. In 1947, the Soviet leadership prohibited its publication, claiming that the book only described the suffering of the Jews and not that of other victims. The *Black Book* was first published in Jerusalem in 1980.

In Buenos Aires 1954 veröffentlichtes Erinnerungsbuch *Pinkas Byten* mit Złata und Judyta Wyszniackas Brief. Es handelt sich bei ihm wahrscheinlich um eine Kopie aus der in der Sowjetunion erschienenen Sammlung *Merder fun felker*.

Memorial book *Pinkas Byten*, published in Buenos Aires in 1954, containing Złata und Judyta Wyszniacka's letter, which is presumably a copy of the letter published in the collection *Merder fun felker* in the Soviet Union.

Pinkas Byten

Ständige Erschießungsorte
Permanent killing sites

An zahlreichen Orten erschießen die Deutschen und lokale Helfer ihre Opfer innerhalb weniger Tage oder Stunden. In der Nähe einiger Städte dienen ihnen Gruben und Waldstücke allerdings über mehrere Jahre als Erschießungsstätten, so bei Kiew, Minsk, Riga und Wilna.

In many places, the Germans and local collaborators shot their victims within a few hours or days. However, they also used pits and forests on the outskirts of cities including Kiev, Minsk, Riga and Vilnius as killing sites for a number of years.

Babij Jar bei Kiew
Babi Yar near Kiev

In der Hauptstadt der Ukrainischen Sowjetrepublik leben vor dem deutschen Angriff auf die Sowjetunion 850.000 Menschen, etwa ein Viertel sind Juden. Viele von ihnen flüchten vor den deutschen Truppen, die Kiew am 19. September 1941 einnehmen. Der Wehrmacht folgen das Sonderkommando 4a und der Stab der Einsatzgruppe C. Am 29. und 30. September ist das nahe Kiew gelegene Babij Jar (Altweiberschlucht) Schauplatz der umfangreichsten Massenerschießung des Holocaust. 33.771 Männer, Frauen und Kinder melden die Täter anschließend als erschossen nach Berlin. Bis Sommer 1943 ermorden die Deutschen in Babij Jar insgesamt bis zu 100.000 Menschen, vor allem Juden, Roma und sowjetische Kriegsgefangene. Im August 1943 müssen Häftlinge die Massengräber öffnen und die Leichen verbrennen, um die Spuren der Verbrechen zu beseitigen.

When Germany invaded the Soviet Union, the capital of the Ukrainian Soviet Socialist Republic had a population of 850,000, a quarter of which were Jews. Many of them fled Kiev before it was seized by German forces on 19 September 1941. Sonderkommando 4a and members of Einsatzgruppe C followed the advancing Wehrmacht. On 29 and 30 September, the largest single mass shooting of the Holocaust took place at Babi Yar (»Old Women's Ravine«) near Kiev. The perpetrators sent a report back to Berlin stating that 33,771 men, women and children had been shot. By the summer of 1943, the Germans had shot up to 100,000 people at Babi Yar. Most were Jews, Roma and Soviet prisoners of war. In August 1943, prisoners were forced to dig up the mass graves and burn the corpses in order to remove the traces of the crime.

Vorgeschichte

Kiew bis zum deutschen Überfall

Kiew wird Ende des 19. Jahrhunderts zu einem Zentrum jüdischen Lebens in der Ukraine. Allerdings bestehen während der Zarenzeit Ansiedlungsbeschränkungen. Im Mai 1881 fordern erste antijüdische Ausschreitungen Todesopfer. Weitere Pogrome folgen in den Jahren danach. Die sowjetische Regierung fördert Anfang der 1920er Jahre die weltliche jüdische Kultur; führende jüdische wissenschaftliche Einrichtungen und ein jüdisches Staatstheater werden in Kiew ansässig. Die Ausübung der Religion wird hingegen unterdrückt. Stalins Terror beendet Ende der 1930er Jahre schließlich auch das kulturelle Leben der Juden.

Prologue

Kiev before the German invasion

In the late 19th century, Kiev became a centre of Jewish life in the Ukraine. However, restrictions were imposed on Jewish residence in Kiev during the Tsarist period. Lives were lost during the first wave of anti-Jewish pogroms in May 1881. Additional pogroms took place in the years that followed. In the early 1920s, the Soviet government encouraged secular Jewish culture and top-ranking Jewish academic institutions and a national Jewish theatre were located in Kiev. However, Jews were prevented from freely practicing their religion. By the late 1930s, Stalinist terror had also put an end to Jewish cultural life.

Kiew: Postkarte mit Choralsynagoge. Das Gebäude wird 1898 fertiggestellt. Es ist in der Zarenzeit eines von über 20 jüdischen Gotteshäusern der Stadt. 1926 wandeln die sowjetischen Behörden die Synagoge in ein Haus für Künstler um.

Kiev: Postcard of the Great Choral Synagogue. The building was completed in 1898 and was one of over 20 Jewish places of worship located in the city during the Tsarist period. The Soviet authorities converted the synagogue into a centre for artists in 1926.

Babi Yar near Kiev

akg-images

Photochrom, um 1895: Kiewer Innenstadt.
Photochrome of Kiev city centre, around 1895.

Privatbesitz Wisniewski

19. bis 28. September 1941

Kiew in Flammen

Am 19. September 1941 fällt Kiew in die Hände der Wehrmacht. Die Rote Armee und der sowjetische Geheimdienst (NKWD) hatten in zahlreichen wichtigen Gebäuden Sprengsätze platziert, die nun ferngezündet werden. Immer wieder erschüttern schwere Explosionen die Stadt. Sowjetische Agenten entfachen Feuer, ganze Häuserblocks stehen in Flammen. Die Deutschen nehmen dies als Vorwand, um die Verfolgung der Kiewer Juden zu verschärfen. Bereits zuvor hatten deutsche Soldaten Juden in Lager gesperrt. Nun werden hunderte Juden zusammen mit NKWD-Agenten, politischen Offizieren und Partisanen ermordet. Bei einer Besprechung verabreden Vertreter der Wehrmacht und des SS- und Polizeiapparats, die verbliebenen Juden der Stadt in Babij Jar zu erschießen.

19 to 28 September 1941

Kiev in flames

The Wehrmacht seized Kiev on 19 September 1941. The Red Army and the Soviet Secret Police (NKVD) had planted explosives in many important buildings and now detonated them. The city was rocked by explosion after explosion. Soviet agents started fires and soon entire blocks of flats were ablaze. The Germans used this as a pretext to intensify the persecution of Kiev's Jewish population. German soldiers had already started to incarcerate Jews in camps. They now murdered hundreds of Jews, along with NKVD agents, political commissars and partisans. Members of the Wehrmacht, SS and police held a meeting at which they agreed to shoot any Jews remaining in Kiev at Babi Yar.

Babi Yar near Kiev

BArch Bild 183-L20208

Kiew, 19./20. September 1941: Blick von der Zitadelle auf Teile des Höhlenklosters und eine brennende Brücke über den Dnjepr. Am 20. September explodiert in der Zitadelle eine erste ferngezündete Mine. Mehrere Wehrmachtsangehörige kommen ums Leben.

Kiev, 19 – 20 September 1941: View from the citadel showing a section of the Monastery of the Caves and a burning bridge across the Dnieper River. The first remote-controlled mine exploded in the citadel on 20 September. Several Wehrmacht soldiers died in the blast.

bpk

Kiew, 1941: Frauen retten Hausrat vor den Flammen. Tausende Kiewer verlieren in diesen Tagen ihre Wohnungen und Habseligkeiten.

Kiev, 1941: Women salvaging household belongings from the flames. Thousands of Kiev's residents lost their homes and possessions during this time.

BArch VBS 286 6400035255

Dr. Dr. Otto Rasch (1891 – 1948): Führer der Einsatzgruppe C. Ende September 1941 finden mehrere Besprechungen zwischen ranghohen SS-Führern, Vertretern der 6. Armee und der zukünftigen Zivilverwaltung statt. Die Ermordung der Kiewer Juden beschlossen wahrscheinlich Rasch, der Stadtkommandant Kurt Eberhard (1874 – 1947), der Führer des Sonderkommandos 4a Paul Blobel (1894 – 1951) und der Höhere SS- und Polizeiführer Friedrich Jeckeln (1895 – 1946).

Otto Rasch (1891 – 1948), commander of Einsatzgruppe C, held two doctorates. Senior SS officials, representatives of the 6th Army and members of the future civil administration met several times in late September 1941. Paul Blobel (1894 – 1951), the head of Sonderkommando 4a, and Friedrich Jeckeln (1895 – 1946), the Higher SS and Police Leader along with Rasch and Kurt Eberhard (1874 – 1947), the military governor of Kiev made probably a joint decision to murder the Jews of Kiev.

29. bis 30. September 1941

Das Massaker von Babij Jar

Am Morgen des 29. Septembers müssen sich die Kiewer Juden in der Nähe von Babij Jar einfinden. Zwei Bataillone der deutschen Ordnungspolizei und ukrainische Hilfspolizisten sperren das Gelände ab. Unter Schlägen werden die Juden gruppenweise in die Schlucht getrieben. Dort beginnt das Sonderkommando 4a unter dem Kommando von Paul Blobel (1894 – 1951), sie zu erschießen. Am frühen Abend unterbrechen die Deutschen ihre Mordtätigkeit. Die noch lebenden Juden müssen die Nacht in Garagen gepfercht verbringen. Am nächsten Tag werden auch sie getötet.

29 to 30 September 1941

The Babi Yar massacre

Kiev's Jews had to assemble near Babi Yar on the morning of 29 September. Two battalions of the German Order Police and Ukrainian auxiliary police sealed off the area. The Jews were beaten and shoved into the ravine group by group. Sonderkommando 4a then began to shoot them under orders from Paul Blobel (1894 – 1951). The Germans carried on shooting until the early evening. Any Jews who were still alive had to spend the night crowded together in garages. They too were murdered the next day.

Babi Yar near Kiev

United States Holocaust Memorial Museum, Washington, D.C.

Kiew, 2. Juli 1926: Eva (geb. Ficks) und L. Raitzes an ihrem 23. Hochzeitstag. Evas Schwester flieht mit ihren Kindern vor den Deutschen in den Ural, ihr Bruder entkommt nach China. Eva und ihr Mann entschließen sich, in Kiew zu bleiben. Sie hoffen, dass die Rote Armee die Deutschen aufhalten wird. Beide werden im September 1941 Opfer der Massenerschießung in Babij Jar. Über die meisten der Menschen, die mit ihnen in den Tod gingen, ist heute fast nichts bekannt.

Kiev, 2. July 1926: Eva (née Ficks) and L. Raitzes on their 23rd wedding anniversary. Eva's sister fled to the Ural Mountains with her children before the German invasion and her brother escaped to China. Eva and her husband decided to remain in Kiev. They hoped that the Red Army would keep the Germans at bay. The couple both became victims of the mass shooting at Babi Yar in September 1941. Very little is known about most of the victims of this massacre.

Yad Vashem, Jerusalem

Portraitaufnahme von Michail Sidko. Er gehört zu den wenigen Überlebenden des Massakers. Am 29. September gelingt dem Sechsjährigen gemeinsam mit seinem Halbbruder Gregorij Kogan die Flucht vom Sammelpunkt unweit von Babij Jar. Ihre jüdische Mutter und zwei jüngere Geschwister werden an diesem Tag Opfer der Massenerschießung. Michails nicht-jüdischer Vater war zuvor als kriegswichtiger Arbeiter von sowjetischen Behörden evakuiert worden. Michail und sein Halbbruder werden zeitweise von Sofia Kriworot-Baklanowa und ihrer Tochter Galina versteckt. Die Brüder überleben die Besatzungszeit und treffen 1944 Michails Vater wieder.

Portrait photo of Michail Sidko, one of the few survivors of the massacre. On 29 September, the then six year-old and his half-brother Gregory Kogan managed to escape from the assembly point near Babi Yar. Their Jewish mother and two younger siblings died during the mass shooting the same day. Michail's non-Jewish father had already been evacuated by the Soviet authorities as he was classed as a worker important to the war effort. Sofia Krivorot-Baklanova and her daughter Galina hid Michail and his half-brother temporarily. The brothers survived the occupation and were reunited with Michail's father in 1944.

Babij Jar bei Kiew

Babij Jar, Anfang Oktober 1941: Wenige Tage nach dem Massenmord macht der Angehörige der Propagandakompanie 637 Johannes Hähle (1906 – 1944) diese Aufnahmen. Unzählige Kleidungsstücke und persönliche Gegenstände der Opfer sind zu erkennen. Wahrscheinlich mussten sie sich vor ihrer Ermordung an dieser Stelle entkleiden.

Babi Yar at the beginning of October 1941: Johannes Hähle (1906 – 1944), a member of propaganda unit 637, took these photos a few days after the mass murder. They show countless pieces of clothing and personal items belonging to the victims. The victims probably had to undress here before being murdered.

Babi Yar near Kiev

Diese drei Aufnahmen der Serie zeigen Kriegsgefangene, die das Massengrab einebnen und Bäume pflanzen müssen. Im Vordergrund ist ein bewaffneter Angehöriger der Waffen-SS zu erkennen.

These three photos from the series show prisoners of war who were made to level the ground over the mass grave and plant trees on it. An armed member of Waffen-SS can be seen in the foreground.

Alle Bilder: Archiv des Hamburger Instituts für Sozialforschung / Fotograf: Johannes Hähle

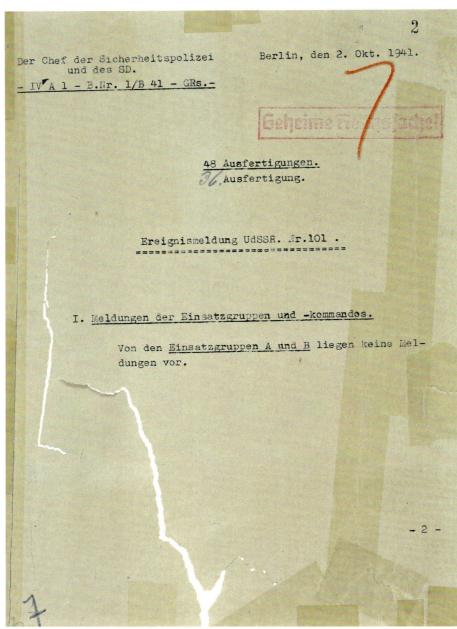

BArch R_58_218_fol. 2 und fol. 3

– 2 –

3

Einsatzgruppe C.

Standort **K i e w**.

Das Sonderkommando 4a hat in Zusammenarbeit mit Gruppenstab und zwei Kommandos des Polizei-Regiments Süd am 29. und 30.9.41 in Kiew 33.771 Juden exekutiert.

Einsatzgruppe D.

Standort **N i k o l a j e w**.

Die Freimachung des Gebietes durch die Kommandos von Juden und kommunistischen Elementen wurde fortgesetzt. Insbesondere wurden in der Berichtszeit die Städte Nikolajew und Cherson von Juden freigemacht und noch vorhandene Funktionäre entsprechend behandelt. Vom 16.9. bis 30.9. wurden 22.467 Juden und Kommunisten exekutiert. Gesamtzahl 35.782. Ermittlungen ergaben wiederum, dass sich die hohen kommunistischen Funktionäre fast überall in Sicherheit gebracht hatten. Gefasst wurden in erster Linie führende Partisanen oder Führer von Sabotagetrupps.

Ermittlungstätigkeit über Partisanengruppen wurden fortgesetzt. Fahndungen ergaben, dass Sowjets schon seit Jahren in Versammlungen nicht nur zum Eintritt in die Rote Armee, sondern auch zur Bildung von Partisanengruppen aufforderten. Kampf der Partisanen und ihre Ausbildung waren wichtige Schulungsthemen. Rekrutierung zunächst freiwillig, nach Ausbruch der Kampfhandlungen wurden Aushebungen ähnlich wie zu Baukompanien auch für Partisanengruppen von Männern im wehrpflichtigen Alter vorgenommen. Aufteilung in Dreier-, Fünfer- und Zehner-Gruppen sollte rasches und sicheres Arbeiten ermöglichen. Es besteht der Eindruck, dass Ausbreitung des Partisanenkriegs dadurch vermindert, dass höhere Partisanenführer vielfach geflohen und Initiative der einzelnen Angehörigen durch jahrzehntelange Erziehung zur Unselbständigkeit und das Warten auf Anweisung weithin erloschen ist.

Ereignismeldung UdSSR vom 2. Oktober 1941. Sie nennt 33.771 Opfer. Nach einer weiteren Ereignismeldung vom 7. Oktober 1941 seien ihre Kleidung und Wertsachen an die Nationalsozialistische Volkswohlfahrt (NSV) und die Stadtverwaltung abgegeben worden. Die Ereignismeldungen werden im Reichssicherheitshauptamt aus den Berichten der Einsatzgruppen zusammengestellt.

Operational situation report USSR (Ereignismeldung UdSSR), 2 October 1941. It gives a total of 33,771 victims. Another report dated 7 October 1941 states that their clothing and valuables had been distributed to the National Socialist People's Welfare Organisation (NSV) and the municipal authorities. The operational situation reports were compiled in the Reich Security Main Office from dispatches submitted by the Einsatzgruppen.

Oktober 1941 bis Juli 1943

Das Morden geht weiter

Nach dem Massaker sprengen Pioniere der Wehrmacht die Ränder der Schlucht, um die Leichen zu begraben. Bis Sommer 1943 dient der Ort den Deutschen weiter als Mordstätte. Regelmäßig werden vor allem weitere Juden, Roma, sowjetische Kriegsgefangene, aber auch Angehörige der Kommunistischen Partei in Babij Jar erschossen oder in sogenannten Gaswagen erstickt und dort verscharrt. In unmittelbarer Nähe der Schlucht finden auf gleiche Weise mehrere Hundert Patienten einer psychiatrischen Anstalt den Tod. Die genaue Zahl der in Babij Jar Ermordeten lässt sich nicht mehr ermitteln. Schätzungen schwanken zwischen 50.000 und 100.000 Menschen.

October 1941 to July 1943

The murders continue

Following the massacre, Wehrmacht pioneer (engineer) units blew up the sides of the ravine in order to bury the bodies. The Germans continued to use the site to carry out murders until summer 1943. Above all Jews, but also Roma, Soviet prisoners of war and members of the Communist Party were regularly shot at Babi Yar or asphyxiated in so-called gas vans before being buried in shallow graves. Several hundred patients from a psychiatric clinic were also killed near the ravine. It is impossible to calculate the exact number of people murdered at Babi Yar, but estimates put this at between 50,000 and 100,000.

Babi Yar near Kiev

United States Holocaust Memorial Museum, Washington, D.C.

Kiew, vermutlich Winter 1941/42: Öffentliche Erhängung. Neben Babij Jar dienen den Deutschen zahlreiche weitere Orte in und um Kiew als Mordstätte. Tausende Menschen fallen der deutschen Besatzungsherrschaft zum Opfer.

Public hanging in Kiev, probably in winter 1941/1942. The Germans carried out murders at many locations in and around Kiev in addition to Babi Yar. Thousands died under the German occupation.

Kurt Eberhard (1874 – 1947): Der Generalmajor ist bis Mitte 1942 Stadtkommandant von Kiew. Unter seinem Befehl werden immer wieder Erschießungen an mehreren hundert Zivilisten verübt. Die Morde werden als Vergeltung für Sabotageakte ausgegeben. Nach dem Krieg nimmt er sich in amerikanischer Gefangenschaft das Leben.

Major General Kurt Eberhard (1874 – 1947) was military governor of Kiev until mid-1942. He repeatedly ordered the shooting of several hundred civilians at a time. These murders were carried out as reprisals for alleged acts of sabotage. Eberhard committed suicide after the war whilst being held prisoner by the Americans.

BArch R/9361/III 522253

August 1943

Verwischen der Spuren und erste Untersuchungen

Mitte August 1943 kehrt Paul Blobel mit dem neu aufgestellten Sonderkommando 1005 A nach Babij Jar zurück. Dieses soll die Spuren der Massenmorde beseitigen. Das Kommando zwingt über 300 Häftlinge des nahegelegenen KZ-Außenlagers Syretz, die Gräber zu öffnen. Die Leichen werden verbrannt und die Knochen anschließend zermahlen. Als die Rote Armee im November 1943 Kiew zurückerobert und die Außerordentliche Staatliche Kommission zur Untersuchung der nationalsozialistischen Verbrechen ihre Arbeit aufnimmt, findet sie fast nur Asche und verkohlte Leichenteile vor.

August 1943

The removal of evidence and the first investigations

In mid-August 1943, Paul Blobel returned to Babi Yar with the newly established Sonderkommando 1005 A. Its task was to remove the evidence of mass murder. The commando forced over 300 prisoners from the nearby Syrets concentration camp to dig up the graves, cremate the corpses and grind up the bones. After the Red Army had regained control of Kiev in November 1943, the Soviet Extraordinary State Commission for the Investigation of National Socialist Crimes went to Babi Yar to gather evidence but it found little more than ashes and charred human remains on the site.

Babi Yar near Kiev

Syretz bei Kiew: Im Frühjahr 1942 wird hier ein Außenlager des KZ Sachsenhausen errichtet. Häftlinge des Lagers müssen im Sommer 1943 die Spuren der Massenerschießungen in Babij Jar beseitigen. Anschließend werden sie ermordet. Einigen wenigen gelingt die Flucht, sie berichten noch im selben Jahr in den sowjetischen Medien. Die Aufnahme zeigt das Lager nach der Befreiung durch die Rote Armee.

Syrets, near Kiev: a sub-camp of the Sachsenhausen concentration camp was established here in spring 1942. In summer 1943, prisoners from the camp were forced to remove evidence of the mass shootings at Babi Yar. They were then murdered. A few did manage to escape. That same year, they gave their accounts in Soviet media. The photo shows the camp following its liberation by the Red Army.

Yad Vashem, Jerusalem

Paul Blobel (1894 – 1951): Als Führer des Sonderkommandos 4a befehligt er die Massenerschießung vom September 1941. Im Frühjahr 1942 bekommt er vom Reichssicherheitshauptamt den Auftrag, die Massengräber in den besetzten Ostgebieten unkenntlich zu machen. Blobel wird nach dem Krieg im Rahmen des Nürnberger Einsatzgruppenprozesses zum Tode verurteilt und hingerichtet.

Paul Blobel (1894 – 1951): As head of Sonderkommando 4a he was in charge of the mass shooting in September 1941. In spring 1942, the Reich Security Main Office instructed him to remove evidence of the mass graves in occupied Eastern Europe. After the war, Blobel was sentenced to death during the Nuremberg SS-Einsatzgruppen Trial and executed.

BArch R/9361 III 517571

Babij Jar, Ende 1943: Aufnahme der Außerordentlichen Staatlichen Kommission während der Untersuchung der Mordstätte.

Babi Yar, late 1943: Photo taken by the Soviet Extraordinary State Commission during its investigations at the execution site.

Rossijskij Gosudarstwennyj Archiv Kinofotodokumentow, Krasnogorsk

1945 bis 1990

»Über Babij Jar stehen keine Denkmäler.«

Die Massenerschießung vom September 1941 ist Teil der Anklage bei den Prozessen gegen die Hauptkriegsverbrecher 1945 und gegen führende Angehörige der Einsatzgruppen 1947/48 in Nürnberg. In der Bundesrepublik stehen einzelne Täter ab den 1960er Jahren vor Gericht. Die Sowjetunion führt ab 1946 Prozesse. Das öffentliche Gedenken an das Massaker von Babij Jar unterdrückt die sowjetische Regierung hingegen. Ende der 1950er Jahre lässt sie auf dem Gelände einen Park errichten. Eine verstärkte öffentliche Auseinandersetzung mit dem Verbrechen beginnt erst im darauffolgenden Jahrzehnt.

1945 to 1990

»No monument stands over Babi Yar«

The mass shooting at Babi Yar in September 1941 formed part of the prosecution's case at the Nuremberg Trials of major war criminals in 1945 and the Einsatzgruppen Trial in 1947/1948. Individual perpetrators were tried by West German courts from the 1960s onwards. The Soviet Union commenced trials in 1946. However, the Soviet government suppressed public commemoration of the Babi Yar massacre. A park was constructed on the site in the late 1950s. It was not until the next decade that public confrontation with the crimes began in earnest.

Babi Yar near Kiev

Kiew, 24. Januar 1946: Dina Pronitschewa (1911 – 1977) sagt beim Prozess gegen 15 deutsche und österreichische Ordnungspolizisten aus. Sie werden wegen Folter und Mordes verurteilt. Die Kiewer Puppenspielerin Pronitschewa hatte sich im September 1941 in die Grube gestürzt und tot gestellt. Ihre Eltern und Geschwister wurden ermordet. Pronitschewas Aussage wird gefilmt und in den sowjetischen Medien ausgestrahlt.

Kiev, 24 January 1946: Dina Pronicheva (1911 – 1977) giving evidence at the trial of 15 German and Austrian members of the Order Police. They were convicted of torture and murder. During the mass shooting in September 1941 Pronicheva, a puppeteer, had thrown herself into the pit and played dead. Her parents and siblings were murdered. Pronicheva's testimony was filmed and broadcast by the Soviet media.

United States Holocaust Memorial Museum, Washington, D.C.

Nürnberg, 1947: Die Angeklagten des Nürnberger Einsatzgruppenprozesses. Für die Verbrechen von Babij Jar sind neben Paul Blobel der Führer der Einsatzgruppe C, Dr. Dr. Otto Rasch, und Waldemar von Radetzky (1910 – 1990), Sonderkommando 4a, angeklagt.

Nuremberg, 1947: the defendants at the Nuremberg SS-Einsatzgruppen trial. The commander of Einsatzgruppe C, Dr Dr Otto Rasch, and Waldemar von Radetzky (1910 – 1990) from Sonderkommando 4a were charged with crimes at Babi Yar along with Paul Blobel.

Babij Jar bei Kiew

akg-images / Universal Images Group / Sovfoto

Moskau, 1962: Jewgenij Jewtuschenko (*1932, r.) und Dmitri Schostakowitsch (1906 – 1975) nach der Uraufführung der 13. Symphonie Babij Jar. Der Komponist vertont darin Jewtuschenkos gleichnamiges Gedicht von 1961. Mit dem Ausruf: »Über Babij Jar stehen keine Denkmäler.« klagt Jewtuschenko das staatlich verordnete Verschweigen des Holocaust an. Die Werke werden von offizieller Seite stark kritisiert, finden bei der Bevölkerung aber großen Zuspruch. Zeugen erinnern sich an »Begeisterungsstürme« nach der Premiere.

Moscow, 1962: Yevgeny Yevtushenko (*1932, right) and Dmitri Shostakovich (1906 – 1975) at the premiere of the composer's 13th Symphony, entitled Babi Yar. Shostakovich set Yevtushenko's eponymous poem from 1961 to music. With the words »No monument stands over Babi Yar« Yevtushenko expressed his opposition to the state's policy of silence on the Holocaust. The two works were heavily criticised by the state but struck a chord with the public. The audience at the premiere recalled that the performance received »tumultuous applause«.

Babi Yar near Kiev

Beit Lohamei Haghetaot, Kibbuz der Ghettokämpfer

Beit Lohamei Haghetaot, Kibbuz der Ghettokämpfer/ Fotograf: Yosef Schneider

Babij Jar, September 1966: erste inoffizielle Gedenkveranstaltung. Etwa 600 Menschen nehmen teil, vor allem Mitglieder der jüdischen Gemeinde. Angehörige des sowjetischen Geheimdienstes machen Aufnahmen. Die Regierung übt Druck auf die Aktivisten aus und drängt einige von ihnen zur Auswanderung.

Babi Yar, September 1966: the first unofficial commemoration at the site. Around 600 people took part, most of them members of the Jewish community. The Soviet secret police photographed the event. The government made life difficult for the activists and forced some of them to emigrate.

Fotograf: Christian Schmittwilken

Kiew, Mai 2016: Sowjetisches Denkmal von 1976. Nachdem Proteste aus der Öffentlichkeit in den 1960er Jahren zugenommen hatten, ließ die Stadtverwaltung dieses Denkmal in der Nähe von Babij Jar errichten. Statt die Juden als Opfergruppe zu nennen, erinnert die Inschrift auf dem Denkmal an die 1941 bis 1943 ermordeten »Bürger der Stadt Kiew und die Kriegsgefangenen«.

Kiev, May 2016: Soviet memorial constructed in 1976. In response to increasing public protests in the 1960s, the municipal authorities commissioned this memorial near Babi Yar. Rather than naming the Jews as a victim group, the inscription refers to the »citizens of Kiev and prisoners of war« murdered between 1941 and 1943.

Seit 1991

Gedenken an die jüdischen Opfer und die Retter

Unmittelbar nachdem die Ukraine 1991 unabhängig wird, findet erstmals eine staatliche Gedenkveranstaltung statt, bei der offiziell der jüdischen Opfer von Babij Jar gedacht wird. Einem ersten Denkmal für die ermordeten Juden folgend, entstehen Denkmäler unterschiedlicher Initiativen in der Umgebung der Grube. Eine zentrale Gedenkstätte gibt es in Babij Jar nicht. An anderen Orten in Kiew und der übrigen Ukraine behandeln Museen und Ausstellungen das Verbrechen.

Since 1991

Remembering the Jewish victims and the rescuers

The first national commemoration officially dedicated to the Jewish victims of Babi Yar took place soon after Ukraine declared independence in 1991. The first memorial to the murdered Jews was inaugurated and additional memorials have been built around the ravine as the result of various initiatives. There is no central memorial at Babi Yar. A number of museums and exhibitions in Kiev and the Ukraine document the crimes.

Babi Yar near Kiev

Bundesregierung / Fotografin: Julia Fassbender

Babij Jar, 18. Oktober 1991: Der deutsche Außenminister Hans-Dietrich Genscher (1927 – 2016) legt einen Kranz nieder. Die Menora war kurz zuvor als erstes Denkmal für die jüdischen Opfer errichtet worden.

Babi Yar, 18 October 1991: the German foreign minister, Hans-Dietrich Genscher (1927 – 2016) laying a wreath. The Menorah-shaped sculpture had recently been inaugurated as the first memorial to the Jewish victims of the massacre.

Yad Vashem, Jerusalem

Die Lehrerin Sofia Kriworot (r., 1896 – 1976) und ihre Tochter Galina (1926 – ?). Im Januar 1942 wird ihr Haus durch eine Bombe zerstört. Sie suchen Schutz im Keller eines anderen Gebäudes. Dort treffen sie auf den sechsjährigen Michail Sidko und seinen Halbbruder Gregorij, die der Massenerschießung vom September 1941 entkommen waren. Sofia gibt die Jungen als ihre Söhne aus. 2004 ehrt Yad Vashem Sofia und ihre Tochter Galina als »Gerechte unter den Völkern«.

The teacher Sofia Krivorot (right, 1896 – 1976) with her daughter Galina (1926 – ?). Their house was destroyed during a bombing raid in January 1942. They took shelter in the cellar of another building. Here they met the six year-old Michail Sidko and his half-brother Gregory, who had fled the mass shooting in September 1941. Sofia pretended that the boys were her sons. In 2004, Yad Vashem awarded Sofia and her daughter Galina the title of »Righteous Among the Nations«.

Malyj Trostenez bei Minsk
Maly Trostenets near Minsk

In der Umgebung der vormaligen Kolchose Malyj Trostenez bei Minsk ermorden die deutschen Besatzer und ihre Hilfswilligen zwischen 1942 und 1944 mindestens 60.000 Menschen: Juden aus Weißrussland und dem Deutschen Reich sowie Kriegsgefangene, Partisanen und Widerstandskämpfer. Sie erschießen ihre Opfer im Umfeld des Lagers oder ersticken sie in Gaswagen. Im Herbst 1943 lassen die Besatzer die Leichen der ermordeten Menschen ausgraben und verbrennen.

Between 1942 and 1944, German occupying forces and local volunteers murdered at least 60,000 people in the area around the former kolkhoz (collective farm) in Maly Trostenets near Minsk. The victims included Jews from Belarus and the territory of the German Reich as well as prisoners of war, partisans and resistance fighters. They were either shot near the camp or asphyxiated in gas vans. In autumn 1943, the occupying forces had the corpses of the murder victims exhumed and cremated.

Vorgeschichte

Minsk bis zum deutschen Überfall

In Minsk leben verschiedene Nationalitäten friedlich zusammen, die Stadt hat einen jüdischen Bevölkerungsanteil von etwa 30 Prozent. 1922 wird sie nach der bolschewistischen Revolution Hauptstadt der Weißrussischen Sowjetrepublik. Unter dem kommunistischen Regime dürfen Juden sowie katholische und orthodoxe Christen ihre Religion nicht öffentlich ausüben. Das Regime unter Josef Stalin (1878 – 1953) zerschlägt Ende der 1930er Jahre fast vollständig auch die weltliche jüdische Kultur, die zunächst noch gefördert worden war. Am Vorabend des deutschen Einmarsches sind die Minsker Juden jeder Möglichkeit beraubt, ihr Leben als Minderheit selbst zu gestalten.

Prologue

Minsk before the German invasion

Various nationalities coexisted peacefully in Minsk. Around 30 percent of the population was Jewish. Minsk became the capital of the Belarusian Soviet Socialist Republic in 1922 following the Bolshevik (October) Revolution. Jews, Catholics and Orthodox Christians were not allowed to practice their religion freely under the Communist regime. In the late 1930s, the regime led by Josef Stalin (1878 – 1953) also eradicated almost all aspects of secular Jewish culture, which had initially been welcomed. The Jewish minority in Minsk lost all autonomy in the period leading up to the German invasion.

Maly Trostenets near Minsk

Beit Hatfutsot, Tel Aviv

Minsk, um 1900: Choralsynagoge. Anfang der 1920er Jahre wandeln die Behörden das Gotteshaus in das Jüdische Staatstheater um. Es muss 1949 schließen.

Choral synagogue in Minsk, around 1900. In the early 1920s, the authorities converted this place of worship into the Jewish National Theatre. It had to close in 1949.

Archives of the YIVO Institute for Jewish Research, New York

Minsk, Bahnhof: Mehrsprachige Beschriftung. Weißrussisch, Russisch, Polnisch und Jiddisch sind seit 1924 Amtssprachen in der Weißrussischen Sowjetrepublik.

Minsk station: Inscription in several languages. In 1942, Belarusian, Russian, Polish and Jewish all became official languages of the Belarusian Soviet Socialist Republic.

Belorusskij Gosudarstwennyj Muzej istorii Welikoj Otetschestwennoj Wojny, Minsk

Minsk, 1939: »Sportparade« vor dem nach Plänen von Josif Langbard (1882 – 1951) errichteten Regierungsgebäude.

Minsk, 1939: »Sports parade« in front of the government building designed by Josif Langbard (1882 – 1951).

Juni bis Juli 1941

Minsk wird besetzt – erzwungener Umzug ins Ghetto

Ende Juni 1941 besetzen deutsche Verbände Minsk. Die Wehrmachtsverwaltung zwingt männliche Bewohner ab 15 Jahren, sich registrieren zu lassen. Nördlich der Stadt werden sie tagelang ohne Versorgung in einem Lager festgehalten. Ein großer Teil der Bevölkerung muss in den folgenden Jahren Zwangsarbeit leisten, viele werden als »Ostarbeiter« ins Deutsche Reich verschleppt. Am 19. Juli 1941 befiehlt die Wehrmacht der jüdischen Bevölkerung im Gebiet Minsk, ins Ghetto im Stadtzentrum zu ziehen. Bis zu 50.000 Menschen leben nun auf zwei Quadratkilometern. Es gibt weder Strom, Trinkwasser noch ausreichend Lebensmittel oder Medikamente. Bis Ende August erschießen die Deutschen mehrere tausend, mehrheitlich männliche Ghettoinsassen.

June to July 1941

The occupation of Minsk and forced resettlement into the ghetto

German troops occupied Minsk at the end of June 1941. The Wehrmacht administration made it compulsory for males over the age of 15 to register with the authorities. They were detained in a camp in the north of the city for days without food or water. In the years that followed, a large number of residents had to work as forced labourers and many others were deported to the territory of the German Reich to work as »Ostarbeiter« (East European workers). On 19 July 1941, the Wehrmacht forced Jewish residents of the Minsk area to move into the ghetto in the city centre. Up to 50,000 people were now living in an area measuring two square kilometres. There was no electricity or drinking water and food and medical supplies were scarce. By the end of August the Germans had shot several thousand ghetto residents, most of them male.

Maly Trostenets near Minsk

BStU-Kopie MfS ZUV 9 Bd. 32

Minsk, Regierungsgebäude, 15. August 1941: Der Reichsführer-SS und Chef der deutschen Polizei, Heinrich Himmler (1900 – 1945, Nummer 2). Besuche ranghoher Angehöriger des SS-und Polizeiapparats im Besatzungsgebiet treiben die Verbrechen voran. Die Nummerierungen auf dem Bild entstanden im Zuge von Ermittlungen der Staatssicherheit der DDR.

Government building in Minsk, 15 August 1941: The Reichsführer-SS and Chief of German Police, Heinrich Himmler (1900 – 1945, number 2). Visits to the occupied territories by high-ranking members of the SS and police provided the impetus to push ahead with the crimes. The numbers were added to this photo during investigations conducted by the Stasi (Secret Police) in East Germany after the war.

Minsk, 1941: Der Zaun, der das von den deutschen Besatzern eingerichtete Ghetto von den anderen Stadtteilen abtrennt.

Minsk, 1941: The fence dividing the ghetto set up by the German occupying forces from the rest of the city.

United States Holocaust Memorial Museum, Washington, D.C.

Malyj Trostenez bei Minsk

November 1941

Minsk als Zielort von Deportationen aus dem Deutschen Reich

In Erwartung des Sieges über die Sowjetunion radikalisiert die deutsche Führung ihre Verfolgungspolitik gegenüber den Juden im Deutschen Reich. Im Oktober 1941 beginnen dort systematische Deportationen in den besetzten Osten, darunter nach Minsk. Im November 1941 verschleppt das Berliner Reichssicherheitshauptamt dorthin knapp 7.000 deutsche, österreichische und tschechische Juden. Angehörige der Dienststelle des Kommandeurs der Sicherheitspolizei und des SD erschießen zuvor in Minsk mindestens 7.500 weißrussische jüdische Kinder, Frauen und Männer. Die Juden aus dem Deutschen Reich werden in den Häusern der zuvor Ermordeten einquartiert. Der Kontakt zu weißrussischen Juden ist ihnen verboten.

Eine Minsker Familie vor der Auslöschung

linke Spalte, von oben nach unten:
Um 1930: Der Schuhhändler Nachum Aig und seine Frau Tauba.
Um 1935: Die Aig-Söhne Meir (hinten), Lova (r.) und Kopel (2.v.l.) sowie ihr Schwager Mordechai Kaplan (l.).
1939: Larissa (Mitte), eines der Enkelkinder von Nachum und Tauba Aig, mit ihren Eltern Mordechai Kaplan und Mania geb. Aig.

Eine Hamburger Familie vor der Deportation nach Minsk. Dort verliert sich ihre Spur.

rechte Spalte, von oben nach unten:
Helene (l.) und Alfred Bielefeld mit ihrem Sohn Kurt und der Schwiegertochter Marion. Alfred Bielefeld betreibt in Hamburg-Eppendorf ein kleines Elektromonteurgeschäft.
Kurt Bielefeld war Motorradliebhaber. Das Foto blieb bei nichtjüdischen Freunden erhalten.
Um 1938: Kurt und Marion Bielefeld mit ihrer Tochter Hella.

November 1941

Minsk as a destination for deportations from the Reich territory

Anticipating victory over the Soviet Union, the German leadership radicalised its anti-Jewish policies on Reich territory. Systematic deportations from Germany to occupied Eastern Europe began in October 1941, with Minsk one of the destinations. The Reich Security Main Office in Berlin deported some 7,000 German, Austrian and Czech Jews in November 1941 to capital of Belarus. Prior to this, staff from the headquarters of the Commanding Officer of the Security Police and SD (KdS) shot at least 7,500 Jewish men, women and children from Belarus in Minsk. Jews arriving from Third Reich territory were moved into the houses belonging to those who had just been murdered. They were not allowed any contact with Belarusian Jews.

A Minsk family murdered during occupation

left column from top:
Around 1930: The shoe merchant Nachum Aig with his wife, Tauba.
Around 1935: The Aig's sons Meir (back), Lova (right) and Kopel (second from left) with their brother-in-law Mordechai Kaplan (left).
1939: Larissa (centre), one of Nachum and Tauba Aig's grandchildren, with her parents Mordechai Kaplan and Mania, née Aig.

A Hamburg family before deportation to Minsk. It is not known what happened to them next.

righ column from top:
Helene (left) and Alfred Bielefeld with their son Kurt and daughter-in-law, Marion. Alfred Bielefeld ran a small electrical installation company in Hamburg-Eppendorf.
Kurt Bielefeld loved motorbikes. Non-Jewish friends kept hold of this photo.
Around 1938: Kurt and Marion Bielefeld with their daughter Hella.

Maly Trostenets near Minsk

Privatbesitz Romanenko

Privatbesitz Olsen

Malyj Trostenez bei Minsk

Januar bis März 1942

Auseinandersetzungen unter den Tätern

Chef der Zivilverwaltung im Generalkommissariat Weißruthenien, zu dem Minsk gehört, ist Wilhelm Kube. Als Anfang 1942 die Deportationen aus dem Deutschen Reich wieder aufgenommen werden sollen, protestieren Kube und der ihm unterstellte Minsker Stadtkommissar Wilhelm Janetzke (1911 – 1964) dagegen bei vorgesetzten Stellen. Sie verweisen auf die katastrophale Wohnraum- und Ernährungslage. Das Reichssicherheitshauptamt unter Reinhard Heydrich bleibt bei seinem Plan.

January to March 1941

Disagreement between the perpetrators

Wilhelm Kube headed the civil administration in the General Commissariat for Weißruthenien, which included Minsk. Deportations from German Reich territory were set to resume at the start of 1942. Kube and Wilhelm Janetzke (1911 – 1964), who worked under Kube as Commissioner for Minsk, complained to their superiors, stressing there was an acute shortage of food and accommodation. Reinhard Heydrich's Reich Security Main Office stuck to its plan.

Maly Trostenets near Minsk

BArch Bild183-B07894

Minsk, Februar 1942: Juden bei der Zwangsarbeit.

Minsk, February 1942: Jewish forced labourers.

BArch Bild 146-1976-127-31A

Minsk, 1943: Generalkommissar Wilhelm Kube (1887 – 1943, 2.v.l.). Kube treibt die Massenerschießungen an den weißrussischen Juden voran, bemüht sich aber zunächst um den Schutz einzelner Deportierter aus dem Deutschen Reich – Veteranen des Ersten Weltkriegs und jener, die dem Regime als »Mischlinge« gelten. Reinhard Heydrich (1904 – 1942) zeigt sich in einem Schreiben an Kube vom März 1942 verärgert.

Minsk, 1943: Commissioner General Wilhelm Kube (1887 – 1943, second from left). Kube continued to organise mass shootings of Belarusian Jews, but initially made efforts to protect certain deportees from German Reich territory – World War One veterans and those designated as »Mischlinge« (of »mixed race«). Reinhard Heydrich (1904 – 1942) sent an angry letter to Kube on this matter in March 1942.

Malyj Trostenez bei Minsk

April 1942

Auf Befehl Heydrichs: Suche nach einer Mordstätte

Ende März kommt Heydrich nach Minsk. Er kündigt für die nahe Zukunft neue Verschleppungen an. Der Zivilverwaltung unter Kube wird die Verfügungsgewalt über die ankommenden Menschen entzogen. Die Deportierten sollen nicht mehr in das Ghetto gebracht, sondern sofort ermordet werden. Heydrich beauftragt damit den Kommandeur der Sicherheitspolizei und des SD (KdS), Eduard Strauch. Dieser sucht nun einen Ort für das Verbrechen. Im April übernimmt seine Dienststelle eine Kolchose bei dem Dorf Malyj Trostenez und wandelt sie in das »Gut des Kommandeurs« um. Dort wird ein Lager eingerichtet. Im nahegelegenen Wald Blagowtschina macht der KdS eine schwer einsehbare Lichtung aus – hier soll geschossen werden.

April 1942

On Heydrich's orders: locating a murder site

Heydrich came to Minsk at the end of March. He announced that additional deportations were imminent. Kube's civil administration was stripped of its authority over the new arrivals. The deportees were now to be murdered on arrival instead of being transferred to the ghetto. Heydrich handed the responsibility for coordinating the murders to Eduard Strauch, Commanding Officer of the Security Police and SD (KdS). Strauch began to search for a location to carry out the murders. In April, his staff took over a kolkhoz near the village of Maly Trostenets and converted it into the »Commanding Officer's Estate«. A camp was set up here. The KdS selected a secluded glade in Blagovshchina forest to carry out the shootings.

Maly Trostenets near Minsk

Staatsarchiv Hamburg, Best. 213-12 Staatsanwaltschaft Landgericht – Nationalsozialistische Gewaltverbrechen Nr. 0597 Band 066

Malyj Trostenez, vermutlich Sommer 1943: Angehörige der volksdeutschen Kompanie; sie gehört offiziell zur Waffen-SS und wird zur Bewachung der Häftlinge eingesetzt. Unter ihren Angehörigen befinden sich Volksdeutsche aus Rumänien, Ungarn und Jugoslawien.

Maly Trostenets, probably in summer 1943: Members of the ethnic German (»Volksdeutsche«) unit in charge of guarding the prisoners. The unit was officially part of the Waffen-SS. Its members included ethnic Germans from Rumania, Hungary and Yugoslavia.

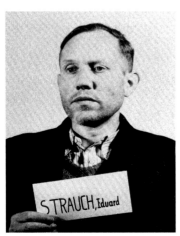

United States Holocaust Memorial Museum, Washington, D.C.

Eduard Strauch (1906 – 1955), Führer des Einsatzkommandos 2 der Einsatzgruppe A, später KdS in Minsk. Die Einrichtung des Lagers und Landgutes Malyj Trostenez geht auf ihn zurück. Der schwer alkoholkranke Strauch lässt sich häufig auf das Gut fahren, um hier seinen Rausch auszuschlafen. Er plant, sich nach dem Krieg in Malyj Trostenez niederzulassen. Er verstirbt in belgischer Haft.

Eduard Strauch (1906 – 1955), head of Einsatzkommando 2 of Einsatzgruppe A and later KdS in Minsk. He was responsible for setting up the camp and agricultural estate at Maly Trostenets. Strauch was a chronic alcoholic who often had himself driven to the estate so that he could sleep off his hangover. He planned to live in Maly Trostenets after the war. He died in a Belgian prison.

Mai 1942

Aus Mitteleuropa in den Tod

Am 6. Mai 1942 müssen etwa 1.000 jüdische Männer, Frauen und Kinder einen Zug im Wiener Aspangbahnhof besteigen. Der Transport nach Minsk ist fünf Tage unterwegs. Acht Menschen überleben die Strapazen nicht. Nahezu alle anderen werden am 11. Mai im Blagowtschina-Wald bei Malyj Trostenez durch Genickschüsse getötet. Bis September 1942 kommen über 14.000 weitere Juden aus dem Deutschen Reich hier an. Die meisten von ihnen lässt der KdS sofort erschießen oder in Gaswagen ersticken. Einige wenige werden zur Zwangsarbeit in den Betrieben des Zwangsarbeitslagers Malyj Trostenez ausgewählt. Auch tausende weißrussische Juden sterben bei Malyj Trostenez.

May 1942

Deportation from Central Europe to certain death

On 6 May 1942, around 1,000 Jewish men, women and children had to board a train at Aspang station in Vienna. The train took five days to get to Minsk. Eight people died during the traumatic journey. Virtually all of the others were shot in the back of the neck in Blagovshchina forest near Maly Trostenets on 11 May. Over 14,000 more Jews had been deported here from the territory of the German Reich by September 1942. The KdS had most of them shot or asphyxiated in gas vans upon arrival. A few were selected to carry out forced labour around the Maly Trostenets camp. Thousands of Belarusian Jews also died at Maly Trostenets.

Maly Trostenets near Minsk

Der 46-jährige Richard Hirsch aus Prag wird zusammen mit 1.000 anderen Juden am 22. August 1942 aus dem Ghettolager Theresienstadt nach Malyj Trostenez deportiert. Drei Tage später wird er bei der Ankunft in der Blagowtschina ermordet.

Richard Hirsch from Prague was deported from the Theresienstadt ghetto and concentration camp to Maly Trostenets on 22 August 1942 along with 1,000 other Jews. He was 46. He was murdered in Blagovshchina forest upon arrival at Maly Trostenets three days later.

Národní archiv, Prag, fond Policejní ředitelství Praha II., 1941-1950, H - Hirsch Richard sign. H 2485/1, karton 3294

Belorusskij Gosudarstwennyj Muzej istorii Welikoj Otetschestwennoj Wojny, Minsk

Im Sommer 1944 findet die sowjetische Außerordentliche Staatliche Kommission Richard Hirschs Koffer auf dem Gelände.

The Soviet Extraordinary State Commission found Richard Hirsch's suitcase on the site in summer 1944.

Malyj Trostenez bei Minsk

Juni 1942

Gaswagen

Juden und nichtjüdische Weißrussen werden bei Malyj Trostenez nicht nur erschossen. Der KdS setzt auch sogenannte Gaswagen ein, um Menschen umzubringen. Dabei handelt es sich um LKW, in deren abgedichteten Laderaum der Fahrer Abgase einleitet. Giftgas verwenden die Nationalsozialisten bereits seit 1940 zur Ermordung von Anstaltspatienten. Der systematische Mord an polnischen Juden in mobilen Gaswagen beginnt im Dezember 1941 im Lager Kulmhof (Chełmno). In Minsk sind solche Wagen möglicherweise bereits im gleichen Monat oder ab Anfang 1942 im Einsatz. Nach Zeugenaussagen morden die Deutschen mit fünf bis sechs, zeitweise zehn Fahrzeugen.

Juni 1942

Gas vans

Shooting was not the only method used to kill Jews and non-Jewish Belarusians at Maly Trostenets. The KdS also murdered people in so-called gas vans. The drivers pumped exhaust fumes into the hermetically sealed container at the back of these vans. The National Socialists had begun to use poison gas to kill psychiatric patients since 1940. The systematic murder of Polish Jews using mobile gas chambers started in December 1941 at the Chełmno camp. Gas vans began to operate in Minsk either in the same month or from early 1942. According to eyewitness reports, the Germans used five, six or sometimes ten vehicles at a time to carry out the murders.

Maly Trostenets near Minsk

Malyj Trostenez mit Dorfteich: Das Bild entsteht 1962 im Rahmen von Ermittlungen. Bei den Gaswagentötungen bildet der Teich zeitweise den Endpunkt des Mordprozesses. Nach dem Todeskampf der Menschen in den Wagen, müssen Zwangsarbeiter die Leichen, die oft ineinander verkrampft und mit Blut, Kot, Urin und Erbrochenem beschmiert sind, in Gruben werfen. Anschließend wird die Ladefläche am Teich abgewaschen. Die Angehörigen der Kommandos werden nach kurzer Zeit selbst erstickt.

Photo of Maly Trostenets showing the village lake. The picture dates from the investigations in 1962. At times, the final stage of the gas van murders took place at the lake. After the victims had lost their battle for life in the vans, forced labourers had to remove the corpses – which were often twisted together and covered in blood, faeces, urine and vomit – and throw them into pits. The back of the vans would then be washed out at the lake. Members of these prisoner commandos were themselves asphyxiated soon afterwards.

Legende der wichtigsten Erläuterungen
der sowjetischen Ermittler:

6   Standort des Hauses des Lagerkommandanten

8   Standort der Räume, in denen sich die Häftlinge befanden

10 Standort der Scheune, in der sich der Besitz befand, der den Verhafteten abgenommen wurde

12 Standort der Räume des früheren Wachpersonals

15 Standort des ehemaligen befestigten Bunkers des Kommandos

16 Standort der Scheune, in der die Gefangenen 1943 gehalten wurden

18 Richtung zum Erschießungsort

Key to the main features
identified by the Soviet investigators:

6   The camp commander's house

8   Prisoner barracks

10 Barn storing property taken from the prisoners

12 Accommodation for former guards

15 Site of the commando's former fortified bunker

16 Barn where the prisoners were held in 1943

18 Direction of the shooting ground

Latvijas Valsts arhīvs, Riga

Malyj Trostenez bei Minsk

Herbst 1943

Spurenbeseitigung und immer neue Morde

Im Oktober 1943 lösen die deutschen Besatzer das Minsker Ghetto auf und ermorden fast alle dort noch lebenden 2.000 Menschen. Etwa zur gleichen Zeit trifft in Malyj Trostenez das Sonderkommando 1005-Mitte ein. Unter seiner Leitung werden Insassen von Haftanstalten gezwungen, die Massengräber in der Blagowtschina zu öffnen und die Leichen zu verbrennen. Da die Deutschen weitere Morde planen, entsteht im Wald Schaschkowka bei Malyj Trostenez ein Krematorium. Gaswagen fahren nun bis hierhin. Angehörige der volksdeutschen Kompanie vernichten die Leichen anschließend. Ab März 1944 finden an diesem Ort auch Erschießungen statt. Die Getöteten sind oft nichtjüdische Zivilisten.

Autumn 1943

Removing the evidence and continuing the murders

The German occupying forces liquidated the Minsk ghetto in October 1943 and murdered virtually all of the 2,000 people still living there. At around the same time, Sonderkommando 1005-Mitte arrived at Maly Trostenets. This commando ordered prison inmates to dig up the mass graves in Blagovshchina forest and to burn the bodies. A crematorium was constructed in Shashkovka forest near Maly Trostenets because the Germans were planning to murder more people. Gas vans were now sent to this forest. Members of the ethnic German unit destroyed the bodies of the victims. Shootings were also carried out here from March 1944. Many non-Jewish civilians were among those murdered.

Georg Heuser (1913 – 1989), 1959. Heuser gehört zwischen Herbst 1941 und Sommer 1944 der Dienststelle des KdS bzw. BdS in Minsk an. Als Leiter der Abteilung IV (Gestapo) treibt er den Massenmord voran. Er erschießt eigenhändig Ghettobewohner und Insassen von Deportationszügen aus dem Deutschen Reich, im Herbst 1943 wohnt er der Verbrennung zweier Menschen bei lebendigen Leibe bei.

Georg Heuser (1913 – 1989) 1959. Heuser worked at the headquarters of the KdS and BdS in Minsk between autumn 1941 and summer 1944. As head of department IV (Gestapo) he pushed ahead with the programme of mass murder. In 1942, he shot ghetto residents and inmates of deportation trains arriving from the territory of the Reich. In autumn 1943, he witnessed two people being burnt alive.

Maly Trostenets near Minsk

Schaschkowka bei Minsk, Juli 1944: Foto der Außerordentlichen Staatlichen Kommission bei der Begehung der Vernichtungsstätte.

Shashkovka forest near Minsk, July 1944: Photo of the former extermination site taken by the Soviet Extraordinary State Commission.

Belorusskij Gosudarstwennyj Muzej istorii Welikoj Otetschestwennoj Woiny, Minsk

Erich Ehrlinger (1910 – 2004). Als Befehlshaber der Sicherheitspolizei und des SD (BdS) Rußland-Mitte und Weißruthenien ist er ab Oktober 1943 verantwortlich für die Ermordung nahezu aller noch in Minsk lebenden Juden.

Erich Ehrlinger (1910 – 2004). As Commander of the Security Police and SD (BdS) for Rußland-Mitte and Weißruthenien, Ehrlinger was responsible for organising the murder of almost all of the Jews left in Minsk from October 1943 onwards.

BArch R 9361_III_522639

Landeshauptarchiv Koblenz Best. 584,001 Nr. 8800 Bild Nr. 267

Malyj Trostenez bei Minsk

1943 bis Juni 1944

Partisanenkrieg und das letzte Verbrechen

Mit Andauern der Besatzung verstärkt sich der Widerstand gegen die Deutschen. Diese antworten mit Terror gegen Zivilisten. Allein im Februar 1943 soll der KdS bei Malyj Trostenez etwa 3.000 Zivilgefangene in Gaswagen erstickt haben. Die Geschichte der Vernichtungsstätte endet im Juni 1944 mit einem Massaker an bis zu 6.500 Insassen von Minsker Gefängnissen und den Häftlingen des Arbeitslagers wenige Tage vor dem Eintreffen der Roten Armee. Die Opfer werden in eine große Scheune am Südrand des Lagers gebracht, dort erschossen und anschließend verbrannt.

1943 to June 1944

Partisan warfare and the final crime

Resistance to the Germans increased as the occupation went on. The Germans responded with acts of terror against civilians. The KdS is said to have asphyxiated around 3,000 civilian prisoners in gas vans near Maly Trostenets in February 1943 alone. The extermination site was used for the last time in June 1944, when up to 6,500 inmates of Minsk prisons and the prisoners of the labour camp were massacred a few days before the arrival of the Red Army. The victims were taken to a large barn on the south side of the camp, where they were shot before being cremated.

Maly Trostenets near Minsk

Belorusskij Gosudarstwennyj Muzej istorii Welikoj Otetschestwennoj Wojny, Minsk

Da vom Lager- bzw. Gutskomplex aus Partisanen bekämpft werden, greifen diese den Ort vermehrt an. Im Januar 1944 wird Malyj Trostenez zum »Wehrdorf Klein Trostenieze« erklärt.

Partisans increasingly attacked the camp and estate at Maly Trostenets as campaigns against them were often launched from here. In January 1944, Maly Trostenets was declared the »Little Trostenets Combat Village« (sign).

Belorusskij Gosudarstwennyj Muzej istorii Welikoj Otetschestwennoj Wojny, Minsk

Aufnahmen der Außerordentlichen Staatlichen Kommission von den ausgebrannten Resten der Scheune mit den verkohlten Leichen hunderter Menschen. Die Kommission nennt für Malyj Trostenez eine Opferzahl von 206.500.

Photographs taken by the Soviet Extraordinary State Commission showing the burnt-out shell of the barn and the charred corpses of hundreds of people. The Commission gave a figure of 206,500 victims for Maly Trostenets.

1946 bis 1970

Juristische Aufarbeitung

Mit dem Prozess des sowjetischen »Volksgerichtes« in Minsk Anfang 1946 beginnt die Aufarbeitung der deutschen Verbrechen in Weißrussland. Rechtsstaatliche Prinzipien werden dabei allerdings nicht eingehalten. Die Richter verurteilen 14 der 18 angeklagten Wehrmachts- und Polizeiangehörigen zum Tode. Tausende verfolgen deren Erhängung auf der Minsker Pferderennbahn. In der Bundesrepublik findet 1949 ein erster Prozess zu den Morden im Minsker Ghetto statt, weitere Verfahren zu Minsk und Malyj Trostenez mit insgesamt 29 Angeklagten folgen erst in den 1960er Jahren. Die Justiz der DDR erhebt zum Tatkomplex Malyj Trostenez keine Anklage. Die österreichische Justiz sammelt zwar Ermittlungsergebnisse westdeutscher Behörden, stellt ein eingeleitetes Sammelverfahren jedoch 1968 ein. 1970 wird in Wien ein Gaswagenfahrer trotz Tatnachweis freigesprochen.

1946 to 1970

Trials

The trial held by the Soviet »People's Court« in Minsk in early 1946 marked the onset of confrontation with German crimes in Belarus. However, the tribunal did not operate according to the rule of law. The judges handed out death sentences to 14 of the 18 members of the Wehrmacht and police who had been charged. Thousands watched their hanging at Minsk racecourse. The first West German trial related to the murders in the Minsk ghetto took place in 1949, but additional trials related to crimes at Minsk and Maly Trostenets did not follow until the 1960s, when 29 men were put on trial. East Germany did not initiate any trials related to crimes at Maly Trostenets. The Austrian judiciary consulted the findings of the investigations conducted by the West German authorities and filed a class-action lawsuit, but the case was dropped in 1968. In 1970, one of the drivers of the gas vans was released without charge in Vienna despite there being evidence against him.

Georg Heuser auf dem Weg ins Landgericht Koblenz, 15. Februar 1962: Nachdem Ehrlinger bei Befragungen Heusers Namen erwähnt hatte, wird dieser im Juli 1959 verhaftet. Heuser war kurz zuvor zum Chef des Landeskriminalamts Rheinland-Pfalz ernannt worden. Das Gericht verurteilt Heuser 1963 wegen der gemeinschaftlichen Beihilfe zum Mord in 11.102 Fällen und weiterer Verbrechen zu 15 Jahren Zuchthaus. 1969 wird er aus der Haft entlassen.

Georg Heuser on his way to Koblenz district court, 15 February 1962. Heuser was arrested in 1959 after Ehrlinger mentioned his name whilst being interrogated. Heuser had just been appointed head of the Criminal Police Office for the State of Rhineland-Palatinate. In 1963, the court found him guilty of 11,102 counts of accessory to murder and of additional crimes. He was sentenced to 15 years in jail. He was released in 1969.

Maly Trostenets near Minsk

picture alliance / dpa / Fotograf: Harry Flesch

Erich Ehrlinger auf dem Weg ins Landgericht Karlsruhe, 16. Oktober 1961. Er wird wegen seiner Verbrechen in der besetzten Sowjetunion – seine Zeit als BdS in Minsk bleibt dabei ausgeklammert – zu 12 Jahren Haft verurteilt. Das Urteil erhält nie Rechtskraft. Ab 1965 befindet er sich auf freiem Fuß, 1969 erklärt ihn die Justiz für dauerhaft haft- und verhandlungsunfähig. Er stirbt 2004.

Erich Ehrlinger on his way to Karlsruhe State court, 16 October 1961. He was sentenced to 12 years in prison for crimes in the occupied Soviet Union – his time as BdS in Minsk was excluded from the conviction. The sentence was never finalised. He was released in 1965 and in 1969 the courts declared him permanently unfit to stand trial or to be imprisoned. He died in 2004.

dpa / Süddeutsche Zeitung Photo

Malyj Trostenez bei Minsk

Neues Deutschland vom 1. Februar 1963

»Opfer klagen an«, Neues Deutschland (ND), 1. Februar 1963. Der Heuser-Prozess wird zum bislang größten Verfahren zu den nationalsozialistischen Verbrechen in der Bundesrepublik. Zur gleichen Zeit produziert die Sowjetunion den Film »Die Opfer klagen an« über die Verbrechen in Malyj Trostenez und stellt Belastungsmaterial gegen Heuser auf einer Pressekonferenz vor. Das ND erhebt in seiner Ausgabe vom 1. Februar 1963 im Zusammenhang mit dem Prozess schwere Vorwürfe gegen die Bundesregierung.

»Victims are accusing« (»Opfer klagen an«), Neues Deutschland (ND), 1 February 1963. The Heuser trial was the most extensive trial of National Socialist crimes to take place in West Germany up to that time. The Soviet Union released the film » Victims are accusing« about the crimes in Maly Trostenets to coincide with the trial and presented incriminating evidence against Heuser at a press conference. The 1 February 1963 edition of the ND delivered a stinging critique of West Germany in connection with the trial.

„Opfer klagen an"

Erschütternder sowjetischer Dokumentarfilm über SS-Verbrechen

Berlin (ND). Millionen Menschen in beiden deutschen Staaten sahen am Donnerstagabend den sowjetischen Dokumentarfilm „Opfer klagen an". Er wurde vom Deutschen Fernsehfunk gesendet.

Mit erschütternden Originaldokumenten überführt der Film den in Koblenz vor Gericht stehenden langjährigen Chef der Kriminalpolizei von Rheinland-Pfalz, Georg Heuser, des hunderttausendfachen Mordes an Sowjetbürgern. Als SS-Führer erteilte er 1942 in Minsk seine Befehle zur Ermordung von Juden, Belorussen und Russen, von Männern, Frauen, Kindern und Greisen.

Vergeblich haben sich die Bonner Behörden bemüht, die wenigen Überlebenden der Massaker des Heuser und seiner zum Teil auf hohen Bonner Staatsposten sitzenden Komplicen durch Verweigerung der Einreisevisa an einer Zeugenaussage in Koblenz zu hindern. Die Sowjetbürger tun es in dem Dokumentarfilm, der mit der Mahnung an die Bonner Justiz endet, um der Gerechtigkeit, der Menschlichkeit und des Friedens willen Heuser und alle in Westdeutschland frei lebenden SS-Bestien, an deren Händen das Blut von Millionen klebt, ihrer gerechten Strafe zuzuführen.

Nur Nazis als Zeugen

Bonn (ADN). Mit verlogenen Behauptungen und Verleumdungen reagieren Bonn und die von ihm gelenkte Presse auf die internationale Pressekonferenz in Moskau, auf der am Mittwoch dokumentarisches Beweismaterial über die bestialischen Kriegsverbrechen der im Koblenzer SS-Prozeß angeklagten Faschisten der Weltöffentlichkeit zur Kenntnis gebracht wurde.

Der in Moskau getroffenen Feststellung, daß die westdeutsche Regierung sowjetischen Zeugen, die vor dem Koblenzer Gericht aussagen wollten, kein Einreisevisum erteilt hat, versuchte das Bonner Außenministerium mit einem „Dementi" zu begegnen. Es behauptete — wie DPA berichtet —, es würde „gegenwärtig die rechtlichen Möglichkeiten für die Gewährung der Visen" prüfen. Bisher traten als Zeugen nur Faschisten zur Entlastung der Mörder auf.

Der Bonner „Generalanzeiger" stellt sich schützend vor die auf der Pressekonferenz schwerbelasteten faschistischen Verbrecher, indem er die Sowjetunion beschuldigt, mit der Veröffentlichung des dokumentarischen Beweismaterials „in ein schwebendes Verfahren" einzugreifen.

Die offiziöse westdeutsche Nachrichtenagentur DPA läßt durchblicken, daß die Bonner Botschaft in Moskau nach einer Möglichkeit sucht, die Annahme der in Moskau veröffentlichten Dokumente zu verweigern.

1944 bis heute

Erinnerung

Nach dem Ende des Zweiten Weltkriegs ist Malyj Trostenez in der sowjetischen Erinnerungskultur auf vielfältige Weise sichtbar: in Gedenkveranstaltungen, im Schulunterricht oder anhand von Denkmälern. So entsteht 1963 ein Obelisk zum Gedenken an die Opfer. Wie auch anderswo in der Sowjetunion bleibt dort jedoch unerwähnt, dass es sich bei den meisten Ermordeten um Juden gehandelt hatte. In dem seit 1991 unabhängigen Weißrussland entstehen neue Dokumentations- und Erinnerungsinitiativen wie die deutsch-weißrussische Geschichtswerkstatt. Sie widmet sich der Forschung, der politischen Bildung und der Unterstützung von Überlebenden. Das Projekt zeugt auch davon, dass die in Malyj Trostenez begangenen Verbrechen in Deutschland verstärkt wahrgenommen werden.

Since 1944

Commemoration

Maly Trostenets was present in many aspects of Soviet commemorative culture in the post-war period, for example in remembrance ceremonies, school curricula or memorials. An obelisk was dedicated to the victims in 1963. However, as elsewhere in the Soviet Union there was no mention of the fact that most of those murdered were Jews. After Belarus gained independence in 1991, a new set of initiatives emerged with the aim of documenting the crimes and commemorating the victims. One example is the German-Belarusian History Project (Geschichtswerkstatt), which conducts research and political education projects and provides support to survivors. This project is also evidence that there is greater public awareness in Germany of the crimes committed in Maly Trostenets.

Maly Trostenets near Minsk

Belorusskij Gosudarstwennyj Muzej istorii Welikoj Otetschestwennoj Wojny, Minsk

Malyj Trostenez. 3. September 1944: Trauerkundgebung.
Die ersten Erinnerungszeichen werden nach und nach durch Gedenksteine ersetzt.

Maly Trostenets. 3 September 1944: Rally to mourn the victims.
The wooden crosses initially put on the site were gradually replaced with memorial stones.

Stiftung Denkmal für die ermordeten Juden Europas

Minsk, Geschichtswerkstatt, Modell der Gedenkanlage im Blagowtschina-Wald. Der von dem Bildhauer Leonid Lewin (1936 – 2014) entworfene Erinnerungsort soll 2017 gebaut werden.

Minsk, Rooms of the German-Belarusian History Project, model of the memorial complex in Blagovshchina forest. Designed by the sculptor Leonid Lewin (1936 – 2014), the memorial site is set for completion in 2017.

Biķernieki bei Riga
Biķernieki near Riga

Am 1. Juli 1941 besetzt die deutsche Wehrmacht die lettische Hauptstadt Riga. Lettland war seit 1918 unabhängig und 1940 von der Sowjetunion annektiert worden. Bereits in den ersten Tagen der deutschen Besatzung werden Juden in Riga ermordet, der Wald von Biķernieki (Hochwald, auch Bickern) im Osten der Stadt dient schon bald als Erschießungsstätte. Hier töten deutsche und lettische Täter bis 1944 über 30.000 Menschen in 55 Gruben. Unter ihnen sind jüdische und nichtjüdische Letten, sowjetische Kriegsgefangene und Juden aus dem Deutschen Reich. An keinem anderen Ort im besetzten Lettland werden mehr Menschen ermordet.

The German Wehrmacht occupied Riga, the Latvian capital, on 1 July 1941. Latvia had gained independence in 1918 but was annexed by the Soviet Union in 1940. Jews were murdered in Riga just a few days after the start of the German occupation. The woods at Biķernieki in the east of the city were soon used to carry out shootings. By 1944, German and Latvian perpetrators had killed over 30,000 people in 55 pits in this forest. The victims included Jewish and non-Jewish Latvians, Soviet prisoners of war and Jews from the territory of the German Reich. Biķernieki was the place where most people were killed in occupied Latvia.

Vorgeschichte

Riga bis zum deutschen Überfall

Die jüdische Minderheit hat einen festen Platz in der lettischen Gesellschaft. 1919 beteiligen sich viele Juden am Kampf für die Unabhängigkeit Lettlands. Ende der 1930er Jahre leben über 40.000 Juden in der Hauptstadt. Nach der sowjetischen Besetzung des Landes 1940 enteignet das Regime unter Diktator Josef Stalin (1878 – 1953) private Unternehmen, darunter viele Betriebe jüdischer Einwohner. Von den 15.000 Letten, die die sowjetischen Behörden im Juni 1941 nach Sibirien deportieren, ist etwa ein Drittel jüdisch. Als die Wehrmacht naht, hoffen tausende Juden – trotz der zuvor erlittenen Unterdrückung – im Inneren der Sowjetunion Schutz zu finden. Doch viele werden an der Grenze abgewiesen und müssen umkehren.

Prologue

Riga before the German invasion

The Jewish minority had an important place in Latvian society. Many Jews joined the war of Latvian independence in 1919. Over 40,000 Jews were living in the Latvian capital in the late 1930s. Following the Soviet occupation of Latvia in 1940, the dictatorship under Josef Stalin (1878 – 1953) appropriated private businesses, including many run by Jews. Around a third of the 15,000 Latvians deported to Siberia by the Soviet authorities in June 1941 were Jews. As the Wehrmacht approached, thousands of Jews hoped to find refuge inside the Soviet Union, despite the repression they had suffered under the regime. Many, however, were turned away at the border and had to go back.

Biķernieki near Riga

Choralsynagoge von Riga, Vorkriegszeit.

Riga's Great Choral Synagogue before the war.

Gemeinfrei

Latvijas Okupācijas muzejs, Riga

Riga, 1941: das Lettische Nationaltheater, geschmückt mit sowjetischen Fahnen und dem Schriftzug »Es lebe die UdSSR«. Hier war 1918 die lettische Republik ausgerufen worden. Im Sommer 1940 verliert das Land durch die sowjetische Besatzung seine Unabhängigkeit.

Riga, 1941: the Latvian National Theatre decorated with Soviet flags and the slogan »Long Live the USSR«. The Latvian Republic had been declared here in 1918. The country lost its independence in summer 1940, when it was occupied by the Soviets.

Juli bis September 1941

Der Beginn des Massenmords

Unmittelbar nach der Einnahme Rigas durch die Wehrmacht misshandeln und töten lettische Nationalisten unter Führung von Viktors Arājs Juden auf offener Straße und zerstören die Synagogen der Stadt. Die Führung der Einsatzgruppe A bezieht in Riga Quartier und ernennt Arājs zum Führer der lettischen Hilfssicherheitspolizei. Unter dem Kommando der Deutschen ermorden Arājs und seine Männer gemeinsam mit den Besatzern in Biķernieki bis September etwa 5.000 Menschen. Zunächst erschießen sie hauptsächlich jüdische Männer und Kommunisten.

July to September 1941

The start of mass murder

As soon as the Wehrmacht had taken Riga, a squad of Latvian nationalists led by Viktors Arājs hunted down and murdered Jews all over the city and destroyed the synagogues. The leadership of Einsatzgruppe A took up their quarters in Riga and appointed Arājs as commander of the Latvian auxiliary security police. Under German command, he and his men together with the occupants murdered several thousand people in Biķernieki forest. At first they mainly shot Jewish men and Communists. Around 5,000 people had died by September 1941.

Biķernieki near Riga

Riga, Anfang Juli 1941: Letten identifizieren Angehörige, die im Zentralgefängnis ermordet worden sind. Der sowjetische Geheimdienst hatte in den letzten Tagen vor dem Einmarsch der Wehrmacht zahlreiche Menschen verhaftet und erschossen. Die Deutschen zeigen die Leichen öffentlich. Sie geben Juden die Schuld am sowjetischen Terror, um den Hass der Letten zu schüren.

Riga, early July 1941: Latvians identifying family members who had been murdered in the city's central prison. In the days leading up to the German invasion, the Soviet secret service had arrested and shot a large number of people. The Germans put the corpses on public display. They blamed the Jews for the acts of Soviet terror in order to incite hatred of Jews among the Latvians.

Latvijas Okupācijas muzejs, Riga

Unbekannter Ort, 1943: Viktors Arājs (1910 – 1988, erste Reihe, 3.v.l.) mit seinem Kommando. Diesem gehören zunächst etwa 100, später über 1.500 Freiwillige an. Arājs und seine Männer töten in ganz Lettland zehntausende Juden.

Unknown location, 1943: Viktors Arājs (1910 – 1988, first row, third from left) with his commando. The commando started off with around 100 men but later had over 1,500 volunteers. Arājs and his men killed tens of thousands of Jews throughout Latvia.

Staatsarchiv Hamburg, Best. 213-12 Staatsanwaltschaft Landgericht – Nationalsozialistische Gewaltverbrechen Nr. 0044 Band 008

Dr. Rudolf Lange (1910 – 1945) ist zunächst Leiter eines Teilkommandos der Einsatzgruppe A und ab 1. Dezember 1941 Kommandeur der Sicherheitspolizei und des SD (KdS) in Riga. Die Männer von Viktors Arājs stehen unter seinem Befehl.

Dr. Rudolf Lange (1910 – 1945) was leader of a sub-commando of Einsatzgruppe A and appointed Commanding Officer of the Security Police and SD (KdS) in Riga on 1 December 1941. Viktors Arājs' commando took orders from him.

BArch VBS286_6400025453

Oktober bis Dezember 1941

Die Ermordung der Juden von Riga

Die deutschen Besatzer zerstören Rigas jüdisches Leben. Juden müssen sich registrieren lassen, den gelben Stern auf der Kleidung tragen und Zwangsarbeit verrichten. Im Oktober werden sie gezwungen, in ein Ghetto zu ziehen. In dieser Zeit entscheidet die nationalsozialistische Führung, tausende Juden aus dem Deutschen Reich nach Riga zu deportieren. Um Platz für die deutschen Juden zu schaffen, ordnet der Reichsführer-SS und Chef der deutschen Polizei, Heinrich Himmler (1900 – 1945), die Ermordung der lettischen Juden im Rigaer Ghetto an. Am 30. November und 8. Dezember erschießen deutsche und lettische Polizisten auf Befehl des Höheren SS- und Polizeiführers Friedrich Jeckeln (1895 – 1946) fast 27.000 Juden im Wald von Rumbula im Südosten der Stadt.

October to December 1941

The murder of Jews from Riga

The German occupying forces destroyed Jewish life in Riga. Jews had to register with the authorities, wear a yellow star on their clothing and work as forced labourers. They were forced to move into a ghetto in October. During this period, the National Socialist leadership decided to deport thousands of German Jews to Riga. Heinrich Himmler (1900 – 1945), Reich SS Leader and Chief of German Police, ordered the murder of the Latvian Jews in the Riga ghetto in order to make space for the German Jews. By command of Higher SS and Police Leader, Friedrich Jeckeln (1895 – 1946), German and Latvian policemen shot almost 27,000 Jews in Rumbula forest in the south-east of the city on 30 November and 8 December.

Bikernieki near Riga

Walter Stahlecker (1900 – 1942), um 1930. Er ist enger Mitarbeiter des Chefs des Reichssicherheitshauptamts Reinhard Heydrich (1904–1942). Als Führer der Einsatzgruppe A und später als Befehlshaber der Sicherheitspolizei und des SD Ostland ist Stahlecker wesentlich am Massenmord beteiligt.

Walter Stahlecker (1900 – 1942), around 1930. He was a close associate of Reinhard Heydrich (1904–1942), who was in charge of the Reich Security Main Office. Stahlecker was heavily involved in the mass murders as head of Einsatzgruppe A and later as Commander of the Security Police and SD (BdS) for Ostland.

Staatsarchiv Ludwigsburg

Anfang 1942 sendet Stahlecker einen Bericht über das Vorgehen der Mordkommandos im Reichskommissariat Ostland an Heydrich. Er fügt eine Karte bei. Darauf verzeichnet er die zwischen Oktober 1941 und Januar 1942 ermordeten sowie die geschätzte Zahl der noch lebenden Juden. Ein weiteres Exemplar der Karte – das hier gezeigte – verbleibt in Riga.

In early 1942, Stahlecker sent a report to Heydrich outlining the activities of the murder squads in the Reich Commissariat Ostland. He included a map, on which he marked the number of Jews murdered between October 1941 and January 1942 and the estimated number of Jews still alive. An additional copy of the map – reproduced here – was kept in Riga.

Latvijas Valsts vēstures Arhīvs, Riga

Dezember 1941 bis März 1942

Die Deportation mitteleuropäischer Juden nach Riga

Die nach Riga deportierten Juden – über 25.000 Menschen – werden ins Ghetto und das verfallene Gut Jungfernhof in der Nähe der Stadt gepfercht. Tausende müssen Zwangsarbeit leisten. Im März 1942 wählen Angehörige der KdS-Dienststelle im Jungfernhof etwa 5.000 Frauen und Kinder aus, angeblich für leichtere Arbeiten in einer Konservenfabrik. Tatsächlich werden sie in Biķernieki erschossen. Wie im Rahmen dieser »Aktion Dünamünde« töten Deutsche und lokale Helfer immer wieder Menschen in Biķernieki.

December 1941 to March 1942

The deportation of central european Jews to Riga

Over 25,000 Jews were deported to Riga. They were crammed into the ghetto or the rundown Jungfernhof estate near the city. Thousands had to work as forced labourers. In March 1942, members of the KdS office selected 5,000 women and children at Jungfernhof, claiming that they were going to be doing non-strenuous work in a preserves factory. They were in fact shot at Biķernieki. This »Aktion Dünamünde« was one of a series of murders carried out by Germans and local collaborators in Biķernieki forest.

Biķernieki near Riga

Stadtarchiv Stuttgart

Durchgangslager Killesberg bei Stuttgart, November 1941, Standbild aus einem Propagandafilm. Über tausend württembergische Juden müssen sich hier zur Deportation nach Riga einfinden.

Still of Killesberg transit camp near Stuttgart taken from a propaganda film, November 1941. Over a thousand Jews from Württemberg had to assemble here prior to their deportation to Riga.

Städtisches Kunstmuseum Spendhaus, Reutlingen

Selbstportrait Alice Haarburger (1891 – 1942), 1930er Jahre. Die erfolgreiche Reutlinger Malerin ist unter den Juden, die vom Stuttgarter Killesberg nach Riga deportiert werden. Während der Fahrt kümmert sie sich um Kranke und Schwache. Laut einer Zeugenaussage wird sie am 26. März 1942 im Rahmen der »Aktion Dünamünde« in Riga Biķernieki ermordet.

Self-portrait of Alice Haarburger (1891 – 1942), 1930s. Haarburger, a succesful painter, was among the Jews who were deported from Stuttgart Killesberg to Riga. She looked after sick and physically weak deportees during the journey. According to a witness statement, she was killed in Riga Biķernieķi as part of »Aktion Dünamünde« on 26 March 1942.

Biķernieki bei Riga

Staatsarchiv Hamburg, Best. 213-12 Staatsanwaltschaft Landgericht –
Nationalsozialistische Gewaltverbrechen Nr. 0044 Band 034

Ghetto von Riga, vermutlich Dezember 1941: Die Juden aus dem Reich, die hier ankommen, finden das Ghetto verwüstet vor. Die dort zuvor eingesperrten lettischen Juden waren kurz zuvor ermordet worden.

Riga ghetto, probably in December 1941. Jews arriving here from the German Reich found it in a state of devastation. The Latvian Jews previously held here had been murdered shortly before.

BArch Bild 101 III-Duerr-053-30 / Fotograf: Dürr

Salaspils, Winter 1941/42: Die Aufnahmen eines Angehörigen einer Propaganda-Kompanie der Wehrmacht zeigen jüdische Männer bei der Zwangsarbeit. 1.500 deutsche Juden müssen das Lager errichten. Über die Hälfte von ihnen stirbt an Kälte und Hunger. Die Überlebenden werden ins Ghetto verschleppt. Das »erweiterte Arbeits- und Erziehungslager Salaspils« ist ab Mai 1942 besonders für lettische »Arbeitsverweigerer« und politische Gefangene vorgesehen. Es ist das größte Lager im besetzten Lettland.

Salaspils, winter 1941/42: Jewish forced labourers photographed by a member of a Wehrmacht propaganda unit. 1,500 German Jews were forced to set up the camp. More than half of them died of hunger and cold. The survivors were transferred to the ghetto. The »expanded police prison and labour correctional camp« was the biggest camp in occupied Latvia. After May 1942, the inmates were mainly Latvian »work shirkers« and political prisoners.

Biķernieki near Riga

Muzejs »Ebreji Latvijā«, Riga

Bei Ankunft der jüdischen Deportierten ist das Gut Jungfernhof verwahrlost. Sie müssen bei eisigen Temperaturen und spärlicher Nahrung Baracken errichten. Zwischen Winter 1941 und Frühjahr 1942 sind hier insgesamt über 10.000 Menschen eingepfercht. Das Foto zeigt die Überreste des Jungfernhofs heute.

The Jungfernhof estate was very run down when the Jewish deportees arrived. They had to set up barracks in freezing temperatures. Food was extremely scarce. Over 10,000 people were crammed into the estate between winter 1941 and spring 1942. The photo shows the remains of Jungfernhof today.

BArch R_9361_III_113921

Rudolf Seck (1908 – 1974). Der Landwirt wird 1941 nach Riga versetzt. KdS Rudolf Lange beauftragt ihn mit der Bewachung der auf dem Jungfernhof eingepferchten Juden. Seck wählt unter anderem im Rahmen der »Aktion Dünamünde« Juden zur Ermordung aus, die als nicht arbeitsfähig gelten. Seck muss sich nach dem Krieg vor Gericht verantworten. Er wird 1951 für den Mord an acht Menschen auf dem Jungfernhof, nicht jedoch für seine Beteiligung an der »Aktion Dünamünde« zu lebenslanger Haft verurteilt.

Rudolf Seck (1908 – 1974). Seck, a farmer, was transferred to Riga in 1941. KdS Rudolf Lange gave him the task of guarding the Jews detained at Jungfernhof. Seck selected Jews who were considered unfit to work to be murdered during »Aktion Dünamünde«. Seck was brought to trial after the war. He received a life sentence in 1951 for the murder of eight people at Jungfernhof, but was not charged with involvement in »Aktion Dünamünde«.

April 1942 bis Dezember 1943

**Zwangsarbeit und Vernichtung.
Konzentrationslager**

Nach der »Aktion Dünamünde« befinden sich noch etwa 12.000 deutsche und 2.000 lettische Juden im Rigaer Ghetto. Im Sommer 1943 befiehlt Himmler die Auflösung des Ghettos und die Überführung der Häftlinge ins Konzentrationslager Kaiserwald im Norden der Stadt. Er verbietet, jüdische Zwangsarbeiter außerhalb des Lagers einzusetzen. Daraufhin entscheidet Friedrich Jeckeln, die Juden direkt an deren Arbeitsstätten unterzubringen. Diese Orte werden offiziell zu KZ-Außenlagern erklärt. Den Häftlingen, die keine Arbeit verrichten können, droht die Ermordung. In den letzten Tagen des Ghettos im November werden etwa 2.000 Kinder und Geschwächte nach Auschwitz deportiert.

April 1942 to December 1943

**Forced labour and annihilation.
The concentration camps**

Following »Aktion Dünamünde« there were still around 12,000 German and 2,000 Latvian Jews in the Riga ghetto. In summer 1943, Himmler ordered the liquidation of the ghetto and for the prisoners to be transferred to Kaiserwald concentration camp in the north of the city. He refused permission for Jewish forced labourers to be deployed outside the camp. Friedrich Jeckeln subsequently decided to house the Jews where they were working. These sites were officially designated as sub-camps of the concentration camps. Prisoners who could not work were likely to be killed. Around 2,000 children and frail prisoners were deported to Auschwitz in the final days of the ghetto that November.

Biķernieki near Riga

Staatsarchiv Hamburg, Best. 213-12 Staatsanwaltschaft Landgericht –
Nationalsozialistische Gewaltverbrechen Nr. 0044 Band 034

Baracken des 1943 errichteten Konzentrationslagers Riga-Kaiserwald. Hier registriert die SS zunächst Insassen der in Lettland und Litauen aufgelösten Ghettos. Sie weist sie in Außenlager ein, in denen häufig nicht einmal Baracken vorhanden sind. Die Juden müssen Schwerstarbeit für die Industrie oder im Straßenbau leisten. Wöchentlich sucht die Lagerkommandantur geschwächte Häftlinge aus, die erschossen werden. Die Bilder entstehen nach der Befreiung.

Barracks at the Riga-Kaiserwald concentration camp, which was established in 1943. The SS registered inmates of the liquidated ghettos of Latvia and Lithuania here. They assigned them to sub-camps, which in many cases did not even have any barracks. The Jews had to carry out back-breaking manual labour for the industry or to build roads. Every week, the camp commandants singled out frail prisoners and shot them. These photographs were taken after liberation.

Biķernieki bei Riga

Januar bis Dezember 1944

Deportationen nach Westen und Kriegsende

Als im Januar die Rote Armee naht, müssen jüdische Häftlinge aus Kaiserwald die Massengräber in Biķernieki und Rumbula öffnen und die Leichen verbrennen. Anschließend werden sie getötet. Gleichzeitig weiten die Kommandanten der Lager die »Selektionen« aus: Tausende Kinder und Kranke werden in Biķernieki erschossen. Ab August deportieren die Deutschen die Mehrheit der arbeitsfähigen Häftlinge ins Konzentrationslager Stutthof bei Danzig. Wer ihnen zu schwach scheint, wird getötet. Das deutsche Besatzungspersonal kann ins Reichsinnere fliehen. Bei der Einnahme Rigas im Oktober 1944 findet die Rote Armee die Lager geräumt vor.

January to December 1944

Deportations westwards and the end of the war

As the Red Army advanced in January, Jewish prisoners from Kaiserwald were forced to open up the mass graves at Biķernieki and Rumbula and cremate the bodies. They were then killed. During this period, the camp commandants also extended the number of »selections« and thousands of children and sick prisoners were shot at Biķernieki. In August, the Germans deported most of the prisoners who were able to work to the Stutthof concentration camp near Danzig. They killed anyone who they considered to be too weak. The German occupying forces managed to flee back into Reich territory. By the time that the Red Army regained control of Riga in October 1944, the camps had been vacated.

Biķernieki near Riga

Biķernieki, November 1944: Angehörige der sowjetischen Außerordentlichen Staatlichen Kommission beim Öffnen der Massengräber. Die Bilder stammen aus Akten zu einem Gerichtsverfahren. Sie zeigen außerdem Wertsachen der Ermordeten, die die Kommission bei der Untersuchung der Mordstätte fand.

Biķernieki, November 1944: Members of the Soviet Extraordinary State Commission at the excavation of mass graves and valuables belonging to the murdered. The commission found these objects while investigating the execution site. The pictures are from files prepared for a criminal proceeding.

Staatsarchiv Hamburg, Best. 213-12 Staatsanwaltschaft Landgericht – Nationalsozialistische Gewaltverbrechen Nr. 0044 Band 034

1945 bis 1990

Verschwundene Täter, vergessene Opfer?

In den letzten Kriegsmonaten evakuieren die Deutschen auch zehntausende Letten, die führend in den Besatzungsapparat eingebunden sind, in das Gebiet des Deutschen Reichs. Ab 1945 fahnden die Besatzungsmächte dort auch in den Kriegsgefangenen- und Flüchtlingslagern nach Tätern. Viele können jedoch in Deutschland, Amerika und Australien untertauchen. In der Sowjetunion verurteilen Gerichte hunderte Letten in meist nichtöffentlichen Verfahren wegen Kollaboration zu Lagerhaft in Sibirien oder zum Tode. Die lettische Presse berichtet über die Verbrechen in Biķernieki, Rumbula und Salaspils. Selten wird jedoch erwähnt, dass die Opfer Juden waren.

1945 to 1990

Invisible perpetrators, forgotten victims?

During the last few months of the war, the Germans also evacuated tens of thousands of Latvians who held leading positions in the occupation administration to German Reich territory. The Allied occupation forces searched for perpetrators in the former prisoner of war and refugee camps in Germany after 1945. However, many perpetrators went into hiding in Germany, America and Australia. The Soviet Union held a series of mainly secret trials during which they convicted hundreds of Latvians of collaboration and either sent them to labour camps in Siberia or sentenced them to death. The Latvian press reported on the crimes in the forests of Biķernieki and Rumbula and in Salaspils but rarely mentioned that the victims were Jews.

Biķernieki near Riga

Salaspils, 1969: Einweihung der größten Gedenkstätte des Landes. Die sowjetische Regierung setzt in Salaspils den Kampf der Sowjetunion gegen das nationalsozialistische Regime in Szene.

Salaspils, 1969: Inauguration of the largest memorial site in Latvia. At the memorial, the Soviet government placed the emphasis on the Soviet struggle against the National Socialist regime.

Valsts kultūras pieminekļu aizsardzības inspekcija, Riga, Inv.Nr. P-3329-4

Staatsarchiv Hamburg, Best. 213-12 Staatsanwaltschaft Landgericht – Nationalsozialistische Gewaltverbrechen Nr. 0044 Band 022

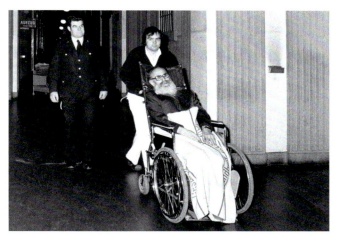

Foto: Kai Greiser

Reisepass, ausgestellt auf den »Staatenlosen« Viktor Zeibots, 1975. Viktors Arājs gerät nach Kriegsende in britische Gefangenschaft, kann jedoch unter dem Geburtsnamen seiner Ehefrau, Zeibots, untertauchen.

Passport for the »stateless« Viktor Zeibots, 1975. Viktors Arājs was captured by the British after the war but he managed to escape and went into hiding, adopting the surname Zeibots, his wife's maiden name.

Hamburg, 8. Dezember 1978: Viktors Arājs während des Prozesses gegen ihn. 1979 verurteilt ihn das Landgericht Hamburg wegen Mordes an 13.000 Menschen in Rumbula am 8. Dezember 1941 zu einer lebenslangen Freiheitsstrafe. Die Verbrechen in Biķernieki können ihm nicht nachgewiesen werden.

Hamburg, 8 December 1978: Viktors Arājs during his trial. In 1979, Hamburg district court sentenced him to life for the murder of 13,000 people in Rumbula on 8 December 1941. There was not enough evidence to charge him with the crimes at Biķernieki.

1991 bis 2016

Ein würdiger Gedenkort

Lettland erlangt 1991 die staatliche Unabhängigkeit wieder. Nach einem bald drauf geschlossenen Abkommen mit der Bundesrepublik Deutschland errichtet der Volksbund Deutsche Kriegsgräberfürsorge mit Mitteln des Auswärtigen Amts eine Gedenkstätte für die in Riga ermordeten jüdischen Deutschen. 2001 wird die Anlage in Biķernieki eröffnet. Betreut wird sie unter anderem von deutschen Städten, aus denen 1941/42 Deportationszüge nach Riga abgingen. An anderen Orten der nationalsozialistischen Verbrechen in Riga erinnern seit den 1960er Jahren Denkmäler an die Opfer.

1991 to 2016

A fitting memorial

Latvia regained independence in 1991. Soon afterwards, the country signed an agreement with Germany, which gave the German War Graves Commission the responsibility for establishing a memorial site for the German Jews murdered in Riga. The Biķernieki memorial site was inaugurated in 2001. It was financed by the German Foreign Office. German towns from which deportation trains left for Riga in 1941/42 contribute to the upkeep of the site. Since the 1960s, memorials to the victims of National Socialist crimes in Riga have been put up at a number of sites where crimes took place.

Biķernieki near Riga

Stiftung Denkmal für die ermordeten Juden Europas / Fotograf: Ronnie Golz

Stiftung Denkmal für die ermordeten Juden Europas / Fotograf: Ronnie Golz

Gedenkstätte Biķernieki, 2001: Das zentrale Mahnmal ist von Granitsteinen umgeben. Sie benennen die deutschen, österreichischen und tschechischen Städte, aus denen Juden nach Riga deportiert wurden.

Biķernieki memorial site, 2001: The central memorial is surrounded by granite stones with inscriptions listing the German, Austrian and Czech cities from which Jews were deported to Riga.

Gedenkstätte Rumbula, eingeweiht 2002. Im Zentrum steht eine Menora. Um sie herum sind Granitsteine angebracht, die die Namen der Ermordeten tragen. Bereits in den 1960er Jahren hatten jüdische Aktivisten damit begonnen, die Gräber mit Steinen zu markieren. Sie hielten Gedenkveranstaltungen ab und errichteten ein erstes Denkmal.

The Rumbula memorial site, which dates from 2002. There is a menorah in the centre surrounded by granite stones bearing the names of the murdered. Back in the 1960s, Jewish activists started to place stones on the graves. They held commemorations and constructed the first memorial.

Fotografin: Joana Pape

Reutlingen, Sandbergerstraße 12: Stolpersteine für Alice Haarburger, ihre Mutter Fanny und ihre Tante Emma Hess. 1992 widmet sich in Baden-Württemberg eine Ausstellung dem Schicksal der Künstlerin, eine 2016 eröffnete Schau stellt ihre Gemälde in den Vordergrund.

Reutlingen, Sandbergerstraße 12: »Stolpersteine« (stumbling stones) for Alice Haarburger, her mother Fanny and her aunt Emma Hess. There was an exhibition on the life of the artist in Baden-Württemberg in 1992 and a 2016 exhibition focuses on her works.

Ponary bei Wilna
Paneriai near Vilnius

Der kleine Ort Ponary (Paneriai) unweit von Wilna (Wilno, Vilnius) gehört zwischen den Weltkriegen zu Polen. 1939 besetzt die Rote Armee die Region Wilna, die Litauen zugeschlagen wird. Ab 1940 ist Litauen Teil der Sowjetunion. Am 24. Juni 1941 marschiert die Wehrmacht in Wilna ein. Bereits in den ersten Tagen der Besatzung beginnen Angehörige der Einsatzgruppe B und litauische Nationalisten, Juden aus Wilna in Ponary zu ermorden. Der Ort wird zwischen Juli 1941 und September 1944 zur Mordstätte von 60.000 bis 100.000 Juden, Polen, Kriegsgefangenen und politisch Verfolgten.

The small village of Paneriai (Ponary), near Vilnius (Wilno), was part of Poland during the inter-war period. In 1939, the Red Army occupied the region of Vilnius. It was given over to Lithuania. Lithuania was incorporated into the Soviet Union in 1940. The Wehrmacht occupied Vilnius on 24 June 1941. Just a few days later, members of Einsatzgruppe B and Lithuanian nationalists began murdering Jews from Vilnius in Paneriai. From July 1941 to September 1944, between 60,000 and 100,000 Jews, Poles, prisoners of war and political opponents were murdered at the site.

Vorgeschichte

Wilna und Ponary bis zum deutschen Überfall

Wilna, das »Jerusalem des Nordens«, ist bis 1941 eines der weltweit bedeutendsten Zentren jüdischer Gelehrsamkeit. Mehrere Talmud-Hochschulen und zahlreiche Synagogen prägen das Stadtbild. In der Zwischenkriegszeit leben 60.000 Juden in der Stadt. Mit der sowjetischen Besetzung 1940 erfährt das jüdische Leben auch in Wilna einen jähen Einschnitt. Die Behörden unterdrücken die jüdische Kultur und beschlagnahmen Eigentum von Juden.
Im malerischen Vorort Ponary, das einst Napoleon »auf Händen nach Frankreich tragen« wollte, beginnt die Rote Armee mit Baumaßnahmen. Sie hebt Gruben für eine Heizöl-Tankanlage aus, die jedoch nie fertiggestellt wird. Diesen Ort wählen die deutschen Besatzer später für den Massenmord aus.

Prologue

Vilnius and Paneriai before the German invasion

Before 1941, Vilnius was one of the most important centres of Jewish scholarship in the world and became known as the »Jerusalem of the North«. The city had several Talmud schools and a large number of synagogues. 60,000 Jews lived in Vilnius in the inter-war period. The Soviet occupation of 1940 marked the end of Jewish life as it had been in Vilnius. The Soviet authorities suppressed Jewish culture and confiscated Jewish property.
Paneriai was a picturesque suburb of Vilnius that Napoleon had once wanted to »put in the palm of his hands and take back to France«. Following the occupation, the Red Army began construction work in Paneriai. They dug pits for a fuel oil storage facility, but the project was never completed. The German occupying forces later chose Paneriai as a location to carry out mass murders.

Ponary, 23. Mai 1939: Schüler des jüdischen Wirtschaftsgymnasiums von Wilna bei einem Ausflug. In der Zwischenkriegszeit ist Ponary ein beliebter Ferienort für die Einwohner Wilnas. Über das Schicksal der abgebildeten Personen ist nichts bekannt.

Paneriai, 23 May 1939: Pupils from the Jewish Commercial Grammar School in Vilnius on a school trip. Paneriai was a popular holiday resort for the residents of Vilnius during the inter-war period. Nothing is known about what happened to the group pictured here.

Paneriai near Vilnius

Lietuvos centrinis valstybės archyvas, Wilna

Wilna, Stadtansicht, Zwischenkriegszeit.
View of the city of Vilnius during the interwar period.

Beit Lohamei Haghetaot, Kibbuz der Ghettokämpfer

Juni bis August 1941

Der Beginn der Massenmorde

Direkt nach der Einnahme Wilnas durch die Wehrmacht beginnen litauische Nationalisten, Juden anzugreifen und zu töten. Mit Ankunft des Einsatzkommandos 9 Anfang Juli wird das Morden systematisch: Über 5.000 Wilnaer Juden werden inhaftiert und in Ponary erschossen, wie an vielen Orten zunächst hauptsächlich Männer. Anfang August erreicht das Einsatzkommando 3 unter der Führung Karl Jägers (1888 – 1959) die Stadt. Seine Männer töten nun auch jüdische Frauen und Kinder. Jäger koordiniert bis Ende des Monats den Mord an über 50.000 Juden in ganz Litauen.

June to August 1941

The start of mass murder

Lithuanian nationalists started attacking and killing Jews as soon as the Wehrmacht had captured Vilnius. Systematic murder began with the arrival of Einsatzkommando 9 at the start of July. Over 5,000 Jews from Vilnius were detained and shot in Paneriai. As in many other regions, most of the initial victims were men. Einsatzkommando 3, which was headed by Karl Jäger (1888 – 1959), reached the city at the beginning of August. Its members now also started killing Jewish women and children. By the end of the month, Jäger had overseen the murder of at least 50,000 Jews in the whole country.

Paneriai near Vilnius

Ponary, Juli 1941: Jüdische Männer in den Gruben. Auf den Bildern sind auch litauische Hilfswillige und Deutsche in Uniform zu erkennen, vermutlich Angehörige des Einsatzkommandos 9.

Paneriai, July 1941: Jewish men in the pits. The picture also shows Lithuanian volunteers and Germans in uniform, probably members of Einsatzkommando 9.

Archives of the YIVO Institute for Jewish Research, New York

September bis Oktober 1941

Das Ghetto

Nach kurzer Zeit übernimmt die Zivilverwaltung die Kontrolle über Litauen: Das Land wird Teil des Reichskommissariats Ostland. Am 6. September zwingt die Zivilverwaltung die Juden in zwei abgeriegelte Bereiche der Altstadt. Im »großen Ghetto« werden 45.000 Zwangsarbeiter, im »kleinen Ghetto« 12.000 Alte und Schwache zusammengedrängt. Bis Ende Oktober erschießen Angehörige der inzwischen eingerichteten stationären Polizeidienststelle fast alle Insassen des »kleinen Ghettos« in Ponary.

September to October 1941

The ghetto

The civil administration soon took control of Lithuania, which was now amalgamated into the Reich Commissariat Ostland. The civil administration forced the Jews to move into two sectioned-off districts of the old town on 6 September. 45,000 forced labourers were crowded together in the »large ghetto« and 12,000 elderly and physically weak Jews in the »small ghetto«. By the end of October, officers from the stationary police office now established in the city had shot virtually all of those living in the »small ghetto« in Paneriai.

Paneriai near Vilnius

Beit Lohamei Haghetaot, Kibbuz der Ghettokämpfer

Der Gebietskommissar von Wilna Hans Christian Hingst (Mitte, in Uniform) und sein Referent für Judenangelegenheiten Franz Murer (hinten rechts, 1912 – 1994). Sie haben die Aufsicht über das Ghetto. Murer ist unter den Juden Wilnas für seine Brutalität bekannt. So schlägt der »Herr des Ghettos« zwei Männern, die er mit Lebensmitteln aufgreift, die Zähne aus und erschießt Mütter vor den Augen ihrer Kinder.

Hans Christian Hingst (centre, wearing a uniform), the District Commissar of Vilnius, and Franz Murer (at the back, right, 1912 – 1994), his deputy for Jewish affairs. The two men were in charge of the ghetto. Murer was known for his brutality towards the Jews in Vilnius. On one occasion, the self-styled »Master of the Ghetto« knocked two men's teeth out after he caught them with food and he shot mothers in front of their children.

Ponary bei Wilna

Yad Vashem, Jerusalem

Martin Weiss (1903 – 1984) ist Angehöriger des Einsatzkommandos 3 und ab September 1941 bei der Außenstelle des Kommandeurs der Sicherheitspolizei und des SD (KdS) Litauen in Wilna beschäftigt. Er ist unter anderem Befehlshaber des dortigen litauischen Sonderkommandos. Weiss ist direkt an der Ermordung der Wilnaer Juden in Ponary beteiligt. Im Ghetto demütigt, prügelt und tötet er immer wieder Männer, Frauen und Kinder.

Martin Weiss (1903 – 1984) was a member of Einsatzkommando 3. In September 1941, he worked at the office of the Commanding Officer of the Security Police and SD (KdS) for Lithuania in Vilnius. One of his posts was as head of the Lithuanian Sonderkommando in Vilnius. Weiss was directly involved in the murder of Jews from Vilnius in Paneriai. He repeatedly humiliated, beat and murdered men, women and children in the ghetto.

Archives of the YIVO Institute for Jewish Research, New York

Ponary, Juli 1941: Jüdische Männer in den Gruben der ehemaligen Heizöl-Tankanlage, offenbar kurz vor ihrer Ermordung.

Paneriai, July 1941: Jewish men in the pits of the former fuel oil storage facility, apparently just before their murder.

Paneriai near Vilnius

Valstybinis Vilniaus Gaono žydų muziejus, Wilna

Aufzeichnungen von Kazimierz Sakowicz (1894 – 1944) auf einem Kalenderblatt vom Oktober 1941. Der in Ponary lebende polnische Journalist beschreibt in seinem Tagebuch von 1941 bis 1943 die Morde und beobachtet Anwohner, die sich am Eigentum der Opfer bereichern. Aus Angst, entdeckt zu werden, schreibt Sakowicz auf losen Blättern oder Kalenderseiten, die er vergräbt. Im Juli 1944 wird er angeschossen und erliegt seinen Verletzungen. Sein erstmals 1999 veröffentlichtes Tagebuch gehört zu den umfangreichsten Quellen des Holocaust in Litauen.

Diary entry by Kazimierz Sakowicz (1894 – 1944) on a calendar list of October 1941. The Polish journalist lived in Paneriai and kept a diary between 1941 and 1943. He witnessed the murders and described how residents were profiting from the property of the victims. Fearful of being found out, Sakowicz wrote on loose sheets of paper or on calendars, which he would bury. He was shot at in July 1944 and died of his injuries. His diary was published for the first time in 1999 and is one of the most detailed sources on the Holocaust in Lithuania.

November bis Dezember 1941

»Wo sind unsere Brüder aus dem zweiten Ghetto?«

Ende Oktober befinden sich noch etwa 27.000 Menschen im »großen Ghetto«. Als Zwangsarbeiter können viele sich und ihre Angehörigen vorerst vor der Ermordung retten. Aus dem Umland fliehen zahlreiche Juden nach Wilna, um unterzutauchen. Doch die litauischen Schutzmänner machen Jagd auf diese Versteckten. Über 33.500 Juden werden bis Mitte Dezember angeblich in ein »zweites Ghetto« in Ponary gebracht. Tatsächlich erschießen die Täter sie dort. Trotz der Bemühungen der Deutschen, diese Massenmorde geheim zu halten, verbreiten sich in der Bevölkerung Gerüchte.

November to December 1941

»Where are our brothers from the second ghetto?«

At the end of October, there were still around 27,000 people living in the »large ghetto«. Many were initially able to save themselves and their relatives by working as forced labourers. Many Jews fled the outlying regions in order to go into hiding in Vilnius. However, the Lithuanian police hunted them down. More than 33,500 Jews were allegedly brought to a »second ghetto« in Paneriai until mid-December. In fact, the perpetrators killed them there. Rumours of the mass murders spread throughout the city despite German attempts to keep them quiet.

Paneriai near Vilnius

Yad Vashem, Jerusalem

Zitat Kovner, deutsch:
Ehrenburg, Ilja; Grossman, Wassili; Lustiger, Arno (Hrsg.):
Das Schwarzbuch. Der Genozid an den sowjetischen Juden,
Reinbeck bei Hamburg 1994.

Jonischken (Joniškis, Litauen), Nachkriegszeit: Abba Kovner (links, 1918 – 1988) und ein weiterer Partisan. Kovner hatte sich 1941 der jüdischen Widerstandsbewegung angeschlossen. Eine von ihm verfasste Erklärung war am Silvesterabend 1941 bei einem heimlichen Treffen einiger Ghettoinsassen vorgetragen und anschließend im Ghetto von Wilna verteilt worden. Kovner rief zum Widerstand auf:

Joniškis (Lithuania) after the war: Abba Kovner (left, 1918 – 1988) and another partisan. Kovner joined the Jewish resistance in 1941. A manifesto written by him and presented at a secret meeting attended by a number of ghetto residents on New Year's Eve 1941 was then distributed throughout the Vilnius ghetto. Kovner called for Jewish resistance:

»Wo sind unsere Brüder aus dem zweiten Ghetto? Von denen, die vor das Ghetto-Tor geführt wurden, kehrte kein einziger zurück. (…) Ponary ist kein Lager. 15.000 wurden dort durch Erschießungen getötet. Hitler beabsichtigt, alle Juden Europas zu vernichten. Es ist das Schicksal der Juden Litauens, als erste an der Reihe zu sein. Lassen wir uns nicht wie Schafe zur Schlachtbank führen!«

»Where are our brothers from the second ghetto? No one taken out of the gates of the ghetto has ever come back. (…) Paneriai is not a camp. 15.000 were shot there. Hitler is planning to annihilate all European Jews. It is the fate of the Lithuanian Jews to be the first on the list. Let us not go like lambs to the slaughter!«

Ponary bei Wilna

1942 bis 1943

Die Morde werden ausgedehnt – die Rote Armee naht

1942 töten die Deutschen und ihre litauischen Helfer in Ponary neben Juden vermehrt Kriegsgefangene sowie polnische und litauische politische Häftlinge. Im April ermorden sie 4.000 Juden aus Kaunas und ländlichen Gebieten Litauens. Nach der »Räumung« des Ghettos am 23. September 1943 müssen noch arbeitsfähige Häftlinge in einer Pelzfabrik in der Nähe von Wilna Zwangsarbeit verrichten oder werden nach Riga deportiert. Die übrigen finden in Ponary oder den Vernichtungslagern Majdanek und Treblinka den Tod. Als die Rote Armee naht, beginnen die Deutschen mit dem Verwischen der Spuren der Massenmorde: Das Sonderkommando 1005 zwingt jüdische Häftlinge, die Massengräber in Ponary zu öffnen und die Leichen zu verbrennen.

1942 to 1943

The spread of mass murder and the advance of the Red Army

In 1942, the Germans and their Lithuanian auxiliaries killed an increasing number of prisoners of war and Polish and Lithuanian political prisoners in Paneriai in addition to Jews. That April they murdered 4,000 Jews from Kaunas and rural parts of Lithuania. After the »liquidation« of the ghetto on 23 September 1943, prisoners who were fit to work were either deployed as forced labourers in a fur factory near Vilnius or deported to Riga. The rest of the prisoners died in Paneriai or in the extermination camps Majdanek or Treblinka. As the Red Army approached, the Germans began to remove the traces of mass murder. Sonderkommando 1005 forced Jewish prisoners to dig up the mass graves in Paneriai and to burn the bodies.

Paneriai near Vilnius

Yad Vashem, Jerusalem

Anton Schmid (1900 – 1942): Der Wiener Elektrotechniker ist ab August 1941 als Wehrmachtssoldat in Wilna stationiert. Dort hilft er der jüdischen Untergrundbewegung. Anfang 1942 wird er inhaftiert. Er schreibt aus dem Gefängnis an seine Frau:

Anton Schmid (1900 – 1942). Schmid was an electrical engineer from Vienna. From August 1941, he was stationed in Vilnius as a Wehrmacht soldier. There, he helped the Jewish underground movement. He was arrested in early 1942. In prison he wrote a letter to his wife:

»hier waren sehr viele Juden, die vom Litauischen Militär zusammengetrieben und auf einer Wiese außerhalb der Stadt erschossen wurden immer so 2.000 – 3.000 Menschen. Die Kinder haben sie auf dem Weg gleich an die Bäume angeschlagen. (…) ich konnte nicht viel nachdenken und half ihnen.«

» many of the Jews here were rounded up by the Lithuanian military and shot in a field outside the city – always around 2,000 – 3,000 at a time. They bashed the children against the trees on the way. (…) I could not think about it and helped them. «

Schmid wird am 13. April hingerichtet.

Schmid was executed on 13 April.

Erste Seiten des Abschiedsbriefs von Anton Schmid vom 9. April 1942.

The first two sides of Anton Schmid's farewell letter written on 9 April 1942.

Brief und Abschrift: Simon Wiesenthal Archiv, Wien

1944

Letzte Verbrechen und erste Ermittlungen

Während das Sonderkommando 1005 die Leichen früherer Massenerschießungen in Ponary verbrennt, werden dort weiterhin Juden ermordet. Den letzten Erschießungen fallen Anfang Juli 1944 die jüdischen Zwangsarbeiter der nahegelegenen Pelzfabrik zum Opfer. Am 11. Juli müssen sich die Deutschen aus Wilna zurückziehen. Zwei Tage später nimmt die Rote Armee die Stadt ein. Bereits einen Monat später beginnt eine sowjetische Kommission mit der Untersuchung der Verbrechen in Ponary.

1944

The final crimes and initial investigations

The murder of Jews continued in Paneriai at the same time as Sonderkommando 1005 was burning the corpses from previous mass shootings. At the beginning of July 1944, the Jewish forced labourers at the nearby fur factory were the final victims to be shot. The Germans were forced to retreat from Vilnius on 11 July. The Red Army took the city two days later. The following month, a Soviet commission began to investigate the crimes at Paneriai.

Paneriai near Vilnius

Beit Lohamei Haghetaot, Kibbuz der Ghettokämpfer

Arie Farber (links) und Kolya Sanin, zwei Häftlinge des Sonderkommandos 1005. Sie gehören möglicherweise zu einer Gruppe von Häftlingen, denen im Februar 1944 die Flucht durch einen selbst gebauten Tunnel gelingt. Einige Häftlinge berichten nach dem Krieg, dass sie etwa 800 Leichen am Tag verbrennen mussten. Manch einer erkannte seine Angehörigen unter den Toten.

Arie Farber (left) and Kolya Sanin, two prisoners from Sonderkommando 1005. It is possible that they were among the prisoners who dug a tunnel through which they managed to escape in February 1944. After the war, some former prisoners reported that they had had to burn around 800 corpses a day. A number of them recognised their relatives among the dead.

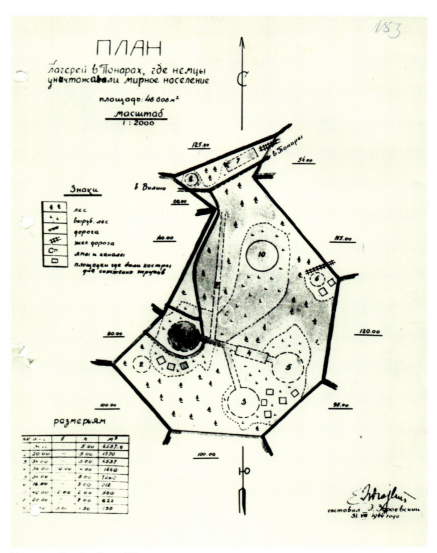

Lietuvos ypatingasis archyvas, Wilna

Plan von Ponary 1944, erstellt von der sowjetischen Außerordentlichen Staatlichen Kommission zur Untersuchung der nationalsozialistischen Verbrechen. Die unterbrochenen Kreise zeigen die Gruben, in denen die Menschen erschossen wurden, die Quadrate die Orte, an denen die Häftlinge des Sonderkommandos 1005 die Leichen verbrennen mussten.

Plan of Paneriai from 1944, produced by the Soviet Extraordinary State Commission for the Investigation of National Socialist Crimes. The dotted circles show the pits where people were shot and the squares represent the areas where prisoners from Sonderkommando 1005 had to burn the bodies.

1945 bis 2016

**Die Mörder finden,
der Opfer gedenken**

Nach dem Krieg müssen sich nur wenige Täter von Ponary vor deutschen Gerichten verantworten. Wie viele Litauer in der Sowjetunion verurteilt werden, ist bisher nicht bekannt. Viele entziehen sich der juristischen Verfolgung durch Flucht in die USA. Nachdem Litauen 1991 unabhängig wird, kommen keine weiteren Prozesse zustande.

Die Erinnerung an die Opfer setzt in Litauen früh ein. Bereits 1945 errichten Überlebende aus Wilna ein Mahnmal in Ponary. Dieses wird jedoch von der Regierung entfernt. Erst nach dem Ende der Sowjetunion entstehen neue Denkmäler für die jüdischen und nichtjüdischen Litauer und Polen. Das Gedenken an Ponary sorgt bis heute für Debatten in der litauischen Öffentlichkeit.

1945 to 2016

Tracking down the murderers and commemorating the victims

Only a few of those who had committed crimes at Paneriai faced trial in post-war Germany. It is not known how many Lithuanians were sentenced in the Soviet Union. Many evaded prosecution by fleeing to the US. There have been no further trials since Lithuania gained independence in 1991.

In Lithuania, commemoration of the victims began soon after the war. Survivors from Vilnius put up a memorial in Paneriai in 1945, but this was removed by the government. It was not until the break-up of the Soviet Union that new memorials were dedicated to Jewish and non-Jewish Lithuanians and Poles who died in Paneriai. There are still public debates in Lithuania on how to commemorate the victims of Paneriai.

Die zwei Seelen in seiner Brust, *Main-Post*, Würzburg, 2. Februar 1950: Bericht über den Prozess gegen die ehemaligen Angehörigen der Außenstelle des KdS Litauen in Wilna Martin Weiss und August Hering (1910 – 1992). Aussagen von Überlebenden über Weiss' grausame Taten schockieren die Öffentlichkeit. Das Gericht verurteilt Weiss zu lebenslanger Haft unter anderem wegen Beihilfe zum Mord in 30.000 Fällen. 1971 wird er nach einem Gnadengesuch aus dem Gefängnis entlassen.

»The Two Souls Dwelling Within His Breast«, *Main-Post*, Würzburg, 2 February 1950. Report on the trial of Martin Weiss and August Hering (1910 – 1992), former members of the office of the KdS for Lithuania in Vilnius. Survivors gave evidence at the trial. Their accounts of Weiss' brutality shocked the public. The court sentenced Weiss to life in prison for crimes including being an accessory to 30.000 counts of murder. He was released from prison in 1971 following an appeal for clemency.

Paneriai near Vilnius

Graz (Österreich), 18. Juni 1963:
Franz Murer vor Gericht. Er wird ab 1947 als Kriegsverbrecher international gesucht. Österreich liefert Murer nach Wilna aus, wo er zu 25 Jahren Arbeitslager verurteilt wird. 1955 kann er jedoch nach Österreich zurückkehren. Dort spürt ihn der Holocaust-Überlebende Simon Wiesenthal (1908 – 2005) auf und Murer kommt wegen seiner Verbrechen im Ghetto von Wilna vor Gericht. Während des Prozesses verunglimpft Murers Verteidiger jüdische Zeugen, Murers Söhne lachen sie aus. Er selbst streitet alle Taten ab und wird freigesprochen.

Graz (Austria), 18 June 1963:
Franz Murer on trial. He was charged with war crimes in 1947 and an international warrant issued for his arrest. Murer was extradited from Austria to Vilnius, where he was sentenced to 25 years in a labour camp. However, he was allowed to return to Austria in 1955. There, the Holocaust survivor Simon Wiesenthal (1908 – 2005) tracked him down. Murer was put on trial because of his crimes in the Vilnius ghetto. During the trial, Murer's defence vilified the Jewish witnesses and his sons ridiculed them. He denied all charges and was found not guilty.

Egon Blaschka, Graz, Prozeß gegen Franz Murer 18.6.1963 (Multimediale Sammlungen /UMJ)

Die zwei Seelen in seiner Brust
Weiß als „Schöngeist" — Auch das Ausland nimmt regen Anteil an dem Prozeß

Als die überlebenden Juden Wilnas nach Kriegsende zum erstenmal ein Treffen abhielten, gelobten sie feierlich, nicht eher zu ruhen, bis sie den Mörder Zehntausender ihrer Angehörigen und Freunde gefunden hätten. Keiner der bisher vernommenen Zeugen benötigte auch nur eine Sekunde, um Weiß wiederzuerkennen. Seine Züge, sein Name scheinen unauslöschlich in ihre Erinnerung eingegraben zu sein. Das starke Polizeiaufgebot hatte vor und nach den Verhandlungen Mühe, Weiß und Hering vor der erbitterten Menge zu schützen.

Lieblingslektüre Adalbert Stifter!
Wenn man einige Tage den erschütterndsten, grauenvollsten Berichten über die Taten von Martin Weiß gelauscht hat, erkennt man, ohne es je begreifen zu können, was alles in der Seele eines einzigen Menschen Platz finden kann. Der Mann, der nach Zeugenaussagen ohne Gefühlsregung Kinder am Arm ihrer Mütter erschoß, wird von seinen Karlsruher Mitbürgern als unbescholtener, treusorgender Familienvater geschildert, der seine Familie liebte und niemand etwas zuleide tun konnte. Von demselben Mann, der drei Jahre lang Menschen wie Ungeziefer behandelte und ungerührt Zehntausende liquidierte, berichtet eine Zeugin aus Karlsruhe, er sei ein Mensch „mit einer idealistischen Lebensauffassung, mit einem ausgesprochenen Sinn für alles Schöne und Gute"! Adalbert Stifters „Nachsommer" sei die Lieblingslektüre in der Familie gewesen. Ausgerechnet Stifter!

Diese eine, harmlose, biedere Seite des Hauptangeklagten wird von der Verteidigung tunlichst herausgestellt. Und gerade dadurch läßt sie den paradoxen Gegensatz der zwei Seelen um so schärfer hervortreten und macht ihn unzugänglicher für jeden Erklärungsversuch.

Von „guten" und „bösen" Deutschen
Niemand weiß besser, als jene täglich vom Tod bedrohten jüdischen Einwohner Wilnas, daß jede kollektive Be- und Verurteilung eines Volkes abwegig ist. Ihr eigenes kollektives Schicksal sagt es ihnen ebenso, wie die Gegensätze unter den Deutschen selbst, mit denen sie zusammenkamen. „Es gab solche und solche, gute und böse", wie ein Zeuge sagt. — Da trat z. B. der ehemalige Oberzahlmeister Schönbrunner als Zeuge vor Gericht auf, wiedererkannt von vielen. Das Gericht konnte nur mühsam Beifallskundgebungen unterdrücken. Er half, wo er konnte, trat gegen den SD auf, holte seine Leute, wenn sie eines Tages nicht zur Arbeit kamen, persönlich aus den Todeszellen des Gefängnisses und rettete vielleicht manchem der Anwesenden das Leben.

Weiß (links) wollte nicht in die Zeitung kommen. Er „schützte" sich hinter der Anklageschrift. Rechts: Hering ist nicht kamerascheu.

Nach ihm sagte ein ehemaliger Beamter der Sicherheitspolizei in Wilna aus. Er war längere Zeit dort, traf Weiß oft, saß in einem Zimmer mit dem SD-Chef und will von Erschießungen nie etwas gemerkt haben! Dabei waren es nahezu 40 000 Menschen, die dort systematisch ausgerottet wurden!

Die Zeugenvernehmungen sind im wesentlichen abgeschlossen. Es war eine schier endlose Kette grauenvoller Einzelereignisse. Immer wieder schlossen die Berichte mit den in der Gleichförmigkeit allmählich quälenden Wendungen: „... daraufhin zog Weiß die Pistole und schoß ihn (sie) vor unseren Augen auf der Stelle nieder" oder „... dann wurden sie nach Ponary gebracht und sind nicht mehr zurückgekehrt".

Die Verhandlung wird heute nachmittag fortgesetzt. Das Interesse der Öffentlichkeit ist weiterhin außerordentlich stark. Zahlreiche Beobachter aus dem Ausland nehmen am Prozeß teil.

Während der Vernehmung der Belastungszeugen — Links: Hering, aufmerksamer Zuhörer. Rechts daneben: Weiß, immer gespannt den Aussagen folgend. Manchmal schüttelt er, kaum wahrnehmbar, den Kopf. Dahinter: Staatsanwalt Heß, der Vertreter der Anklage.

Die zwei Seelen in seiner Brust, in: Main-Post, Würzburg 2. Februar 1950, S. 3.

Ponary bei Wilna

Lietuvos ypatingasis archyvas, Wilna

Yad Vashem, Jerusalem

Ponary, 1949: Der 1945 von Überlebenden errichtete Obelisk »im ewigen Gedenken an die Juden, die von den deutschen faschistischen Mördern, dem größten Feind der Menschheit, ermordet wurden«. 1952 lässt die Regierung das Denkmal abreißen.

Paneriai, 1949: The obelisk inaugurated in 1945 by survivors »in eternal remembrance of the Jews murdered by the German fascist murderers, humanity's greatest foe«. The government had the monument pulled down in 1952.

Das Denkmal von 1991 soll auf die litauische Beteiligung am Massenmord hinweisen. Darauf folgende Debatten führen dazu, dass die Inschrift nur auf Hebräisch und Jiddisch erscheint. Ein späteres Mahnmal thematisiert die Rolle der örtlichen Täter auch auf Litauisch und Russisch.

This 1991 memorial was supposed to mention Lithuanian involvement in the mass murder. However, following public debate on the memorial the inscription only appeared in Hebrew and Yiddish. A more recent memorial has text in Lithuanian and Russian referring to the role of local perpetrators.

Paneriai near Vilnius

Ponary, 2004: Denkmal für die ermordeten Juden in einer der Gruben für die einstige Heizöl-Tankanlage. Die Gedenkanlage im Wald bei Ponary besteht aus mehreren Denkmälern. 1989 und 1993 entstehen Gedenksteine für die in Ponary ermordeten Polen und Litauer.

Paneriai, 2004: Memorial to the murdered Jews in one of the pits originally dug for the fuel oil storage facility. The memorial complex in Paneriai forest comprises a number of monuments. Memorial stones for the Poles and Lithuanians murdered at Paneriai were placed on the site in 1989 and 1993.

Stiftung Denkmal für die ermordeten Juden Europas

Essays
Essays

Die Erschießungen in der Sowjetunion 1941 – 1944

Martin Cüppers

Massaker an hunderten, wenn nicht tausenden Orten, Verbrechen als Alltag: Am 28. August 1941 erschossen Angehörige des Sonderkommandos 10b der Einsatzgruppe D in Ananjew, etwa 150 Kilometer nördlich von Odessa, 300 Juden. 100 weitere sowie mehrere »Bolschewistenführer« waren es am Tag darauf in Cherson nahe des Schwarzen Meers. Am 30. August starben 600 Witebsker Juden – sie wurden außerhalb der weißrussischen Stadt erschossen, die Kinder von den deutschen Tätern lebendig begraben. Am 31. August und an den folgenden drei Tagen wurden insgesamt 8.000 Jüdinnen und Juden aus dem Ghetto von Wilna im Wald von Ponary ermordet. Am 1. September töteten Litauer und Angehörige der Einsatzgruppe A im litauischen Mariampole fast 5.000 jüdische Menschen und mehr als 100 Psychiatriepatienten. Als Deutsche am 2. September 1942 die Insassen des Ghettos im weißrussischen Lachwa vernichten wollten, leisteten diese Widerstand, vielen gelang die Flucht. Die meisten der 6.000 Juden wurden dennoch erschossen. Für das gesamte Kalenderjahr ließe sich die exemplarische Aufzählung für die deutsch besetzten Gebiete der Sowjetunion fortführen. Oft genug verübten deutsche Einheiten und ihre Helfer am selben Tag an ganz unterschiedlichen Orten Massaker. Die Mordtaten ereigneten sich während des gesamten Ostfeldzugs der Jahre 1941 bis 1944.

Der Umfang der Erschießungen

Seit Jahrzehnten gilt Auschwitz als Synonym für die Ermordung der west- und mittel-europäischen Juden. Die Vernichtung des polnischen Judentums in Gaskammern ist mit Namen wie Treblinka, Sobibor und Belzec verknüpft. Lidice oder Oradour-sur-Glane stehen für nationalsozialistische Verbrechen an der Zivilbevölkerung, während die Konzentrationslager im einstigen Deutschen Reich seit langem weltweit bekannte Erinnerungsorte sind. Für die Geschichte des Holocaust – oder zutreffender: der Shoah – in der Sowjetunion haben diese Tatorte jedoch kaum Bedeutung. Das dortige millionen-fache Töten bleibt in der kollektiven Erinnerung in Deutschland bis heute seltsam ausgespart.

Die Juden aus Riga, Minsk, Kiew, Odessa, aus Ananjew, Mariampole oder Lachwa, aus ungezählten und einer deutschen Allgemeinheit in der Regel unbekannten Städten, Dörfern und kleinsten Siedlungen der damaligen Sowjetunion wurden nicht in Vernichtungslager deportiert, sondern eines Tages zusammengetrieben und unweit des eigenen Zuhauses erschossen und verscharrt. Es sind hunderte, wenn nicht tausende von Ortsnamen, die für den Massenmord durch Kugeln stehen. Darin unterscheidet sich die Shoah in der Sowjetunion ganz wesentlich vom übrigen Europa. Opfer dieser tödlichen Systematik wurden zwischen November 1941 und Oktober 1942 auch

Shootings in the Soviet Union
1941 – 1944

Martin Cüppers

During the war in the Soviet Union, massacres took place in hundreds if not thousands of different places and atrocities were a routine occurrence, as indicated by the following examples. On 28 August 1941, members of Sonderkommando 10b, a sub-division of Einsatzgruppe D, shot 300 Jews in Ananjew, around 150 kilometres north of Odessa. 100 more Jews and several »Bolshevist leaders« were shot the next day in Kherson, near the Black Sea. A further 600 Jews from Vitebsk (Belarus) died on 30 August. The Germans shot them on the outskirts of the town and buried their children alive. On 31 August and over the three days that followed, a total of 8,000 Jewish men and women from the Vilnius ghetto were murdered in Paneriai forest. On 1 September, Lithuanians and soldiers from Einsatzgruppe A shot almost 5,000 Jews and over 100 psychiatric patients in Marijampolė (Lithuania). On 2 September 1942, the Jews in Lakhva (Belarus) staged an uprising against the Germans who had come to liquidate the ghetto and many managed to escape. However, most of the 6,000 Jews from the ghetto were shot. The shootings in the German-occupied territories of the Soviet Union continued in a similar vein throughout the entire year. It was not uncommon for German units and their auxiliaries to carry out massacres in completely different places on the same day. The murders continued for the duration of the war in the Soviet Union between 1941 and 1944.

The scale of the shootings

For decades, Auschwitz has been synonymous with the murder of Jews from Central and Western Europe. Names such as Treblinka, Sobibor and Belzec evoke the annihilation of Polish Jews in the gas chambers. Lidice and Oradour-sur-Glane exemplify National Socialist crimes against civilians. People all over the world have heard of the former concentration camps located in what was the German Reich, which now serve as memorial sites. However, these sites have very little to do with the history of the Holocaust – or, to term it more accurately, the Shoah – in the Soviet Union. It is puzzling that the millions of lives lost there are still largely absent from German collective memory.

The Jews from Riga, Minsk, Kiev, Odessa, Ananjew, Marijampolė or Lakhva, or from countless towns, villages and hamlets in the former Soviet Union, most of which are unknown in Germany, were not deported to the extermination camps but instead rounded up, shot and buried in shallow graves near their own homes. Mass shootings took place in hundreds if not thousands of different places. This illustrates a significant distinction

Die Erschießungen in der Sowjetunion 1941 – 1944

55.000 deutsche, österreichische und tschechische Juden, die das Berliner Reichssicherheitshauptamt in 32 Deportationszügen nach Minsk, Kowno, Riga und Raasiku deportieren ließ. Dort wurden die Menschen entweder gleich erschossen oder zunächst noch in Ghettos und Arbeitslager gezwungen, bevor sie in den folgenden Monaten ebenfalls fast alle ermordet wurden.

Das mittlerweile breitere historische Wissen über die Erschießungen mit wenigen oder bis zu mehreren zehntausend Opfern widerlegt lange vorherrschende Vorstellungen. Die Nationalsozialisten haben ihre jüdischen Opfer eben nicht nur in einem industriell organisierten Prozess unter quasi klinischen Begleitumständen getötet, in dem sich Opfer und Täter kaum begegneten und individuell begangene Verbrechen gar nicht vorkamen. Vielmehr standen Unschuldige vor ihren Mördern, bis diese den Abzug betätigten. Menschen mussten sich auf die toten oder schwerverletzten Körper ihrer Nachbarn oder Freunde legen, bevor sie selbst erschossen wurden. Die Luft an den Tatorten roch nach Blut, während oft genug betrunkene Schützen torkelten, grölten und ihre Opfer mitunter kaum noch zu treffen vermochten.

Opfer der Massenerschießungen waren nicht nur Juden. Zeitlich wie regional uneinheitlich und ohne überlieferte eindeutige Befehle wurden in der Sowjetunion auch etwa 30.000 Roma ermordet. SS und Polizei erschossen außerdem schätzungsweise 17.000 Patienten psychiatrischer Einrichtungen oder erstickten sie in Gaswagen. Dies war die Fortsetzung der bereits 1939 im Deutschen Reich begonnenen Mordkampagne gegen »lebensunwerte« Menschen. In weit größerem Umfang traf es außerdem nichtjüdische Zivilpersonen, die mit Kriegsbeginn als tatsächliche oder vermeintliche Unterstützer des Kommunismus getötet wurden. Nach dem Aufbau einer Partisanenbewegung ab Anfang Juli 1941 und ersten operativen Erfolgen im Jahr darauf wurden Männer, Frauen und Kinder häufig entweder als »Ortsfremde« oder angebliches Sicherheitsrisiko ermordet und in immer brutaleren »Vergeltungsmaßnahmen« als »Unterstützer« oder »Verdächtige« erschossen. Zahlreiche Dörfer wurden auf diese Weise ausgelöscht, ganze Gebiete entvölkert. Die Gesamtzahl der Opfer von systematischen Erschießungen unter der nichtjüdischen Zivilbevölkerung auf sowjetischem Boden beläuft sich auf bis zu 200.000 Menschen; bis heute gibt es kaum verlässliche Angaben. Die Gesamtbilanz der Besatzung ist weitaus verheerender. Millionen weiterer Zivilisten starben durch gezieltes Aushungern und die Politik der »verbrannten Erde«. Als todbringend erwiesen sich die Bedingungen nicht zuletzt auch für die Kriegsgefangenen. Allein zehntausende Rotarmisten wurden direkt bei der Gefangennahme, auf dem Weg in die Lager oder im Verlauf ungezählter Exzesstaten von ihren deutschen Bewachern umgebracht. Über drei der insgesamt fünf Millionen überlebten die Lager nicht.

So umfassend die Vernichtungspolitik in der besetzten Sowjetunion war, so unterschiedlich war dennoch ihre Durchsetzung gegenüber den verschiedenen Opfergruppen. So verfolgten die Nationalsozialisten Kommunisten nicht nur im Deutschen Reich, sondern auch in der Sowjetunion unerbittlich. Nur war vielfach unklar, wer überhaupt als Träger

between the characteristics of the Shoah in the Soviet Union and in the rest of Europe. 55,000 German, Austrian and Czech Jews also fell victim to this programme of systematic murder. The Reich Security Main Office in Berlin had them deported to Minsk, Kovno, Riga and Raasiku on 32 separate trains between November 1941 and October 1942. They were either shot on arrival or initially made to reside in ghettos and forced labour camps, where the vast majority were also murdered in the months that followed.

As more historical facts have come to light about the shootings, which targeted groups ranging from just a few to tens of thousands of victims, a picture has emerged that contradicts the longstanding version of events. It is now known that the National Socialists did not always murder their Jewish victims using an industrial – and almost clinical – method, whereby perpetrators and victims had little contact with each other and atrocities committed by individuals did not occur. It was rather the case that the murderers stood face to face with their innocent victims before pulling the trigger. People were made to lie on top of the lifeless or critically injured bodies of their neighbours or friends before being shot themselves. With the stench of blood in the air, the marksmen – often blind drunk – would stagger around bawling and shouting, at times barely able to hit their targets.

The victims of the mass shootings were not just Jews. Around 30,000 Roma were also killed in the Soviet Union. The scale and timing of these shootings varied from region to region and there is no evidence of any official mandate. In addition, the SS and police shot an estimated 17,000 patients from psychiatric clinics or asphyxiated them in gas vans. These murders marked the continuation of the policy to kill people deemed »unworthy of life« that had come into effect in the German Reich in 1939. Non-Jewish civilians were targeted to an even greater extent and killed right from the start of the war for being genuine or suspected supporters of Communism. The partisan movement was established in early July 1941 and had carried out a number of successful operations by the following year. The Germans reacted by repeatedly murdering men, women and children for being »suspicious strangers« or alleged security threats, or by shooting them in a series of increasingly brutal »reprisal measures« that targeted Communist »supporters« or »suspects«. This led to many villages being obliterated and to the population of entire regions wiped out. It is estimated that up to 200,000 non-Jewish civilians were killed in systematic shootings on Soviet territory, but there are still no reliable figures. The full extent of the devastation wrought by the occupying forces was far greater than this. Millions more civilians died as a result of the ›Hunger Plan‹ designed to starve them to death as well as the »scorched earth policy«. The conditions faced by prisoners of war also caused many of them to perish. Tens of thousands of Red Army troops alone were murdered directly after their capture, on their way to the prisoner of war camps or as the targets of countless acts of excessive violence committed by German guards. Of a total of five million prisoners of war, three million did not survive the camps.

The policy of annihilation was applied in all of the occupied territories of the Soviet Union, but the method of doing so varied widely depending on the victim group concerned.

dieser Ideologie gelten konnte. Letztlich blieben viele unerkannt, andere waren fortan für die deutschen Besatzer tätig. Auch der Massenmord an den Roma wies eine unterschiedliche Systematik auf. So wurden Angehörige der Volksgruppe in manchen Regionen wie der Krim ausnahmslos ermordet. Anderswo blieben sie unbehelligt, weil die Täter am Ort keine Initiative zu ihrer Tötung ergriffen. Und auch die Mordpolitik gegen die nichtjüdische Zivilbevölkerung (Ukrainer, Weißrussen oder Russen und andere) – ein Wesensmerkmal des Vernichtungskriegs in der Sowjetunion – war keineswegs gleichförmig. Die jüdische Bevölkerung wurde hingegen mit einer Systematik verfolgt, die ohne Ausnahmen auf Vernichtung abzielte – und dies flächendeckend.

Den ungezählten Erschießungen fielen während des Krieges zwischen 1941 und 1944 – rechnet man die Opfer unter rumänischer Herrschaft hinzu – bis zu 2,4 Millionen jüdische Kinder, Frauen und Männer zum Opfer. Damit starben in den zwischen der Ostsee und dem Kaukasus ausgehobenen Gruben mehr als doppelt so viele Menschen durch Kugeln aus Pistolen oder Gewehren wie in den Gaskammern von Auschwitz. Die historische Forschung hat zwei unterschiedliche Tötungswellen ausgemacht. Die erste setzte mit dem deutschen Angriff auf die Sowjetunion am 22. Juni 1941 ein. Anfangs schossen hauptsächlich die mobilen Einheiten von Sicherheitspolizei und SD sowie Bataillone der Ordnungspolizei. Nach den ersten Kriegswochen kamen Einheiten der Waffen-SS, rumänische Verbände sowie litauische, lettische, estnische, weißrussische und ukrainische Helfer hinzu, die zusammen in vorher nie dagewesenem Umfang die jüdische Zivilbevölkerung ermordeten. Von den westlichen Grenzgebieten ausgehend, wurden zuerst fast ausschließlich erwachsene männliche Juden getötet. Nach einigen Wochen folgten erste Vernichtungen ganzer Gemeinden. In anderen Gegenden wurde die nicht arbeitsfähige jüdische Bevölkerung erschossen, während Zwangsarbeiter in vielerorts eigens eingerichteten Ghettos im einstigen Ostpolen sowie in wenigen Städten Litauens und Lettlands vorerst überlebten.

Regional und zeitlich unterschiedlich, begann im Frühjahr 1942 eine zweite Tötungswelle. In Litauen, Weißrussland und der Ukraine wurden Ghettos aufgelöst und noch bestehende jüdische Gemeinden bei »Aktionen« ausgelöscht. Zudem verstärkten die Besatzungsinstitutionen ihre Suche nach Juden auf dem Land, die häufig unter dem Deckmantel der sogenannten Partisanenbekämpfung ermordet wurden. Sowohl die Zahl der Opfer als auch die der Täter überstieg dabei die der ersten Tötungswelle bei weitem. War es im Zuge der nationalsozialistischen Vernichtungspolitik 1941 kaum zu Widerstand gekommen, nahmen Aufstände, organisierte Fluchtversuche und der Zulauf zu den Partisanen ab 1942 beträchtlich zu.

Opfer und Überlebende

Anfangs traf das Morden die Gemeinden gänzlich unvorbereitet. 1939 waren zahlreiche polnische Juden vor den Nationalsozialisten Richtung Osten geflohen. Als sich die Lage in

Hence, the National Socialists pursued a relentless crusade against Communists on the territory of both the German Reich and the Soviet Union. And yet it was often unclear who was actually spreading this ideology. Many Communists remained undetected, whilst others now worked for the German occupation forces. There was also no uniform approach to the mass murder of Roma. In some regions, for example Crimea, Roma were murdered without exception. In other places they were spared as the perpetrators did not use the opportunity to kill them. The policy of murdering non-Jewish civilians (for example Ukrainians, Belarusians and Russians), in itself a hallmark of the war of annihilation in the Soviet Union, was also by no means consistent in practice. By contrast, the persecution of the Jewish population was systematic as it occurred throughout the occupied territories of the Soviet Union with the sole objective of annihilating this group.

If the victims of the Rumanian regime are included, up to 2.4 million Jewish men, women and children fell victim to the countless mass shootings that took place between 1941 and 1944 in the context of World War Two. More than twice as many people were gunned down in the pits dug in the region stretching from the Baltic Sea to the Caucasus than in the gas chambers of Auschwitz. Historians have identified two distinct waves of murder. The first began with the German invasion of the Soviet Union on 22 June 1941. At first, the shootings were mainly carried out by the mobile killing squads made up of troops from the Security Police or SD (SS Security Service), or by Order Police battalions. After the first few weeks of the conflict, Waffen-SS units, Rumanian divisions and Lithuanian, Latvian, Estonian, Belarusian and Ukrainian auxiliary troops also began to participate in the mass murder of Jewish civilians, which assumed unprecedented dimensions. Starting at the western border, the initial targets were almost exclusively Jewish men. Within a few weeks, a number of entire communities had been destroyed. Elsewhere, Jews unfit to work were shot whilst forced labourers initially survived in designated ghettos established in many parts of what was then eastern Poland and in a number of towns in Latvia and Lithuania.

The second wave of murder began in the spring of 1942, with its scale and timing varying from region to region. In Lithuania, Belarus and the Ukraine, the ghettos were liquidated and »operations« carried out to obliterate any remaining Jewish communities. At the same time, the occupation forces intensified their efforts to root out Jews in rural areas, often killing them under the pretext of the so-called anti-partisan combat. This second wave of killing involved far greater numbers of both victims and perpetrators. Whilst the National Socialist extermination policy had barely encountered any resistance in 1941, the period after 1942 saw a sharp increase in the number of uprisings, organised escape attempts and in people joining the partisans.

Victims and survivors

The murders initially took communities completely by surprise. In 1939, a large number of Polish Jews had fled east to escape the National Socialist advance. However, many returned

der deutsch besetzten Heimat aber beruhigt zu haben schien, kehrten viele wieder zurück. Angesichts des überraschenden deutschen Angriffs im Juni 1941 hatten gerade in den grenznahen Regionen der Sowjetunion die Wenigsten Gelegenheit, rechtzeitig zu fliehen. Erst im weiteren Kriegsverlauf, als mehr Zeit zur Fluchtvorbereitung bestand und erste Berichte über die weiter westlich verübten Morde die Gemeinden erreichten, stieg der Anteil jüdischer Flüchtlinge deutlich an.

Das erste Erscheinen deutscher Soldaten erschien oft wenig bedrohlich. Doch als plötzlich Menschen zusammengetrieben wurden, Wertsachen abgegeben werden mussten und bewaffnete Deutsche auf der Suche nach weiteren Juden in Häuser eindrangen, ahnten viele, was bevorstand. Handlungsmöglichkeiten gab es zu diesem Zeitpunkt allerdings kaum mehr. Schnell trieben SS-Männer, Ordnungspolizisten oder andere Täter die Juden aus ihren Häusern zu bereits vorbereiteten oder nun hastig auszuhebenden Gruben, wo umgehend die Erschießungen begannen. Solche Abläufe wiederholten sich täglich, ganze Gemeinden hörten an einem Tag auf, zu bestehen. Dort, wo zunächst ausschließlich Ältere und Kranke getötet wurden, mussten gesunde und arbeitsfähige Männer und Frauen fortan in eigens abgetrennten Ghettos Zwangsarbeit für die Deutschen leisten. Monate später, oft erst 1942 oder 1943, wurden die Menschen, die auf ein Überleben durch Arbeit gehofft hatten, auch erschossen.

Vielerorts konnten nur mehr die nichtjüdischen Nachbarn von den Verbrechen erzählen. Häufig waren sie von den Tätern gezwungen worden, die Gruben auszuheben oder die Kleider der Ermordeten zu sortieren. Nur wenige Verfolgte überlebten die Massaker: Manchen gelang die Flucht in die Wälder, andere konnten sich – verletzt – nach Stunden aus einem Leichenberg befreien, um anschließend mit Glück von Nichtjuden irgendwo aufgenommen und versteckt zu werden. So entstanden Berichte einzelner Überlebender, die vom Vorgehen der Täter und dem Sterben der Liebsten erzählen und der Nachwelt Einblicke in Details des alltäglichen Grauens erlauben.

Die Massenerschießungen des Sommers 1941 bildeten den eigentlichen Auftakt und die Vorbedingung für die erst in den folgenden Monaten allmählich auf ganz Europa ausgedehnte Vernichtung der Juden. Ganz offenbar diente die Sowjetunion den Nationalsozialisten als Experimentierfeld, um die gewonnenen Kenntnisse zur Realisierung des Völkermords dann im europäischen Maßstab anzuwenden.

Der Weg in den Völkermord

In der Vergangenheit ist der Ursprung der Shoah häufig auf grundsätzliche Befehle des Führers und Reichskanzlers Adolf Hitler (1889 – 1945) zurückgeführt worden, die dann von Gefolgsleuten nur noch befolgt worden seien. Zahlreiche Quellen vermitteln heute jedoch, dass die Genese der Shoah in der Sowjetunion in hohem Maße auf Initiativen unterer Ebenen beruhte. Diese führten der nationalsozialistischen Führung um Hitler

once the situation appeared to have eased in their German-occupied homeland. Having not reckoned with the German invasion of the Soviet Union in June 1941, very few residents of the Soviet border regions had chance to get out in time. The number of Jewish refugees only began to multiply as the conflict progressed and there was more time to make arrangements to flee, and also as a result of initial reports being circulated about atrocities committed further to the west.

The arrival of German troops did not seem to pose much of a threat at first. However, when they suddenly started rounding people up and making them hand over their valuables, and when armed German troops began forcing their way into people's homes to hunt down Jews, many had an idea of what was about to happen to them. Yet by now there was very little the Jews could do. Members of the SS, Order Police or other perpetrators soon began dragging Jews out of their homes and taking them to pits that had either been hastily dug in advance or that the victims were made to dig themselves. The shootings then commenced without delay. The same thing happened day after day, obliterating entire communities in one go. In many locations at first only the sick and elderly were killed. Healthy men and women able to work were then made to carry out forced labour for the Germans in segregated ghettos designated for this purpose. Those who had hoped to survive as workers were also shot dead, but not until months later, often not until 1942 or 1943.

In many places, only the non-Jewish neighbours of the victims were left to report on the atrocities. The perpetrators often forced the Jews to dig their own graves or to sort through the clothing belonging to those murdered. There were very few survivors of the massacres. Some managed to flee into the forests. Others were able to extricate themselves from the pile of corpses after lying there injured for hours. If they were lucky, they were then taken in and hidden by non-Jews. A number of survivors were thus able to recount what the perpetrators had done and how their loved ones had died, giving future generations an insight into the atrocities occurring on a daily basis at the time.

The mass shootings in summer 1941 heralded both the onset of and the precondition for the extermination of the Jews, a process that gradually extended to the rest of Europe in the months that followed. It is evident that the National Socialists saw the Soviet Union as a kind of testing ground for the practice of genocide, subsequently applying what they had learned to the rest of Europe.

The stages leading up to the genocide

In the past, the origins of the Shoah were frequently attributed to a series of fundamental orders issued by the Führer and Reich Chancellor, Adolf Hitler (1889 – 1945), and obeyed by his henchmen. However, many sources now indicate that in the Soviet Union the Shoah largely came about as a result of the lower ranks of the hierarchy taking the initiative. Those scopes of these lower ranks actually provided Hitler's National Socialist leadership with

Die Erschießungen in der Sowjetunion 1941 – 1944

überhaupt erst vor Augen, dass die eigenen Mordeinheiten vor Ort tatsächlich willens und fähig sein würden, Hunderttausende zu töten und damit die »Endlösung der Judenfrage« umzusetzen. Da ein solches Vorhaben bis dahin ohne Beispiel war, konnten Adolf Hitler oder der Reichsführer-SS und Chef der deutschen Polizei Heinrich Himmler (1900 – 1945) im Voraus gar nicht wissen, ob ihre Gefolgsleute in Osteuropa psychisch in der Lage wären, Tag für Tag Menschen umzubringen. Daher beschränkten Hitler und seine engsten Gefolgsleute sich in einem ersten Experimentierstadium mit Beginn des Krieges gegen die Sowjetunion im Juni 1941 auf den Erlass vager Anordnungen und die Formulierung breit interpretierbarer Anweisungen. Dadurch waren Handlungsspielräume eröffnet, die entscheidend zur weiteren Radikalisierung beitrugen.

Ende Juli 1941 begannen zwei SS-Kavallerieregimenter ihre Einsätze in der Region der weißrussischen Pripjetsümpfe. Das Gebiet sollte »befriedet« werden; weitere radikale, aber auffällig offen formulierte Anweisungen folgten. Die im Norden vorrückenden SS-Reiter des 1. Regiments gingen sofort dazu über, sämtliche jüdische Gemeinden zu vernichten und als erste Einheit überhaupt täglich neben mehreren tausend jüdischen Männern auch Frauen mit ihren Kindern zu erschießen. »Entjudung« nannte SS-Sturmbannführer Gustav Lombard (1895 – 1992) dieses Vorgehen – ein Begriff, mit dem bis dahin die Ausschaltung von Juden aus dem Wirtschaftsleben im Deutschen Reich bezeichnet worden war. Weiter südlich gingen die Reiter des 2. SS-Kavallerieregiments weniger umfassend vor: Sie erschossen anfangs ausschließlich jüdische Männer. Mit fadenscheinigen Begründungen versuchte Kommandeur Franz Magill (1900 – nach 1964) in späteren Berichten das Vorgehen seiner Truppe zu rechtfertigen. Während sein Gegenspieler Lombard für seine Vorreiterrolle bei der Ermordung der jüdischen Bevölkerung mit militärischen Orden ausgezeichnet und befördert wurde, blieb Magill die Anerkennung der Vorgesetzten verwehrt. Er wurde wegen seines weniger mörderischen Handelns vielmehr wenig später seines Kommandos entbunden und anderweitig eingesetzt.

Die Entwicklung des Massenmords ist also keine im Voraus erdachte und dann nur mehr umzusetzende Planung, sondern ein variables System von Ausprobieren und anschließender Anwendung oder Ausschluss. Dabei setzten sich in der Regel die in den Augen der Mörder effektivsten Maßnahmen durch. Im Vorfeld waren umfassende Lösungsansätze zur »Judenfrage« wie der »Madagaskarplan« zur Deportation der europäischen Juden erwogen, jedoch alsbald aus praktischen Gründen wieder verworfen worden. Bei ihrem zweiwöchigen Einsatz in Weißrussland mit etwa 25.000 jüdischen Opfern hatten die Einheiten der SS-Kavallerie erstmals bewiesen, dass deutsche Verbände ohne nennenswerte Probleme bereit waren, Tag für Tag jüdische Männer, Frauen und Kinder zu ermorden. Vor diesem Hintergrund wies Himmler andere SS- und Polizeieinheiten persönlich an, ebenso vorzugehen: Innerhalb weniger Wochen gingen alle Mordeinheiten von SS, Polizei oder einheimischen Helfern im Sommer und Herbst 1941 überall in den deutsch besetzten Gebieten der Sowjetunion zur ausnahmslosen Ermordung der jüdischen Bevölkerung über.

the confirmation that the murder squads deployed there were indeed willing and able to kill hundreds of thousands of people and therefore to implement the »Final Solution of the Jewish Question«. As this was an unprecedented operation, neither Adolf Hitler nor the Reich SS Leader and Chief of German Police, Heinrich Himmler (1900 – 1945), could have known beforehand whether their men in Eastern Europe had the mental capacity to kill people on a day to day basis. While testing the waters at the start of the war against the Soviet Union in June 1941, Hitler and his henchmen thus limited themselves to issuing vague orders and sending lists of instructions that were open to interpretation. This gave the perpetrators a certain degree of autonomy and was instrumental in the increased radicalisation of violence.

Two SS cavalry brigades were posted to the Pripet Marshes in Belarus at the end of July 1941. They were instructed to »pacify« the region. Further instructions followed that called for radical action but were worded in extremely general terms. As they advanced northwards, the SS cavalry from the 1st brigade immediately proceeded to annihilate entire Jewish communities. This was the first unit to start shooting women and children along with several thousands of Jewish men per day. SS-Sturmbannführer Gustav Lombard (1895 – 1992) termed this approach »De-Jewification« (Entjudung) – a term previously been used to describe the exclusion of Jews from the German economy. Further to the south, the 2nd SS cavalry brigade was not as thorough and only shot Jewish men at first. When later questioned, brigade commander Franz Magill (1900 – 1964 or later) gave feeble excuses for the performance of his troops. Whereas his counterpart Lombard was decorated with military honours and promoted for his pioneering role in the murder of the Jews, Magill received no recognition from his superiors. His less bloodthirsty approach indeed led to him being relieved of his command and stationed elsewhere.

From the above it is clear that the mass murder was not simply the implementation of a strategy worked out in advance, but rather a shifting process of trial and error. The methods considered most effective by the murderers were usually the ones adopted. Comprehensive solutions to the »Jewish Question« such as the »Madagascar Plan« to deport European Jews had initially been considered, but were soon rejected for practical reasons. Having murdered around 25,000 Jewish victims during their two-week posting in Belarus, the SS cavalry units had proven for the first time that German troops had no real problem in killing Jewish men, women and children on a daily basis. Himmler therefore approached other SS and police units directly and instructed them to do the same. Within a few weeks, all of the murder squads manned by the SS, police or local auxiliaries began efforts to kill the entire Jewish population of the German-occupied Soviet Union in summer and autumn 1942.

The four Einsatzgruppen had shot around 55,000 Jews in the Soviet Union by the end of July 1941. As the year reached its end, the death toll was ten times greater. Massacres were now a routine occurrence in the »German East«. At the end of August 1941, units headed by the Higher SS and Police Leader, Friedrich Jeckeln (1895 – 1946), killed around 23,600

Die Erschießungen in der Sowjetunion 1941 – 1944

Hatten die vier Einsatzgruppen in der Sowjetunion bis Ende Juli 1941 ungefähr 55.000 Juden erschossen, belief sich die Bilanz zum Jahresende auf das Zehnfache. Massaker gehörten nun zum Alltag im »deutschen Osten«. Ende August 1941 ermordeten Einheiten des Höheren SS- und Polizeiführers Friedrich Jeckeln (1895 – 1946) im ukrainischen Kamenez-Podolsk an drei Tagen ungefähr 23.600 Juden. Einen Monat später töteten SS- und Polizeieinheiten in der Schlucht Babij Jar einen Großteil der verbliebenen jüdischen Gemeinde von Kiew und meldeten 33.771 Opfer nach Berlin. Entsetzt kommentierten britische Abhörspezialisten, die den Funkcode der Ordnungspolizei entschlüsselt hatten und so die täglichen Mordmeldungen mitlasen, SS-Führer würden offenbar miteinander um die höchsten Zahlen »wetteifern«.

Darüber hinaus wurde Mitte August in der Sowjetunion noch eine weitere Entwicklung in Gang gesetzt: Himmler sorgte sich ernsthaft, seine Männer könnten angesichts ihres mörderischen Alltags seelischen Schaden nehmen. Daher wies er hohe SS-Führer an, nach anderen Tötungsmethoden zu suchen. Bald darauf experimentierten Fachleute aus Berlin in Weißrussland an Psychiatriepatienten. Während sich Sprengstoff als ungeeignet erwies, erwiesen sich kohlenmonoxidhaltige Abgase von Benzinmotoren als vielversprechend. Wochen später tauchten in der Ukraine die ersten Lastkraftwagen auf, in deren dicht verschließbaren Kastenaufbauten Menschen durch die Einleitung der Fahrzeugabgase innerhalb weniger Minuten getötet werden konnten. Mehr als 20 dieser Gaswagen wurden von Sicherheitspolizei und SD in der Sowjetunion eingesetzt. Bis 1944 kamen in solchen mobilen Gaskammern mindestens 200.000 Juden, Roma, Patienten psychiatrischer Anstalten und weitere Zivilpersonen ums Leben. Dieses im Warthegau und Weißrussland erprobte Verfahren wurde ab 1942 dann in den Vernichtungslagern Belzec, Sobibor und Treblinka vor allem zur Ermordung der polnischen Juden angewandt. Weil es jedoch schlicht zu aufwändig war, die Menschen aus den weit entfernten Gebieten der Sowjetunion in die neuen Lager im besetzten Polen zu transportieren, weil nicht genug Gaswagen konstruiert wurden oder die zur Verfügung stehenden Fahrzeuge öfter ausfielen, fanden weiterhin Erschießungen in großem Umfang statt.

Die Täter

Die verantwortlich Handelnden gehörten vor allem Himmlers SS- und Polizeiapparat an. Die Personalstärke der vier Einsatzgruppen des Reichssicherheitshauptamts in der Sowjetunion belief sich auf gerade einmal 3.000 Mann. Nur zu einem verhältnismäßig geringen Teil waren sie Angehörige der Gestapo, der Kriminalpolizei oder des SD. Den Hauptanteil stellten vielmehr Soldaten der Waffen-SS (drei Brigaden mit zusammen fast 20.000 Mann) und etliche Bataillone der Ordnungspolizei in einer Gesamtstärke von mehreren 10.000. Hinzu kamen Fahrer, Funker und weiteres technisches Personal, das teils über Notdienstverpflichtungen zu den Einsatzgruppen versetzt worden war, außerdem mitunter einheimische Dolmetscher und Hilfspolizisten sowie teilweise weibliche Verwaltungsangestellte.

Jews in the space of three days in Kamianets-Podilsky (Ukraine). A month later, SS and police units massacred most of the Jews left in Kiev in the nearby Babi Yar ravine and put the total of victims at 33,771 in a report sent back to Berlin. British code breakers who had cracked the secret codes used in radio messages from the Order Police and therefore read the daily reports on the murders, were horrified to establish that SS leaders were evidently »competing« with each other to boast the highest number of victims.

There was an additional development in the Soviet Union in mid-August. Himmler was genuinely concerned that his men might suffer psychological damage as a result of committing murders day after day. He therefore instructed senior SS commanders to come up with other methods of killing. Soon afterwards, experts from Berlin experimented on psychiatric patients in Belarus. Blowing them up did not prove very effective, but initial tests using carbon monoxide fumes from vehicle engines were very promising. Several weeks later, the first gas vans were dispatched to the Ukraine. Exhaust fumes were pumped into the hermetically-sealed containers on the back of these vans, killing those inside within minutes. The Security Police and SD employed over 20 such vans in the Soviet Union. At least 200,000 Jews, Roma, psychiatric patients and civilians had died in these mobile gas chambers by 1944. After piloting the procedure in the Warthegau province and in Belarus, it was subsequently introduced in the extermination camps at Belzec, Sobibor und Treblinka in 1942, primarily to kill Polish Jews. However, it was simply too much work to transport people from the far-flung regions of the Soviet Union to the new camps in occupied Poland. Moreover, not enough gas vans could be produced and the vehicles available often broke down. For all these reasons, the shootings continued on a vast scale.

The perpetrators

Most of those responsible for the crimes were members of Himmler's SS and police divisions. The four Einsatzgruppen established by the Reich Security Main Office and deployed in the Soviet Union had some 3,000 members in total. Relatively few were recruited from the Gestapo, Criminal Police or SD. In addition, there were men belonging to the Waffen-SS and Order Police, drivers, radio operators and other technical staff, some of whom had been assigned to the Einsatzgruppen in order to provide additional personnel. Finally, there were interpreters and police reservists from the local area and administrative staff, some of whom were women. The majority of the perpetrators were soldiers from the Waffen-SS (three brigades with a total of almost 20,000 men) or were from the tens of thousands of troops belonging to the Order Police battalions.

At the end of July 1941, Himmler also ordered that volunteer units be assembled from the local population. These so-called auxiliary police forces (Schutzmannschaften) were nominally affiliated with the German Order Police. Additional collaborators worked for the Security Police and SD. The auxiliary forces had recruited some 300,000 men by the end of 1942 and played a key role in the shootings. The number of potential perpetrators from

Die Erschießungen in der Sowjetunion 1941 – 1944

Ende Juli 1941 hatte Himmler zudem die Aufstellung von Freiwilligenverbänden aus Einheimischen verfügt. Sogenannte Schutzmannschaften wurden nominell der deutschen Ordnungspolizei unterstellt, weitere Kollaborateure waren für Sicherheitspolizei und SD tätig. Dieses Personal, das in hohem Maße auch bei Erschießungen mitwirkte, umfasste Ende 1942 mehr als 300.000 Mann. Allein für SS und Polizei summiert sich der potenzielle Täterkreis damit auf über 350.000 Personen, von denen ab 1942 eine deutliche Mehrheit aus einheimischen Helfern bestand.

Die Wehrmacht war ebenfalls beteiligt, lobte die Zusammenarbeit mit SS und Polizei, mithin die Verbrechen in höchsten Tönen und war selbst oft genug für Morde verantwortlich. In Kamenez-Podolsk etwa notierten Wehrmachtsoffiziere im Vorfeld des Massakers angesichts der Abschiebung vieler tausend Juden aus den von Ungarn besetzten Gebieten in völligem Einvernehmen, der verantwortliche Höhere SS- und Polizeiführer hoffe, »die Liquidation dieser Juden bis zum 1.9.1941 durchgeführt zu haben«. Einige Wehrmachtseinheiten wie die 707. Sicherungsdivision beteiligten sich aktiv an der Shoah. Deren Divisionskommandeur Gustav Freiherr von Bechtolsheim (1889–1969), ein überzeugter Nationalsozialist und radikaler Antisemit, stachelte seine Truppe dazu an, in Weißrussland weit hinter der Front im Rahmen zahlreicher Erschießungen tausende Juden zu ermorden.

Überall in den deutsch besetzten Gebieten entwickelten sich Judenerschießungen zu öffentlichen Aufführungen, die von deutschen und einheimischen Gaffern bestaunt wurden. Und oft fanden sich ganz gewöhnliche Soldaten, die sich unbedingt am Morden beteiligen wollten. Als die Einsatzgruppe D im südukrainischen Cherson ein Judenmassaker verübte, beobachteten die Täter: »Vorbeifahrende Wehrmacht(s)angehörige hielten vielfach an und nahmen für kurze Zeit an der Erschießung teil.« Ebenfalls freiwillig beteiligten sich Soldaten bei Erschießungen auf der Krim. Die Übereinstimmung mit der SS zeigt sich in einer ergänzenden Erinnerung: »Diese Wehrmachtsangehörigen haben dann zusammen mit (SS-Sturmbannführer) Persterer am Abend des betreffenden Tages noch ein großes Saufgelage veranstaltet.«

Antisemitismus und Rassenhass waren entscheidende Motive von Schützen bei den alltäglich gewordenen Massakern in der Sowjetunion. Eine auf der nationalsozialistischen Ideologie basierende und etwa über Propagandaschriften oder regelmäßige weltanschauliche Schulungen bei den Einheiten gespeiste Prägung wurde vielfach durch individuell ganz unterschiedliche Beweggründe ergänzt. Gehorsam und Gruppendruck haben eine wichtige Rolle gespielt, Habgier oder die Befriedigung sexueller Triebe ebenfalls. Über Kameraden seiner Mordeinheit berichtete ein Ordnungspolizist, dass diese bei Erschießungen regelmäßig von einer »Art Blutrausch« erfasst worden seien. Allerdings habe die Täter gar nicht Lust am Töten angetrieben. Zentrale Motivation sei vielmehr gewesen, »dass es bei solchen Aktionen immer etwas zu ›organisieren‹ gab, was von diesen Leuten dann ausgenützt wurde«. Massenhaft raubten Täter ihren Opfern noch vor den Morden Bargeld, Uhren, Eheringe, allen erdenklichen Schmuck und Kleidungsstücke. Oder sie durchsuchten im Anschluss die Leichen und sicherten sich Beute.

the SS and police alone thus totalled over 350,000, a clear majority of whom were local volunteers after 1942.

The Wehrmacht was also implicated in the crimes. Its men were full of praise for the good working relations established with the SS and police and, by association, for the atrocities and they were themselves guilty of murder on a good number of occasions. Prior to the massacre in Kamianets-Podilsky, for example, which was carried out to kill thousands of Jews deported from Hungarian-occupied territory, Wehrmacht officers expressed their support for the Higher SS and Police Leader's objective »to have completed the liquidation of these Jews by 1 September 1941«. Next to the deported, also the local Jews were murdered. Some Wehrmacht units, such as the 707th infantry division, played an active part in the Shoah. The commander of this division, Gustav Freiherr von Bechtolsheim (1889–1969), was a staunch National Socialist with radical anti-semitic views. He incited his troops to carry out a large number of shootings in Belarus, far away from the front, killing thousands of Jews.

The shooting of Jews became public spectacles throughout German-occupied territory, drawing crowds of Germans and locals eager to have a look. It was often the most ›ordinary‹ soldiers who were keen to get involved in the murders. Whilst Einsatzgruppe D was massacring Jews in Kherson in southern Ukraine, the perpetrators observed that: »Wehrmacht soldiers who were passing by often stopped to help out with the shooting for a while.« Soldiers also willingly participated in the shootings in the Crimea. An additional account illustrates the good rapport between the Wehrmacht and SS: »That evening, the same Wehrmacht soldiers then went out on a drinking spree with (SS-Sturmbannführer) Persterer.«

Antisemitism and racial hatred would definitely have spurred on the marksmen responsible for what were now regarded as routine massacres in the Soviet Union. A mindset shaped by National Socialist ideology and reinforced by propaganda or regular indoctrination during their military training was often coupled with other motivational factors that varied widely from individual to individual. Obedience and peer pressure played a key role, as did greed and the desire to satisfy sexual urges. One member of the Order Police recalled that the men from his murder squad regularly succumbed to a kind of »blood lust«. However, he also maintained that the perpetrators were not driven by the desire to kill. Instead they were primarily motivated by the fact »that there was always something to ›sort‹ during these operations, which these men then took advantage of«. The perpetrators stripped their victims of money, watches, wedding rings, clothing and any jewellery they had before murdering them. Alternatively, they searched and looted the bodies afterwards.

Although »racial defilement« was known to be strictly out of bounds, especially for the self-appointed SS elite, many of the perpetrators had no qualms about raping Jewish women or sexually exploiting them over lengthy periods. When they eventually lost interest, they simply shot these inconvenient witnesses at the next available opportunity. It was common

Die Erschießungen in der Sowjetunion 1941 – 1944

Obwohl gerade für die selbsternannte SS-Elite »Rassenschande« bekanntlich strengstens verboten war, scheuten sich viele Täter keineswegs, jüdische Frauen zu vergewaltigen oder im Rahmen vorgeschobener Dienstverhältnisse über längere Zeit sexuell auszubeuten. Waren sie der Frauen irgendwann überdrüssig, erschossen die Täter solche unbequemen Zeuginnen bei nächster Gelegenheit. Dass Vergewaltigungen, Raub oder Plünderungen gegen die strafbewehrte nationalsozialistische Moral verstießen, war allgemein bekannt. Dass derartige »Verfehlungen« im deutsch besetzten Osten dennoch gang und gäbe waren, offenbart ein bemerkenswertes Maß an selbstgestrickter Doppelmoral. So wähnten sich deutsche Polizisten, Soldaten und SS-Angehörige einerseits als Vorkämpfer einer neuen Ordnung, die mittels besonderer Wertmaßstäbe mit vermeintlichen Missständen rücksichtslos aufräumte. Andererseits wurde dieser nationalsozialistische Kodex im Alltag von den gleichen Personen ständig unterlaufen, um sich persönliche Vorteile zu verschaffen. Die Erkenntnis, dass individuelle Gewalt verschiedenster Täter ein Massenphänomen darstellte, weist wiederum auf den Charakter des deutschen Vernichtungskriegs hin. Erschießungen, Hunger, individueller Terror und alltägliche Gewalt bildeten ein alptraumhaftes und zugleich geplantes Gesamtbild, das heute nur noch ansatzweise rekonstruiert werden kann. Ohne einheimische Helfer wären die Verbrechen nicht so reibungslos umzusetzen gewesen. Kollaborateure haben damit einen bedeutenden, noch längst nicht hinreichend erforschten Anteil an der Umsetzung der Vernichtungspolitik, die allerdings ohne deutsche Urheber nicht in Gang gesetzt worden wäre.

Festzuhalten bleibt: Das nationalsozialistische Deutschland hatte mit den grundlegenden verbrecherischen Befehlen und vielfältigen weiteren Initiativen den maßgeblichen Rahmen geschaffen, um mit Beginn des Krieges gegen die Sowjetunion ein Gewaltpotenzial neuen Ausmaßes zu entfesseln. Schon nach wenigen Wochen brachen letzte zivilisatorische Dämme und deutsche Polizei- und SS-Angehörige gingen bereitwillig dazu über, unterschiedslos Kinder, Frauen und Männer zu ermorden. Damit mündete die deutsche Vernichtungspolitik unverkennbar in das, was wir heute als Shoah oder Holocaust bezeichnen. Die ungezählten Erschießungen auf dem Gebiet der Sowjetunion endeten erst, als auch die Juden der letzten verbliebenen Ghettos und Arbeitslager ermordet worden waren und der erzwungene deutsche Rückzug 1944 weitere Verbrechen an der Zivilbevölkerung unmöglich machte.

knowledge that rape, theft and looting contravened the National Socialists' strict moral code. The fact that such »misdemeanours« were nonetheless rife in Eastern Europe under the German occupation is indicative of the extent to which the National Socialists operated according to their own double standards. Hence, German police, soldiers and SS members on the one hand perceived themselves as the trailblazers of a new world order who adhered to a distinct set of values in the ruthless drive to eliminate supposed evils. Yet on the other hand, the same individuals breached this National Socialist moral code time and time again for their own personal gain. The realisation that the individual atrocities committed by a broad spectrum of perpetrators were a mass phenomenon in turn sheds light on the nature of the German war of annihilation. Shootings, starvation, individual acts of terror and routine violence fit into a nightmarish but equally preordained scenario that can only be partially reconstructed today. The atrocities could not have run so smoothly without the input of local volunteers. The collaborators thus played a significant and as yet under-researched role in implementing National Socialist extermination policy, although without the Germans behind it this policy would of course have never come into effect.

The fact remains that through a series of decisive criminal orders and a wealth of additional initiatives, National Socialist Germany constructed a definitive framework for the unprecedented displays of brutality unleashed with the start of the war against the Soviet Union. In just a few weeks, civilised society broke down and members of the German police and SS willingly crossed the line to start murdering men, women and children indiscriminately. This marked the unmistakeable shift of German extermination policy towards what we now know as the Shoah or the Holocaust. The countless shootings on Soviet soil only ceased when the Jews from the last remaining ghettos and labour camps had also been murdered and after German troops were forced to retreat in 1944, making it impossible for them to commit any additional crimes against the civilian population.

Die Aktion 1005 oder
Vom Verschwinden der Massengräber
Andrej Angrick

Bereits zur Jahreswende 1941/42 beschloss die deutsche Führung, die Spuren des staatlich angeordneten Völkermordes an den europäischen Juden zu beseitigen. Dabei ging es um die Unkenntlichmachung aller Massengräber in den Vernichtungs- und Konzentrationslagern wie an den Erschießungsstätten im nationalsozialistisch besetzten Europa, indem die Leichen der ermordeten Männer, Frauen und Kinder zerstört werden sollten. Die Entschlussbildung und die Anfänge dieser Maßnahme liegen fast völlig im Dunkeln. Jedoch scheint die Durchführung eines solch personal- und ressourcenintensiven, vor allem aber zentral gesteuerten Projekts ohne eine Grundsatzentscheidung Adolf Hitlers kaum vorstellbar. Diese Aufgabe erhielten Heinrich Himmler und sein SS- und Polizeiapparat. Aus Geheimhaltungsgründen wurde von vornherein auf Codenamen verzichtet, wie sie sonst im NS-Jargon üblich waren – etwa Aktion Reinhardt, Endlösung oder Aktion Erntefest. Vielmehr wählten die Täter als Tarnbegriff das Aktenzeichen eines neu anzulegenden Verwaltungsvorgangs, bei dem es sich einer internen Zählung folgend um die Nr. 1005 des Reichssicherheitshauptamts (RSHA) handelte. Fortan lief die Umsetzung des Befehls unter dem Begriff Aktion 1005 oder schlicht 1005. Für eine Geheime Reichssache als höchste Geheimhaltungsstufe des »Dritten Reichs« schien eine gewöhnliche Registraturnummer am besten geeignet, da sich ihre Bedeutung lediglich Eingeweihten erschloss.

Anhand der zeitgenössischen Quellen – von denen nur eine Handvoll und zudem unvollständig Auskunft über die Aktion 1005 gibt – lässt sich diese Frage nach den Beweggründen für dieses Unternehmen nicht beantworten. Zieht man jedoch die Nachkriegsvernehmungen hauptverantwortlich Beteiligter heran, kann das Puzzle zusammengesetzt werden. Zum einen ist es die militärische Situation: Das Deutsche Reich hatte die Sowjetunion nicht wie vorgesehen erobert, sich vielmehr an einigen Stellen bereits wieder zurückziehen müssen, sei es in Rostow am Don oder in Kaluga. Man konnte sich also von deutscher Seite nicht mehr sicher sein, Herr über die oft nur unzureichend getarnten Massengräber zu bleiben und lief Gefahr, dass die Gegenseite diese für den Propagandakrieg nutzen würde – wie es das »Dritte Reich« selbst (beispielsweise nach der Eroberung Lembergs oder Rigas) getan hatte. So waren die Verbrechen des sowjetischen Geheimdienstes NKWD in alle Welt verbreitet worden.

Entgegen den ursprünglichen Vorhersagen, das Unternehmen Barbarossa schnell siegreich zu beenden, lagen deutsche Truppen im Osten fest. Daher setzte das Regime alles daran, die Moral an der Heimatfront aufrechtzuerhalten und die Verbundenheit

Operation 1005:
On the disappearance of mass graves

Andrej Angrick

As early as late 1941 or early 1942, the German leadership decided to eliminate the traces of the state-sanctioned genocide of European Jews. The aim was to remove evidence of all mass graves at the concentration and extermination camps and at the sites of mass shootings throughout Nazi-occupied territory by destroying the corpses of the men, women and children who had been murdered. There is barely any information on the origins and drafting of this decision. However, it is very unlikely that a centrally-coordinated operation on this scale, requiring vast amounts of personnel and other resources, would have gone ahead without a ›fundamental decision‹ from Adolf Hitler. Heinrich Himmler and his SS and police departments were put in charge of the project. Codenames regularly featured in National Socialist jargon, examples being Operation Reinhardt (Aktion Reinhardt), Final Solution (Endlösung) or Operation Harvest Festival (Aktion Erntefest). However, to keep it secret this plan was not given a codename. Instead the perpetrators referred to it as 1005, which related to a reference number for a new administrative procedure generated by staff at the Reich Security Main Office (RSHA). Henceforth, the project was termed Operation 1005 or simply 1005. A standard reference number seemed most appropriate for a ›Secret Reich Matter‹, the highest security classification in the »Third Reich«, as only a select few would have known what it meant.

It is impossible to ascertain the reasoning behind the plan from the scant number of resources from the period that mention Operation 1005, none of which provide a complete account. However, it is possible to piece together the motives from the post-war interrogations of major war criminals. One of the contributing factors was the military situation. The German Reich's anticipated victory over the Soviet Union had not come to pass. German troops had instead already been forced to retreat from a number of Soviet cities including Rostov-on-Don and Kaluga. The Germans could therefore no longer be certain of retaining control over the mass graves, which were often poorly camouflaged, and they ran the risk of the enemy using the existence of these graves for propaganda purposes. The »Third Reich« had done the very same thing following the capture of Lvov or Riga for example, letting the world know about the crimes of the Soviet Secret Police (NKVD).

Counter to initial expectations, Operation Barbarossa had not come to a speedy and victorious conclusion and German troops were now stuck in Eastern Europe. The regime therefore did everything in its power to keep up morale on the home front and to avoid horror stories reported by the intelligence services of enemy or neutral states from

von Führung und Volksgemeinschaft nicht durch Horrormeldungen gegnerischer und neutraler Nachrichtendienste in Funk und Presse schwächen zu lassen. Folgerichtig erging an Sicherheitspolizei, SD, Ordnungspolizei und Waffen-SS die Anweisung, alle Fotos (Negative und Positive) von Massenerschießungen – egal ob dienstlich oder privat angefertigt – an das RSHA abzugeben; einer der Gründe, warum heute so wenige Aufnahmen dieser Art vorliegen. Diese verfänglichen Fotos wurden zentral verwahrt und gehörten – wahrscheinlich – zu dem bei Kriegsende vernichteten Archivgut des Geheimen Staatspolizeiamtes (Gestapa). Schließlich handelte es sich auch um Beweismittel gegen die Täter. Und hier kommt ein weiteres Element zur Begründung der Aktion 1005 zum Tragen: die befürchtete Strafverfolgung.

Im Jahr 1941 mochten die Staatsmörder sich in völliger Sicherheit gewogen haben, selbst wenn sie in die Hand des Feindes gerieten, nie für ihre Taten zur Verantwortung gezogen zu werden. Wenngleich die Sowjetregierung in diplomatischen Erklärungen bereits früh eine Ahndung der Gräueltaten angekündigt hatte, versammelten sich am 13. Januar 1942 Vertreter von neun Exilregierungen im Londoner St. James Palace, um dort die sogenannte Inter-Alliierte-Kommission zur Bestrafung von Kriegsverbrechern ins Leben zu rufen. In der »Erklärung von St. James« betonten diese klar, dass es ihren Nationen nicht auf Rache oder Vergeltung ankomme, sondern dass man die beschuldigten Personen – egal ob sie die Verbrechen befohlen, allein oder zusammen mit anderen begangen hatten – vor ein ordentliches Gericht stellen wolle. Dieser Appell war auch im Reich gehört worden.

Ein letzter Anstoß für die Aktion 1005 dürfte gewesen sein, dass immer mehr Details über das Ausmaß des Massenmordes an die Öffentlichkeit gelangten, wozu insbesondere verstörende Nachrichten über das Vernichtungslager Kulmhof zählten, die das Warschauer Ghetto-Archiv in den Westen schmuggeln ließ. Man kann mutmaßen, dass diese Entwicklung, die in den Augen der SS-Führung und des Auswärtigen Amtes die bereits geschilderten ›Sachzwänge‹ zur Beweisvernichtung – also die Beseitigung der Leichen an den Tatorten – noch verstärkte. Mit Vorbereitung und Durchführung betraute Heinrich Himmler das RSHA und dessen Chef Reinhardt Heydrich (1904 – 1942). Dieser wiederum suchte unter seinen Leuten den geeigneten Mann aus, der das Geheimprojekt gemäß der Vorgaben umsetzen würde: SS-Standartenführer Paul Blobel (1894 – 1951), Führer des Sonderkommandos 4a, der im Winter 1942 mit seiner Einheit weit im Osten – in Charkow – stationiert war. Blobel galt im Gegensatz zu seinen Kollegen, den Einsatz- und Sonderkommandoführern, nicht als Intellektueller vom Schlage anderer führender Köpfe des SD (Sicherheitsdienstes), sondern als grobschlächtige Natur. Der studierte Architekt war bereits vor der Machübernahme 1933 der NSDAP und SS beigetreten und somit kein ›Spätberufener‹, sondern ein Mann, der sich früh in den Dienst der ›Bewegung‹ gestellt hatte. Dies empfahl ihn für die anstehende Aufgabe. Neben dem erlernten Beruf hatte er Erfahrungen als Heerespionier im Ersten Weltkrieg gesammelt; Blobel kannte sich also im weitesten Sinne mit Bodenbeschaffenheiten aus. Viel wichtiger noch, er gehörte zu den Führern der Mordkommandos. Sein Sonderkommando 4a hatte initiativ am Völkermord mitgewirkt; wobei das Massaker von Babij Jar mit 33.771 von den Tätern gezählten

appearing in the media and potentially weakening the Volksgemeinschaft's support for the Nazi leadership. The Security Police, SS Security Service (SD), Order Police and Waffen-SS were consequently instructed to hand in all photos of mass shootings (both negatives and printed images) to the RSHA, irrespective of whether these had been officially commissioned or taken in a personal capacity. This is one of the reasons why so few photographs of these events have survived. The incriminating images were stored centrally and were probably among the archived materials of the Secret State Police that were destroyed at the end of the war. These photos could of course serve as evidence to implicate the perpetrators in the crimes. The fear of criminal proceedings provided an additional motive for Operation 1005.

In 1941, the National Socialist murderers must have been under the illusion that they would never be brought to justice, even if captured by the enemy. The Soviet government had already issued declarations stating the intention to exact revenge for the atrocities. However, the representatives of nine governments in exile who met at St James's Palace in London on 13 January 1942 to establish the so-called Inter-Allied Commission on the Punishment of War Crimes adopted a different approach. The resulting »Declaration of St James's« clearly stated that the nations concerned were not out for revenge or retribution but that the priority was to subject the people charged with crimes to a proper trial – regardless of whether they had ordered crimes or had acted alone or with others. This message had also been understood in the German Reich.

A final impetus to carry out Operation 1005 was likely the fact that details of the scale of the mass murder were increasingly being made public, in particular with a number of disturbing reports about the Chełmno extermination camp, which those running the secret archive in the Warsaw ghetto had managed to have smuggled into the West. One can imagine that this development further reinforced what SS leaders and the Foreign Office viewed as the ›inherent necessity‹ to destroy the evidence, in other words to remove the corpses from the scenes of the crime. Heinrich Himmler gave the RSHA and its head, Reinhard Heydrich (1904 – 1942), the task of preparing and implementing Operation 1005. Heydrich in turn selected SS-Standartenführer Paul Blobel (1894 – 1951), the head of Sonderkommando 4a, as the best man to carry out the secret plan according to instructions. Blobel and his unit were stationed in Kharkov – in the depths of Eastern Europe – in the winter of 1942. Unlike his colleagues who headed the Einsatzkommandos and Sonderkommandos, Blobel was not regarded as an intellectual in the same mould as elite members of the SD, but as rather rough around the edges. An architect by profession, Blobel had joined the NSDAP and SS before the Nazis assumed power in 1933 and he was thus not a ›latecomer‹ to the ›movement‹ but someone who had offered his services at an early stage. He was therefore seen as having the right credentials for the task. Along with his training as an architect, Blobel had also gained experience as an army engineer in World War One. He was therefore familiar with ground conditions in the broadest sense of the term. More importantly, he was at the helm of a murder squad. Under his leadership, Sonderkommando 4a had played an instrumental role in the genocide, one of the most

Die Aktion 1005 oder Vom Verschwinden der Massengräber

Ermordeten hervorsticht. Im Zuge dessen hatte Blobel – man ist gezwungen, es so zu benennen – an der Weiterentwicklung der Mordmethoden mitgewirkt.

Blobel verabschiedete sich Ende März 1942 von seiner alten Einheit und reiste zusammen mit seinem Fahrer und Vertrauten Julius Bauer von Charkow nach Warschau, wo er mit Heydrich zusammentraf. Dieser weihte Blobel in seinen Geheimauftrag ein und übertrug ihm offiziell die Aktion 1005. Einige Zeit später – Blobel war nach Berlin in die Zentrale des Terrors weitergereist – erhielt er von Gestapo-Chef Heinrich Müller (1900 – 1945) weiterreichende Anweisungen.

Damit Blobel seinen Auftrag ohne Widerstände der SS- und Polizeifunktionäre ausführen konnte und keiner anderen Einrichtung oder anderen Amtsträgern Rechenschaft über sein Tun abzulegen brauchte, erhielt er von Himmler einen Sonderausweis ausgestellt. Dieser ist als zeithistorisches Artefakt nicht überliefert, jedoch hatten ihn viele SS-Funktionäre gesehen – man hatte ihnen das Dokument buchstäblich vorgehalten. Auf diesem Stück Papier stand sinngemäß, dass Blobel durch Himmler umfassende Sondervollmachten eingeräumt worden seien und insbesondere jede SS- und Polizeidienststelle ihn zu unterstützen habe, sich seinen Anweisungen nicht verweigern dürfe. Mit diesem Zettel war – für diesen Fall – die SS-Rangfolge außer Kraft gesetzt worden. Selbst ranghöhere Funktionsträger hätten sich Weisungen Blobels zu fügen und andere – mitunter in Wettstreit stehende – Ämter wie das SS-Wirtschafts- und Verwaltungshauptamt, das Hauptamt Ordnungspolizei oder die Verwaltung der drei Vernichtungslager der Aktion Reinhardt im besetzten Polen (Treblinka, Belzec und Sobibor) dem Mann Heydrichs und somit dem RSHA zu Diensten sein müssen. Durch die Übernahme der Aktion 1005 war es Heydrich so auch gelungen – ergänzend zum Befehl Hermann Görings vom 31. Juli 1941, die »erforderlichen Vorbereitungen in organisatorischer, sachlicher und materieller Hinsicht« bei der »Gesamtlösung der Judenfrage in Europa« einzuleiten –, zugleich für die Spurenbeseitigung verantwortlich zu sein. Damit erfuhr Heydrichs Apparat einen Machtzuwachs gegenüber anderen mit der »Endlösung« betrauten Organisationen, ja Heydrich und das RSHA durften sich erstmals als umfassend für dieses von staatlicher Seite geplante und ausgeführte Verbrechen zuständig ansehen.

Blobel dagegen dürfte die verwaltungsmäßige Anbindung weniger interessiert haben, für ihn galt es zunächst, zwei Fragen zu lösen: Zum einen musste er die Anzahl der ermordeten Menschen und die Lage der Massengräber in Erfahrung bringen, zum anderen ein geeignetes Verfahren zur rückstandslosen Beseitigung der Leichen entwickeln.
Das erste ›Problem‹ versuchte Blobel aus den Unterlagen des Referates von Adolf Eichmann (1906 – 1962), Referent für »Judenangelegenheiten, Räumungsangelegenheiten« im RSHA, zu lösen. Dabei ging es darum, im Nachgang die Mordvorgänge zu rekonstruieren. Auch wurden zu einem späteren Zeitpunkt die einzelnen Gestapo- und Polizeidienststellen angehalten, ihre Unterlagen zu überprüfen und die genaue Lage der Gräber sowie die Zahl der verscharrten Personen zu melden. Da die Aktion 1005 über kein eigenes Stabsquartier in Berlin verfügte, bezog Blobel im Rahmen seines Auftrages im Gästehaus am Wannsee

notable examples being the Babi Yar massacre, at which the perpetrators put the death toll at 33,771. In this role, Blobel had been involved in what one can only describe as the perfecting of murder methods.

Blobel took leave of his former unit in Kharkov at the end of March 1942 and travelled to Warsaw with Julius Bauer, his driver and confidante, to meet Heydrich. Heydrich filled him in on the secret plans and gave him the official responsibility for Operation 1005. Blobel travelled on to Berlin, where National Socialist terror was coordinated, and received further instructions from the Gestapo chief, Heinrich Müller (1900 – 1945).

Himmler issued Blobel with a special permit enabling him to implement the plans without resistance from SS or police officials and without having to be accountable to any other authority or official. This permit no longer exists but many SS officials saw it at the time as it was literally held in front of their noses. The permit stated that Himmler had granted Blobel a special mandate and that each and every SS and police department in particular was to support him and had no authority to refuse to obey his instructions. The permit served to dissolve the SS hierarchy in this particular case. Even elite officials were to follow Blobel's orders and bodies such as the SS Economic and Administration Main Office, the headquarters of the Order Police or the administration of the three extermination camps in occupied Poland established under Operation Reinhardt (Treblinka, Belzec and Sobibor) – which by now were vying with each other for responsibility – had to answer to Heydrich and therefore the Reich Security Main Office (RSHA). In taking on Operation 1005, Heydrich had succeeded in taking charge of the process of removing evidence, in addition to the responsibility already conferred on him through the order from Hermann Göring on 31 July 1941 commissioning him to carry out »all necessary preparations with regard to organisational, practical and material aspects for a complete solution (Gesamtlösung) of the Jewish question in Europe«. In this way, Heydrich's administration saw its power increase compared to other organisations charged with implementing the »Final Solution«. For the first time, Heydrich and the RSHA could indeed now consider themselves to have the overall responsibility for this state-planned and centrally-coordinated crime.

However, Blobel was probably not that interested in the administrative side of things. His priority was to solve two problems. Firstly, he had to find out how many people had been killed and ascertain where the mass graves were located, and secondly he had to establish a workable procedure for removing the bodies and all traces of them.
Blobel attempted to solve the first ›problem‹ by consulting documents from the section for »Jewish Affairs and Clearing Activities« at the Reich Security Main Office, which was headed by Adolf Eichmann (1906 – 1962). The task was to reconstruct the murders one by one. At a later stage, the individual Gestapo and police departments were also called upon to check their files and notify Blobel of the exact location of the mass graves and the number of people buried in shallow graves. As Operation 1005 did not have its own headquarters in Berlin, Blobel moved into the SS guesthouse at Wannsee while he was working on it. Just a few months before, senior officials from German ministries and authorities together with

Die Aktion 1005 oder Vom Verschwinden der Massengräber

seine Unterkunft. Von dem Ort aus, an dem wenige Monate zuvor führende Vertreter deutscher Ministerien bzw. Behörden mit der SS- und Polizeiführung das nähere Vorgehen bei der Ermordung der europäischen Juden besprochen hatten, wurde nunmehr auch die Spurenbeseitigung gesteuert. Zudem lief über das benachbarte Havel-Institut, einer Funkanlage des SD, die Kurierpost der Aktion 1005. Das andere ›Problem‹ konnte allerdings nicht durch Aktenstudium oder Nachforschungen vor Ort gelöst werden: Wie konnten die Leichen zerstört werden, wie die Massengräber verschwinden?

Blobel reiste mit Bauer nach Kulmhof, um sich mit einem anderen ›Experten‹, dem Leiter des Vernichtungslagers, Kriminalkommissar und SS-Hauptsturmführer Hans Bothmann (1911 – 1946), aufgrund seiner Erfahrungen zu besprechen. Beide Männer kamen schnell zur Erkenntnis, dass es mehr bräuchte, als »nur Benzin auf die geöffneten Gräber zu gießen« – wie man »fälschlicherweise in Berlin annahm«. Im Sommer des Jahres 1942 experimentierten Blobel und Bothmann – jeweils mit ihren Stäben – mit Flammenwerfern, Termit-Sprengsätzen oder Chemikalien; alles erwies sich als unzureichend. Es wurde deutlich, dass die Leichen nicht in der Tiefe zu beseitigen waren, sondern aus den Massengräbern hervorgeholt werden mussten. Nach einiger Zeit entwickelte man in Kulmhof die Methode, die fortan – in verschiedenen Varianten – angewandt werden sollte: Nach ihrer Bergung waren die Leichen in einen Erdofen zu ziehen und dort aufeinanderzulegen. Der Ofen befand sich tief in der Erde, seine Begrenzung war aus Ziegelsteinen gemauert. Um die Luftzufuhr steuern zu können, war ein Belüftungsschacht mit der Verbrennungsanlage verbunden worden.
Als Rost dienten Eisenbahnschienen, während vom Forstamt gelieferte Hölzer und Reisigbündel für die kontrollierte Befeuerung genutzt wurden. Diese Vorgehensweise brachte den gewünschten Erfolg. Nachdem eine gewisse Erfahrung vorlag, bedurfte die Aktion an anderer Stelle nicht zwingend Erdgruben, es reichte aus, die Leichen auf Eisenbahnschienen oder massivem Holz aufzutürmen. Die Täter sollten die veraltet anmutende, aber wirksame Vorgehensweise im Laufe ihrer Einsätze vervollkommnen und sich rühmen, Leichenpyramiden mit bis zu 2.000 Körpern schichten zu können.

Indes war es mit dem Verbrennen allein nicht getan. Die Knochenrückstände mussten zerstört werden: durch Handmörser oder ergänzende Knochenmühlen (Betonmischer oder industrielle Kaffeemühlen). Die Rückstände durchsuchte man nach wertvollen Hinterlassenschaften wie Goldzähnen oder Edelsteinen. Letztendlich sammelte man die Asche und verstreute sie entweder (etwa zur Düngung), schüttete sie in einen Fluss oder vergrub sie an geeigneter Stelle – je nachdem, was am Ort als sinnvoll erschien.
Zur eigentlichen Arbeit zwangen die Täter von ihnen eigens ausgewählte, körperlich kräftige Häftlinge des jüdischen Arbeitskommandos von Kulmhof. Auch an allen anderen Orten griff man dann in erster Linie auf jüdische Männer zurück. Nur wenn eine Ortschaft bereits als »judenfrei« galt, griff man für die Aktion 1005 auf andere Gefangene (zumeist aus Zuchthäusern der Gestapo) zurück. Als ›Geheimnisträger‹ wurden sie spätestens nach Beendigung der Arbeiten getötet oder bei einer längeren Dauer der Grabungs- und Zerstörungsarbeiten in regelmäßigen Zeitabschnitten ›ausgetauscht‹, also ermordet und durch neue Häftlinge ›ersetzt‹.

SS and police leaders had met at Wannsee to finalise the plan to murder European Jews. It was here that a project was now coordinated to remove the evidence of these murders. Messages related to Operation 1005 were sent via the neighbouring Havel Institute, a radio facility run by the SD. The second ›problem‹ could however not be solved just by looking through files or investigating the site of the crimes. How could the bodies be destroyed and how could the evidence of mass graves be hidden?

Blobel and Bauer travelled to Chełmno (Kulmhof) to meet another ›expert‹, the police commissioner and SS-Hauptsturmführer Hans Bothmann (1911 – 1946), who had experience in this area as head of the Kulmhof extermination camp. Blobel and Bothmann soon realised that it would take more than »simply pouring petrol on the open graves« as had »been wrongly assumed in Berlin«. During the summer of 1942, the two men and their staff experimented with flame-throwers, incendiary devices and chemicals, but none of these worked well enough. It became clear that the bodies could not be destroyed while they were still in the ground but instead they needed to be removed from the mass graves. After some time, a standard method to dispose of the bodies was developed at Kulmhof and subsequently adopted in a variety of formats. The bodies were to be dug up and laid one on top of the other in an underground oven. The oven was located deep underground and surrounded by a brick wall. An air vent was connected to the cremation device in order to control the airflow. Rails were laid to form a grate and timber and brushwood supplied by the forestry commission were used to light and stoke the fire. This method yielded the desired results. Once the technique had been established, it became apparent that underground ovens were not always essential – the bodies could be simply piled up on wooden boards or rails. The perpetrators perfected this method, which seemed old-fashioned but worked, until they could boast of stacking up piles of up to 2,000 bodies in human pyramids.

However, simply burning the bodies was not enough. Any remaining pieces of bone had to be destroyed using a hand-held mortar mixer or additional crushing devices (concrete mixers or industrial coffee grinders). The fragments were searched for valuables such as gold teeth or precious stones. Finally, the ashes were collected and either scattered (for example as fertiliser), poured into a river or buried in an appropriate place, depending on what worked best at the respective sites.
The perpetrators personally selected physically strong prisoners from the Jewish labour commando at Kulmhof and forced them to carry out the dirty work. Jewish men formed the bulk of the workers in other locations too. Other prisoners (mainly from Gestapo prisons) were only assigned to Operation 1005 if a location was already deemed »Jew free«. As they had ›access to secret information‹ the prisoners were murdered once the work was completed, if not before. In cases where the process of exhuming and destroying the bodies was fairly lengthy they were regularly ›swapped‹, in other words murdered and ›replaced‹ with new prisoners.

Die Aktion 1005 oder Vom Verschwinden der Massengräber

Vor all diesen Menschen lag eine nicht zu beschreibende Qual: Sie wurden zuerst gezwungen, die Erdschichten über den Massengräbern abzutragen. Dabei schlugen Wachhabende zu, wenn es zu langsam ging, die Gefangenen kurz miteinander redeten oder Fehler begingen. Sie mussten auch ansonsten Hiebe, ständige Beschimpfungen und sonstige schikanöse Launen ihrer Wächter ertragen und dennoch ›aufmerksam‹ ihrer grausigen Arbeit nachkommen. Viele gingen an dieser Behandlung rasch innerlich zu Grunde. Schließlich war es keine Seltenheit, dass sie die halb verwesten Körper von Verwandten oder Freunden aus der Erde ziehen mussten. Andere verkrafteten die schreckliche Tätigkeit auch körperlich nicht mehr. Die Mörder gingen bald dazu über, die Gefangenen als »Figuren« zu bezeichnen, um ihnen das Menschsein abzusprechen. Die Häftlinge hatten zumeist nur noch wenige Tage zu leben, dann wurden sie – seelisch gebrochen und körperlich ausgelaugt – getötet.

Zu einem späteren Zeitpunkt änderten die Täter ihr Vorgehen. Sie meinten, es sei (zumeist) effektiver, ihre Zwangsarbeiter besser zu behandeln, sie mit ausreichend Nahrung zu versorgen, ihnen – bei »guter Arbeit« – Hoffnungen auf eine Entlassung zu machen, ja Freizeitbeschäftigungen wie Musik oder Kartenspiele zu gestatten, um sie in Sicherheit zu wiegen, ihre Motivation zu heben und einer Flucht so vorzubeugen. In der Tat ist aus Nachkriegsvernehmungen bekannt, dass einige wenige Häftlinge Vertrauen fassten, die Mehrheit sich aber keiner Illusion über die Pläne und den Charakter ihrer Bewacher hingab und zu Recht annahm, dass man sie am Ende der Leichenbeseitigung ermorden würde.

Blobel verfügte im Sommer 1942 über eine überall verwendbare Brenn- und Zerstörungstechnik, die gleichermaßen einfach und wirksam war. Nun hieß es, die Aktion 1005 nach Abschluss dieser Testphase auszuweiten. Einer Weisung Himmlers folgend waren als erstes die Leichenfelder von Auschwitz-Birkenau – vornehmlich handelte es sich bei den Ermordeten um sowjetische Kriegsgefangene sowie im Bunker I und II um Juden aus der Slowakei und Frankreich – mit der entwickelten Methode zu beseitigen. Dies war eine Voraussetzung für den weiteren Ausbau der Vernichtungsstätte mit großräumigen Gasanlagen und modernen Krematorien. Zu diesem Zweck erfolgte (in Kulmhof und in Auschwitz-Birkenau) die Ausbildung einiger SS-Angehöriger um den SS-Obersturmführer Franz Hössler (1906 – 1945). Diese gaben wiederum ihre Kenntnisse über die ›ideale‹ Art der Verbrennung später an ihre Kollegen im Konzentrationslager Majdanek bei Lublin weiter. Blobel selbst ließ das Personal der Lager der Aktion Reinhardt entsprechend ausbilden. Nicht wenige seiner ›Schüler‹ verfügten bereits über Erfahrung bei der Einäscherung der Opfer der T4-Aktion, des Mordes an Anstaltspatienten im Deutschen Reich. Im ersten Drittel des Jahres 1943 war die Aktion 1005 in allen Vernichtungslagern des Regimes abgeschlossen. Blobels eigentliches Betätigungsfeld tat sich fortan hauptsächlich auf dem Gebiet der besetzten Sowjetunion, aber auch im Generalgouvernement für das besetzte Polen und in Serbien auf.

Im Zuge der Niederlage der 6. Armee vor Stalingrad war klar geworden, dass man die Spurenbeseitigung der Verbrechen an der Ostfront sträflich vernachlässigt hatte.

These prisoners faced inconceivable horrors. They were firstly forced to clear away the layers of earth covering the mass graves. Guards would beat them if they were too slow, exchanged words with each other or made a mistake. They had to endure random beatings, constant abuse and other forms of bullying from the guards whilst being expected to carry out this horrendous task in a ›conscientious‹ fashion. These conditions soon caused many to shut down emotionally. After all, some of them had to pull the semi-decomposed bodies of their friends or family out of the ground. Others could not cope physically with the horrific work. The murderers soon began to describe the prisoners as »Figuren« (bodies), no longer acknowledging them as humans. Pushed to the ultimate limits of their mental and physical capabilities, the prisoners mostly had just days to live before being murdered.

The perpetrators later changed their approach. They thought that it would (usually) be most effective to treat their forced labourers better, to feed them enough, to let them hope that they would be released as a reward for »good work«, even to allow them to play music or cards when they were not working. The aim was to lull them into a false sense of security, to motivate them and to deter them from escaping. Post-war interrogations reveal that the strategy did in fact win over a few of the prisoners, but the majority were under no illusions over the intentions and the true character of their guards and they were right in presuming that they would be killed once they had disposed of the bodies.

By the summer of 1942, Blobel had developed a tried and tested method of cremating and destroying bodies that was both straightforward and effective and could be employed anywhere. Now that the pilot phase was over, the task was to roll out the implementation of Operation 1005. Following instructions from Himmler, the process was to be firstly used to clear the mass graves at Auschwitz-Birkenau. These mainly contained the corpses of Soviet prisoners of war and of Jews from Slovakia and France killed in the gas chambers of Bunkers I and II. The removal of bodies was necessary here to allow the extension of the extermination site with the addition of large-scale gas chambers and modern crematoria. SS-Obersturmführer Franz Hössler (1906 – 1945) trained a number of SS officers in the disposal methods at Kulmhof and Auschwitz-Birkenau. These officers later passed on what they had learnt about the ›ideal‹ method of cremation to their colleagues at the Majdanek extermination camp near Lublin. Blobel himself ensured that staff at the camps established under Operation Reinhardt got the right training. Quite a few of his ›trainees‹ already had experience of cremating the victims of Operation T4, the programme of murdering patients with physical and mental disabilities on Third Reich territory. Operation 1005 was completed in all National Socialist extermination camps within the first four months of 1943. From this point onwards, Blobel's work mainly took place in the occupied Soviet Union, but also in the General Government in occupied Poland and in Serbia.

As the German 6th Army was losing the Battle of Stalingrad, it became clear that the troops had been shockingly remiss in removing the traces of crimes on the Eastern front. The realisation dawned when the Soviets launched a propaganda offensive after the Extraordinary Soviet Commission for the Investigation of National Socialist Crimes had

Die Aktion 1005 oder Vom Verschwinden der Massengräber

Auslöser dieser Erkenntnis war die propagandistische Offensive der Sowjets, nachdem die Außerordentliche Staatliche Kommission zur Untersuchung der nationalsozialistischen Verbrechen die Massengräber von Rostow am Don mit etwa 20.000 Leichen der Weltöffentlichkeit bekannt gemacht hatte. Propagandaminister Dr. Joseph Goebbels (1897 – 1945) gab die Order aus, darauf nicht zu reagieren, doch Blobel sollte dafür Sorge tragen, dass sich dies nicht wiederhole.

Blobel gründete daher zunächst zwei Sonderkommandos 1005 – A und B. Das Sonderkommando B war für den Einsatz im Generalkommissariat Dnjepropetrowsk vorgesehen, A für das Generalkommissariat Kiew. Es folgten weitere Gründungen: Das Sonderkommando Mitte (oder auch C) für Zentral- und Weißrussland sowie die in der Forschung bisher weitgehend im Dunkeln gebliebenen Einheiten D und E für den Nordabschnitt, vor allem Lettland und Litauen. Diese Truppen konnten die Unmengen von Gräbern nicht beseitigen, nicht alle Leichen verbrennen. Daher waren lokale Gestapostellen angehalten, selbstständige 1005-Kommandos zu bilden, um ihre speziell geschulten Kollegen zu entlasten. Außerdem bestand seit spätestens Juni 1943 ein Grundsatzbefehl Blobels, keine weiteren Gräber mehr anzulegen. Vielmehr galt es, die Leichen unmittelbar nach Massenerschießungen zu verbrennen.

Für die interne Kommunikation, die häufig per Fernschreiben oder Funk erfolgte, war eine Tarnsprache unerlässlich. Ein Vertrauter Blobels entwickelte Tarnbegriffe: »Vorkommen« bedeutete Massengrab, »Niederschlagsgebiet« den Einsatzraum, »Baustelle« das Öffnen der Gräber und »Wolkenhöhe« die Zahl der jeweils verbrannten Leichen. Der erste Einsatzort des Sonderkommandos 1005 A war die Schlucht von Babij Jar, wo sich neben dem Gelände des Septembermassakers noch weitere Massengräber befanden. Hier lagen die von Oktober 1941 bis August 1943 ermordeten Menschen verscharrt. Insgesamt muss man von etwa 50.000 Leichen ausgehen. Das Gräberfeld war so riesig, dass das Sonderkommando 1005 A für diesen Einsatz durch Kollegen des Sonderkommandos 1005 B verstärkt werden musste. »Einsatz« bedeutete hier das Schinden von 300 Gefangenen aus dem Lager Syretz im Norden Kiews. Einigen wenigen von ihnen gelang die Flucht.

Für Blobel war das Ergebnis von Babij Jar daher zwiespältig. Zwar war es ihm gelungen, die Gräber rechtzeitig vor der Aufgabe der ukrainischen Hauptstadt zu beseitigen. Doch die erfolgreiche Flucht der Häftlinge und deren Berichte über die Aktion 1005 bei Radio Moskau waren in seinen Augen ein nicht wieder gutzumachendes Versäumnis. Seine beiden im Süden operierenden 1005-Kommandos folgten dem Weg der Einsatzgruppen nun in umgekehrter Richtung von West nach Ost. Sie suchten Stätten der Massenmorde der Jahre 1941/42 auf – Einsätze erfolgten bei Berditschew, Belaja Zerkow, Kriwoj Rog, Nikolajew, Kamenez-Podolsk oder Lemberg – und sollten nie wieder eine größere Zahl von Häftlingen entkommen lassen.

Einige Massengräber blieben gänzlich unberührt; gehetzt und offenbar von der Wucht und Dynamik der sowjetischen Offensiven überrascht, kamen die Sonderkommandos

informed the world's media about the mass graves in Rostov-on-Don, which contained some 20,000 bodies. The German Propaganda Minister Dr Joseph Goebbels (1897 – 1945) ordered that no statement should be issued in response, but warned Blobel to ensure that this would not happen again.

As a result, Blobel firstly formed Sonderkommandos A and B to carry out Operation 1005. Sonderkommando B was assigned to the General Commissariat in Dnipropetrovsk and Sonderkommando A to the General Commissariat in Kiev. Additional units were subsequently established: Sonderkommando Mitte (or C) for Central Russia and Belarus and units D and E for the occupied territories in the north, primarily Latvia and Lithuania. There is very little research to date on the latter units. The commandos were unable to obliterate the countless mass graves or to burn all the bodies. Local Gestapo departments were therefore instructed to form their own 1005 commandos to relieve their specially trained colleagues. Moreover, by June 1943 at the latest Blobel had issued an order forbidding the digging of any more graves. Bodies were now to be cremated straight after mass shootings rather than being buried.

A secret code was essential for internal communications, which were often transmitted via telex or radio. One of Blobel's close associates developed the following code words: »Vorkommen« (deposit) stood for mass grave, »Niederschlagsgebiet« (precipitation area) for the operational area, »Baustelle« (building site) for opening up the graves and »Wolkenhöhe« (cloud height) for the number of corpses cremated in each case. Sonderkommando A was firstly sent to the Babi Yar ravine, where there were mass graves of the September massacre but also additional shallow graves containing the bodies of those murdered between October 1941 and August 1943. There must have been around 50,000 bodies here in total. The field of graves was so vast that Sonderkommando 1005 A required back-up from Sonderkommando 1005 B to complete the task. The »assignment« itself was carried out by 300 prisoners dispatched as forced labourers from the Syrets camp in the north of Kiev. A few of these prisoners managed to escape.

For Blobel, the outcome of the operation at Babi Yar thus had both a positive and a negative outcome. He had managed to destroy the graves before Kiev was recaptured by the Red Army. However, he considered the failure to stop the prisoners from escaping and their subsequent accounts of Operation 1005 to Radio Moscow to represent a serious blunder that could not be rectified. His two 1005 commandos operating in the South now followed the paths of the Einsatzgruppen in the opposite direction from West to East. They went in search of mass murder sites used in 1941/42 and went to Berdichev, Bila Tserkva, Krivoy Rog, Nikolaev, Kamianets-Podilsky and Lvov. Never again would they allow such a large group of prisoners to escape.

Some of the mass graves remained untouched. Under pressure and clearly stunned by the force and momentum of the Soviet offensive, the Sonderkommandos did not even manage to reach some of the locations of the crimes, such as Lubny. Elsewhere the regional

erst gar nicht dazu, einige Tatorte – wie beispielsweise Lubny – aufzusuchen. An anderer Stelle versagten die regionalen Kräfte. Zwar sind aus sowjetischen Erhebungen einzelne »Einerdungen« in den Amtsbezirken Wolhynien und Podolien nachweisbar. Doch ein Großteil der Massengräber blieb bestehen, war bestenfalls getarnt und mit Chlorkalk bestreut worden, nicht zuletzt weil die 1005er sich unversehens absetzen und ihre letzten Wirkungsstätten nur unzureichend beräumt zurücklassen mussten.

Überall fehlte Blobels Trupps die Zeit, häufig ebenso das Material und schließlich ging – wenn überhaupt vorhanden – auch die Motivation verloren. Die Männer der 1005-Kommandos, deren Mannschaftsdienstgrade und somit die Mehrheit des abgestellten Personals zur Ordnungspolizei zählten, hatten aufgrund ihrer Tätigkeit früher als andere erkannt und gespürt, dass der Krieg unwiderruflich verloren war und sie als Spurenbeseitiger Gefahr liefen, dafür die Konsequenzen zu tragen. Auch die SS-Führung sah das Problem; Himmler wollte seine Leute nicht an der Ostfront belassen, sie nicht der Gefahr aussetzen, in sowjetische Gefangenschaft zu geraten. Aus diesem Grund wurde der Großteil der Angehörigen der 1005-Sonderkommandos im Sommer 1944 abgezogen und Richtung Salzburg in Marsch gesetzt. Dort bildeten diese Männer das Sonderkommando Iltis, das zur Partisanenbekämpfung in Slowenien eingesetzt wurde.

Im Rückblick hatte sich die SS-Führung in zweierlei Hinsicht getäuscht. Durch die Aktion 1005 war es keineswegs gelungen, den Völkermord zu vertuschen – weder die Zahl der Opfer noch die Stätten des Massenmords. An zahlreichen dieser Orte entstanden zur sowjetischen Zeit Gedenkzeichen. Bis heute stellen weitere Projekte, in denen sich Menschen für das Sichern und die Herrichtung noch nicht geborgener Massengräber engagieren, eine späte, aber endgültige Niederlage für die Aktion 1005 dar. Diese Arbeiten können angesichts der Vielzahl der Orte aber kein flächendeckendes Erinnern gewährleisten. Eine unbekannte Zahl von Stätten ist für die Nachkommen heute kaum mehr auffindbar; dort fehlen weiterhin Orte des Trauerns, Mahnens und Erinnerns.

Auch die Strafverfolgung blieb nicht aus: Blobel wurde im Rahmen des Nürnberger Einsatzgruppenprozesses als Führer des Sonderkommandos 4a zum Tode verurteilt und seine Begnadigung abgelehnt. Am 7. Juni 1951 wurde er in Landsberg am Lech hingerichtet. Allerdings handelt es sich bei ihm um eine Ausnahme. In der Bundesrepublik erhob nur in wenigen Strafverfahren die Staatsanwaltschaft Anklage gegen Führungskräfte einzelner 1005-Kommandos – allerdings wegen der Ermordung der Arbeitshäftlinge und nicht wegen (der verjährten) Spurenbeseitigung. Immerhin drei Funktionsträger wurden zu lebenslanger Haft verurteilt, andere zu zeitlichen Strafen. Jedoch blieb die Gesamtzahl der Verurteilungen der im Rahmen der Aktion 1005 begangenen Morde gering. Die Mehrheit des Personals hatte, schon wegen der ihnen häufig im Vorfeld zugestandenen nachrangigen Funktion als Wache oder einfacher Befehlsempfänger von den Strafverfolgungsbehörden kaum etwas zu befürchten. So konnte sich der Einzelne, ohne dass in der Öffentlichkeit etwas über seine Taten bekannt wurde, als respektabler Bürger am Wiederaufbau einer nunmehr demokratisch konstituierten Gesellschaft beteiligen …

forces were not up to the task. Soviet investigators found some evidence of »burying« in the administrative districts of Volhynia and Podolia. However, many of the mass graves remained untouched and were at best camouflaged and scattered with chlorinated lime, not least because the Operation 1005 commandos must have had to beat a hasty retreat without properly clearing the sites of their final assignments.

Wherever they were, Blobel's men lacked time and often also materials and they ultimately lost motivation for the task, if they had this to start with. The 1005 commandos held the same rank as the Order Police and so most of their members were drafted from this organisation. Their activities in this role had led them to sense and to realise that the war had been lost once and for all before other members of the armed forces and that their involvement in eliminating the evidence put them at risk of facing the consequences. The SS leadership also recognised the problem: Himmler did not want to leave his men on the Eastern front, where they were in danger of being captured by the Soviets. For this reason, most of the Operation 1005 Sonderkommandos were recalled in summer 1944 and put on a march towards Salzburg. Here they were used to form Sonderkommando Iltis, which was deployed to combat partisans in Slovenia.

In retrospect, the SS leadership had erred on two counts. Operation 1005 by no means succeeded in concealing either the number of victims of the genocide or the locations where mass murder had been committed. Memorials were put up at many of these locations during the Soviet era. Initiatives to preserve or identify mass graves are still ongoing today and seal the late, but irrevocable, defeat of Operation 1005. As so many sites are involved, such projects have not, however, been able to fill all the gaps in commemoration. Post-war generations are unlikely to locate an unknown number of additional sites, which therefore continue to lack facilities to mourn, admonish and remember.

And Operation 1005 was indeed the subject of criminal proceedings. Blobel was sentenced to death at the Nuremberg Einsatzgruppen Trial for his role as head of Sonderkommando 4a and his request for clemency was overturned. He was executed on 7 June 1951 in Landsberg prison. However, his conviction was an exception. The West German courts only initiated criminal proceedings against the heads of individual Operation 1005 commandos in a few cases and the men concerned were charged with murdering forced labourers of the commando rather than for their role in removing the evidence (a crime which came under the statute of limitations). This being said, three commando chiefs did receive life sentences and others were sentenced to time in prison. However, the total number of convictions for murders committed during Operation 1005 was low. Most of those involved had held low-ranking roles as guards or simply took orders and as such they had little to fear from the criminal justice system. This meant that such individuals were able to play the role of respectable citizens in the reconstruction of what was now a democratic society without their crimes ever coming to light …

Gewaltbilder. Über das Zeigen und Betrachten von Fotografien der Extreme

Michaela Christ [*]

I.

Auf einer Wiese in einer Senke sitzt, zwischen mehreren Dutzend nackter Frauenleichen, ein Junge. Er ist fünf, sechs, vielleicht sieben Jahre alt. Ein Mann in Uniform, die Maschinenpistole schussbereit in der ausgestreckten Hand, steht vor dem Kind. Ein zweiter Uniformierter mit gesenkter Waffe befindet sich wenige Meter hinter dem ersten. Es sieht aus, als beobachte er das Geschehen.

Das Foto stammt aus einer Serie von fünf Schwarz-Weiß-Bildern. Sie wurden während der Erschießung von bis zu 1.500 jüdischen Kindern, Frauen und Männern aufgenommen, die im Oktober 1942 in der ostpolnischen Stadt Mizocz stattfand. Verantwortlich für den Mord war ein Kommando der Sicherheitspolizei und des SD – mit Unterstützung deutscher Gendarmerie und einheimischer Hilfskräfte. In der Ausstellung »Massenerschießungen. Der Holocaust zwischen Ostsee und Schwarzem Meer 1941 – 1944« steht die Bilderserie beispielhaft für die Verfolgung und das Sterben der jüdischen Bevölkerung unter deutscher Besatzung. Sie verdeutlicht und verdichtet gleichzeitig, was die Ausstellung in den übrigen Kapiteln – auch anhand weiterer gewalthaltiger Fotografien – darstellt. Die Aufnahmen stammen in der Regel von Angehörigen der deutschen Besatzungsmacht.

Im Folgenden soll es um die Frage nach der Bedeutung des Zeigens und Betrachtens solcher Bilder gehen. Immer wieder wird in Wissenschaft und Öffentlichkeit diskutiert, ob ein solches Zurschaustellen menschlichen Leids legitim ist. Und wenn ja: Aus welchem Grund? Ziel dieses Textes ist es nicht, die Frage nach der Rechtmäßigkeit eindeutig zu beantworten, vielmehr sollen hier einige der Ambivalenzen, die mit dem Zeigen und Betrachten verbunden sind, aufgezeigt werden. Zugleich werden Überlegungen dazu vorgestellt, was man aus Fotos, die das Zufügen von Gewalt und das Erleiden von Schmerz zeigen, erfahren kann, das andere Quellen nicht oder nur indirekt vermitteln.

Seit Langem gehören die in Mizocz gemachten Aufnahmen zum bekannten Bildmaterial des Holocaust. Sie sind, wenngleich selten als Serie und nicht immer mit richtiger Orts- oder Zeitangabe, vielfach veröffentlicht worden. Sie wurden und werden in verschiedenen Ausstellungen, darunter in Yad Vashem (Israel) und in der sogenannten ersten Wehrmachtsausstellung gezeigt, können auf zahlreichen Seiten und in mehreren Datenbanken im Internet abgerufen werden. Mit anderen Worten: Die Bilder sind ›in der Welt‹. Weshalb also soll hier darüber nachgedacht werden, was es heißt, sie auszustellen? »Man braucht gute Gründe, um manche Fotos zu zeigen«, schreibt die Historikerin

---

[*] Andrea Rudorff, Ute Wrocklage und die Kuratorin und Kuratoren der Ausstellung haben eine frühere Fassung des Textes gelesen und mit hilfreichen Anmerkungen kommentiert. Ihnen sei hierfür herzlich gedankt.

Photographs of violence. Exhibiting and viewing images of brutality and suffering

Michaela Christ *

I.

A boy is sitting in a ravine surrounded by the naked corpses of several dozen women. He is five or six, maybe seven years old. A man in uniform is pointing a gun at the child, poised to shoot. There is a second man a few metres behind him. He has lowered his weapon and appears to be watching.

The photo is one of a series of five black and white images. They were taken in October 1942 during the shooting of up to 1,500 Jewish children, women and men in the town of Mizocz in eastern Poland. The murders were committed by a Security Police and SD commando with assistance from German police and local auxiliaries. The photos were selected for the exhibition »Mass Shootings. The Holocaust from the Baltic to the Black Sea 1941 – 1944« to exemplify the persecution and death of Jews under the German occupation. They illustrate and consolidate the contents of the rest of the exhibition, which features additional photographic images. Most of the photographs were taken by members of the German occupying forces.

This essay considers the impact of exhibiting and viewing such images. There are repeated public and academic debates on whether it is legitimate to display images of human suffering in this way and, if so, for what purpose. This article does not seek to provide a definitive answer to this question but rather to explore some of the contradictions involved in exhibiting and viewing such images. It will also consider what photos of violence and suffering reveal that other sources lack or only imply.

The photos taken in Mizocz have long been part of the iconography of the Holocaust. They have been reproduced on many occasions, although rarely as a series and not always with the correct date or location. They have often been displayed – and still are – in various exhibitions, for example at Yad Vashem (Israel) and in the first Wehrmachtsausstellung (Exhibition on the Crimes of the Wehrmacht). They can be accessed via many websites and a range of online databases. In other words, the images are ›out there‹. Why then should we reflect on the implications of exhibiting them? With reference to acts of violence photographed against the will of the victims concerned, the historian Cornelia Brink[1] maintains that »certain images should only be shown with good reason«. The mere fact that the images exist does not seem to be reason enough. Just because they exist does not mean that one has to show them.

---

* The author would like to express her sincere thanks to Andrea Rudorff, Ute Wrocklage and the curators of the exhibition for reading and commenting on the first draft of this article.

[1] Brink, Cornelia, Vor aller Augen: Fotografien-wider-Willen in der Geschichtsschreibung, p. 74, in: WerkstattGeschichte 47/2008, pp. 61–74.

Gewaltbilder. Über das Zeigen und Betrachten von Fotografien der Extreme

Cornelia Brink[1] mit Blick auf Fotografien von Gewaltereignissen, die gegen den Willen der fotografierten Opfer gemacht wurden. Ihr bloßes Vorhandensein jedenfalls scheint aus mehreren Gründen als Begründung unzureichend. Nur weil es sie gibt, muss man sie noch lange nicht zeigen.

II.

Die Bilder aus Mizocz dokumentieren ein Ereignis, fotografiert von einer Person. Sie erfassen unterschiedliche Zeitpunkte der Massenerschießung. Der Fotograf, der Reservepolizist Gustav Hille, hat aus unbekannten Gründen vier verschiedene Stationen auf dem Weg zur Erschießung sowie den Ort der Ermordung festgehalten. Hille nahm auf, wie eine große Gruppe von Ghettoinsassen sich auszog. Offenbar hatten die Deutschen Männer und Frauen voneinander getrennt. Auf einem Bild sind nur Frauen und einige Kinder zu sehen. Die Senke ist fast leer, der Boden übersät mit Kleidungsstücken. Es folgt das Foto mit Frauen und Kindern in der Schlange. Schließlich zwei Bilder mit mehreren Dutzend nackter Frauen- und Kinderleichen – aus unterschiedlichen Blickwinkeln. Das Töten scheint beinahe beendet, nur Einzelne sind erkennbar noch am Leben. Möglicherweise hat hier eine Szene Hilles Interesse geweckt: In der Bildmitte sitzen zwei angezogene Kinder, ein Mädchen und ein Junge. Ein Deutscher mit Maschinenpistole steht daneben und hält seine Waffe gesenkt. Das nächste und vermutlich letzte Bild der Serie ist das eingangs beschriebene.

Aus den Bildern lässt sich der Ablauf des Gewaltaktes erkennen, zugleich eröffnen sie verschiedene Perspektiven auf die Begebenheit. Man sieht das Gelände von unterschiedlichen Seiten, umkreist und begleitet mit dem Fotografen gewissermaßen das Geschehen. Aus der Bilderserie schließen lässt sich auch, wie die Täter agierten. Sie teilten und ordneten die Masse, trennten Gruppen ab, wiesen diese an, sich auszuziehen und befahlen jenen, sich in einer Reihe aufzustellen. Alle Bilder geben Hinweise auf die große Machtungleichheit zwischen den Abgebildeten. Nur auf einem Foto hält ein Täter eine Waffe im Anschlag. Die Machtfülle der deutschen Besatzer war offensichtlich so groß, dass es keiner direkten Bedrohung mit Waffen bedurfte und vergleichsweise wenige Uniformierte ausreichten, um Hunderte Menschen zu bewachen und zu töten. Auf den Bildern sieht man weder einen Zaun noch eine Postenkette, die die Menschen aus Mizocz daran gehindert hätten, dem Ort zu entfliehen. Die Beschaffenheit des Geländes, die zu beiden Seiten der Senke ansteigende Wiese sowie eine zahlenmäßig deutlich unterlegene, jedoch bewaffnete Zahl an Tätern reichten aus. Nur wenige Menschen wagten einen Fluchtversuch. Die meisten wurden dabei erschossen.

III.

Aus dem Bestand der bekannten Aufnahmen von Massenerschießungen stechen die Bilder aus Mizocz hervor, weil sie die Opfer in besonderer Weise als verletzliche und

---

1   Brink, Cornelia, Vor aller Augen: Fotografien-wider-Willen in der Geschichtsschreibung, S. 74, in: WerkstattGeschichte 47/2008, S. 61–74.

II.

The Mizocz photos show an event captured by a single person. They document various phases of the mass shooting. The photos were taken by Gustav Hille, a police reservist. For unknown reasons, he took pictures of four stages of the process of mass murder as well as of the site where the murders took place. Hille photographed a large group of ghetto inmates undressing. The Germans had evidently separated the men from the women. On one photo, only women and a few children can be seen. The ravine is almost empty and articles of clothing are strewn over the ground. The next photo shows women and children standing in a line. Finally, there are two photos showing the naked corpses of several dozen women and children from different angles. On these photos, it appears that the killing has stopped; only a few individuals are definitely still alive. It is possible that one particular scene captured Hille's interest. In the centre of the photo are a boy and a girl, both fully clothed. The German standing next to them has lowered his machine gun. The next photo, probably the final one of the set, features the image described at the beginning of this chapter.

The photos show how this violent event unfolded and present it from a range of perspectives. We see the site from a number of angles; in a sense we accompany the photographer as he walks around and observes what is happening. The photos also provide insights into the actions of the perpetrators. They divided up and managed the crowds and split people into groups, ordering some to undress and others to line up. All of the photos indicate the complete imbalance of power between those pictured. There is only one photo where a perpetrator has raised his weapon. The German occupying forces clearly exuded such power that relatively few uniformed men were able to guard and kill hundreds of people without needing to threaten them directly with their guns. The photos give no indication that there was a fence or line of guards preventing the residents of Mizocz from escaping. The layout of the site, the upward slope from both sides of the ravine and the presence of the perpetrators – very much in the minority in terms of numbers, but armed – all provided a deterrent. Only a few people attempted to flee. Most of them were shot in the process.

III.

Of all the known images of the mass shootings, the pictures from Mizocz are particularly striking as they show the victims as truly vulnerable and defenceless. Four of the five photos show some of the victims naked; in three of the pictures almost all of them are without clothes. Their nakedness is disturbing as it exposes the anguish of the women and children. It is immediately apparent that these people did not wish to be seen in this state. Whenever I look at the photos of Mizocz I want to avert my eyes as they make me extremely uncomfortable and I feel ashamed to adopt what is unavoidably a voyeur's stance. The women and children on the photos were defenceless in two aspects. German SS officers,

Gewaltbilder. Über das Zeigen und Betrachten von Fotografien der Extreme

schutzlose Menschen zeigen. Auf vier der fünf Bilder sind mehrere, auf dreien fast alle Opfer vollständig unbekleidet. Ihre Nacktheit verstört, tritt durch sie doch die Verletzungsoffenheit der Frauen und Kinder besonders deutlich hervor. Augenblicklich ist klar: Diese Menschen stellen ihre Blöße nicht freiwillig zur Schau. Wann immer ich die Fotos aus Mizocz betrachte, möchte ich den Blick diskret abwenden, weil sie mich peinlich berühren und mich der mir aufgedrängte Voyeurismus beschämt. Die Frauen und Kinder auf den Bildern waren den Tätern in doppeltem Sinn schutzlos ausgeliefert. Deutsche SS-Männer, Polizisten und ihre einheimischen Zuarbeiter waren in der Lage durchzusetzen, was immer sie wollten. Dazu gehörte auch, den Opfern die Kleider zu nehmen, die ihre Körper gegen die Blicke der Anwesenden abschirmten.

Unfreiwillige Nacktheit wird sicherlich von den meisten Menschen als beschämend und erniedrigend wahrgenommen, selbst in freizügigen Gesellschaften wie der unsrigen. Wenn man die zeitgenössischen Normen und Werte in Bezug auf Nacktheit – zumal in traditionell lebenden Gesellschaftsschichten wie den oft orthodoxen jüdischen Gemeinden im ländlichen Ostpolen – mitbedenkt, die deutlich mehr Tabus kannten, ist vielleicht zu erahnen, wie groß die Demütigung war.

Zur langen Liste von Entrechtung und Gewalt, die die Deutschen ihren Opfern zugefügt haben, gehört auch das Filmen und Fotografieren der Verfolgten. Man mag einwenden, angesichts ihrer Ermordung sei diese Form der übergriffigen Handlung geringfügig. Die Frage aber bleibt, ob man sich mit dem Zeigen und dem Betrachten der Bilder nicht zu Komplizen der Verbrechen macht und – wie Janina Struk argumentiert – die Opfer erneut zu Opfern macht.[2] Denn die Bilder belegen das Verbrechen nicht nur, sie sind Bestandteil von Entrechtung, Entmündigung und Gewalt. Sie machen die Gezeigten zu Objekten, deren Interessen noch weit über den Zeitraum des Ereignisses hinaus missachtet werden können. Die nackten Frauen und Kinder mussten sich nicht nur damals begaffen lassen, sie sind bis heute, noch 70 Jahre nach dem Geschehen, dem Angestarrtwerden ausgeliefert.

Die Bilder sind, wie gesagt, in der Welt. Wer sie in welchem Kontext, mit welcher Motivation benutzt und mit welchem Interesse betrachtet, konnte niemals von den Fotografierten kontrolliert oder auch nur beeinflusst werden. Mir scheint, das Unbehagen, das diese Bilder auslösen, die »soziale Nervosität«[3], die sich beim Ansehen von Fotos dieser Art breitmacht, ist ein Hinweis darauf, dass den Betrachterinnen und Betrachtern das Übergriffige, das ihrem Schauen innewohnt, mindestens unbewusst gegenwärtig ist. Der Zwang zur Entblößung, die beschämende Prozedur, sich anderen Menschen gegen den eigenen Willen nackt zu zeigen, der die Täter ihre Opfer ausgesetzt haben, setzt sich, ob gewollt oder nicht, in dem Moment fort, in dem wir die Bilder betrachten. Sicher ist: Die Erkenntnisse, die man aus diesen Bildern gewinnen kann, sind ohne den Preis des übergriffigen Blicks nicht zu bekommen.

---

2 Struk, Janina, Photographing the Holocaust. Interpretations of the Evidence, London, New York 2004.
3 Brink, Vor aller Augen, S. 66.

policemen and their local auxiliaries could do whatever they wanted. This included taking the clothes belonging to the victims, who now tried to shield their bodies from the gaze of those around them.

Even in liberal societies such as ours, most people find it embarrassing and humiliating to be seen naked against their will. If we consider nakedness in the context of the greater number of taboos inherent in the norms and values of the time – especially in traditional social classes such as the largely Orthodox Jewish communities in rural Poland – one perhaps has an inkling of how humiliating this must have been.

Filming and photographing the victims was one of the many ways in which the Germans showed violence towards them and deprived them of their rights. One could argue that such intrusive behaviour towards the victims pales into insignificance when compared to their murder. However, the question remains as to whether showing and viewing such images in fact implicates one in the crimes and – as Janina Struk argues – whether in doing so the victims are made to suffer for a second time.[2] After all, these images do not just testify to the crime but they are also part of a process of humiliation, violence and deprivation of rights. They turn the people photographed into mere objects, whose interests can be disregarded way after the crimes actually took place. The naked women and children not only had to endure being stared at then but continue to be stared at right up to the present day, 70 years afterwards.

As already stated, the images are ›out there‹. The people in the photos never had any control over or even a say in who used them, why, and in what context, or who viewed them and for what purpose. I would argue that the sense of discomfort triggered by these photos and the »social unease«[3] initiated by exposure to this type of image are an indication that anyone viewing them has a sense, at least unconsciously, of the intrusive nature of their gaze. Whether we like it or not, the process whereby the perpetrators forced the victims to undress and to show themselves naked to others against their will continues from the moment that we view the pictures. What is certain is that we cannot glean any insights from these images without adopting an intrusive gaze ourselves.

IV.

What do we then see on the photos that Gustav Hille took at the site where the Jews of Mizocz were shot in October 1942? What do they tell us? The victims were often forced to participate in the process of mass murder, making this more efficient and less onerous for the perpetrators. They were, for example, made to remove their clothes, which were then re-used, or to dig their own graves. Clothing does not just afford protection from the sun, cold or rain; it is also an expression of our personality and social standing. Moreover, clothing gives an indication of the limits of decency mediated within a society.[4] In taking away the victims' clothing, the perpetrators not only stripped them of significant markers

2   Struk, Janina, Photographing the Holocaust. Interpretations of the Evidence, London, New York 2004.
3   Brink, Vor aller Augen, p. 66.
4   For a detailed discussion of this point see Christ, Michaela, Die Dynamik des Tötens. Die Ermordung der Juden in Berditschew.
    Ukraine 1941–1944, Frankfurt/M. 2011, p. 40, 250ff.

IV.

Was also sieht man auf den Bildern, die Gustav Hille im Oktober 1942 am Erschießungsort der Mizoczer Juden aufnahm? Welche Informationen halten sie bereit? Häufig wurden die Opfer gezwungen, sich am Prozess ihrer Ermordung zu beteiligen, was diesen effizienter und für die Täter weniger beschwerlich machte. Das Ausziehen der Kleidung zur Weiterverwertung dieser ist hierfür ein Beispiel, das Ausheben der eigenen Gräber ein anderes. Kleider dienen nicht nur als Schutz gegen Sonne, Kälte oder Regen, sie sind Ausdruck der Persönlichkeit und der Positionen ihrer Trägerinnen und Träger in der Gesellschaft. Sie geben darüber hinaus Auskunft über sozial vereinbarte Schamgrenzen.[4] Entsprechend nahm man den Opfern mit ihrer Kleidung nicht nur bedeutsame Merkmale ihres Selbst, sondern auch die schützende Hülle, die Menschen im gewöhnlichen Miteinander tragen, auch im Sinne eines geteilten Verständnisses von Werten und Normen. Die erzwungene Nacktheit hatte unverkennbar eine symbolische Funktion[5]: Die Täter entzogen den Opfern mit ihrer Kleidung ein zentrales Symbol ihres Gleich- und Subjektseins. Und so tritt das extreme Machtungleichgewicht zwischen den Menschen auf den Bildern aus Mizocz besonders durch den Umstand hervor, dass die einen nackt und die anderen vollständig bekleidet sind.

Häufiger wurde argumentiert, den Tätern sei ihr Tun leichter gemacht worden, da die Opfer ohne Kleidung weniger als einzelne Subjekte, als Adressaten von Empathie oder Mitleid, erkennbar waren, sondern zu einer nackten Menge von Menschen verschmolzen.[6] Für manche Täter mag dies zugetroffen haben, für viele andere nicht. Sicher, das Bewachen der Opfer wurde erleichtert, da nur wenigen unbekleidet die Flucht vom Ort einer Massenerschießung gelungen sein dürfte. Und einfacher wurde obendrein die Verwertung ihres Besitzes; dieser blieb zurück auf Wiesen und Feldern.

Überdeutlich tritt aus den Bildern die körperliche und sinnliche Dimension gewalttätigen Handelns hervor: Täter und Opfer, Zuarbeiter und Zuschauer konnten einander nicht nur sehen, sondern auch hören und riechen. Berührungen blieben nicht aus. Die Mizoczer Serie belegt, wie nahe sich Täter und Opfer am Ort der Erschießung waren. Der Deutsche mit der Waffe auf dem eingangs beschriebenen Bild ist von denen, die er erschoss und noch erschießen wird, nur eine Armeslänge entfernt. Aus anderen Beschreibungen von Massenerschießungen ist bekannt, dass manche Schützen sich aus Zeltbahnen und anderen Utensilien behelfsmäßige Schutzkleidung machten, damit ihre Uniformen nicht von Blut, Knochen oder Gehirnmasse der Opfer beschmutzt würden.[7] Beim Töten standen sich Täter und Opfer Auge in Auge gegenüber, waren einander praktisch ausgesetzt: der Geruch von Angst, Blut und Fäkalien aufseiten der Opfer, der Schweiß körperlicher Anstrengung oder Nervosität aufseiten der Täter.

Auf den ersten drei Bildern der Serie fällt auf, wie eng die Mizoczer beieinander sitzen oder stehen. Auf der ersten Aufnahme ist eine Gruppe von etwa 350 Menschen zu sehen. Frauen, Männer und Kinder kauern in einem lang gezogenen Pulk in einer Senke auf

---

4   hierzu ausführlich: Christ, Michaela, Die Dynamik des Tötens. Die Ermordung der Juden in Berditschew. Ukraine 1941–1944, Frankfurt/M. 2011, S. 40, 250ff
5   Zur symbolischen Funktion von Nacktheit zum Beispiel Suderland, Maja, Ein Extremfall des Sozialen. Die Häftlingsgesellschaft in den nationalsozialistischen Konzentrationslagern, Frankfurt/M., New York 2009, S. 168.
6   Stellvertretend für viele sei hier genannt: Sofsky, Wolfgang, Ordnung des Terrors. Das Konzentrationslager, Frankfurt/M. 1993, S. 101.
7   Welzer, Harald (Mitarbeit Michaela Christ), Täter. Wie aus ganz normalen Menschen Massenmörder werden, Frankfurt/M. 2005.

of their identity but also of the sense of protection that clothing affords in everyday social interaction, also as a reflection of diverging norms and values. This enforced nakedness undoubtedly had a symbolic function.[5] In forcing the victims to remove their clothes, the perpetrators stripped them of a core element of their Commonness and of their sense of self. The extreme imbalance of power between the people pictured at Mizocz is thus reinforced by the fact that some are naked and others fully clothed.

It has frequently been argued that the victims being without clothes made it easier for the perpetrators to commit the crime as their targets blurred into a mass of naked bodies rather than being recognisable as individuals who might attract empathy or sympathy.[6] This may have been the case for some of the perpetrators, but by no means for all of them. It goes without saying that it was easier to guard the victims this way as only very few would have managed to escape from the site of a mass execution without any clothes on. It was also simpler to sort through their belongings, which were left behind on the fields.

The physical and sensual dimensions of violence are plain to see on these images. Victims, perpetrators, auxiliaries and witnesses could not only see but also smell and hear each other. There was physical contact between them. The series of photos from Mizocz shows just how near the victims and perpetrators were to each other at the site of the shooting. On the picture described above, the German with the gun is standing right next to the people he has shot and is about to shoot. Additional accounts of mass shootings reveal that some of the marksmen fashioned makeshift protective clothing out of tarpaulins and other materials so that their uniforms would not get spattered with the blood, bones or brain tissue of the victims.[7] As the killings took place, the perpetrators and victims were looking into each other's eyes and literally had nowhere to hide, with the stench of fear, blood and faeces coming from the victims and the reek of sweat from the perpetrators generated by physical exertion or nerves.

In the first three pictures in the series it is striking just how close the Mizocz Jews are sitting or standing next to each other. The first photo shows a group of around 350 people. A large crowd of men, women and children can be seen cowering together in a ravine. Only a few are standing and there are just two people sitting to the side, a short distance away from the rest of the group. The picture of around two dozen women and children surrounded by items of abandoned clothing in the now almost empty ravine also shows them in close physical proximity. They are evidently getting undressed. A small group huddling together was easier to control than a crowd of hundreds spread over a larger area, especially as the number of guards was relatively small and positioned at the top of a steep-sided ravine. Yet it also seems as if the Jewish men, women and children sought physical closeness. The third and best-known of the photos shows a line of 20 naked women. Several of them carry infants or toddlers in their arms; a larger child is clinging to one of the women. On one side a naked pregnant women can be seen moving in haste towards the group, covering her bare breasts with her arms. Behind the row of women and thus barely visible are two members of the

---

5   On the symbolism of nakedness see, for example, Suderland, Maja, Ein Extremfall des Sozialen. Die Häftlingsgesellschaft in den nationalsozialistischen Konzentrationslagern, Frankfurt/M., New York 2009, p. 168.
6   See, for example, Sofsky, Wolfgang, Ordnung des Terrors. Das Konzentrationslager, Frankfurt/M. 1993, p. 101.
7   Welzer, Harald (with contributions from Michaela Christ), Täter. Wie aus ganz normalen Menschen Massenmörder werden, Frankfurt/M. 2005.

dem Boden. Nur vereinzelt steht noch jemand, nur zwei Personen sitzen in kurzer Distanz zum Rest des Pulks an dessen Rändern. Auch auf dem Bild, das die fast entleerte Senke zeigt, in der sich zwischen zurückgelassener Kleidung noch etwa zwei Dutzend Frauen und Kinder aufhalten, stehen die Menschen nah beieinander. Sie sind offenkundig dabei, sich auszuziehen. Eine zusammengedrängte Gruppe lässt sich – zumal von den erhöhten Flanken der Senke und mit einer verhältnismäßig kleinen Zahl von Männern – einfacher überwachen, als Hunderte, die über eine größere Fläche verstreut sind. Und doch scheint es auch, als suchten die jüdischen Männer, Frauen und Kinder die Nähe untereinander. Auf dem dritten und wohl bekanntesten der Bilder stehen 20 nackte Frauen in einer Reihe. Mehrere haben Säuglinge oder Kleinkinder auf dem Arm, ein größeres Kind drängt sich an eine der Frauen. Von der Seite hastet eine unbekleidete Schwangere, die Arme schützend vor die Brust gelegt, auf die Gruppe zu. Hinter der Reihe, die die Frauen bilden und von diesen für die Betrachtenden halb verdeckt, halten sich zwei Angehörige der ukrainischen Hilfstruppen auf – erkennbar an ihren weißen Armbinden. Die Frauen stehen mit ihren Kindern Schlange, sie warten gemeinsam auf den Tod.

Vielleicht ist es die Gleichzeitigkeit der völlig alltäglichen Routine des Schlangestehens, die, gepaart mit dem Schrecken dessen, wofür die Frauen anstehen, dieses Bild zum festen Bestandteil des kollektiven visuellen Gedächtnisses des Holocaust hat werden lassen. Ordnung und Grausamkeit sind in diesem Bild auf verstörende Weise gleichberechtigte Partner. Hinzu kommen Zärtlichkeit und Fürsorge, die aus den Berührungen der Wartenden untereinander sprechen. Nicht nur halten die Frauen ihre Kinder eng umarmt; auch zwischen den Frauen gibt es intensiven körperlichen Kontakt. Sie schmiegen sich aneinander, vermutlich – es ist Mitte Oktober – um sich gegenseitig zu wärmen, sich Halt zu geben und sich vor den Blicken der Männer zu schützen.

V.

Keines der Bilder erweckt den Eindruck, die Täter hätten es besonders eilig gehabt. Schon allein der Umstand, dass Gustav Hille umhergehen und offenbar ungestört fotografieren konnte, spricht dafür, dass die Zeit nicht knapp war. Nahezu alle Bewegungen gehen von den Opfern aus. Sie hasten zur Erschießung, ziehen sich aus, bemühen sich anscheinend, Befehlen Folge zu leisten. Die Täter wiederum stehen beisammen, die Waffen gesenkt, und unterhalten sich. Sie widmen ihren Opfern kaum Aufmerksamkeit, sondern scheinen zu warten und zu schauen, als sei das Geschehen um sie herum alltäglich. Tatsächlich war dies nicht die erste Erschießung dieser Einheit. Und man kann annehmen, dass sich nach über einem Jahr Krieg gegen die Sowjetunion bei denjenigen unter den deutschen Besatzern, zu deren Aufgabe es gehörte, Juden zu töten, eine Art Routine entwickelt hatte. Die entspannte Körperhaltung der Deutschen auf den Bildern wäre dafür ein Indiz.

Es gibt noch einen Hinweis, der für Ruhe und – man kann es nicht anders sagen – Gelassenheit aufseiten der Täter spricht. Er betrifft die beiden Kinder, von denen bereits die

Ukrainian auxiliary police, who can be identified by their white armbands. The women are queuing up with their children, all waiting to die.

It is perhaps the everyday practice of queuing coupled with the horrific reason why the women are doing so that has lent this image such iconic status within the collective visual memory of the Holocaust. The photo shows a disturbing symmetry of order and inhumanity. Added to this are the expressions of tenderness and care reflected in the physical gestures of the women in the queue. The women are hugging their children tightly but are also in close physical contact with each other. They are huddled together, presumably to keep each other warm – the photo was taken in mid-October – but also to support each other and to shield themselves from the men's gaze.

V.

None of the photos gives the impression that the perpetrators were in any particular hurry. The very fact that Gustav Hille was able to walk around freely taking pictures indicates that time was not short. Virtually all of the signs of movement are on the part of the victims. They can be seen racing towards the shooting site, taking off their clothes and apparently attempting to comply with orders. In contrast, the perpetrators are standing around chatting with their guns lowered. They are barely paying any attention to the victims but rather seem to be watching and waiting as if the events around them were an everyday occurrence. This was indeed not the first time that this unit had been involved in a mass shooting. Moreover, one can imagine that after over a year in combat against the Soviet Union, the men from the occupying forces whose job it was to kill Jews had come to see this as part of their routine. The relaxed body language of the Germans on the photos lends weight to this argument.

There is one further indicator of the calm and what can only be described as casual attitude of the perpetrators. This relates to the two children mentioned above. They are still fully clothed at the execution site. Perhaps they were brought there after the others, perhaps they had tried and failed to hide or escape, or perhaps they had refused to get undressed? Surrounded by dead bodies, the marksman bides his time until these children are also naked and therefore in his view ready for what he is about to do.

VI.

One can only speculate as to what motivated Gustav Hille, a photographer and reserve police officer, to wander around with his camera while the shootings were taking place. What is certain is that Hille, like thousands of others, was flouting the ban on photography that had been repeatedly imposed by Heinrich Himmler and a range of authorities under his control. For Dieter Reifarth and Viktoria Schmidt-Linsenhoff, the personal photos taken

Rede war. Sie sind noch am Ort der Erschießung vollständig bekleidet. Vielleicht wurden sie nachträglich dazu geholt, vielleicht hatten sie versucht, sich zu verstecken oder zu fliehen, und waren entdeckt worden, vielleicht hatten sie sich nicht ausziehen wollen? Umgeben von Dutzenden Leichen, bringt der Schütze genug Zeit auf, abzuwarten, bis auch diese Kinder nackt und damit in seinen Augen für sein Tun bereit sind.

VI.

Was Gustav Hille, den Fotografen und Reservepolizisten, motiviert haben mag, während der Erschießungen mit der Kamera umherzugehen, darüber kann man nur spekulieren. Fest steht, dass Hille, wie Tausende andere, gegen das ausdrückliche Fotografierverbot, das wiederholt von Heinrich Himmler und diversen nachgeordneten Dienststellen ausgesprochen worden war, handelte. Dieter Reifarth und Viktoria Schmidt-Linsenhoff haben das private Fotografieren im Zweiten Weltkrieg als »Steigerung der Schaulust« interpretiert.[8] Ob die Bilder Ausdruck von Hilles Lust am Betrachten waren, ob er sich durch die Linse der Kamera einen zugleich voyeuristisch intensiven und – die Bilder würden bleiben – dauerhaften Blick auf die entblößten Frauenkörper verschaffte, geht aus den Fotos selbst nicht hervor. Genauso wenig wie man abschließend bewerten kann, ob die Fotos Souvenirs sein sollten, Belege dafür, dabei gewesen zu sein und mit eigenen Augen gesehen zu haben. War das Fotografieren eine Geste der Überlegenheit oder gar des Sieges über ›die Feinde‹? War das Festhalten des Verbrechens der Versuch, Unrecht für die Nachwelt zu dokumentieren, oder war es Ergebnis sexueller Erregung? Unklar ist ebenfalls, welche Gefühle den Mann bewegten, als er die Bilder machte. Genugtuung, sadistischer Genuss, Zorn, Staunen, Freude, Lust, Furcht, Überwältigung, Mitleid oder Neugier?

Wir sehen das Geschehen aus Hilles Perspektive, jedoch nicht zwangsläufig so, wie er es gesehen hat. Der Blick des Fotografen ist nicht zwingend der Blick der heutigen Betrachterinnen und Betrachter. Denn Blicke sind, so wie Gewalt selbst, sozial, zeitlich und kulturell gerahmt. Was die Bilder zeigen, ist in hohem Maße abhängig von dem, der sie betrachtet. Roland Barthes bemerkte dazu: Die Fotografie »wird nicht einfach wahrgenommen, sie wird gelesen, sie wird von dem Publikum, das sie konsumiert mehr oder weniger bewusst mit einem traditionellen Bestand von Zeichen verknüpft«[9]. Wie also Bilder gesehen werden, unterliegt den Deutungen und Interpretationen derer, die sie anschauen. Anders formuliert, Deutsche im Jahr 1942 sahen auf und in den Bildern aus Mizocz sicherlich anderes als die Besucherinnen und Besucher der Ausstellung im Jahr 2016. Ihnen fallen heute Elemente der Bilder auf, die damaligen Betrachtern möglicherweise völlig normal erschienen. Zum Beispiel: Keiner der gezeigten Täter scheint von dem Fotografen Notiz zu nehmen; er störte sie offenbar nicht. Auch nutzte niemand die Gelegenheit, für die Kamera zu posieren um das Geschehen für sich zu rekurrieren. Allein der Umstand, dass es die Bilder gibt, dass jemand auf die Idee kam, an solchen Orten zu fotografieren und anscheinend keiner der fotografierten Deutschen daran Anstoß nahm, in einer solchen Situation abgelichtet zu werden, ist aus heutiger Sicht mindestens

[8] Reifarth, Dieter und Schmidt-Linsenhoff, Viktoria, Die Kamera der Täter, in: Hannes Heer und Klaus Naumann (Hrsg.), Vernichtungskrieg: Verbrechen der Wehrmacht 1941 bis 1944, Hamburg 1995, S. 475–503.
[9] zitiert nach: Boltanski, Luc, Die Rethorik des Bildes, S. 153, in: Pierre Bourdieu, et al. (Hrsg.), Eine illegitime Kunst. Die sozialen Gebrauchsweisen der Photographie, Hamburg 2006 [1965], S. 134–167.

during World War Two were evidence of a »heightened curiosity«.[8] It is impossible to tell whether the photos reflected Hille's enjoyment at watching was happening and whether looking through the lens gave him an intense, voyeuristic view of the naked women that he could also retain in photo form. It is equally impossible to judge whether the photos were intended as mementos, as proof that he had been there and seen what happened with his own eyes. Was the act of taking photos an attempt to demonstrate superiority or even victory over ›the enemy‹? In capturing the crimes on camera, was Hille trying to document the injustice as evidence for future generations or giving vent to his sexual desires? Moreover, it is unclear what he would have been feeling whilst taking the pictures: gratification, sadistic pleasure, rage, shock, pleasure, desire, fear, stupefaction, sympathy or curiosity?

We can see what was happening from Hille's perspective, but not necessarily as he saw it at the time. A photographer back then would not always view things in the same way as someone looking at the pictures today. This is because our view is shaped by social, temporal and cultural factors, as is our understanding of violence itself. What the pictures reveal is largely dependent on who is looking at them. For Roland Barthes, photographs »are not just taken at face value, rather the public interprets them – whether unconsciously or not – by drawing associations with a stock of conventional symbols«[9]. People view pictures through their own prism of meanings and interpretations. To put it another way, a German in 1942 would undoubtedly have viewed and interpreted the photos from Mizocz differently than a visitor to the exhibition in 2016. Looking at the pictures from today's perspective, certain elements stand out that would perhaps have appeared completely normal to someone seeing the photos at the time. For example, none of the perpetrators seem to take any notice of the photographer; they are clearly not vexed by his presence. Moreover, no one has taken the opportunity to pose for the camera in order to record the event for posterity. The very fact that the pictures exist, that someone would take it into their head to photograph such scenes and that none of the Germans appeared to mind being caught on camera in these circumstances, would certainly raise eyebrows today. At the same time, during this period it was generally understood by the members of the occupying forces that the persecution and murder of Jews, especially on Soviet territory, was part and parcel of the occupation. Hence, the photos not only provide insights into their visual content, but also into the context in which they were taken. The photos were not commissioned, indeed they were taken without permission, but at the same time they reveal things from the perpetrators' perspective. They provide a visual record of the violence, which is also accessible to future generations. In this way, the photos are both evidence of war crimes and documents that were themselves produced as a result of criminal behaviour.

Looking at Hille's photos does not necessarily mean that we share his viewpoint, but his choice of subject does influence the way that we look at the pictures. We do not have to understand the feelings or motives of the photographer to recognise that these photos represent the perpetrator perspective in many respects. They are in themselves an

---

8   Reifarth, Dieter und Schmidt-Linsenhoff, Viktoria, Die Kamera der Täter, in: Hannes Heer und Klaus Naumann (eds.), Vernichtungskrieg: Verbrechen der Wehrmacht 1941 bis 1944, Hamburg 1995, pp. 475–503.
9   Cited in Boltanski, Luc, Die Rethorik des Bildes, p. 153, in: Pierre Bourdieu, et al. (Hrsg.), Eine illegitime Kunst. Die sozialen Gebrauchsweisen der Photographie, Hamburg 2006 [1965], pp. 134–167.

bemerkenswert. Nach der zeitgenössischen Logik hingegen gehörte die Verfolgung und Ermordung von Juden, zumal in den besetzten Gebieten der Sowjetunion, zum Alltag der Besatzer. Das heißt, wir erfahren aus den Bildern nicht nur etwas über das, was sie enthüllen, sondern auch etwas über den Kontext, in dem sie entstanden sind. Die Fotos waren keine Auftragsarbeiten und sind ohne Genehmigung entstanden, gleichwohl zeichnen sie die Blickrichtung der Täter nach. Die Gewalt wird dokumentiert und damit auch für die Nachwelt zugänglich. So sind die Fotos gleichzeitig Belege für Kriegsverbrechen und Dokumente, die ihrerseits unter verbrecherischen Umständen entstanden sind.

Obgleich Hilles Bilder anzuschauen nicht zwangsläufig heißt, auch seinen Blick zu übernehmen, prägt seine Motivwahl das heutige Schauen. Man muss weder die Gefühle noch die Motive des Fotografen kennen, um zu bemerken, dass die Bilder in mannigfaltiger Hinsicht die Perspektive der Täter darstellen. Sie sind auf ihre Weise beredt. Die Fotos aus Mizocz dokumentieren nicht zuletzt Hilles Parteilichkeit, sondern auch – indirekt – seine Zugehörigkeit zum Kreis der Täter. Er bewegte sich augenscheinlich am Rand der Senke – dort, wo sich kein Opfer aufhalten konnte. Das heißt, man blickt durch seine Bilder von oben herab auf die Menschen, sieht sie kaum als einzelne Personen, sondern als Teile einer Menge. Aus seiner Blickrichtung entspringen Aufnahmen, auf denen die Täter größer als die Opfer sind und sich, weil sie einzeln stehen, deutlich von der Masse der zusammengetriebenen Menschen abheben. Auf diese Weise schreiben die Bilder eine Erzählung fort, in der jüdische Verfolgte ausschließlich als untätige, namenlose Opfer vorkommen. Nicht zuletzt ist dies einer der Gründe, weshalb über die weitere Verbreitung dieser und anderer Bilder aus Gewaltsituationen diskutiert wird.

VII.

Fotos, die Gewaltereignisse zeigen, berühren. Sie gehen über das, was die meisten von uns im Alltag zu sehen gewohnt sind, hinaus. Man sieht, wie Menschen anderen Menschen etwas antun, das ihnen den Tod bringt. Die Ausstellung bedient sich einer Vielzahl ungeheuer gewalthaltiger Bilder. Sie sollen informieren und belegen, bebildern und vielleicht Beweis dafür sein, dass das, wovon die Texte berichten, tatsächlich stattgefunden hat. Nicht zuletzt bedienen die Bilder die Erwartungen und die Schaulust der Besucher. Ausstellungsmacher wollen nicht nur informieren, sondern auch bewegen, genauso wie Besucher nicht nur kognitiv, sondern auch emotional angesprochen werden möchten.

Was es heißt, das Leiden anderer zu betrachten, damit beschäftigte sich Susan Sontag in ihrem gleichnamigen Essay[10], der wie kaum eine andere Veröffentlichung die Debatte um das Zeigen oder Nicht-Zeigen von Bildern, die das Zufügen und Erleiden von Gewalt und Schmerz abbilden, prägte. Sontag arbeitete heraus, wie vielschichtig Fotografieren, Zeigen und Schauen aufeinander bezogen sind. Sie wies darauf hin, dass sich bisweilen beim Anschauen von Bildern der Gewalt eine Art Nähe zwischen Betrachtenden und Fotografierten einstelle und dass diese Vertrautheit eine Täuschung ist. Der Abgrund

---

10 Sontag, Susan, Das Leiden anderer betrachten, München 2003.

eloquent testimony to the crime. The photos of Mizocz not only prove Hille's affiliation with but also – indirectly – his status as one of the perpetrators. He is evidently walking around the edges of the ravine, where no victims were allowed. The pictures of the victims are thus taken from above and show them as part of a crowd rather than as individuals. From this vantage point, the perpetrators appear larger than the victims and as they are standing separately they are clearly distinguishable from the mass of people crowded together. In this way, the pictures perpetuate a narrative in which Jews who were persecuted only ever appear as passive, nameless victims. This is in itself one of the reasons why the continued dissemination of this and other graphic images raises questions.

VII.

Photographs of violence have an emotional impact. They present us with scenes that go way beyond what most of us encounter in daily life. They show us people committing acts that result in the death of others. This exhibition displays a large number of extremely graphic images. They are intended to inform, testify, illustrate and perhaps confirm that the events described in words actually took place. The images not least respond to the expectations and curiosity of visitors. Exhibition curators do not just want to provide information but also to initiate a response from visitors, just as the visitors themselves do not just want to be presented with facts but also to be emotionally engaged by an exhibition.

In the essay *Regarding the Pain of Others*[10], Susan Sontag made an unparalleled contribution to the debate on whether images of violence, pain and suffering should be shown. Sontag demonstrated how the process of taking, showing and looking at photographs is interlinked on many levels. She pointed out that when looking at pictures of violence we sometimes feel a connection with the subject of the photograph, but that this sense of closeness is illusory. In her view, there is an insurmountable gulf between those looking at the photos and those who are being looked at. Even pictures cannot communicate what it is like to inflict pain and death or to experience suffering. Sontag also emphasised that one feels overwhelmed, helpless and powerless when confronted with images of suffering and death. There are thus a number of arguments against putting images of extreme violence on display. Among these is the fact the victims did not give their permission for the images to be circulated. And yet one can also counter this by pointing out that many survivors give a no holds barred account of the Holocaust in order to bear witness to what happened. The victims of Mizocz would perhaps have granted permission for the photos to be exhibited in order to demonstrate what each and every one of them had to endure, to ensure that their agony and that of their friends and family is remembered and talked about even 70 years after the event, and finally so that their death can be mourned. These photographs and this exhibition provide the impetus and the opportunity to do so.

---

10 Sontag, Susan, Regarding the pain of others, London 2003.

zwischen denjenigen, die betrachten, und denjenigen, die betrachtet werden, ist unüberbrückbar. Was es bedeutet, Schmerz und Tod zuzufügen und vor allem zu erleiden, können auch Bilder nicht vermitteln. Sontag macht auch darauf aufmerksam, dass sich Betrachter beim Anblick von Leid und Tod überwältigt, hilflos und ohnmächtig fühlen. Es gibt also einige Aspekte, die gegen das Ausstellen extrem gewalthaltiger Bilder sprechen. Die fehlende Zustimmung der Opfer zur Veröffentlichung ist einer davon. Doch denkbar ist auch das Gegenteil: Viele Überlebende haben sich in Berichten über den Holocaust nicht geschont, um Zeugnis abzulegen. Die Opfer auf den Fotos aus Mizocz würden sich möglicherweise ebenfalls für das Ausstellen der Bilder aussprechen, damit das, was sie persönlich erleiden mussten, sichtbar wird. Damit das, was ihnen und ihren Familien und Freunden angetan wurde, auch 70 Jahre danach noch in Erinnerung ist und diskutiert wird. Und schließlich auch, damit ihr Tod betrauert werden kann. Nicht zuletzt dazu geben diese Bilder, gibt die Ausstellung Anlass und Gelegenheit.

Herausgeber | Publishers
Stiftung Denkmal für die ermordeten Juden Europas | Foundation Memorial to the Murdered Jews of Europe, Uwe Neumärker
Stiftung Topographie des Terrors | Topography of Terror Foundation, Prof. Dr. Andreas Nachama

Kuratoren | Curators
Dr. Ulrich Baumann, Stiftung Denkmal für die ermordeten Juden Europas (Projektleiter | Project Director)
Paula Oppermann, Stiftung Topographie des Terrors
Christian Schmittwilken, Stiftung Topographie des Terrors

Texte | Texts
Dr. Ulrich Baumann, Paula Oppermann, Christian Schmittwilken

Wissenschaftliche Recherche | Research
Benno Auras, Dr. Ulrich Baumann, Nikolaj Bessonow, Ray Brandon, Hannes Bock, Dr. Alexander Dolgowskij, Amélie Gräfin zu Eulenburg, Adam Kerpel-Fronius, Dr. Alexander Kruglov, Sarah Kunte, Lennart Mängli, Jana Mechelhoff-Herezi, Dr. Roman Michaltschuk, Doron Oberhand, Paula Oppermann, Veronika Patočková, Christian Schmittwilken, Regina Schulz, Dr. Andrej Umansky, Aleksandra Wroblewska, Nina Zellerhoff

Wissenschaftliche Erarbeitung der Karten zur jüdischen Bevölkerung und zu den Massenerschießungen
Research Maps Jewish Population and Mass Shootings
Dr. Andrej Umansky, Dr. Alexander Kruglov

Wissenschaftlicher Beirat | Advisory Board
Dr. Andrej Angrick, Prof. Dr. Wolfgang Benz, Dr. Michaela Christ, PD Dr. Martin Cüppers,
Dr. Jörg Skriebeleit, Prof. Dr. Peter Steinbach, Prof. Dr. Michael Wildt

Konzeptionelle und inhaltliche Beratung | Historical Consultants
Dr. Andrej Angrick, Ray Brandon, Eva Brücker

Projektkoordination | Project Coordination
Britta Scherer

Verwaltung | Administration
Marianne Emge, Anja Lieweke

Redaktion und Lektorat | Editing
Uwe Neumärker, Britta Scherer

Bildverwaltung und -rechte | Image Management
Sarah Kunte

Öffentlichkeitsarbeit | Public Relations
Kay-Uwe von Damaros, Sarah Friedrich, Jenifer Stolz

Übersetzungen | Translations
Pamela Hirsinger, Dr. Caroline Pearce

Die deutsche Übersetzung von Semens Tagebuch basiert auf | German Translation Semen's Diary based on
Die Verfolgung und Ermordung der europäischen Juden durch das nationalsozialistische Deutschland 1933 - 1945; Band 8, Teil II, Sowjetunion mit annektierten Gebieten

Englische Übersetzung Semens Tagebuch | English Translation Semen's Diary
Ray Brandon

Kartografie | Cartography
mr-kartographie - Ingenieurbüro und Verlag, Manfred Müller

Ausstellungsgestaltung, Grafik und Katalog | Exhibition Design, Graphics and Catalogue
Ursula Wilms

Ausstellungsbau, Medientechnik, Grafikproduktion
Exhibition Construction, Media Technology, Graphics Production
format Atelier für Messe + Design GmbH

Druck Katalog | Print Catalogue
ARNOLD group

Der Katalog enthält nahezu alle gedruckten Teile der Ausstellung.
Die Inhalte der Medien- und Hörstationen fanden keine Aufnahme.
The catalogue comprises almost all printed parts of the exhibition.
Contents of media and audio stations are not included in the book.

IT, Medienpräsentation | IT, Media Presentation
Uwe Seemann, Kaj Kunstheim

Interviews | Interviews
Stiftung Denkmal für die ermordeten Juden Europas, Videoarchiv »Sprechen trotz allem«
Fortunoff Video Archive for Holocaust Testimonies, Yale University

Film | Film
Benjamin Ferencz. Von Nürnberg nach Den Haag. Ein Film von Ullabritt Horn (28 min),
Kurzfassung von | Abridgment of *A man can make a difference*
Verleih für beide Filme | Distributor for both films W-film Distribution, Köln

Hörstationen | Audio Stations
G 7 Tontechnik

Unser Dank gilt | We would like to thank
Edward Anders, Michael und Nicolas Becker, Nikolaj Bessonow, Dr. Ruth Bettina Birn, Maja Böhm,
Ray Brandon, Gennadij Chenkin, Judith Cohen, Jekaterina Danova, Dr. Martin Dean, Christian Diesner,
Wladimir Gorodokin, Christine Heitmann, Prof. Dr. Hartmut von Hentig, Familie Hille, Ilana Ivanova,
Kamil Jaworski, Jessica Kensicki, Dr. Magnus Koch, Dr. Ingo Loose, Dr. Jared McBride, Tatiana Manykina,
Dr. Beate Meyer, Dr. Roman Michaltschuk, Joana Pape, Horst Sassin, Katharina Schmitten, Mikhail Tyaglyy,
Sima Tsyskin, Caroline Lydia Tupikowski, Berit Walter, Familie von Weizsäcker, Nina Zellerhoff

Kooperationspartner | Cooperation Partners
Yahad – In Unum, Paris, France

Gefördert durch | Supported by
Auswärtiges Amt

Unterstützt durch | Supported by
Die Beauftragte der Bundesregierung für Kultur und Medien
Der Regierende Bürgermeister von Berlin, Senatskanzlei – Kulturelle Angelegenheiten

In Fällen, in denen Rechteinhaber nicht ermittelt werden konnten, bitten die Herausgeber um entsprechende
Mitteilung zur Klärung von Urheberrechtsansprüchen.
In cases where the holder of rights could not be traced, the publishers invite information
that might assist in making compensation for any copyright claims.

© 2016 bei den Herausgebern und den Autoren | by the Publishers and Authors
Printed in Germany

ISBN 978-3-941772-22-9